AMERICAN PRESS OPINION
WASHINGTON TO COOLIDGE

AMERICAN PRESS OPINION

Washington to Coolidge

A DOCUMENTARY RECORD OF EDITORIAL
LEADERSHIP AND CRITICISM
1785–1927

BY

ALLAN NEVINS

Of Columbia University
and The New York
World

VOLUME
ONE

KENNIKAT PRESS/Port Washington, N.Y.

AMERICAN PRESS OPINION

First published 1928
Reissued 1969 by Kennikat Press

Library of Congress Catalog Card No: 68-8206
SBN 8046-0332-4
Manufactured in the United States of America

TO
WALTER LIPPMANN

PREFACE

The editor, no matter how distinguished, writes in water; his page is a palimpsest, on which he expends all his talents, wit, learning and judgment for the day alone, to be erased with the next sun. Nearly as much as the actor and more than the orator, his fame is based not on any achievement that succeeding generations can test for themselves, but simply upon contemporary records of his effect upon his own generation. At best, some small fragments — a few biting phrases, a fulmination which perhaps accidentally has made a distinct mark in history — are kept currently alive.

Hence it is that whereas everyone knows the names of our greatest editors — Greeley, Dana, Bennett, Raymond, Bowles — few except research workers in history have really read anything that they wrote; that while Bryant's poetry is familiar to every school-child, nobody has read the editorials into which Bryant actually put a much greater amount of time and effort. It is taken for granted that these men wrote admirably, as journalism goes; that for their passing day and purpose their work was valuable; but that it is as dead as the snows and blooms of those long past years.

With this verdict the present volume has a decided quarrel. That specimens of the best work of Greeley, Dana, and Godkin are of immediate present-day interest to journalists, students, and many general readers; that some outstanding American editorials possess qualities entitling them to permanent preservation in easily accessible form; above all, that a wide variety of typical editorials from representative journals, chronologically arranged, will furnish a valuable record of the history of public opinion — these are the beliefs upon which this collection is founded. It is not meant as an attempt at a mere selection of "famous" editorials. There are, to be sure, long-remembered editorials here included: Hamilton's attacks on Jefferson, Bache's diatribe against Washington, Bennett's announcement of his forthcoming marriage, the editorial in *Niles's Register* which gave Van Buren's candidacy in 1844 its death-blow, Greeley's exposure of the Kansas-Nebraska Bill, Bryant's denunciation of the Dred Scott decision, Greeley's "Prayer of Twenty Millions," the New York

Times's announcement of its Tweed Ring revelations, and so on down to William Allen White's "What's the Matter with Kansas?" and Henry Watterson's "Vae Victis." It is not meant as a collection of model editorials, though many fine models are here. It is intended as a representative body of the work of the best American editors, so selected as to throw light on the chief events of American history.

There can be little doubt that the vigor, point, and shrewdness of a great deal of this writing, from the early days of Cobbett and Freneau, will surprise many readers. Probably nobody needs to be told that Godkin was a master of English style, that for blunt, homely, forcible exposition or argument Greeley was admirable, that Bryant could attain moving heights of eloquence, and that Dana possessed a wit which could sting or amuse, as he pleased. But the specimens here reprinted will convince the ordinary man or woman of the truth of these statements as mere assertion never could. It will also show beyond any cavil that the work of some minor editors — for example, Hezekiah Niles of *Niles's Register*, or Gales and Seaton of the *Intelligencer* — had excellent journalistic and even literary quality. The sobriety and solidity of the editorials, taken as a whole, should be a pleasing surprise to those who think this form of writing peculiarly characterized by controversial intemperance, by sloppy sentimentality, and by inflated rhetoric. This is an impression which is widely held, and which has not been lessened by certain recent peculiar awards of the Pulitzer judges for the best editorial of each year. No class of writers are less charitable to sentimental banalities or to pompous rhetoric than hardened newspapermen. No class place a greater value on terseness, lucidity, restraint, and genuine thought.

Some editorial pages wear well; some do not. The editor of this compilation, who has turned over so many dusty, yellowing volumes of files, may perhaps be pardoned a few expressions of personal judgment upon the relative editorial merits of different journals. One of these is that no other single American newspaper has quite the long record of distinction which the *Evening Post*, under Coleman, Bryant, Schurz, Godkin, Rollo Ogden, and Simeon Strunsky, almost a century and a quarter, maintained. Another is that among American editors Horace Greeley stands preëminent for the vigor, vitality, and persuasiveness of his writings, and that anyone who wishes to study the best example of the editorial page as a great democratic force must still go back to the New York *Tribune* of 1850–1860. A third is that, admirable though the third Bowles was as an editor and writer, his father, the second Bowles, stood head and shoulders

above him and above all but a few of his contemporaries. Another
is that while E. L. Godkin is almost beyond praise·in small doses,
ordinary human nature rejects him if the dose be made too large
or long-continued.   Finally, he is convinced that, despite many
lamentations over the sad estate of journalism, editorial leadership
still vigorously survives, and that there are editors who are carrying
on the great tradition of their calling in a way to give it fresh lustre;
it is to one of these that this volume is dedicated.

NOTE

Editorial titles which have been supplied — for in the early days
titles were rare, and some of later periods proved unusable — have
been indicated by brackets.   Obvious errors of proofreading and
grammar have been corrected, and the typographical form of the
earlier editorials has been brought to sufficient conformity with
modern usage to make them easily readable.   Numerous editorials
have been abbreviated, but excisions from the actual body of any
piece of writing are always indicated by asterisks.

CONTENTS

CONTENTS   xi
PAGE

CONTENTS   xi

PAGE

The New England Threat of Secession 53
Columbian Centinel, January 13, 1813

New Orleans 54
New York *Evening Post*, February 7, 1815

Peace 55
New York *Evening Post*, February 13, 1815

[Effects of the News of Peace] 56
New York *Evening Post*, February 14, 1815

[President Monroe's Tour and the Era of Good Feeling] 57
Washington *Intelligencer*, April 23, 1817, July 24, 1817

[Effects of the Panic of 1819] 58
Niles's Register, September 16, 1820

Slavery and the Missouri Compromise 59
Niles's Register, December 23, 1820

[Cruelty to Dumb Animals] 60
Niles's Register, July 7, 1821

[Why We Need a Protective Tariff] 61
Niles's Register, June 23, 1821

[The Erie Canal: "The Meeting of the Water"] 63
New York *Commercial Advertiser*, October 11, 1822

[States Which Refuse Political Equality] 65
Niles's Register, November 29, 1823

[The Monroe Doctrine Enunciated] 66
Niles's Register, December 6, 1823

[Albert Gallatin as a "Foreigner"] 67
Niles's Register, April 17, 1824

[The Death of Adams and Jefferson] 68
Niles's Register, July 15, 1826

[Aspects of American Social History, 1827] 68
National Intelligencer

The Argument against General Jackson 72
National Intelligencer, August 4, 1827

[The Argument against J. Q. Adams] 72
Natchez *Gazette*, November 1, 1827

President Adams's Regard for Merit 74
Washington *National Intelligencer*, November 17, 1827

[The Baltimore and Ohio Railroad] 76
Baltimore *Gazette*, April 30, 1828

[John Quincy Adams Gives Way to Jackson] 77
New York *Evening Post*, March 5, 1829

A Declaration of Anti-Masonic Principles 77
Albany *Evening Journal*, March 22, 1830

[President Jackson's Toast: A Southern Interpretation] 79
Charleston *Mercury*, April 24, 1830

President Jackson and Internal Improvements 80
Richmond *Enquirer*, June 1, 1830

The Argument against Free Public Schools 81
Philadelphia *National Gazette*, July 10, 1830, August 19, 1830

PART II

CONTENTS

PART III

CONTENTS

CONTENTS xxi

PART IV

CONTENTS

PAGE

CARTOONS

PART ONE

THE AMERICAN PRESS AND PUBLIC OPINION
1783–1835

THE AMERICAN PRESS AND PUBLIC OPINION
1783–1835

The nineteenth century, to the historian of public opinion, is the century of the newspaper. The sphere of influence which had previously been shared by the preacher, the pamphleteer, and the politician was more and more largely engrossed, as the century wore on, by the journalist. When James Russell Lowell spoke in 1884 in London to the Provincial Newspaper Society he was able to declare that a revolution had taken place, in both America and Great Britain, in the methods of forming public opinion. "I am not sure that you are always aware," he said, "to how great an extent you have supplanted the pulpit, to how great an extent you have supplanted even the deliberative assembly. You have assumed responsibilities, I should say, heavier than ever man assumed before. You wield an influence entirely without precedent hitherto in human history." This was in essence what Carlyle had meant a generation earlier in writing that "the journalists are now the true kings and clergy," the "dynasts," of the earth. In America even more than England did the newspaper rise to a paramount position, and the greatest editors became figures almost as prominent and powerful as the greatest statesmen. This was hardly due to superior literacy in America — we should not forget that in 1840, for example, our republic of 17,000,000 people contained 500,000 illiterate adults. It was due to the diffused prosperity, enabling everyone to buy a newspaper, to our political democracy, giving every voter an interest in the newspaper discussion of politics, and to the editorial alertness which, taking advantage of the great distances and paucity of contacts in America, created a newspaper habit.

At the outset this alertness was not in evidence; for in 1783 the line between the editor and the pamphleteer was still very blurred. Historically, the editor had usually been a pamphleteer, and the greatest journalists, like Defoe in England, Franklin in America, and Cobbett in both, were the greatest of pamphleteers. The important newspapers in the generation after the Revolution, like the *Minerva*, the *Columbian Centinel*, the *Gazette of the United States*, and the *Aurora*,

3

were small, dingy, once-folded sheets which printed fragmentary commercial and political intelligence, some advertisements, and long editorials which usually resembled daily instalments of a pamphlet, or were actually such instalments. If written by the editor himself, they might unreservedly be called editorials. More often they were written by an outsider of political distinction, and signed Agricola, Publicola, or Cato. The style was that of a pamphlet: the writer thought of the cumulative effect of a series of articles, not of the individual effect of a single essay, and modeled himself upon Junius, Wilkes, or some other great pamphleteer.

The men who were interested in American public opinion between the Treaty of Paris and the Missouri Compromise were with few exceptions interested in it for political purposes. The birth of clear-cut, intensely antagonistic parties in Washington's first Administration was accompanied by the founding of a Federalist press by Hamilton, who assisted John Fenno and Noah Webster to establish newspapers, and whose papers signed "Camillus" and "Philo-Camillus" were as effective during the discussion of Jay's Treaty as his "Federalist" series had been during the debate on the Constitution; while Jefferson eagerly encouraged James T. Callender to set up a journal, and believing himself unfit for editorial controversies, wrote to Madison appealing that he answer Hamilton's fire. North and south, from Boston to Savannah, minor political leaders tended to establish, to assist, or to ally themselves with minor newspapers. Thus George Clinton in New York had his *American Citizen*, edited by the noted English immigrant James Cheetham, and Levi Lincoln in Massachusetts had his Worcester *National Ægis*. The true newspaper, independent of politics, had not yet been born even at the close of the second war with England, and the only sheets which were not supported by some party leader or party group were those which, led by the *Pennsylvania Packet*, devoted themselves to trade and markets. In these latter the editorial was almost entirely lacking; while in the other papers it dealt almost exclusively with politics.

The close connection between the political pamphlet and the newspaper editorial is amply illustrated by such journalists as Alexander Hamilton, William Cobbett, John Fenno, and J. T. Callender. The "Federalist" essays which Hamilton, Madison, and John Jay composed in 1787–1788 were essentially a pamphlet enterprise, published in a newspaper instead of pamphlet form for convenience and wide circulation, and then reprinted together. Appearing in the New York *Independent Journal* and another sheet friendly to the new Constitution, the New York *Packet*, they were copied by sympathetic newspapers throughout the country. Later Hamilton became virtually an over-editor or general supervisor of three journals in turn — Fenno's *Gazette of the United States*, Noah Webster's *Minerva*, and William Coleman's *Evening Post*. His "Camillus" series in the *Minerva* was practically a pamphlet — an argument for Jay's Treaty in thirty-six short chapters. In another aspect, they were a series of thirty-six editorials, for they had all the weight of the newspaper's editorial power behind them. Cobbett began his American career as a pamphleteer, and even after he had established *Porcupine's Gazette and Daily Advertiser* in 1797, he kept reprinting his material in pamphlet form. Callender first appears in history as the author of a pamphlet attack on William Pitt entitled "The Political Progress of Britain."

But a pamphlet, chopped into sections for the editorial page, had evident weaknesses from the standpoint of either the journalist or the party leader. Its sections sometimes lacked completeness; the length of the series made it dull; there was a lack of variety and vivacity. While the ponderous series of articles might serve as heavy artillery, small guns and rifle fire were needed. After 1795 the dashing franc-tireurs of journalism, such as William Duane of the *Aurora*, showed a marked preference for the brief editorial, peppered with denunciatory epithets and harsh accusations, and casting to the winds the dignity of the chief Federalist penmen. Their methods soon became characteristic of journalism. In the opposite camp such capable editors as Noah Webster of the *Minerva* and Coleman of the *Evening Post* began to intersperse the pamphlet-style articles by Hamilton, Rufus King, Oliver Wolcott, and other leaders with shorter, livelier comments of their own. Later, feeling that the public demands were best met by brief immediate comment, they concentrated their attention upon it, and the pamphlet matter began to fade away entirely from their pages. By 1815 there was little of it left. Meanwhile, such a versatile and talented journalist as Philip Freneau, who edited the *National Gazette* in Jefferson's behalf, made a contribution of different nature to the editorial page. Freneau, possessing high literary gifts and familiar with the best British essayists and poets, imparted sprightliness and grace to this journal and even more to his subsequent venture, the New York *Time-Piece*, by using poems, skits, dialogues, and epigram.

The really tremendous political influence of newspapers in this period — an influence attested by Hamilton, Jefferson, and Adams in emphatic language — was based largely upon the fact that the electorate was small. Property qualifications hedged it about, and all who voted read the press. These political journals, circulating among a small and very political-minded class, would even under favorable conditions have been slow to range outside the political field. But conditions were anything but favorable. It was impossible to present a varied editorial fare in an era which lacked varied social and intellectual interests. A raw young nation which had no independent literature, no drama, no art, no music, intent upon conquering a living from the wild forest and prairie — how much could this nation expect beyond politics; beyond underbred personalities, ill-tempered campaign harangues, and a none-too-intelligent discussion of fiscal topics? Certainly most journals gave it nothing better. In the larger cities, the obvious questions of municipal administration — paving, lighting, fires, the suppression of crime, epidemics, and accidents — obtained more and more attention, but their treatment lacked systematic energy. For the most part the editorials upon these subjects did not apply a definite reformative policy, but were casual in nature, and often did no more than supply the lack of news-stories upon them. Indeed, one function of the editorial columns until the thirties was to furnish news regarding even events of the greatest importance. When the Erie Canal was built, when the Baltimore & Ohio Railroad was opened, when John Quincy Adams was inaugurated, many newspapers had no way of treating the occurrence except by combining news with editorial comment. Reporting was in its infancy and correspondence was all but unknown, though letters were sometimes contributed by a benevolent friend. The most enterprising editors would either clip the needed news-story from some journal near the scene, or would furnish a second-hand account of the event in the guise of tepid comment; the unenterprising editors would print nothing at all.

The character of the editorial columns of the pre-Jacksonian era, it is clear, was determined by factors of environment that were slow to change. Those who turn over the yellowed files find the monotony of subject-matter, the woodenness of the treatment, and the lack of perspective painful. The shrillness of tone is often still more repugnant. Benjamin Russell, the Federalist editor of the *Columbian Centinel*, wrote in 1799 that his party had never employed Cobbett as a judicious writer in its cause, but had used him to assail the Democratic "foxes, skunks, and serpents" — the verminous newspapers which "ejected their mud, filth, and venom" upon even George Washington. John Fenno, in a moment of pique, wrote that same year that "the American newspapers are the most base, false, servile, and venal publications that ever polluted the fountains of society — their editors the most ignorant, mercenary, and vulgar automatons that ever were moved by the constantly rusting wires of sordid mercantile avarice." Yet again and again we do come, in the arid waste of governmental theorizing and intemperate political attacks, upon elevated and effective pieces of editorial writing, upon bits of eloquence and wit, upon utterances which arrest us by their sincerity or their lucid reasoning. We cannot help liking the directness and informality with which many editors, especially after 1800, wrote; addressing a familiar audience of perhaps 2,000 buyers they assumed no pontifical airs, but used the pronoun "I" and took an understanding of their personal crotchets for granted. Nor can we avoid being impressed by the intensity of conviction, the warmth of emotion, with which opinions upon political issues were often stated.

Of eminent editors in this period there were but a small number, and perhaps none of them can be said to have attained real greatness. The most important, viewed purely as a journalist, was indubitably William Cobbett — the irascible Englishman who, remaining but a few years (1794–1800), left nevertheless a deep imprint upon our newspapers. His ability lay in his earnestness, combativeness, and courage, in his homely, sinewy, picturesque English style, and in his reformative temper. Like every real publicist, he had an intense desire to make himself a power in the world. It was this which led him, a penniless ex-sergeant newly arrived in the United States, to challenge notice by his pamphlet upon Dr. Joseph Priestley, "Observations on the Emigration of a Martyr," and to follow it by his "Prospect from the Congress Gallery" and his "Political Censor." He gloried in the attention soon given him. In *Porcupine's Gazette* he published a naïve editorial which reveals how much he enjoyed the abuse he received. "'Dear father,'" (so it ran) — "'When you used to set me off in the morning, dressed in my blue smock-frock and woolen spatterdashes, with my bag of bread and cheese and bottle of small-beer swung over my shoulder on the little crook that my old godfather Boxall gave me, little did you imagine that I should one day become so great a man as to have my picture stuck in the windows, and have four whole books published about me in the course of one week.' Thus begins a letter which I wrote to my father yesterday morning, and which, if it reaches him, will make the old man drink an extraordinary pot of ale to my health. Heaven bless him! I think I see him now, by the old-fashioned fire-side, reading the letter to his neighbors. 'Ay, ay,' says he. 'Will will stand his ground wherever he goes.' And so I will, father, in spite of all the hell of democracy." The pages of the *Gazette* show how this doughty John Bull did telling service for the Federalist party and for Mother England against France, and how he repaid the attacks of Franklin's grandson, Ben Bache, with shot in kind:

> Everyone will, I hope, have the goodness to believe that *my* grandfather was no philosopher. Indeed he was not. He never made a lightning rod, nor bottled up a single quart of sunshine, in the whole course of his life; he was no almanac-maker, nor quack, nor chimney-doctor, nor soap-boiler, nor ambassador, nor printer's devil; neither was he a deist; and all his children were born in wedlock. The legacies he left were his scythe, his reaping-hook, and his flail; he bequeathed no old and irrevocable debts to a hospital; he never cheated the poor during his life; nor mocked them at his death. He has, it is true, been suffered to sleep quietly beneath the green sward; but if his descendants cannot point to his statue over the door of a library, they have not the mortification of hearing him spoken of as a libertine, a hypocrite, and an infidel.

More combative still and even more vituperative, were two lesser men of British training, who remained in America permanently and who were identified with the Republican or anti-Federalist side — James T. Callender and William Duane. Of Callender, an English-man born, it is sufficient to say that he founded the Richmond *Examiner* as an anti-Federalist organ, was imprisoned under the Sedition Act, and later in the columns of the Richmond *Reporter* foully slandered and abused his original patron Jefferson. Duane, a man of greater capacity and principle, was born in America, but spent more than a decade in India and England (1784–1795) before he became associated with Benjamin Franklin Bache in editing the *Aurora*. He succeeded to the chief editorship in 1798, and made the journal the leading Republican newspaper of the country, Jefferson ascribing his election as President largely to it. The *Aurora* remained of importance until 1822, when Duane resigned the editorship; but it lost its place as the head of the national Democratic press soon after the capital was removed from Philadelphia to Washington. Other of the most energetic editors of the time were foreign-born or foreign-trained: Thomas Cooper, James Cheetham, Joseph Gales, and Mathew Lyon. The chagrined John Adams, surveying this array of alien editors, wrote in 1801 after his defeat that "A group of foreign liars encouraged by a few ambitious native gentlemen have discomfited the education, the talents, the virtues, and the prosperity of the country."

One of the outstanding American newspapers of the nineteenth century commenced its career in Washington in the fall of 1800, when Samuel H. Smith founded the *National Intelligencer* to support Jefferson. The next year Hamilton and his friends brought into existence in New York a far greater journal, William Coleman's *Evening Post*. For three years Coleman, a man of talent who had left a Massachusetts editorship to join the New York bar, enjoyed the close collaboration of Hamilton himself. Inspired by these two men, the *Post* led in that editorial improvement in range, taste, and intellectual quality which was inevitable. Just a decade later, in 1811, a third distinguished newspaper appeared in the *Register* of Hezekiah Niles, published first in Baltimore and later in Washington; a weekly journal which is familiar to everyone as a repository of historical information, but which is not usually regarded as an organ of opinion. It was one, however — and a very effective one. Niles, who was of New England origin, made it a telling exponent first of Federalist and later of Whig doctrines, and argued unweariedly for a protective tariff. The second decade of the century brought in Thomas Ritchie's Richmond *Enquirer*, the vigorous editorials of which were soon read and discussed all over the country. In New England a little later (1814), Nathan Hale established the Boston *Daily Advertiser*, and gave special emphasis to editorials. He was an able, fearless, and responsible writer; but the claim sometimes made for Hale, that the unsigned editorial was his invention, is quite untenable.

A word of especial praise is due to the Washington *National Intelligencer* as conducted by Joseph W. Gales, Jr., and his brother-in-law, William Winston Seaton. Gales became editor in 1810, and remained in the harness till his death in 1860; Seaton joined him in 1812, and did not retire until 1864. Supporting Jefferson and Madison in its early years, the *Intelligencer* later turned to J. Q. Adams, and at the opening of the Jacksonian era adhered to Henry Clay and the American or Whig party of which he was one of the founders. It long derived a peculiar authority from the fact that, both Gales and Seaton being stenographers, it offered the only trustworthy report of the debates of Congress. Webster is quoted as having said that Gales and Seaton possessed the two wisest heads in the country, and that Gales's knowledge of our governmental history surpassed that of "all the other political writers of the day put together." Edward Everett late in life spoke of the *Intelligencer's* editorials as written "with an unsurpassed journalistic breadth of view and weight of authority"; and the *Atlantic Monthly* declared that the venerable editors had been for decades "a power and safety in the land." The influence of the *Intelligencer* was at its height in the thirties and early forties, declining when the slavery controversy overshot its mild and conciliatory views.

By the year 1830 journalism was showing greater breadth, elasticity, and energy in every department. It had spread far to the West. In New York William Cullen Bryant had joined the *Evening Post*, and James Watson Webb and M. M. Noah were making the *Courier and Enquirer* well known. The *Journal of Commerce*, established in 1827 by Arthur Tappan as a commercial journal of austerely moral standards, vied with the *Courier* in running pony expresses from Washington and in keeping news schooners off the harbor entrance. But despite the fresh and vigorous impulses of the time, politics still dominated the editorial pages. The most important of the newspapers which emerged into prominence with Jackson was the Washington *Globe*, which the stern old President decided to establish when Duff Green's *United States Telegraph*, previously the Administration organ, turned to follow the leadership of John C. Calhoun, with whom Green was connected by marriage. Jackson brought to Washington a Kentucky editor named Francis P. Blair, who issued the first number of the *Globe* on December 7, 1830. With the aid of the lucrative public printing contracts and of Federal officeholders throughout the country, the "government paper" flourished. Its editor was the shrewdest of politicians, and not a man of excessive scruple; and by virtue of his headship of the "Kitchen Cabinet," and of his contacts with the Albany "Regency" and Richmond "Junta," he played a part in what has been well called the most powerful political and journalistic cabal the nation has ever known.

It is interesting to note the close parallel which the relations between Andrew Jackson and Francis P. Blair furnished with those which had existed between Alexander Hamilton and William Coleman a generation earlier. Coleman had been wont, when any public question of importance was pending, to go — usually late at night — to Hamilton's home. "He (Hamilton) always keeps himself minutely informed upon all political matters," Coleman informed an acquaintance, Jeremiah Mason. "As soon as I see him he begins in a deliberate manner to dictate, and I to note down in shorthand; when he stops, my article is completed." In the same way, the chief editorial writer for the *Globe*, Amos Kendall, would come by night for a private conference with Andrew Jackson. The President would lie on a sofa and smoke, dictating his ideas as well as he could express them, while Kendall wrote, read, and rewrote his editorial until it approximated the model which the Chief Executive had in mind. Jackson, according to Henry A. Wise, needed just such an expert amanuensis. "He could think but could not write; he knew what nerve to touch, but he was no surgeon skilled in the instrument of dissection. Kendall was." In the same way that the *Evening Post* during and after Hamilton's time, till the close of the War of 1812, was the precentor of Hamiltonian Federalism, the *Globe* from 1830 to 1840 was the leader of the whole Jacksonian Democratic press.

Journalism developed mightily, in most material respects, in the first forty years of the republic; it improved its mechanical equipment, multiplied its offices and sheets, and strode to and beyond the Mississippi, till Illinois alone had more dailies in 1830 than the whole nation had possessed in 1790. It increased with greater slowness, but still steadily and creditably, in accuracy and editorial enterprise. Henry Adams was hardly too severe in characterizing the infant press of the country, about 1800, as simply a storehouse of political calumny; in saying that intermingled with its scanty advertisements, its marine lists, its extracts from English newspapers, one might find long dull columns of political disquisition, but hardly any real news or really pungent comment. However, even by 1812 this was no longer true. By 1830 a very decided turning point had been reached. The Washington correspondent had been invented, and James Gordon Bennett was about to make him important. A few newspapers in the largest cities were printing letters from other distant points. Reporting was beginning to become a profession. The basis was being laid for a newer, more popular, more broadly effective journalism, in touch with the strong currents of national life released by Jacksonian democracy; and the improvement in the news columns and distribution of intelligence was being already reflected in a greater vitality and strength in the editorial pages, and in a lessened dependence upon politics and politicians.

[WILL NEW YORK REJECT THE IMPOST?] [1]

Pennsylvania Packet, March 22, 1786

The State of Rhode Island having at length acceded to the impost and the supplementary aids, according to the last proposition of Congress, and there remaining but little doubt of the same national spirit animating the councils of every other government on this side the Hudson, the eyes of the friends of the Union, the very existence of which has been brought into jeopardy by our past neglect of this salutary expedient to retrieve the credit of America, will now be turned to the State of New York, which, it is to be hoped, will not long be deficient in exhibiting this last proof of its attachment to our federal interest. It seems no less strange than remarkable that the influence of Congress should be least regarded in the place of their immediate residence: an argument, among others, in demonstrating the little probability there is of the authority of that truly respectable body being suddenly extended so as to endanger the existence of that democratic spirit which still, and we flatter ourselves will ever, flourish in full vigour throughout this continent. But at the same time, it is most ardently to be wished, that in guarding against this unhappy extreme, we should not run into all the horrors of anarchy and civil dissension, which are far more to be dreaded. A true American will feel for the reputation and interest of his country as keenly as for the immediate emolument of the State of which he is a member, and it is apparent beyond the necessity of language to explain it, that a government without the means of performing its engagements must soon be contemptible. There must therefore be some strong motives that immediately affect themselves to account for such a pointed opposition to the united views and wishes of almost every part of our federal government. If it proceeds from any little benefit which that State may derive from its peculiar situation as to commerce, it is an object so different from those which governed our conduct in the early days of our independence, and so repugnant to every principle of honor, policy, and the love of our country, that we must hope it will soon give place to a mode of procedure more consonant to their past glory and the present hopes of every real friend of America.

[1] The Pennsylvania *Packet* was the leading commercial newspaper of the United States and as such was heartily in favor of all measures to strengthen the Confederation. New York, swayed by Governor George Clinton, was successful in defeating the proposal for a national impost or customs tax. The measure was beaten in the Legislature in May, 1786 (though a much-mangled substitute, quite unsatisfactory in nature, did pass); and Governor Clinton refused to call a special session to take it up again. Many New Yorkers had just the selfish motive denounced by the *Packet*.

[THE HARD TIMES ARE ONLY TEMPORARY] [1]

Pennsylvania Gazette, May 21, 1786

We see in the public newspapers of different States frequent complaints of *hard times, deadness of trade, scarcity of money,* and so on. It is not our intention to assert or maintain that these complaints are entirely without foundation. There can be no country or nation existing in which there will not be some people so circumstanced as to find it hard to gain a livelihood, people who are not in the way of any profitable trade, and with whom money is scarce because they have nothing to give in exchange for it. And it is always in the power of a small number to make a great clamor. But let us take a cool view of the general state of our affairs, and perhaps the prospect will appear less gloomy than has been imagined.

The great business of the continent is agriculture. For one citizen or merchant, I suppose we have at least one hundred farmers, by far the greatest part cultivators of their own fertile lands, from whence many of them draw not only the food necessary for their subsistence, but the materials of their clothing, so as to need very few foreign supplies; while they have a surplus of production to dispose of, whereby wealth is gradually accumulated. Such has been the goodness of Divine Providence to these regions, and so favorable the climate, that since the three or four years of hardship in the first settlement of our fathers here, a famine or scarcity has never been heard of among us; on the contrary, though some years may have been more, and others less plentiful, there has always been provision enough for ourselves, and a quantity to spare for exportation. And although the crops of last year were generally good, never was the farmer better paid for the part he can spare to commerce, as the published price currents abundantly testify. The lands he possesses are also continually rising in value with the increase of population. And on the whole, he is able to give such good wages to all who work for him that all who are acquainted with the Old World must agree that in no part of it are the laboring poor so generally well fed, well clothed, well lodged, and well paid as in the United States of America.

If we enter the cities, we find that since the Revolution the owners of houses and lots of ground there have had their interest vastly augmented in value; rents have risen to an astonishing height, and thence encouragement to increased building, which gives employment to an abundance of workmen, as does also the increased luxury and splendor of living among the inhabitants thus made

[1] The Revolution was followed by severe business depression, acutest in 1785–1786. Its subsidence coincided with the adoption of the Constitution in 1788.

richer. These workmen all demand and obtain much higher wages than any other part of the world would afford them, and are paid in ready money. This rank of people therefore do not or ought not to complain of hard times, and they make a very considerable part of the city inhabitants.

At the distance we live from the American fisheries, we cannot speak of them with certainty; but we have not heard that the labour of the valuable race of men employed in them is worse paid, or that they meet with less success than before the Revolution. The whale-men indeed have been deprived of one market for their oil, but another we hear is opening for them, which it is hoped may be equally advantageous. And the demand is constantly increasing for spermaceti candles, which therefore bear a much higher rate than formerly. . . .

Whoever has travelled through the various parts of Europe, and observed how small is the proportion of people in affluence or easy circumstances there, compared with those in poverty or misery, the few rich and haughty landlords, the multitude of poor, abject, rack-rented, tithe-paying tenants, and half-paid and half-starved ragged laborers; and who views here the happy mediocrity that so generally prevails throughout these States, where the cultivator works for himself and supports his family in decent plenty, will, we think, feel abundant reason to bless Divine Providence for the evident and great difference in our favour, and be convinced that no nation known to us enjoys a greater share of human felicity.

[PHILADELPHIA SHOULD BE THE NATIONAL CAPITAL]

Pennsylvania Packet, September 6, 1786

It seems a great hardship upon the people of the United States . . . that so great a majority as voted for Philadelphia should not determine the residence of Congress — New Hampshire, Connecticut, Pennsylvania, Maryland, Virginia, and North Carolina, having 1,480,000 people, according to the statements of the Federal Convention, voted for Philadelphia; and Massachusetts, New York, New Jersey, and South Carolina, having only 920,000 people, were for New York. Delaware and Georgia were divided.

We cannot but wonder at the want of reflection in the writer of a New York paragraph of August 30, who complains that Congress have not determined the question of the residence of the new government, although a ninth State has adopted the Constitution above two months. Surely this gentleman will not complain as a New Yorker that Congress delayed for many weeks to determine the matter, when New York was not in a capacity to be fixed on, or even to be put in nomination. . . . . This writer tells us that the sufferings of New York ought to influence Congress to fix the government there. Upon that principle it should go to New Jersey. But does he remember that half the ships and cargoes belonging to Philadelphia that were captured in the war would rebuild all they had lost? Our greater proportion of voluntary public loans, now reduced three-fourths in value, would also rebuild it. But they have been amply repaid for this loss by the confiscation of a great number of the most capital city estates. Philadelphia, he says, wishes to become the arbitress of the United States. This we deny and despise. Let New York remember how firmly she refused to make common cause even with her sister States, by refusing the impost; and let the worthy citizens of Connecticut and New Jersey remember how safe it would be for New York, with such an unjust spirit, to become the arbitress of America. The dispositions of this State are, and always have been, *national*. When Boston suffered before the war, Pennsylvania subscribed to their relief. When the South Carolinians were exiled, Pennsylvania subscribed for their poor and lent to their rich citizens. How much did New York do on these two occasions? They did not furnish in gifts or loans a tenth penny. When our Philosophical Society, or Bank, our Manufacturing Society, etc., were established, all America were publicly and heartily invited to partake. Our little societies have offered premiums for inventions, improvements, and new articles of produce to the citizens of the most distant States. Our spirit has always been Federal, both before and since the Revolution, as is well known.

[VIRGINIA RATIFIES THE CONSTITUTION] [1]

Pennsylvania Packet, August 9, 1788

It would be difficult to convey an adequate idea of the general enthusiastic happiness which this fortunate event has diffused. The acquisition of Virginia to the new confederated States would of itself have been highly important; but at this crisis, when it was considered that her accession, by being the ninth approving State, has established the liberty, independence, and public credit of this rising Western Union, our joy is not to be described. A general sympathy unites all. Hope, rational hope, animates every rank

---

[1] Virginia ratified the Constitution June 25, 1788, after a struggle in which Patrick Henry and George Mason led the opposition. She was the tenth State to take the step, and her action made the success of the new government certain. New Hampshire ratified only a few days earlier, which explains the *Packet's* erroneous reference to the "ninth State."

and profession. The prospect of justice, parent of liberty and support of virtue, being speedily and impartially administered; public faith and dignity supported; a consistent productive commerce disseminating its happy consequences through every rank of citizens, arrested the attention and feelings of every lover of liberty and mankind.

Shortly shall we begin to reap the blessings of the glorious revolution, purchased with difficulties and anxieties which none but a sufferer can truly comprehend. No longer shall the useful artisan be paid with procrastinated promises; no longer shall the planter sweat for a hard-earned, narrow, uncertain competence, but receive the just reward of his labor; no longer shall we be insulted with the tantalizing name of wealth, depreciated to a shadow, even while we contemplate its nominal amount. Specie (that valuable quid pro quo attendant on all well-regulated efficient governments) will again circulate; the price of imports and exports will be regulated; in short, it is to be expected as a natural consequence, that industry and ingenuity will be rewarded with peace, plenty, and content under this well-digested, approved confederation, framed by some of the wisest and most virtuous men now existing, and by the most strenuous supporters of liberty through the mazes of the late war.

[THE FUNDING OF THE NATIONAL DEBT] [1]

National Gazette, September 11, 1792

Much declamation has been indulged against certain characters, who are charged with advocating the pernicious doctrine, that "public debts are public blessings," and with being friends to a perpetuation of the public debt of the country. Among these characters, if the Secretary of the Treasury has not been named, he has been pretty plainly alluded to. It is proper to examine what foundation there is then for these charges.

That officer, it is very certain, explicitly maintained, that the *funding* of the existing debt of the United States would render it a national blessing; and a man has only to travel through the United States with his eyes open, and to observe the invigoration of industry in every branch, to be convinced that the position is well founded.

But, whether right or wrong, it is quite a different thing from maintaining, as a general proposition, that a public debt is a public blessing; particular and temporary circumstances might render that advantageous at one time, which at another might be hurtful.

It is known that prior to the Revolution, a great part of the cir-

[1] Written by Alexander Hamilton, Secretary of the Treasury; signed "Fact."

culation was carried on by paper money; that in consequence of the events of the Revolution, that resource was in a great measure destroyed, by being discredited, and that the same events had destroyed a large proportion of the moneyed and mercantile capital of the country, and of personal property generally. It was natural to think that the chasm created by these circumstances required to be supplied, and a just theory was sufficient to demonstrate, that a funded debt would answer the end. To infer that it would have such an effect, was no more to maintain the general doctrine of "public debts being public blessings," than the saying, that paper emissions, by the authority of government, were useful in the early periods of the country, was the maintaining, that they would be useful in all the future stages of its progress. . . .

Extract from a report of the Secretary of the Treasury on the subject of a provision for the public debt, presented the 14th of January, 1790:

> Persuaded, as the Secretary is, that the proper funding of the *present* debt will render it a national blessing; yet he is *so far* from acceding to the position, in the latitude in which it is sometimes laid down, that 'Public debts are public benefits,' a position *inviting to prodigality, and liable to dangerous abuse,* that he ardently wishes to see it incorporated, as a *fundamental maxim* in the *system of public credit* of the United States, that the *creation of debt should be always accompanied with the means of extinguishment.* This he regards as the *true secret of rendering public credit immortal.*

[DID JEFFERSON OPPOSE THE CONSTITUTION?] [1]

Gazette of the United States, September 19, 1792

Mr. Pendleton represents a certain letter of Mr. Jefferson as containing these particulars — a strong wish that the *first nine conventions* may accept the new Constitution because it would secure the *good* it contains, which is *great* and *important.* 2d. A wish that the four latest, whichever they should be, might refuse to accede to it till *amendments were secured.* 3d. A caution to take care that no objection to the form of government should produce a schism in the Union; which Mr. Jefferson admits to be an incurable evil.

From this it appears, that though Mr. Jefferson was of opinion that the Constitution contained "great and important good," and was desirous that the first nine deliberating States should consent to it for the sake of preserving the existence of the Union, yet he had strong objections to the Constitution; so strong, that he was willing

---

[1] Written by Alexander Hamilton, and characteristic of the newspaper attacks which Jefferson, then Secretary of State, keenly resented; signed "Catullus."

to risk an *ultimate dismemberment* in an experiment to obtain the alterations which he deemed necessary.

If the four last deliberating States (particularly if they had happened to be States in geographical contiguity, which was very possible) had refused to ratify the Constitution, what might not have been the consequence? Who knows whether the assenting States would have been willing to have been *coerced* into the amendments which the non-assenting States might have been disposed to dictate? Calculating the intrigues and machinations which were to have been expected to stand in the way, who can say, if even two thirds of both houses of Congress should have been found willing to propose them, or that three fourths of the legislatures, or conventions, in three fourths of the States, would have been brought to adopt the required amendments?

Could anything but objections to the Constitution of the most *serious* kind have justified the hazarding an eventual schism in the Union, in so great a degree as would have attended an adherence to the advice given by Mr. Jefferson? Can there be any perversion of truth in affirming that the person who entertained those objections was opposed to the Constitution?

The opposition which was experienced in every part of the United States, acknowledged the necessity and utility of the Union; and, generally speaking, that the Constitution contained many valuable features; contending only that it wanted some essential alterations to render it upon the whole a safe and good government.

[THE UNFAIR ATTACK ON JAY'S TREATY] [1]

American Minerva, July 22, 1795

It was known, that the resentment produced by our revolution war with Great Britain, had never been entirely extinguished, and that recent injuries had rekindled the flame with additional violence. It was a natural consequence of this, that many should be disinclined to any amicable relation with Great Britain, and that many others should be prepared to acquiesce only in a treaty which should present advantages of so striking and preponderant a kind, as it was not reasonable to expect could be obtained, unless the United States were in a position to give the law to Great Britain, and as, if obtained under the coercion of such a situation, could only have been the short-lived prelude of a speedy rupture to get rid of them. . . .

It was not to be mistaken, that an enthusiasm for France and her revolution, throughout all its wonderful vicissitudes, has continued to possess the minds of the great body of the people of this country;

[1] By Alexander Hamilton; one of the Camillus series.

and it was to be inferred, that this sentiment would predispose to a jealousy of any agreement or treaty with her most persevering competitor — a jealousy so excessive, as would give the fullest scope to insidious arts to perplex and mislead the public opinion. It is well understood, that a numerous party among us, though disavowing the design, because the avowal would defeat it, have been steadily endeavoring to make the United States a party in the present European war, by advocating all those measures which would widen the breach between us and Great Britain, and by resisting all those which would tend to close it; and it was morally certain, that this party would eagerly improve every circumstance which could serve to render the treaty odious, and to frustrate it, as the most effectual road to their favorite goal.

It was also known beforehand, that personal and party rivalships, of the most active kind, would assail whatever treaty might be made, to disgrace, if possible, its organ. There are three persons prominent in the public eye, as the successor of the actual President of the United States, in the event of his retreat from the station, Mr. Adams, Mr. Jay, and Mr. Jefferson.

No one has forgotten the systematic pains which have been taken to impair the well-earned popularity of the first gentleman. Mr. Jay, too, has been repeatedly the object of attacks with the same view. His friends, as well as his enemies, anticipated that he could make no treaty which would not furnish weapons against him: and it were to have been ignorant of the indefatigable malice of his adversaries, to have doubted that they would be seized with eagerness and wielded with dexterity.

The peculiar circumstances which have attended the two last elections for governor of this State, have been of a nature to give the utmost keenness to party animosity. It was impossible that Mr. Jay should be forgiven for his double, and, in the last instance, triumphant success; or that any prominent opportunity of detaching from him the public confidence, should pass unimproved.[1] . . .

From the combined operation of these different causes, it would have been a vain expectation, that the treaty would be generally contemplated with candor and moderation, or that reason would regulate the first impressions concerning it. It was certain, on the contrary, that however unexceptionable its true character might be, it would have to fight its way through a mass of unreasonable opposition; and that time, examination, and reflection would be requisite to fix the public opinion on a true basis. It was certain

---

[1] Jay stood for Governor in 1792; but though he had an actual majority of votes, a partisan returning board so handled the returns of three counties as to elect George Clinton. But Jay obtained a clear majority at the election of May, 1795.

that it would become the instrument of a systematic effort against the national government and its administration; a decided engine of party to advance its own views at the hazard of the public peace and prosperity.

The events which have already taken place, are a full comment on these positions. If the good sense of the people does not speedily discountenance the projects which are on foot, more melancholy proofs may succeed.

Before the treaty was known, attempts were made to prepossess the public mind against it. It was absurdly asserted, that it was not expected by the people, that Mr. Jay was to make any treaty; as if he had been sent, not to accommodate differences by negotiation and agreement, but to dictate to Great Britain the terms of an unconditional submission.

Before it was published at large, a sketch, calculated to produce false impressions, was handed out to the public, through a medium noted for hostility to the administration of the government. — Emissaries flew through the country, spreading alarm and discontent: the leaders of clubs were everywhere active to seize the passions of the people, and preoccupy their judgments against the treaty.

At Boston it was published one day, and the next a town meeting was convened to condemn it; without ever being read, without any serious discussion, sentence was pronounced against it.

Will any man seriously believe, that in so short a time, an instrument of this nature could have been tolerably understood by the greater part of those who were thus induced to a condemnation of it? Can the result be considered as anything more than a sudden ebullition of popular passion, excited by the artifices of a party, which had adroitly seized a favorable moment to furorize the public opinion? This spirit of precipitation and the intemperance which accompanied it, prevented the body of the merchants and the greater part of the most considerate citizens, from attending the meeting, and left those who met wholly under the guidance of a set of men who, with two or three exceptions, have been the uniform opposers of the government.

The intelligence of this event had no sooner reached New York, than the leaders of the clubs were seen haranguing in every corner of the city, to stir up our citizens into an imitation of the example of the meeting at Boston. An invitation to meet at the city-hall quickly followed, not to consider or discuss the merits of the treaty, but to unite with the meeting at Boston to address the President against its ratification.

This was immediately succeeded by a handbill, full of invectives against the treaty, as absurd as they were inflammatory, and manifestly designed to induce the citizens to surrender their reason to the empire of their passions.

In vain did a respectable meeting of the merchants endeavor, by their advice, to moderate the violence of these views, and to promote a spirit favorable to a fair discussion of the treaty; in vain did a respectable majority of the citizens of every description attend for that purpose. The leaders of the clubs resisted all discussion, and their followers, by their clamors and vociferations, rendered it impracticable, notwithstanding the wish of a manifest majority of the citizens, convened upon the occasion.

Can we believe, that the leaders were really sincere in the objections they made to a discussion, or that the great and mixed mass of citizens then assembled, had so thoroughly mastered the merits of the treaty as that they might not have been enlightened by such a discussion?

It cannot be doubted that the real motive to the opposition, was the fear of a discussion; the desire of excluding light; the adherence to a plan of surprise and deception. Nor need we desire any fuller proof of the spirit of party which has stimulated the opposition to the treaty, than is to be found in the circumstances of that opposition.

WASHINGTON LEAVES THE PRESIDENCY [1]

Philadelphia *Aurora*, March 6, 1797

"Lord, now lettest thou thy servant depart in peace, for mine eyes have seen thy salvation," was the pious ejaculation of a man who beheld a flood of happiness rushing in upon mankind. If ever there was a time that would license the reiteration of the exclamation, that time is now arrived; for the man who is the source of all the misfortunes of our country, is this day reduced to a level with his fellow citizens, and is no longer possessed of power to multiply evils upon the United States. If ever there was a period for rejoicing, this is the moment — every heart in unison with the freedom and happiness of the people ought to beat high, with exultation that the name of Washington from this day ceases to give a currency to political iniquity, and to legalize corruption. A new era is opening upon us, a new era which promises much to the people; for public measures must now stand upon their own merits, and nefarious projects can no longer be supported by a name.

[1] Long famous, or infamous, as the worst of the scurrilous attacks of extremist Anti-Federalists upon Washington. Written by Franklin's grandson, B. F. Bache, this classic of unseemly libel, as Worthington C. Ford calls it, reflects the family's resentment of Washington's frigid treatment of Franklin.

When a retrospect is taken of the Washingtonian Administration for eight years, it is a subject of the greatest astonishment, that a single individual should have canceled the principles of republicanism in an enlightened people, and should have carried his designs against the public liberty so far, as to have put in jeopardy its very existence. Such, however, are the facts, and with these staring us in the face, this day ought to be a *jubilee* in the United States.

THE NATION'S NEW CAPITAL

Washington *Gazette*, June 3, 1797

The city of Washington, or rather the site intended for the city, stands perhaps unrivalled by any in the world in point of advantages for becoming the emporium of a great nation. The scheme is grand and magnificent, and the funds intended for erecting public buildings *were* in the same proportion. But serious doubts are entertained in the minds of many persons, whose situations do not preclude them from examination, whether, in the execution, these funds have not been dissipated in wild and extravagant projects which, after having been carried on at an enormous expense, have been relinquished before being completed, so as not to be in any way beneficial. Instances need not be given; the facts speak for themselves, and are strongly imprinted in the memories of all who have had an opportunity for observing. . . . The enthusiastic spirit in which the operations of the city commenced opened a wide field for speculation, which has been practised in all its various forms, and has terminated in the ruin of all who were drawn into its vortex, and whose capital or talents were inferior to others'. Little is their failure to be regretted, were not a greater number of honest individuals, and useful mechanics and others, involved in its pernicious effects.

[DANGERS OF THE WYOMING LAND DISPUTE][1]

The Time-Piece, March 20, 1797

A bill is before the legislature of Pennsylvania for driving from their estates and burning the houses of the settlers under the Connecticut claims, at Wyoming. The severity of the proposed measure calls forth pointed animadversions in that State, and should the bill pass into a law, and the Executive attempt to enforce it, a civil commotion would probably be the consequence. The settlers on those lands have a strong sense of the justice of their claims, and

[1] These excerpts from the *Time-Piece* of Philip Freneau, a short-lived New York journal, are representative specimens of the editor's direct and telling style.

their right to the soil, which no legal decision has yet shaken; and to attempt to expel two, three, or perhaps five thousand hardy farmers from lands which they *firmly believe* to be their own property, would be a desperate undertaking. If the sword must be the ultimate arbiter between the parties, the blood of five thousand men might leave the controversy undecided. We trust the dreadful alternative will be avoided.

[SLAVERY THE CURSE OF AMERICA]
Idem, May 26, 1797

Mr. Rushton's address to the late President of the United States (see the first page of this paper) is an awful appeal to the moral sentiment of the world on the injustice and cruelty of man holding man in bondage; and in a country, too, that prides itself in having given the first spring to a universal emancipation from the fangs of tyrants. It is a lesson which cannot be soon forgot, and applies to every generous feeling of the heart that has not, from the accumulation of exorbitant wealth, become callous to the miseries of the far greater part of our species. There are not a few in these States who, notwithstanding all that has been said to the contrary, are still of the opinion that the patriotic Washington, who headed the Americans at a crisis that tried the heart of man, in the sublime cause of liberty and virtue, will come forward before the ingress of the approaching century (big with the most tremendous events) and shew an example to the world, that the people of republican America will not be the last to advance this grand object, the emancipation of slaves, by such means as the legislative wisdom of the Union shall deem it advisable to adopt. To suppose the continuance of the old *servile system* in this country, would be to suppose a halt in the progress of man towards that political perfection, which Plato of old and Condorcet in our own times, have given the world reason to believe is not wholly ideal.

[PEACE WITH FRANCE SHOULD BE PRESERVED]
Idem, June 9, 1797

Much is due to that description of men in Congress who have endeavored to prevent the flames of war from being kindled in these States; and it is to be hoped that their virtuous efforts will in the end defeat the hostile projects of the secret enemies of the peace of the United States, and the friends of the orders, checks, and balances of what is called the British Constitution. It is to be suspected that providing for friends in an American army and navy contributes in some degree to the thirst of certain persons for a war with France. Have all these people known what war is? or do they suppose it a frolic, that may be ended at pleasure? — have they ever witnessed the consequences of a battle either at sea or land, and the whole diabolical scene of broken bones, cleft skulls, and mangled carcasses — scenes which can only be justified in cases of resistance to oppression or invasion, and not from lighter considerations? If selfishness be the motive of some for warfare, let it be remembered that a whole nation is never selfish in this respect. It is for the interest of the few that men are turned into bulldogs and butchers — the selfishness of the many is their enjoyment of peace and quiet.

[THE TALK OF NEW ENGLAND'S SECESSION]

Idem, July 7, 1797

On Saturday [in Congress] was exhibited striking evidence of the real designs and views of the party in New England, who are constantly struggling in the House of Representatives for an indefinite increase in the executive power in this country, in the declaration made by Mr. Sewell, a member from Massachusetts, in the reply to those members who opposed the equipping and manning of the three frigates, on the ground of their very great expense and the slight probability of their being of so great a national advantage as would justify such an expenditure under the present circumstances of the country with respect to revenue. The gentleman affected to consider this kind of reasoning as intended to throw out of the protection of the Union all those who were engaged in commerce; and [he] said, Let those States, or that part of the Union who live by commerce, *separate themselves from the Union*, if they are not to be protected by the agricultural part of the country, and they will then be able to defend themselves; or words to that effect. Declarations of this kind, we think, must convince every impartial person that if this party cannot succeed in carrying all their favorite points in the Federal Government (and almost all their projects require a great expenditure of money, which must fall upon the landed interest in pretty heavy taxes), they will not scruple to make attempts to separate themselves from the Union, and form a separate confederacy; and as such a confederacy must be in its nature weak, they will be more easily enabled by that circumstance to carry into effect that favorite object which they must have so long had in view, *the placing themselves under the protection of the British Government.* We are the more confirmed in this opinion, from a recollection of several publications which were not many months since made in the newspapers of Connecticut. . . . Can it be possible that the honest farmers of New England will long support such a party in such a system of measures?

AMERICAN LOTTERIES: ADVICE TO THOSE WHO NEED IT [1]

Porcupine's Gazette, August 25, 1797

Have you an itching propensity to use your wits to advantage? Make a lottery. A splendid scheme is a bait that cannot fail to catch the gulls. Be sure to spangle it with rich prizes: the fewer blanks — on paper — the better; for on winding up the business, you know, it is easy to make as many blanks as you please. Witness a late lottery on the Potowmack. The *winding up*, however, is not absolutely necessary: you know what a noise the winding up of a certain clock once made. The better way is to delay the drawing; or should it *ever begin*, there is no hurry about the *end*, or rather, let it have no end at all. If, in either case, a set of discontented adventurers should happen to say hard things of you, show them that you despise their unmannerly insinuations, by humming the tune of *Yankee Doodle*. This may dumbfound them; but should they persist, there is a mode left that cannot fail to stop their mouths. The scheme of the lottery is your contract with the purchasers of tickets: produce this, and defy them to point out any breach of it on your part. *Entre nous;* I am supposing you discreet enough to avoid in your scheme anything that might look like a promise to commence the drawing on this or that particular day; or to finish at any given period. It would be enough to promise a beginning *when a sufficient number of tickets shall be sold;* of the sufficiency you would be the sole judge. Now they ought to know as well as you that, like Peter Pindar's razors, your tickets were "made to sell"; so that if but one ticket remained unsold, you are under no obligation to draw, a *sufficient number* not having been disposed of.

JOHN ADAMS AND MONARCHY

Philadelphia *Aurora*, August, 1797

The British faction in Boston are making a very great parade with John Adams. It seems they have prepared a "feast of gratitude" to him — for what? What have been his achievements since he became President by three stolen votes? If the "illustrious Adams" has a claim upon the gratitude of a certain set of men in Boston, is it owing to his Whiggism or to the manifestation which he gave in

[1] By William Cobbett.

his waf-whoop to the cause of Great Britain and of tyranny? If to his Revolutionary conduct, is it not extraordinary that the sentiment of gratitude should never have operated before? John Adams was Vice President of the United States for eight years, during which time he travelled to and from the dukedom of Braintree very often, and yet strange to tell, not one feast of gratitude was ever prepared for him by the faction at Boston. What an ungrateful set of monsters to let merit pass so long unnoticed and unrewarded.

. . . The farce of idolatry, however, it seems, must be kept up. The creator must worship the creature, or that order of things cannot be made to come to pass which a detestable and nefarious conspiracy in this country are seeking to bring about — *monarchy*.

[AMERICAN FORBEARANCE TOWARDS FRANCE]

Porcupine's Gazette, September 9, 1797

There never was a nation on earth so unjustly and so contemptuously treated by another, as America has been by France. Nations have been invaded, laid under contribution, conquered, and enslaved; but this has been effected by force or by treachery; it has been the fortune of war, or the result of conspiracy. Never did we before hear of a nation at peace with all the world, and pretending to be in the full enjoyment of independence, suffering a millionth part of what we suffered from the French (even before a whimper of complaint escaped from our lips) without declaring war or making reprisals.

This tameness following so close upon the heels of that Revolution which in its origins, its progress, and its conclusion was so strongly marked with irascibility and stubbornness, will naturally excite astonishment in all those who shall read the American history. When they are told of the innumerable and inexpressible injuries and indignities we have received from the French; that this despicable race of beings lorded it over our bays and rivers; and, not content with plundering and chastising our mariners, made them put the seal to their degradation by exacting from them payment for the shot fired at them; when we are told this, and that we bore it all without even talking of revenge, will they not wonder what was become of the men of 1776 who, with the scroll of their imaginary rights in one hand, and the sword in the other, swore to preserve the full enjoyment of the former, or to perish by the latter? And what will be their astonishment when they are told that the greater part of those very men were still living, and were still the rulers of the land?

Were the bold, the undaunted, the haughty language of the first

Congress, in their public remonstrances and addresses, compared with the faltering, the timid, the tame, the humble, the whining tone of the answer to the President's firm and manly speech, what a contrast, great God! would it present!

Mr. Adams's speech seems to be the last gleam of the spirit of the old Whigs. It was his protest against the degradation of his country — as if he had said to the House of Representatives: "I see that you are resolved to blast your reputation and that of America, but you shall not blast mine."

BENJAMIN FRANKLIN BACHE

Porcupine's Gazette, November 14, 1797

This atrocious wretch (worthy descendant of old Ben) knows that all men of any understanding set him down as an abandoned liar, as a tool and a hireling; and he is content that they should do so. He does not want to be thought anything else. As this *Gazette* is honored with many readers in foreign countries, it may not be improper to give them some little account of this miscreant.

If they have read the old hypocrite Franklin's will, they must have observed that part of his library, with some other things, are left to a certain *grandson;* this is the very identical Market-Street scoundrel. He spent several years in hunting offices under the Federal Government, and being constantly rejected, he at last became its most bitter foe. Hence his abuse of General Washington, whom, at the time he was soliciting a place, he panegyrized to the third heaven.

He was born for a hireling, and therefore when he found that he could not obtain employ in one quarter, he sought it in another. The first effect of his paw being greased, appeared soon after Genet's arrival, and he has from that time to this been as faithful to the cutthroats of Paris, as ever dog was to his master.

He is an ill-looking devil. His eyes never get above your knees. He is of a sallow complexion, hollow-cheeked, dead-eyed, and has a *tout ensemble* just like that of a fellow who has been about a week or ten days on a gibbet.

[THE BENEFITS OF WAR WITH FRANCE]

Porcupine's Gazette, January, 1798

Let us see what would be gained by a war. The immediate effect would be, a free passage over the ocean, without the hazard of seizure, or even of examination.

The commerce of America would immediately raise its drooping head; the confidence of commercial men would be reëstablished, and the spirit of trade and enterprise renewed. American seamen would no longer be shot at, and flogged, within sight of their own shores; nor would the red-headed ruffians add to the twenty millions they have already seized: no peace should be made with them till they refund their plunder, which would amply discharge all the debts incurred by the war.

Louisiana they might be compelled to relinquish; and thus would these States be completely rid of the most alarming danger that ever menaced them; and which, if not soon removed, must and will, in a few years, effect their disunion and destruction.

But above all, the alliance with Great Britain would cut up the French faction here. It is my sincere opinion, that they have formed the diabolical plan of *revolutionizing* (to use one of their execrable terms) the whole continent of America. They have their agents and partizans without number, and very often where we do not imagine. Their immoral and blasphemous principles have made a most alarming progress. They have explored the community to its utmost boundaries and its inmost recesses, and have left a partizan on every spot, ready to preach up *the holy right of insurrection.*

They have no intention of invading these States with the fair and avowed purpose of *subjugating them.* No; they will come as they went to the Brabanters and the Dutch, as "friends and deliverers." A single spark of their fraternity would set all the Southern States in a flame, the progress of which, as far as Connecticut, would be as rapid as the chariot of Apollo. This dreadful scourge nothing can prevent but a war. That would naturally disarm and discredit their adherents; would expel their intriguing agents, who are now in our streets, in our houses, and at our tables. It would cut off the cankering, poisonous, *sans-culottes* connexion, and leave the country once more sound and really independent.

PORCUPINE TO THE PUBLIC

The Rushlight, February 24, 1800

When I determined to discontinue the publication of *Porcupine's Gazette*, I intended to remain for the future if not an unconcerned, at least a silent spectator of public transactions and political events; but the unexpected and sweeping result of a lawsuit, since decided against me, has induced me to abandon my lounging intention. The suit to which I allude was an action of slander, commenced against me in the autumn of 1797 by Dr. Benjamin Rush, the noted bleeding physician of Philadelphia. I was tried on the 14th of December last, when "the upright, enlightened, and impartial

Republican jury" assessed, as damages, *five thousand dollars;* a sum surpassing the aggregate amount of all the damages assessed for all the torts of this kind, ever sued for in these States, from their first settlement to the present day. To the five thousand dollars must be added the costs of suit, the loss incurred by the interruption in collecting debts in Pennsylvania, and by the sacrifice of property taken in execution, and sold by the sheriff at public auction in Philadelphia, where a great number of books in sheets (among which was a part of the new edition of Porcupine's Works) were sold, or rather given away, as waste paper; so that the total of what has been, or will be, wrested away from me by Rush, will fall little short of eight thousand dollars.

To say that I do not feel this stroke, and very sensibly too, would be great affectation; but to repine at it would be folly, and to sink under it would be cowardice. I knew an Englishman in the Royal Province of New Brunswick, who had a very valuable house, which was, I believe, at that time nearly his all; burnt to the ground. He was out of town when the fire broke out, and happened to come just after it had exhausted itself. Everyone, knowing how hard he had earned the property, expected to see him bitterly bewail its loss. He came very leisurely up to the spot, stood about five minutes, looking earnestly at the rubbish, and then, stripping off his coat, *"here goes,"* said he, *"to earn another!"* and immediately went to work, raking the spikes and bits of iron out of the ashes. This noble-spirited man I have the honor to call my friend, and if ever this page should meet his eye, he will have the satisfaction to see that, should it be impossible for me to follow, I at least remember his example.

In the future exertions of my industry, however, pecuniary emolument will be, as it always has been with me, an object of only secondary consideration. Recent incidents, amongst which I reckon the unprecedented proceedings against me at Philadelphia, have imposed on me the discharge of a duty which I owe to my own country as well as this, and the sooner I begin the sooner I shall have done.

NOAH WEBSTER [1]

Philadelphia *Aurora*, July, 1800

There are some beings whose fate it seems to be to run counter from reason and propriety on all occasions. In every attempt

---

[1] Noah Webster's Dictionary, here derided, was successfully published in 1828 in two large volumes of more than 1,000 pages each, containing many more words and definitions than any previous dictionary of the language, and attaining a new level of the lexicographer's art.

which this oddity of literature has made, he appears not only to have made himself ridiculous, but to have rendered what he attempted to elucidate more obscure, and to injure or deface what he has intended to improve.

His spelling-book has done more injury in the common schools of the country than the genius of ignorance herself could have conceived a hope of, by his ridiculous attempts to alter the *syllable* division of words and to *new model* the spelling, by a capricious but utterly incompetent attempt of his own weak conception.

After involving the question of the yellow fever in deeper obscurity, and producing nothing but the profit by the sale of the work, he now appears as a legislator and municipal magistrate of Connecticut; writes nonsense pseudo-political and pseudo-philosophical for his newspaper at New York, and proposes to give to the American world no less than three dictionaries!

This man, who ought to go to school for the regulation of his understanding, has, it appears, undertaken to complete a *system of education*, and as part of these, we are told, is to give us a dictionary for *schools*, a dictionary for the *counting-house*, and a dictionary for the *learned!*

His motives, for they are truly *Gothic*, it appears are that a number of English words have been misapplied — new words introduced — and a considerable number exploded in America; for this reason he says it is necessary to make a new Dictionary. The plain truth is, for the reason given is preposterous, that he means to *make money* by a scheme which ought to be and will be discountenanced by every man who admires the classic English writers, who has sense enough to see the confusion which must arise from such a silly project — and the incapacity of a man who thus undertakes a work which, if it were at all necessary or eligible, would require the labor of a number of learned and competent men to accomplish it.

[JEFFERSON BECOMES PRESIDENT]

New York *American Citizen*, March 13, 1801

Citizen Adams arrived in town the day before yesterday on his way to the eastward. No bells were rung, no cannon were fired, no dinner was provided, no toasts were drunk on the occasion. As a citizen he arrived, as a citizen he was received, and as a citizen he was suffered to depart. Is it not mortifying that while Oliver Wolcott, the Secretary, is toasted and idolized, *Citizen* Adams is neglected? How shall we account for this? Mr. Adams is neglected by some for his political inconsistency in treating with France, and by a still greater proportion because he is no longer President.

[DEMOCRATIC CONTRADICTIONS: MADISON VERSUS JEFFERSON]

New York *Evening Post*, November 23, 1801

To displace a man of high merit, and one who from his station may be supposed a man of extensive influence, will excite jealousies and create an interested opposition in the system, and in the people. He will have his friends, his dependants, and the public sympathy on his side, and if it should not give birth to an impeachment in the legislature, it would probably prove a fatal impeachment before the community at large. Can we suppose that a President of the United States, elected for four years only, dependent on the popular voice, impeachable by the legislature, and not perhaps distinguished in point of wealth or personal talents from the head of the department himself, can we suppose, I say, that in defiance of all these considerations, he will presume wantonly to dismiss a meritorious and virtuous officer from his service?

I own it is *an abuse of power* which exceeds my imagination, and of which I can form no rational conception.

Madison's Speech in Congress.

How are vacancies to be obtained? Those by death are few, by resignation none. Can any other mode then but removal be proposed? This is a painful office, but it is made my duty, and I meet it as such.

Jefferson's Reply to the New Haven Remonstrance.

[THE HORRID CUSTOM OF DUELLING]

New York *Evening Post*, November 24, 1801

Died, this morning, in the twentieth year of his age, PHILIP HAMILTON, eldest son of General Hamilton — murdered in a duel. As the public will be anxious to know the leading particulars of this deplorable event, we have collected the following, which may be relied upon as correct.

On Friday morning last, young Hamilton and young Price, sitting in the same box with Mr. George I. Eacker, began in levity a conversation respecting an oration delivered by the latter in July, and made use of some expressions respecting it, which were overheard by Eacker, who asked Hamilton to step into the lobby. Price followed. Here the expression, *damned rascal*, was used by

Eacker to one of them, and a little scuffle ensued; but they soon adjourned to a public house. An explanation was then demanded, which of them the offensive expression was meant for; after a little hesitation, it was declared to be meant for each. Eacker then said, as they parted, "I expect to hear from you;" they replied, "You shall;" and challenges followed. A meeting took place, between Eacker and Price, on Sunday morning; which, after their exchanging four shots each, was finished by the interference of the seconds.

Yesterday afternoon, the fatal duel was fought between young Hamilton and Eacker. Hamilton received a shot through the body at the first discharge, and fell without firing. He was brought across the ferry to his father's house, where he languished of the wound till this morning, when he expired.

He was a young man of an amiable disposition and cultivated mind; much esteemed and affectionately beloved by all who had the pleasure of his acquaintance.

Reflections on this horrid custom must occur to every man of humanity; but the voice of an individual or of the press must be ineffectual without additional, strong, and pointed legislative interference. Fashion has placed it upon a footing which nothing short of this can control.

[MAKING TAMMANY VOTERS WHOLESALE]

New York *Evening Post*, December 15, 1801

Much public attention having been excited by the late election of charter officers, for the fourth and fifth wards of this city, and the scrutiny that succeeded, we have judged that it would be proper to publish a fair and correct statement of those transactions.

By the charter of the city, the aldermen and assistants are to be annually chosen by the freemen being inhabitants, and the freeholders of each respective ward; and by an act of the legislature the freehold must be of the value of $50 over and above all debts charged upon it, and have been possessed (unless acquired by descent or devise) at least one month before the day of such election. The elector is moreover obliged, if called upon for that purpose, to take an oath that he is not under any obligation or promise to convey to any other person after the election.

In the fourth ward, John Bogert and Nicholas Carmer were the federal, and Cornelius C. Roosevelt and Samuel Wendover the anti-federal candidates; and in the fifth ward the federal candidates were James Roosevelt and John P. Ritter, the anti-federal candidates were Arcularius and Drake.

The election according to law was to be held on the seventeenth day of November. But on the tenth day of October, Jasper Ward, a noted zealot of the anti-federal party, purchased from Abraham Bloodgood, the currier, another person of the same description, a lot of ground in the fifth ward, with a currier's shop upon it, at the price of $2,000, and took a conveyance for the same to thirty-nine persons, as tenants in common. On the same day a similar purchase was made in the fourth ward at the price of $3700, and a conveyance made in like manner to seventy-four persons; but the premises were subjected to a mortgage, upon which $1500, besides interest, were due. Both those purchases were clandestinely made for the sole and avowed purpose of procuring qualifications to vote at the next election of charter officers. In the fifth ward thirty-six of the persons named in the first deed, and in the fourth ward seventy-four named in the last, voted at the late election; and by their aid the anti-federal candidates had an apparent majority of six in the fifth, and of thirty-three in the fourth ward.

A scrutiny was demanded and the federal candidates in the fifth ward objected to the votes of the thirty-six persons named as grantees in the deed from Bloodgood, and to about thirty-three more. The federal candidates in the fourth ward at first objected to all the votes not given for themselves, except two; but being called on by the board to declare upon oath, how many they conscientiously believed to be proper subjects of challenge, they gave up one hundred, and then challenged the remainder, being eighty-one.

[PRESIDENT JEFFERSON'S FIRST ANNUAL MESSAGE] [1]

New York *Evening Post*, December 18, 1801

Instead of delivering a *speech* to the houses of Congress, at the opening of the present session, the President has thought fit to transmit a *message*. Whether this has proceeded from pride or from humility, from a temperate love of reform or from a wild spirit of innovation, is submitted to the conjectures of the curious. A single observation shall be indulged — since all agree that he is unlike his predecessors in essential points, it is a mark of consistency to differ from them in matters of form.

Whoever considers the temper of the day, must be satisfied that this message is likely to add much to the popularity of our chief magistrate. It conforms, as far as would be tolerated at this early stage of our progress in political perfection, to the bewitching tenets of that illuminated doctrine which promises man, ere long, an emancipation from the burdens and restraints of government;

[1] By William Coleman.

giving a foretaste of that pure felicity which the apostles of that doctrine have predicted. After having, with infinite pains and assiduity, formed the public taste for this species of fare, it is certainly right for those whom the people have chosen for their caterers to be attentive to the gratification of that taste. And should the viands which they offer prove baneful poisons instead of wholesome ailments, the justification is both plain and easy — *Good patriots must, at all events, please the people.* But those whose patriotism is of the old school, who differ so widely from the disciples of the new creed that they would rather risk incurring the displeasure of the people by speaking unpalatable truths, than betray their interest by fostering their prejudices, will never be deterred by an impure tide of popular opinion from honestly pointing out the mistakes or the faults of weak or wicked men, who may have been selected as guardians of the public weal.

The message of the President, by whatever motives it may have been dictated, is a performance which ought to alarm all who are anxious for the safety of our government, for the respectability and welfare of our nation. It makes, or aims at making, a most prodigal sacrifice of constitutional energy, of sound principle, and of public interest, to the popularity of one man.

THE DEATH OF HAMILTON [1]

Philadelphia *Political Register*, July 13, 1804

The mail from New York of this morning confirms the melancholy, the heart-rending intelligence of the DEATH of General Hamilton. The mourning countenance of our citizens — the anguish of his friends — the tears of his countrymen, proclaim their sense of his worth, and offer a just tribute of gratitude to his memory. To the honor of our character, let it be recorded, that those who entertained unceasing jealousy of his superior powers, while living — with honorable feeling lament him dead. After Washington (who alone surpassed him), after the first of men and greatest of heroes, who has rivalled Hamilton in usefulness to our country? — in attachment to its interests? in unceasing labour, in the exertion of the most splendid talents for its welfare? The generous and gallant soldier, the wise and virtuous statesman, the eloquent and accomplished orator, the ardent and magnanimous patriot, has fallen the victim of unyielding honor, and inflexible integrity.

His memory is embalmed in the esteem and affection of his con-

---

[1] By a fellow-soldier of Hamilton in the Revolution, Major Jackson. Its abstention from criticism of the custom of duelling, in contrast with the previous editorial, and from censure of Aaron Burr, are noteworthy.

temporaries, and will be consecrated by the gratitude of his country
to future ages.

Thus has fallen, prematurely fallen, the Hero, to whose military
ardor and accomplishments America confessed the highest obligation; the Civilian, from whose luminous and correct mind proceeded that invaluable commentary on the Constitution of the
United States, which essentially contributed to secure its adoption;
the Statesman, to whose talents we are indebted for the organization of our finances, and the establishment of our public credit; the
Jurist and the Scholar, whose combination of intellectual powers
formed the boast and ornament of our country; the Patriot, who
gave, with glowing zeal, to that country, the increasing efforts of
his superior mind; and the Man who, endeared to his friends by
every tender and ennobled quality of the heart, received in return
the truest affection, and the most respectful esteem.

POLITICS FOR FARMERS: [THE FATUOUS CRY FOR WAR][1]

Philadelphia *Aurora*, January, 1807

Foreign governments, whose institutions and interests are dis-
similar from ours, *envy us, and endeavor to disturb our repose.*

Nations whose policy is a combination of commercial monopoly
and war, to maintain that monopoly, look upon the United States
as other sects look upon the *Quakers* — with *jealousy* — because our
Quaker policy exempts us from all the variety of evils to which the
savage and unchristian policy of war exposes them.

Our policy, so salutary for our own people, like all human things,
admits of an alloy; it tempts numbers from those foreign governments to come hither merely for a temporary term — to profit by
our policy, and being enriched, to go away; these persons spread
through our seaports, with the various habits of their own citizen
nations, and contaminate many of our own citizens.

Many of our citizens educated in the prejudices of the government which ruled us as colonies, still retain their early attachment
and prejudices, and even the most peaceful sect exhibits too many
examples of the blunders of prejudice which can maintain a *religious* and a *political* sentiment at variance, and destructive one of
another.

A disposition is evident in many to be discontented with a calm
and tranquil prosperity; and a solicitude in others to bow down
the necks of their fellow citizens, over whom they fancy they possess

[1] By William Duane.

either greater talents or greater riches, which conveys to them a more important idea than talents, genius, or virtue.

Many persons educated after the prejudices and habits of foreign cities, and hostile to the simplicity and equality of a free state, become speculators in commerce and repay their commercial credits by infidelity to their country.

These various classes of men are wrought upon by foreign agents and emissaries — several in the receipt of *stipends* from foreign governments; numerous presses are indirectly bribed and kept in pay by mercantile and consular favor for the purpose of influencing our people, and forming interests, either to retard the growth of our own nation to maturity, or to create interests and alliances with foreign governments.

It is from these various and other subordinate sources that we hear the cry *for war* — *naval establishments* — and extravagant systems.

THE RESPONSIBILITY FOR THE BRITISH OUTRAGE [1]

Washington *National Intelligencer*, July 10, 1807

We are pleased to observe the circumspection of the merchants. If they consult their own interests, or that of the country, they will for a time repress their spirit of adventure, and run as few risks as possible, until an explicit answer shall be given by the British Ministry. As yet it remains a point undetermined whether the late barbarous outrages have emanated directly from the British Cabinet, or are the acts exclusively of subordinate commanders. If they are directly authorized by the Cabinet, then we may calculate upon a scene of violence co-extensive with British power, and for another display of that perfidy so characteristic of its government. Every American vessel on the ocean will be seized and sent into some British port for adjudication, and the courts will take special care, if they do not forthwith proceed to condemnation, at any rate to keep the cases *sub judice*. Indeed, if the recent outrages do not emanate from the government, it is difficult to say whether they will not, notwithstanding, seize what they may consider a favorable opportunity to wreak their vengeance on this country. We know the hostility of the greater part of those who compose the British administration to our principles, and they may be Quixotic enough to imagine themselves able to crush these principles, or seriously arrest our commercial growth. They may, therefore, under some hollow pretext, refuse that satisfaction which we de-

[1] By Samuel Harrison Smith, the young editor whom Jefferson advised to remove from Philadelphia to Washington; his paper had by this date become the official organ of the Administration.

mand, the result of which will be war.   There is indeed no small color of truth in the supposition that this outrage has flowed from the change in the British Ministry, connected with the fate the treaty has received from our government, and that without meaning or expecting war, they have virtually authorized aggressions on us, which they fancied we would tamely submit to; and that however astonished they may be with the manifestation they will soon receive of the temper of the nation, their pride may prevent them from retracting.

Everything is, and must for some time remain, uncertain.   In the meantime it becomes our duty to husband all our strength.   But little injury can accrue to the merchant from a suspension of his export business for a few months, compared with the incalculable evils that might befall him from its active prosecution.   He is, therefore, under a double obligation to pursue this course, arising not only from a regard to his own interest, but likewise from a love of his country.   In the day of danger it will want all its resources, and all its seamen.   Were Congress in session, it is extremely probable that their first step would be the imposition of an embargo.   What they would do, were they sitting, it is the interest and duty of the merchant to do himself.   We have no doubt that the intelligence of this order of men may on this occasion, as it has on all former occasions, be relied on.

[THE *CHESAPEAKE* AND THE *LEOPARD*]

Washington *Federalist*, July 3, 1807

We have never, on any occasion, witnessed the spirit of the people excited to so great a degree of indignation, or such a thirst for revenge, as on hearing of the late unexampled outrage on the *Chesapeake*.   All parties, ranks, and professions were unanimous in their detestation of the dastardly deed, and all cried aloud for vengeance. The accounts which we receive from every quarter tend to show that these sentiments universally prevail.   The Administration may implicitly rely on the cordial support of every American citizen, in whatever manly and dignified steps they may take, to resent the insult and obtain reparation for the injury.

New York *Evening Post*, July 24, 1807

We say and we once more repeat it, that the *Chesapeake*, *being a national ship*, was not liable to be searched for any purpose, nor to have any of her crew taken from her.   This is ground that ought to be maintained at every hazard.   But on the other hand, candor demands the concession, that it was in every way improper in the

American commodore to enlist four deserters from the British man
of war, *knowing them to be such;* and whether they were English subjects, or had voluntarily enlisted and received their bounty (this
being a conduct long since silently permitted by us), is immaterial.
And we say further that if the Administration, on being applied to
by the English consul, refused to accommodate the affair, but insisted on protecting the men by placing them under the national
flag, the Administration thereby became criminal, and are answer-
able to the people for their culpable conduct.

Such are the sentiments we hold on this subject: they have been
often revised, and are believed to be correct.

The result is that our own Administration are considered as having
been to blame; but not so that their misconduct justified the resort
to force on the part of the English. On this point, we are ready to
say that we consider the national sovereignty has been attacked, the
national honor tarnished, and that ample reparations and satisfaction must be given or that war ought to be resorted to by force of
arms.

[THE EVILS OF THE EMBARGO] [1]

Columbian Centinel, January 23, 1808

Since the promulgation of the British Order in Council — which
has certainly been expected ever since the neutral nations have
refused to resent or remonstrate against the abominable and unprecedented decrees of France — some men think the embargo not
so bad a measure! Does not this betray a want of calculation?
Let the following facts reply:

1. France cannot endanger our trade to England more than to
the amount of about four or five per cent. Of course the embargo
is not necessary against her.

2. Great Britain leaves open to us: —

Her own dominions and colonies throughout the world, to
which we now export twenty-six millions per annum.

She relaxes her great Navigation Act in our favor.

She leaves open to us our trade to the colonies of France, Spain,
and Holland, which will take off ten millions more of our produce.

She permits to us the free import of all our West India produce,
which will still give us revenue and luxuries.

We can pursue the Russian, Swedish, African, and much of the
Mediterranean trade; as well as all our India and China trade.

We can export all our present produce, and a very considerable
part of our foreign importations.

---

[1] The Embargo Act, detested by such New England journals as the *Centinel*,
was passed in December, 1807, and repealed March 1, 1809. The Federalists of
New England and New York assailed it as a diabolical scheme to ruin the North
while the South stood unharmed.

Is not this better than an embargo, which destroys all trade, all revenue, all employment? Let those who think it is not, discuss the subject; and they will find that this British decree, bad as it is, is not by far so bad as it was reported to be

[THE EMBARGO AND THE FARMER'S STORY]

Columbian Centinel, May 25, 1808

A zealous Boston Democrat was lately in the country extolling the embargo to a plain farmer, as a wise as well as a strong measure, and urging the farmer to express his opinion upon it. The farmer, however, modestly declined, saying that he lived in the bush where he had not the means of information on which to ground an opinion on political measures; but if Boston folks, who knew more, said it was right, he supposed it was so; but, says he, I will tell you a story. Our minister one day sent his boy to the pasture after a horse. He was gone so long that the parson was afraid the horse had kicked his brains out; he went therefore with anxiety to look after him. In the field he found the boy standing still with his eyes steadily fixed upon the ground. His master inquired with severity what he was doing there. Why, sir, said he, I saw a woodchuck run into this hole, and so I thought I would stand and watch for him until he was starved out; but *I declare I am almost starved to death myself.*

[HATEFUL MEASURES FOR ENFORCING THE EMBARGO]

Boston *Gazette,* February 2, 1809

Within a few days past Colonel Boyd, commanding at the Castle, received orders from the Secretary of War to interdict all vessels from passing Fort Independence; in consequence of this edict the acting Collector has been placed under the necessity of withholding clearances to every description of vessels.

This aggravated repression was not generally known until yesterday, when the vessels in the harbor bound their colors in black, and hoisted them half-mast. The circumstance has created some considerable agitation in the public mind, but to the honor of the town has been yet unattended with any serious consequences.

It is to be presumed that this new edict will at least continue to be enforced until Secretary Dearborn is at leisure to come on, to mark out his favorites, and take upon himself the office, so long reserved for him, of the Customs.

The spirit of our citizens is rising and may burst into a flame. Everything should therefore be done to calm them till the Legislature has had time to mature its plans of redress. It is feared that the caution necessary in such an assembly may protract our relief too long; but we must wait patiently the aid of our *Constitutional Guardians*, rather than stain the character of this metropolis by mobs and riots. If our government cannot do anything now that shall afford full and complete relief, they may at least do enough to calm the public mind and lead the citizens to wait for events, which must place the means for a radical cure completely in our hands.

The spirit of New England is slow in rising; but when once inflamed by oppression, it will never be repressed by anything short of complete *justice*.

THE EMBARGO EXPERIMENT ENDED[1]

Baltimore *Federal Republican*, March, 1809

The embargo now ceases to be in force, and every merchant who can give a bond with good sureties to double the amount of vessel and cargo, is entitled to clear out for any port except in France or England or the dependency of either of them. After depriving government of its means of support for sixteen months, and preventing the people of the United States from pursuing a lawful and profitable commerce, and reducing the whole country to a state of wretchedness and poverty, our infatuated rulers, blinded by a corrupt predilection for France, have been forced to acknowledge their fatal error, and so far to retrace their steps. To the patriotism of the New England States is due the praise of our salvation. By their courage and virtue have we been saved from entanglements in a fatal alliance with France. The whole system of fraud and corruption has been exposed to the people, and those very men who were the first to cast off the yoke of England, have lived to save their country from falling under the command of a more cruel tyrant. The patriot who had the courage to encounter the fury of the political storm, who stepped forth in the hour of danger to give the first alarm to his country, we trust will one day be rewarded with the highest honors in the gift of a grateful people.

[1] The Republican caucus in Congress decided on February 7, 1809, in favor of dropping the embargo and returning to the old non-intercourse plan. President Jefferson signed the repeal on March 1, just before he left office. The opposition "patriot" to whom the Baltimore *Republican* refers was Senator Timothy Pickering of Massachusetts.

EX–PRESIDENT ADAMS ON NATIONAL UNITY AND FOREIGN AFFAIRS [1]

Columbian Centinel, March 25, 1809

The Democrats have attempted to make much electioneering use of their old friend the late President Adams. For nearly a year past they have put their wits in requisition to extract something from the venerable patriot which should serve them as a lift. Numerous demagogues were selected to write to him, to send him pamphlets, and to ask his advice on public affairs; knowing that politeness, etiquette, and habit would induce him to answer them. The mere correspondence they knew would *tell* something; but their chief hope was that good use might be made, at a proper time, of mutilated parts of the answer, and perhaps the escape of a hasty or unguarded expression. Though the impudence of this attempt was without parallel in the annals of Machiavellism, yet as the case was desperate, the attempt must be made. It did not deter these Democratic demagogues that they and the world well knew that only four or five short years ago they themselves, and their hirelings, had branded this same John Adams — this *new* correspondent — with every invective which the lexicography of hatred, malice, and billingsgate could furnish; that he was by them unblushingly proclaimed a "hoary-headed traitor"; an upstart tyrant, the son of a shoemaker, who wished to lord it over an American heritage; whose aim *totis viribus* was to introduce Monarchy, Aristocracy, and Slavery into the United States; who for this purpose was the father of the Alien and Sedition laws, the introducer of a standing army, excise and land taxes, and of eight per cent loans; that he, John Adams, had sold himself to Great Britain; that he had defended, in a book written for the purpose, a government of kings, lords, and commons; and that he was the venal tool of the British Ministry. Nay more, these demagogues knew that there was no epithet too degrading which they had not applied to this same Mr. John Adams; and that of the nicknames they had bestowed on him, that of the "French War-Hawk," "Duke of Braintree," and "skulking, crazy John" were not the most opprobrious. A record of these scurrilities, and of many others, will be found in the files of the Democratic papers.

The new correspondence between Mr. Adams and these demagogues was at first heard of only in rumors and privately shewn to confidential persons. Not one of the old friends of the President

---

[1] By Benjamin Russell, the stout Federalist who had founded the *Centinel* in 1784, and kept it for more than thirty years the leading Boston newspaper, and one of the greatest of the Federalist organs. His arguments against the Embargo were warmly applauded throughout New England.

who had supported him through thick and thin was allowed to take a peep at them. It was thought not quite up to the mark for general publication, and was, perhaps, too strongly tinctured with old-fashioned political morality. Still the names of John Adams and the Embargo were linked together, and capitalized in many a caucus resolution. But the approaching election called for something to cheer up the drooping spirits of Democracy; and two of the Hampshire County managers were selected to write to Mr. Adams and request an answer. The answer was prompt, but only extracts from it have been permitted to meet the public eye. The extracts follow:

Quincy, March 13, 1809.

Gentlemen:

I have received your very civil letter of the third of this month with emotions very similar to those which I felt many years ago.

I have neither power nor influence to do anything for my country, to assist her in her present distresses, or guard her against future calamities. Nothing now remains to me but the right of private judgment, and that I exercise freely, and communicate my sentiments as freely to those who wish to know them.

I am *totis viribus* against any division of the Union, by the North River, or by Delaware River, or by the Potomac, or any other river, or by any chain of mountains. I am for maintaining the independence of the nation at all events. [1]

I am no advocate for Mr. Gore's declaration of war against France. Knowing as I do from personal experience the mutually friendly dispositions between the people of France and the people of America, Bonaparte out of the question, I should be very sorry to see them converted into ill-will, and our old English prejudices revived. Lasting injuries and misfortunes would arise to this country from such a change. [2]

I am averse also to a war with England, and wish to maintain our neutrality as long as possible, without conceding important principles. If either of the belligerent powers force us into a war, I am for fighting that power, whichever it may be. [3]

I always consider the whole nation as my children: but they have almost all been undutiful to me. You two gentlemen are almost the only ones, out of my own house, who have for a long time, and I thank you for it, expressed a filial affection for

JOHN ADAMS. [4]

(1) And who, pray, has ever advocated a dissolution of the Union, excepting indeed Mr. Giles and some other Virginia demagogues during Mr. Adams's Administration? We do not know why this remark was lugged in here. But we defy anyone to produce

a single act adopted, or a single line written by any Federalist, in which a dissolution of the Union has been threatened or advocated. The idea is an absurdity; and the charge one of the most contemptible ever propagated. We appeal to the hundreds of spirited resolutions of the people of New England recently adopted in their primary assemblies; to the resolutions, reports, and addresses of the legislature of Massachusetts for proof of the attachment of the Federalists to the union and independence of the United States.

(2) What does all this mean? Can it be possible that Mr. Adams has adopted the newspaper slang of the day — "Mr. Gore's declaration of War"? O tempora! O mores! The legislature appointed a large committee to report on a certain subject; Mr. Gore signed the report as chairman. The report was in favor of a repeal of the embargo laws, and as the Democrats demanded a substitute, for they insisted upon war or embargo, the report recommended the entire repeal of the embargo laws; and if we must have war with one of the European aggressors, it ought to be with France, who was first aggressor and the enemy likely to do us the least harm. This opinion was not merely that of the committee and Mr. Gore as one of them, but of the Legislature and the people at large. At the town meeting in Boston Mr. Eustis, now Secretary of War, and Mr. Blake, both declared not merely that if war was made it ought to be with France, but that we ought to, and should be, at war with France. Thousands heard and can remember this declaration.

(3) Mr. Adams's aversion to war seems to be among the new doctrines he has embraced. Does he recollect the answer he gave to the young men of Boston in 1798–1799? "*To arms, my young friends, to arms!*" We have not the files before us to copy the war articles of those days. But the language is rather of a different nature from the present, though a war then would have been made against the French people themselves; whereas a war now would be against the Tyrant who governs them.

(4) We have heretofore preserved an unabated respect for the character of the late President. But we must say that thus to lend himself to a party which has loaded him with their execrations and charges, and which he has repeatedly denounced as the worst enemies of their country, solely to serve *electioneering purposes*, is a degradation of conduct unworthy a statesman and a philosopher; and which must blast his fame to all posterity. We say nothing of gratitude due his old friends, and particularly to Mr. Gore, who never injured him in thought, word, or deed.[1]

---

[1] Both John Adams and John Quincy Adams were bitterly opposed to England in these years, denouncing her interferences with neutral trade. Their support of the embargo aroused all Federalist New England against them.

[FRENCH OUTRAGES AGAINST OUR SHIPS AND SAILORS][1]

New York *Evening Post*, July, 1809

Fellow Citizens, for more than two years has your flag been struck on the ocean whenever it has been met with by the flag of France; your vessels have been scornfully burnt or scuttled in the ocean; your property has been seized or confiscated; your sailors robbed and manacled, or forced by cruelties to serve against their own country; the worthless part of them suborned by a public decree to commit perjury, and on their evidence, though charging no crime, the wretched remainder of the crew condemned as prisoners of war, landed as such and marched without shoes to their feet or clothing to their backs in the most inclement weather some hundreds of miles into the interior of France; lashed along the highway like slaves, treated with every possible indignity, and then immured in the infernal dungeons of Arras or Verdun. There, deprived of every comfort and of all intercourse with the rest of the world, there, fellow citizens, have they been lying, some for months and some for years! There they now lie, wasting away the best vigor of their days, counting the hours of their captivity as they turn in vain their imploring eyes towards their own government, and etching down another and another week of grief and despondence. Nineteen cents a day allowed them for subsistence and clothing and medicine! Allow them seven a day, or $25 a year for clothing, and you leave them four cents to purchase each meal. Think of this, ye who live in luxury here, and read their story with more indifference than you listen to the fictitious sorrows of a Robinson Crusoe; think of this, and let it at length engage your attention, and induce you to demand of your government to interfere in earnest.

But after all, what is to be expected? If any one of these wretched men, more fortunate than his fellow sufferers, escapes and brings the tale of their situation, and makes it known to his countrymen, a set of inhuman wretches here, more cruel than the French themselves, turn their wrongs into derision, or exert their miserable faculties in cavillings and criticisms to shew that all these statements are fabrications, because they have not been drawn up by some special pleader. The barbarous impudence of some editors pronounces them forgeries, and every fellow who can set a type repeats the infamous calumny, till the public voice that had begun to raise itself in their favor is stilled, and sympathy extinguished.

---

[1] Under the Bayonne Decree of April 17, 1808, the Napoleonic Government seized many American ships and imprisoned their men, and French frigates even sank American ships at sea.

[THE FOLLY OF JOINING THE ARMY] [1]

New York *Evening Post*, January 24, 1812

"*Tricks upon Travellers*," or "*More Ways than one to kill a Cat.*" — Old saws. We are certainly now to have a war, for Congress have voted to have an army. But let me tell you, there is all the difference in the world between an army on paper, and an army in the field. An army on paper is voted in a whiff, but to raise an army, you must offer men good wages. The wages proposed to be given to induce men to come forward and enlist for five years, leave their homes and march away to take Canada, is a bounty of $16, and $5 a month; and at the end of the war, if they can get a certificate of good behavior, 160 acres of wild land and three months' pay; for the purpose, I presume, of enabling the soldier to walk off and find it, if he can. Now I should really be glad to be informed, whether it is seriously expected that, in a country where a stout able-bodied man can earn $15 a month from May to November, and a dollar a day during mowing and harvesting, he will go into the army for a bounty of $16, $5 a month for five years, if the war should last so long, and 160 acres of wild land, if he happens to be on such good terms with his commanding officer as to obtain a certificate of good behavior? Let the public judge if such inducements as these will ever raise an army of 25,000 men, or ever were seriously expected to do it? If not, can anything be meant more than "sound and fury signifying nothing"? This may be called humbugging on a large scale.

[THEY CALL IT A WAR FOR COMMERCE!]

New York *Evening Post*, January 26, 1812

Look for yourselves, good people all. — The administration tell me that the object for which they are going to war with Great Britain, is to secure our commercial rights; to put the trade of the country on a good footing; to enable our merchants to deal with Great Britain on full as favorable terms as they deal with France, or else not deal at all. Such is the declared object for which all further intercourse is to be suspended with Great Britain and her allies, while we proceed to make war upon her and them until we compel her to pay more respect to American commerce: and, as Mr. Stow truly observed in his late excellent speech, the anxiety of members of Congress to effect this object is always the greater in proportion

---

[1] By William Coleman; his efforts to prevent army enlistments and subscriptions to the national loan on the eve of the War of 1812 explain why he and his newspaper were threatened with mob attack.

to the distance any honorable member lives from the seaboard. To enable you, good people, to judge for yourselves, I have only to beg of you to turn your eyes to Mr. Gallatin's letter in a succeeding column, stating the amount of the exports of the United States for the last year [actually the year ending October 1, 1811]; the particular country to which these exports were sent, and specifying the amount received from us by each. If you will just cast a glance at this document, you will find of the articles of our own growth or manufactures we in that time carried or sent abroad (in round numbers) no less than $45,294,000 worth. You will next find that out of this sum, all the rest of the world (Great Britain and her allies excepted) took about $7,719,366, and that Great Britain and her allies took the remainder, amounting to $38,575,627. Now, after this, let me ask you what you think of making war upon Great Britain and her allies, for the purpose of benefiting commerce?

[WAR SHOULD BE DECLARED]
Washington *National Intelligencer*, April 14, 1812

The public attention has been drawn to the approaching arrival of the *Hornet*, as a period when the measures of our government would take a decisive character, or rather their final cast. We are among those who have attached to this event a high degree of importance, and have therefore looked to it with the utmost solicitude.

But if the reports which we now hear are true, that with England all hope of honorable accommodation is at an end, and that with France our negotiations are in a forwardness encouraging expectations of a favorable result, where is the motive for longer delay? The final step ought to be taken, and that step is WAR. *By what course of measures we have reached the present crisis, is not now a question for patriots and freemen to discuss.* It exists: and it is by open and manly war only that we can get through it with honor and advantage to the country. Our wrongs have been great; our cause is just; and if we are decided and firm, success is inevitable.

Let war therefore be forthwith proclaimed against England. With her there can be no motive for delay. Any further discussion, any new attempt at negotiation, would be as fruitless as it would be dishonorable. With France we shall be at liberty to pursue the course which circumstances may require. The advance she has already made by a repeal of her decrees; the manner of its reception by the government, and the prospect which exists of an amicable accommodation, entitle her to this preference. If she acquits herself to the just claims of the United States, we shall have good cause to applaud our conduct in it, and if she fails we shall always be in time to place her on the ground of her adversary.

But it is said that we are not prepared for war, and ought therefore not to declare it. This is an idle objection, which can have weight with the timid and pusillanimous only. The fact is otherwise. Our preparations are adequate to every essential object. Do we apprehend danger to ourselves? From what quarter will it assail us? From England, and by invasion? The idea is too absurd to merit a moment's consideration. Where are her troops? But lately she dreaded an invasion of her own dominions from her powerful and menacing neighbor. That danger, it is true, has diminished, but it has not entirely and forever disappeared. The war in the Peninsula, which lingers, requires strong armies to support it. She maintains an army in Sicily; another in India; and a strong force in Ireland, and along her own coast, and in the West Indies. Can anyone believe that, under such circumstances, the British government could be so infatuated as to send troops here for the purpose of invasion? The experience and the fortune of our Revolution, when we were comparatively in an infant state, have doubtless taught her a useful lesson that she cannot have forgotten. Since that period our population has increased threefold, whilst hers has remained almost stationary. The condition of the civilized world, too, has changed. Although Great Britain has nothing to fear as to her independence, and her military operations are extensive and distant, the contest is evidently maintained by her rather for safety than for conquest. Have we cause to dread an attack from her neighboring provinces? That apprehension is still more groundless. Seven or eight millions of people have nothing to dread from 300,000. From the moment that war is declared, the British colonies will be put on the defensive. and soon after we get in motion must sink under the pressure.

AN ADDRESS TO THE PEOPLE OF THE EASTERN STATES

New York *Evening Post*, April 21, 1812

In a war with England we shall need numerous armies and ample treasuries for their support. The war-hounds that are howling for war through the continent are not to be the men who are to force entrenchments, and scale ramparts against the bayonet and the cannon's mouth; to perish in sickly camps, or in long marches through sultry heats or wastes of snow. These gowned warriors, who are so loudly seconded by a set of fiery spirits in the great towns, and by a set of office hunters in the country, expect that

their influence with the great body of the people, the honest yeo-
manry of our country, is such that every farmer, every mechanic,
every laborer, will send off his sons, nay, will even shoulder his
firelock himself and march to the field of blood. While these *brave
men* who are "designing or exhorting glorious war," lodged safe
at Monticello or some other secure retreat, will *direct and look on;*
and will receive such pay for their services as they shall see fit to
ask, and such as will answer their purposes.

Citizens, if pecuniary redress is your object in going to war with
England, the measure is perfect madness. You will lose millions
when you will gain a cent. The expense will be enormous. It will
ruin our country. Direct taxes must be resorted to. The people
will have nothing to pay. We once had a revenue; — that has been
destroyed in the destruction of our commerce. For several years
past you have been deceived and abused by the false pretenses of a
full treasury. That phantom of hope will soon vanish. You have
lately seen fifteen millions of dollars wasted in the purchase of a
province we did not want, and never shall possess. And will you
spend thousands of millions in conquering a province which, were
it made a present to us, would not be worth accepting? Our territories are already too large. The desire to annex Canada to the
United States is as base an ambition as ever burned in the bosom
of Alexander. What benefit will it ever be to the great body of
the people, after their wealth is exhausted, and their best blood is
shed in its reduction? — "We wish to clear our continent of foreign
powers." So did the *Madman* of Macedon wish to clear the world
of his enemies, and such as would not bow to his sceptre. So does
Bonaparte wish to clear Europe of all his enemies; yea, and Asia
too. Canada, if annexed to the United States, will furnish offices to
a set of hungry villains, grown quite too numerous for our present
wide limits; and that is *all* the benefit we ever shall derive from it.

These remarks will have little weight with men whose interest
leads them to advocate war. Thousands of lives, millions of money,
the flames of cities, the tears of widows and orphans, with *them* are
light expedients when they lead to wealth and power. But to the
people who must fight, if fighting must be done, — who must pay
if money be wanted — who must march when the trumpet sounds,
and who must die when the "battle bleeds," — to the people I
appeal. To them the warning voice is lifted. From a war they are
to expect nothing but expenses and sufferings; — expenses dis-
proportionate to their means, and sufferings lasting as life.

In our extensive shores and numerous seaports, we know not
where the enemy will strike; or more properly speaking, we know
they will strike when a station is defenceless. Their fleets will hover

on our coasts, and can trace our line from Maine to New Orleans
in a few weeks. *Gunboats* cannot repel them, nor is there a fort on
all our shores in which confidence can be placed. The ruin of our
seaports and loss of all vessels will form an item in the list of expenses.
Fortifications and garrisons numerous and strong must be added.
As to the main points of attack or defence, I shall only say that an
efficient force will be necessary. A handful of men cannot *run up*
and take Canada, in a few weeks, for mere diversion. The conflict
will be long and severe: resistance formidable, and the final result
doubtful. A nation that can debar the conqueror of Europe from
the sea, and resist his armies in Spain, will not surrender its provinces
without a struggle. Those who advocate a British war must be
perfectly aware that the whole revenue arising from all British
America for the ensuing century would not repay the expenses of
that war.

THE GALLATIN LOAN

New York *Evening Post*, April 28, 1812

It has been whispered that two or three merchants here have
expressed an inclination to dabble in the Gallatin loan. If so, I
dare say these gentlemen know how to calculate better than I do;
six per cent they doubtless find to be a good premium, although
they can now purchase government six per cent stock at three per
cent under par. As to the security, those who subscribe must be
such friends of the Administration as to advance their money without even thinking of that. Not a cent of revenue is pledged, and
for a very good reason; they have none to pledge. But even if they
had pledged it, will it not be as easy to destroy the pledge whenever
they please, as it was for the same party to destroy the excise after
it had been solemnly pledged to the public creditors under the
Washington Administration? As it will very much depend on the
filling up of this loan whether we shall or shall not go to war, it is
evident that no man who is averse to that calamity can ever, consistently, lend his assistance to enable the government to plunge
us into it. Let those who are for war subscribe — let those who dread
it avoid doing so, as they value all they hold dear.

[THE SURRENDER OF HULL AT DETROIT]

New York *Evening Post*, August 31, 1812

On the disgraceful and deplorable results of our first military
efforts in Canada, we are not in a temper to say much. How much
soever we deprecated this ruinous war at the outset; however
satisfied we were that the whole plan of the campaign was miserably

imbecile and must be utterly inefficient — yet such a catastrophe as is just announced was beyond our most gloomy apprehensions. Mr. Madison, Mr. Gallatin, Dr. Eustis, and Dr. Hamilton, it was evident, must be utterly unequal to cope with the experienced veteran British officers in Canada. And when, besides this disheartening fact, we beheld how small a force was relied upon, what could reasonable men feel but despair? With inferior numbers and inferior skill, the odds were fearful indeed.

Yet we did not expect so deep a stain upon our country's character.[1] A nation, counting eight millions of souls, deliberating and planning for a whole winter and spring and part of a summer, the invasion and conquest of a neighboring province; at length making that invasion; and in one month its army retiring — captured — and captured almost without firing a gun! Miserably deficient in practical talent must that Administration be which formed the plan of that invasion; or the army which has thus surrendered must be a gang of more cowardly poltroons than ever disgraced a country. A parallel to this melancholy defeat is not to be found in all history. But we do not, we cannot brand our countrymen in General Hull's army with cowardice. We shall not till we are compelled. For when were Americans known to shrink from danger? — when have they not been heroes? But the folly, the weakness, the utter incapacity of our Administration to conduct affairs of difficulty to a successful issue, has not only been the tedious theme of many an appeal to our fellow-citizens, but is felt in the privations and distresses of almost every man, woman, and child in this once happy and prosperous country. And he who can longer doubt that incapacity, would not believe though one should rise from the dead.

What! March an army *into* a country where there were not more than seven or eight hundred soldiers to oppose them, and not make the army large enough! March them *from* a country which is the granary of the world, and let them famish on the very frontiers for want of provisions! Issue a gasconading proclamation threatening to exterminate the enemy, and surrender your whole army to them! If there be judgment in this people, they will see the utter unfitness of our rulers for anything beyond management, intrigue, and electioneering. They have talents enough to inflame a misguided populace against their best friends; but they cannot protect the nation from insult and disgrace. They have talents enough to persecute the pupils and disciples of Washington, but not to meet the enemies whom they have called into the field. "Woe to the people whose King is a child!"

[1] General William Hull marched into Canada with a small American army, laid siege to Malden, hastily retreated to Detroit when British reinforcements approached, and on August 16, 1812, ignominiously surrendered his whole army.

THE *CONSTITUTION* AND THE *GUERRIERE*

New York *Evening Post*, September 2, 1812

After the gloomy accounts which have crowded upon us for some days past, we are happy to be able this day to give our readers something in favor of the courage and activity of our countrymen. We have always contended that our people would fight whenever they should have a chance, and that on an equal footing they would be beaten by no men on earth; the naval action, the particulars of which we publish this day, proves our assertion. Captain Hull, who has immortalized himself in the capture of the *Guerriere*, is a relation of General Hull, who has been sacrificed by an imbecile Administration on the borders of Canada. We have no doubt that General Hull would have fought as manfully as his kinsman, and that the result would have been as favorable, had he been placed in a situation where there had been the least chance of success; but without provisions or munitions of war, what could be done against a veteran and well-appointed army?

Though very little present benefit is to be expected from the war, commenced as it *has been* and carried on as it *will be*, under the present Administration, yet it may have one good effect: it will prove that in a contest where the *freedom of the seas* is the object, a naval force is much superior to an army on the land. It will prove what the Federalists have always advocated, and what the present ruling party have always opposed, the necessity of a maritime force to a commercial people. It will in fact settle the question practically which has so often been debated in our councils, whether a nation can exist as a powerful maritime nation without a well-appointed navy?

We shall not attempt to heap applauses upon Captain Hull and his gallant crew; after what they have achieved, our approbation can be of but little use to them. The thing shows for itself: it shows that man to man and gun to gun, even the veteran British tars can get no advantage over the Americans.

[THE BLAME FOR HULL'S SURRENDER: TWO VIEWS] [1]

Washington *National Intelligencer*, September 3, 1812

The government is not as yet, that we are informed, in possession of any official advices relating to the disaster which seems to have befallen our Northwestern army. The rumor of it has struck every-

[1] By either William Seaton or Joseph Gales, who had taken over the *National Intelligencer* and kept it the Administration organ under Madison and Monroe as it had been under Jefferson.

one here, as it must everywhere, with astonishment. That at the
moment the country was looking with the best-founded and most
justified hope for the intelligence of the success of our arms in that
quarter, we should hear of defeat — of the total surrender of an
army of 2,500 men without a battle — probably without firing a
gun — to a force not greater, perhaps much less, than its own,
is equally extraordinary and mysterious. It might, perhaps, be
premature, in us, at such a moment as this, to hazard any opinion
on an event so vitally important to the character of the commanding
general; but we share largely in the public astonishment which
manifests itself upon the occasion. A very little time must unravel
the cause of this utterly unexpected reverse. We think we do not
misunderstand the character of that army when we say it was
abundantly strong under every calculation of safety and prudence,
and in the previous estimation of the general himself, for the contemplated objects of the expedition on which it set out; that it was
also abundantly supplied with every requisite of ammunition, arms,
stores, provisions, to secure, under judicious and prompt movements, all the advantages that were looked to from its march.

New York *Evening Post*, September 5, 1812[1]

The government gazette has, at last, published the articles of
capitulation by which General Hull surrendered himself and his
army to the British. It will be seen by the editorial article which we
copy from the same paper that the Administration intend to shift
the disgrace of this shameful affair from their own shoulders to
those of General Hull and his abused officers and men. The *Intelligencer* says the army was "abundantly strong for the contemplated
objects of the expedition on which it set out; that it was also abundantly supplied with every requisite of ammunition, arms, stores,
and provisions, to secure, under judicious and prompt movements,
all the advantages that were looked to from its march." By letters
from General Hull and his officers dated previous to the capture and
inserted in the same *Intelligencer*, it appears that such was not the
case: they all agree in stating that the army was without provisions
— and was so weak that if reinforcements did not soon arrive, the
most fatal consequences were to be expected. Now on which statement are we to depend: on the accounts of General Hull and his
officers, written on the spot, or on the speculations of the government editor, written five hundred miles from the scene of action?

[1] The best historical opinion is that, as Henry Adams says, "a good general
would have saved Detroit for some weeks, if not altogether." But he was wretch-
edly supplied.

THE NEW ENGLAND THREAT OF SECESSION

Columbian Centinel, January 13, 1813

North of the Delaware, there is among all who do not bask or expect to bask in the Executive sunshine but one voice for *Peace*. South of that river, the general cry is "Open war, O peers!" There are not two hostile nations upon earth whose views of the principles and polity of a perfect commonwealth, and of men and measures, are more discordant than those of these two great divisions. There is but little of congeniality or sympathy in our notions or feelings; and this small residuum will be extinguished by this withering war.

The sentiment is hourly extending, and in these Northern States will soon be universal, that we are in a condition no better in relation to the South than that of a *conquered people*. We have been compelled without the least necessity or occasion to renounce our habits, occupations, means of happiness, and subsistence. We are plunged into a war, without a sense of enmity, or a perception of sufficient provocation; and obliged to fight the battles of a Cabal which, under the sickening affectation of republican *equality*, aims at trampling into the dust the weight, influence, and power of Commerce and her dependencies. We, whose soil was the hotbed and whose ships were the nursery of Sailors, are insulted with the hypocrisy of a devotedness to Sailors' rights, and the arrogance of a pretended skill in maritime jurisprudence, by those whose country furnishes no navigation beyond the size of a ferryboat or an Indian canoe. We have no more interest in waging this sort of war, at this period and under these circumstances, at the command of Virginia, than Holland in accelerating her ruin by uniting her destiny to France. We resemble Holland in another particular. The officers and power of government are engrossed by executive minions, who are selected on account of *their known infidelity to the interest of their fellow citizens*, to foment divisions and to deceive and distract the people whom they cannot intimidate. The land is literally taken from its Old Possessors and given to strangers. The Cabinet has no confidence in those who enjoy the confidence of this people, and on the other hand the solid mass of the talents and property of this community is wholly unsusceptible of any favorable impressions or dispositions towards an Executive in whose choice they had no part, and by whom they feel that they shall be, as they always have been, degraded and marked as objects of oppression and resentment. The consequence of this state of things must then be, either that the Southern States must *drag* the Northern States farther into the war, or we must *drag* them out of it; or the chain will break. This will be the "imposing attitude" of the next year.

We must no longer be deafened by senseless clamors about a separation of the States. It is an event we do not desire, not because we have derived advantages from the compact, but because we cannot foresee or limit the dangers or effects of revolution. *But the States are separated in fact*, when one section assumes an *imposing attitude*, and with high hand perseveres in measures fatal to the interests and repugnant to the opinions of another section, by dint of a geographical majority.

NEW ORLEANS[1]

New York *Evening Post*, February 7, 1815

We have today the official account of General Jackson, which makes the loss of the enemy much greater than it was reported to be, and on our side still less.

On the subject of this gallant, this extraordinary defence, it is due to truth and justice to observe that on no pretence whatever, are the Administration entitled to the least share of the honor attending this very brilliant affair, or to partake in the smallest of the glory acquired. After being three years at war with a powerful enemy, who had the means of transporting his forces to any part of our sea-coast, the Administration has been so utterly neglectful of this important place, the depôt of immense property belonging to the trading part of the community, that it was not until his forces were actually on the point of landing, that any measures of defence were taken. New Orleans was left to itself. And when at last the militia of the neighboring states voluntarily turned out to defend it, the Administration had not even provided arms, for their use, nor clothing to protect them from the cold. Whatever, therefore, of honor or glory the militia have acquired in this achievement, they alone are exclusively entitled to it; it would be the highest injustice to attempt to divide it with the President or with the Secretary of War. Had New Orleans fallen, I have no doubt that Mr. Madison would have been impeached by his own party. Report is very erroneous if he would not, and surely a different result, not owing to any measure of his, cannot materially alter the complexion of his conduct.

We cannot omit this opportunity to express how much we are pleased, at the unstudied simplicity and modesty of General Jackson's official letter; and we recommend it to American officers as a model for imitation.

---

[1] Jackson's victory of January 8, 1815, over the British army under Pakenham, was one of the few events of the war in which Americans could take pride. It came at a moment when, as Coleman hints, the government of Madison trembled on the brink of disaster. Jackson rightly received the entire credit.

PEACE

New York *Evening Post*, February 13, 1815

On Saturday evening, about eight o'clock, arrived the British sloop of war, *Favorite*, bringing Mr. Carroll, one of the Secretaries attached to the American legation, bearer of a treaty of PEACE between the United States and Great Britain. He came not unexpected to us: Ever since the receipt of the October dispatches, we have entertained and expressed, as our readers know, but one opinion. A critical examination of those dispatches convinced us that the negociations would, nay, must terminate in the restoration of a speedy peace; and the speech of the Prince Regent, in November, contained an implied assurance that the preliminaries waited for little else than the form of signatures. It has come, and the public expressions of tumultuous joy and gladness that spontaneously burst forth from all ranks and degrees of people on Saturday evening, without stopping to enquire the conditions, evinced how really sick at heart they were, of a war that threatened to wring from them the remaining means of subsistence, and of which they could neither see the object nor the end. The public exhilaration shewed itself in the illumination of most of the windows in the lower part of Broadway and the adjoining streets in less than twenty minutes after Mr. Carroll arrived at the City Hotel. The street itself was illuminated by lighted candles, carried in the hands of a large concourse of the populace; the city resounded in all parts with the joyful cry of a peace! a peace! and it was for nearly two hours difficult to make one's way through unnumbered crowds of persons of all descriptions, who came forth to see and to hear and to rejoice. In the truth, the occasion called for the liveliest marks of sincere congratulations. Never, in our opinion, has there occurred so great a one since we became an independent nation. Expresses of the glad tidings were instantly dispatched in all directions, to Boston, Philadelphia, Providence, Albany, &c., &c. The country will now be convinced that the federalists were right in the opinion they have ever held, that during the despotism of Bonaparte, no peace was ever to be expected for their own country, and therefore they publickly rejoiced at his downfall, and celebrated the restoration of the Bourbons. Men of property, particularly, should felicitate themselves, for they may look back upon the perils they have just escaped with the same sensations that the passenger in a ship experiences, when, driving directly on the breakers through the blunders of an ignorant pilot, he is unexpectedly snatched from impending destruction by a sudden shifting of the wind. Fears were entertained, that it was really intended, like losing and desperate gamblers, to find a pretence for never paying the public debt, in the magnitude of the sum: that a spunge would be employed in the last resort, as the favorite instrument to wipe off all scores at once. A principle nearly bordering on this, was, not long ago, openly avowed on the floor of Congress by a member from Virginia. Neither is it a small cause of congratulation that we are now to be delivered from that swarm of leeches that have so long fastened upon the nation, and been sucking its blood. Their day is over. Let the nation rejoice.

What the terms of the peace are, we cannot tell; they will only be made known at Washington, by the dispatches themselves. But one thing I will venture to say now and before they are opened, and I will hazard my reputation upon the correctness of what I say, that when the terms are disclosed, it will be found that the government have not by this negociation obtained one single avowed object for which they involved the country in this bloody and expensive war.

[EFFECTS OF THE NEWS OF PEACE]
New York *Evening Post*, February 14, 1815

In yesterday's paper we gave a rapid sketch of the effects of war; today we give one of the effects of the prospect of peace even before the ratification. Our markets of every kind experienced a sudden and to many a shocking change. Sugar, for instance, fell from $26 per hundredweight to $12.50; tea, which sold at $2.25 on Saturday, yesterday was purchased at $1; specie, which had got up to the enormous rate of 22 per cent premium, dropped down to two. The article in particular of tin fell from the height of $80 the box to $25. Six per cent bonds rose from 76 to 86, or ten per cent, and Treasury notes rose from 92 to 98 per cent. This difference between the two kinds of stock is owing to the interest being the same on both, while the price of the former is much less to the holder; that is, the holder of the former receives six per cent on $100, while the holder of the latter receives the same interest, but the principal costs him 96.

Bank stock rose generally from five to ten per cent. *Sailors' Rights* beat time to the sound of the hammer at every wharf, and *free trade* looked briskly up; no longer did it live in toasts alone. On the other hand, wagons creaked their dying groans on their dry axle-trees. Ships swarm in the columns of our friends Lang & Turner, and glisten in a row in Crooks & Butler's; even a few, from some friendly hand, here and there adorn the *Evening Post* and help to make up a show. We are grateful for what we have received.

It is really wonderful to see the change produced in a few hours in the city of New York. In no place has the war been more felt nor proved more disastrous, putting us back in our growth at least ten years; and no place in the United States will more experience the reviving blessings of a peace. Let us be grateful to that merciful Providence who has kindly interposed for our relief and delivered us from all our fears.

[PRESIDENT MONROE'S TOUR AND THE ERA OF GOOD FEELING]

Washington *National Intelligencer*, April 23, 1817

It has been already intimated in several papers that the President proposes, within a short time, to commence a tour through a part of the United States. . . .

By the Constitution of our country, it is made the duty of the President of the United States to give to Congress information of the state of the Union, and to recommend from time to time such measures as he shall judge necessary and expedient. One of the principal objects of the association of these States, under a Federal head, was to secure adequate provision for the national defence. Such attention has always been paid to that object heretofore as the best information authorized and required. But there is no information so satisfactory, nor upon which so much reliance can be placed, as that obtained by personal observation. It is therefore believed, in the present quiet state of our foreign and domestic concerns, not requiring the presence of the President at the seat of government, that he could not do a more valuable service to his country than by personally inspecting the state of the public works, of the military and naval posts and depots, and all the establishments connected with national defence.

Idem, July 24, 1817

We trace the path of the President by means of the newspapers as far east as Portland, Maine, the remotest point in that direction, and the remotest in any direction ever before visited by a President of the United States. Wherever the President passes, concord attends his steps. So extraordinary is the unanimity of sentiment, and the fraternity of intercourse which the progress of the President has developed, that we are led to believe that an excuse only was wanting for the harmony of society for which the President's conciliating deportment is assigned as a reason. Mr. Monroe was always the same as he now is, and his predecessor was certainly distinguished for urbanity and freedom from the asperities of political controversy.

Let us not, however, too nicely scan the motive when the effect is so valuable. Never before, perhaps, since the institution of civil government, did the same harmony, the same absence of party spirit, the same national feeling, pervade a community. The result is too consoling to dispute too nicely about the cause.

[EFFECTS OF THE PANIC OF 1819] [1]

Niles's Register, September 16, 1820

A large part of the present dullness of trade and "scarcity of money" is owing to a diminished consumption of costly articles for food and raiment, or for ornament and show, whether of foreign or domestic product. It is a hard thing to retrograde in these, but — *necessitas non habet leges;* what "can't be cured must be endured." There are few even of the most wealthy (except some steady-habited old fellows who never conformed to the times), who now live as they did a few years ago, so far as my observation and information extend. Pride, pomp, and splendor, as well as sheer luxury and what is sometimes called comfort, derive much of their real value (if anything they have) from comparison. The black broth of the Lacedemonians was their greatest enjoyment, though the humblest stranger could hardly keep it on his stomach. A little while ago, I frequently saw the streets crowded in an evening with a bustling multitude dashing in carriages to Mrs. Anything's party. An orderly man could hardly get along for them. I have heard of three hundred persons taking tea with the wife of the servant of a bank! But "madam's husband" can't afford it any longer, or so much respects common decency that he won't allow it. So those who may afford it receive the same comparative *éclat* for having thirty or forty which they used to derive from having three or four hundred at their parties; and it is much better, because in a company of the former dimensions you may find a satisfaction not to be expected in the other, designed *only to make a noise.* It is thus also with gentlemen's dinners and suppers — ten or twenty are occasionally invited, instead of having twenty or forty frequently. The style is still maintained, but *fashion* does not call for its exhibition so extensively nor so often. "The top of the wheel" is still held, and that is enough.

But the general retrenchment spoken of may be proven from a multitude of facts. In the New York, Philadelphia, and Baltimore newspapers you may often see the grocers puffing their wines by saying that certain particular pipes were expressly imported for

[1] By Hezekiah Niles. The war with England was followed by severe commercial distress, culminating in something like a financial panic in 1819.

private use. Their sayings are true. The gentlemen who ordered it had found out that there was an end to paper credit when the wine arrived, and though they might have retained some money, it would look too bad to see a pipe of wine going into a bankrupt's cellar; and the fact is that our grocers hardly sell one gallon of their costly wines for ten which they used to dispose of. So also it is for every business, trade, or profession which furnishes us with luxuries, from the wine merchant to the confectioner; and if it was known that a man in an ordinary trade gave his wife a shawl which cost $500, his note would certainly be "turned down" at bank.

SLAVERY AND THE MISSOURI COMPROMISE [1]

Niles's Register, December 23, 1820

It is established (so far as large majorities in both houses of Congress can establish it) that the power to check the progress of a slave population within the territories of the United States exists by the Constitution; but admitted that it was not expedient to exert that power in regard to Missouri and Arkansas. The latter depended on many considerations of no ordinary importance: the safety and feelings of the white population in several of the States appeared to be involved in it, and the rights and feelings of others were as deeply concerned in the subject at large. In this conflict of interests, among persons who possibly desired the same ultimate issue, though their views of it were diametrically opposed, a spirit of conciliation prevailed and a compromise was effected. The people of those sections of country in which there are few or no slaves or persons of color, very imperfectly appreciate the wants, necessity, or general principle of others differently situated. Collectively, the latter deprecate slavery as severely as the former, and deprecate its increase; but individual cupidity and rashness acts against the common sentiment, in the hope that an event which everybody believes must happen, will not happen in their day. It is thus that too many of us act about death; we are sure it must come, yet we commit wrong to acquire property, just as if we should hold and enjoy it forever. That the slave population will, at some certain period, cause the most horrible catastrophe, cannot be doubted; those who possess them act defensively in behalf of all that is nearest and dearest to them, when they endeavor to acquire all the strength and influence to meet that period which they can; and hence the political and civil opposition of these to

[1] A characteristic expression of the strong nationalism of Niles, of his New England aversion to slavery, though his newspaper was conducted in a slave State, Maryland, and in its prophecy of a "horrible catastrophe," of his political shrewdness. The *Register* agreed with Jefferson that the Missouri discussion was like "a firebell in the night."

the restriction which was proposed to be laid on Missouri. They *have* the offensive population, and no feasible plan has yet been contrived to rid them of it, if they were disposed so to do. Will the people of any of the States, so much alive to humanity, pass acts to encourage emancipation by agreeing to receive the emancipated? What will they do, what can they do, to assist the people of others to relieve themselves of their unfortunate condition? It is easy to use severe terms against the practise of slavery; but let us first tell the Southern people what they can safely do to abolish it, before we condemn them wholesale.

No one can hate slavery more than I do — it is a thing opposed to every principle that operates on my mind as an individual — and in my own private circle I do much to discourage it. I am also exceedingly jealous of it, so far as it affects my political rights as a citizen of the United States, entitled to be fairly and fully represented, and no more. But I can make great allowances for those who hold slaves in districts where they abound — where, in many cases, their emancipation might be an act of cruelty to them, and of most serious injury to the white population. Their difference of color is an insuperable barrier to their incorporation within the society; and the mixture of free blacks with slaves is detrimental to the happiness of both, the cause of uncounted crimes. Yet I think that some have urged their defensive character too far; without a proper respect for the rights and feelings of others, as applicable to an extension of the evil. But we advocated the compromise, as fixing certain points for the future government of all the parties concerned; believing that the moral and political evil of spreading slavery over Missouri and even in Arkansas was not greater than that which might have risen from restriction, though to restrict was right in itself. The harmony of the Union, and the peace and prosperity of the white population, most excited our sympathies. We did not fear the dreadful things which some silly folks talked of, but apprehended geographical oppositions which might lead to the worst of calamities. We had no pleasant feeling on the Compromise, for bad was the best that could be done. Nevertheless, we hoped that the contest was at an end, and that things would settle down and adapt themselves to the agreement which necessity imposed.

[CRUELTY TO DUMB ANIMALS]

Niles's Register, July 7, 1821

A person was taken up and committed to prison in New York for so fastening the tongue of a calf that it could not suck its mother, both of which were for sale. Now in Baltimore it is quite a common thing, when cows and calves are driven through our streets for sale, to see the mouths of the latter severely tied up with string; but what is much worse, in passing the Centre market every Wednesday and Saturday, we see calves with their four feet bound together with ropes, and so suffered to lie for hours together on the public pavements, exposed to a burning sun! If there is no law to punish such cruelty, the people might soon check it, if they would act as I do. I inquire what butchers are in the habit of this cruelty, and avoid their stalls as if their meat was as putrid as their hearts are callous to humanity and disregardful of decency.

WHY WE NEED A PROTECTIVE TARIFF [1]

Niles's Register, June 23, 1821

The Waltham manufactory is the largest and probably the most prosperous in the United States. Too much credit cannot be given to the managers for the economy and skill with which it is conducted, or the good order and morality which are so conspicuous among the workmen, women and children. It is a magnificent and truly national establishment, presenting a splendid matter-of-fact illustration of the true principles of political economy; imparting to the mind of one who views its structure, machinery, and management, more conviction and practical information than could be drawn from all the books which its walls could contain.

When foreign or hireling writers tell us, your country is not fit for manufactures, we can with pride tell them — look at Waltham; that manufactures are injurious to morals and agriculture — look at Waltham and its neighborhood; that they will destroy commerce — ask the merchants of Boston and Providence; that they will destroy the market for our produce — look at Mr. Jackson's books; that the Southern planter will suffer — count the bales of cotton in store; that they tax the many and oppress the few — compare the price and quality of their fabrics with the imported; that we have not sufficient capital — examine the list of stockholders and their bankbooks ($600,000 paid in, $600,000 more ready if it could be employed). In short, there is not an objection to the encouragement of manufactures among us that is not put down by an inspection of this establishment, without reasoning

---

[1] Francis Lowell in 1814 invented a power-loom which was at once used successfully in textile manufacturing in Waltham. Here the Boston Manufacturing Company established the first modern factory in the United States. It performed all operations by central power, used specialized labor, organized the workers into departments, and standardized the product. The idea of the factory as America now knows it was thus first demonstrated, and the success of the establishment, with its benefits to the surrounding country, was much used by writers like Niles in the argument for tariffs.

or books, except the book we all neglect too much — the book of observation, practical experience, and active life. It would give me much pleasure to seat myself on an eminence near Waltham with some honest anti-tariffite, and for one day watch the motions of all the in-comers and out-goers at the village and factory; to take a note of what they brought in and took out; to ask the passing farmer what he took to market, the price he obtained, and what he brought home in exchange; to ask the fond mother who had been to see her children, whether their habits were industrious, frugal, moral, and how much of their earnings went to the comforts of their aged parents. I would ask one of the worthy mercantile proprietors what effect it had on his commercial pursuits; and I would cheerfully agree to give up all my tariff doctrines, if the answers of all would not be as I could wish.[1]

If my anti-tariff friend would not be convinced, I would put him this case: Suppose this fine factory should be destroyed by fire, and the proprietors should not rebuild it. We will suppose ourselves sitting on this same hill one year after the establishment had been in ruins, and the same farmer, the same mother, and the same merchant should all join us, and we should join in the conversation, comparing the past with the present, the farmer's market, the mother's children, the merchant's business. Reader, I need not detail our remarks to you, for you will imagine them all: you know there is not one of the group that would not look at the unemployed waterfall, the ruins of the factory, and say there it stood; things were not so when the factory was going. Suppose we come down to the village. It is quiet — a few people seen about the taverns and retail stores, houses decaying, children ragged, old people begging. "What is the matter? It was not so last year." "O, no! but the factory is burnt!" This answer would break from every mouth, and I am much mistaken if any anti-tariff man could stand the scene unconvinced. Every man of this description ought to go to Waltham, or some other manufactory, and imagine to himself the difference between *a factory at work and a factory burnt*. This is the mode of settling questions of political economy and national policy. What Waltham is on a large scale every manufacturing establishment is on a small one; and those are the books which the people must study or they will never understand the subject. When they see the practical difference between a factory stopped and a factory active, the nation will cease to be divided and Congress indifferent.

[1] The tariff act passed in the spring of 1824 placed protective duties, as Niles desired, upon the textile and other industrial interests of the North. Northern shipping interests and Southern agriculturists both opposed such legislation.

[THE ERIE CANAL: "THE MEETING OF THE WATERS"][1]

New York *Commercial Advertiser*, October 11, 1822

Ye shades of ancient heroes! Ye who toiled,
Through long successive ages, to build up
A laboring plan of state; behold, at once,
The wonder done!

Wednesday of the present week was not only a proud day for
New York, but for the Union; for although the joyous festival at
Albany was a celebration of an event in the achievement of which
New York has exerted her enterprise and physical energies single-
handed and alone, yet the stupendous object is not the less important in a national point of view.   In addition to the incalculable
benefits it will confer on our State in respect to commercial affairs,
the canal will long serve as a chain to bind together rich and populous territories, far distant from each other, and whose real or
imaginary diversity of interests might otherwise, and at no very
remote period, cause a dissolution, alike injurious and disastrous
to all.   By means of this great artificial river, and others which will
be formed in consequence of our example, the Atlantic States and
the rich and widely extended regions of the West will become neighbors, and a close community of interests will induce them to cling
together with a degree of tenaciousness and constancy which even
a daily recollection of their consanguinity would not otherwise have
produced. . . .

Whatever party rules, whatever political chief rises or falls, agriculture, manufactures, and commerce must still remain the greatest
of our concerns, and by the opening of the canal these three great
vital interests are all most eminently promoted.   What a widespread
region of cultivated soil has already been brought within the near
vicinity of the greatest market on our continent!   How many manufacturing establishments have had the value of everything connected
with them doubled by this "meeting of the waters"!   How vastly
have the internal resources of this metropolis been, in one day,

---

[1] An interesting example of the literary treatment of a commercial topic.   The
Erie Canal was begun in 1817 and completed in November, 1825; the celebration
here noted marked the completion of its most important stage.   De Witt Clinton
was primarily responsible for beginning and pushing the work, but in 1822 he was
forced by the opposition to his administration to decline to seek a third term as
Governor.   Later he was reëlected triumphantly, serving from 1825 till his death
in 1828.   The editor of the *Commercial Advertiser* alludes to this temporary retirement in a tactful way.   At this date steam navigation was rapidly increasing on
all rivers and along the coast; while the ship *Savannah* had crossed the Atlantic
under sail and steam in 1819.   Americans were greatly interested in the subject.
The Erie Canal was of course destined to make New York the metropolis of the
continent.

practically extended! Without adverting to any long vista of future times, how much has already, at this present hour, been effected in the enhancement of the total value of the whole State! If we justly consider the Hudson, flowing through the densest population and best-cultivated territory, an invaluable blessing, and a leading feature of our local advantages, what must be the opening of a new and additional river, twice the navigable length of the Hudson, and traversing a region whose population and agricultural wealth will soon rival and even surpass those of its banks? A river which, in one year more, will carry our trade to the foot of the falls of St. Mary, and will eventually give us access to the remotest shore of Lake Superior!

Thus has closed one of the greatest, happiest, proudest, most propitious scenes our State has ever witnessed. Excepting that day on which she joined the national confederacy, there is none like it in her history; nor is there likely to be, save that which will commemorate the completion of the same grand design, now so near its consummation. The prominent figure in this scene of the public exultation is a man whose name will be preserved from the stroke of time by the benedictions of remotest posterity; one of those men whom one age is insufficient to appreciate; whose thoughts and purposes run through many ages — and whose minds are never fully developed till their conceptions have been embodied in plans and measures which go on to bless a nation from generation to generation. It is in vain that the efforts of the weak, who cannot comprehend, or the malignant, who comprehend only to hate and envy true greatness, are combined to bring such men into the dust:

> *Like ancient oaks, superior in power,*
> *To all the warring winds of heaven, they rise;*
> *And from their stony promontory tower,*
> *And toss their giant arms amid the skies,*
> *While each assailing blast increase of strength supplies.*

De Witt Clinton, whatever may be his public career, is now a private man; and none of those feelings which public life, in a free country, never fail to arouse, have anything to do with claims to his country's gratitude which rest upon his measures for internal improvement. These claims are clear, acknowledged, irresistible. They have borne down opposition of party feeling, except in heads and hearts which nothing can penetrate; and they will be owned, and paid too, when we are dead and our squabbles forgotten.

[STATES WHICH REFUSE POLITICAL EQUALITY][1]

Niles's Register, November 29, 1823

Delaware, Maryland, Virginia, and North Carolina are the only States whose representation, in their several legislatures, depends upon the long-laughed-at and truly ridiculous, though abominable and unjust, rotten-borough system of England.   That is, a certain district of country, or space of land, whether inhabited by whites, blacks, or mulattoes, or a mixture of all — or by bucks and does, or bears and wolves, or even frogs and mosquitoes, provided it hath certain qualified bipeds enough in it to fill the place of representatives of the people — is entitled to an equal degree of power in the passage of laws to regulate the affairs of the several commonwealths.   It is no matter whether a district is fertile or barren, large or small, ten feet square or an hundred miles — whether it contains five militia-men or fifty thousand, or pays one dollar tax or one million — such is the virtue of the Constitution that the very pine-trees and stunted oaks, whortleberry bushes or chestnut sprouts, are transformed into somethings that make great men out of very little ones, investing them with the sovereign power of legislation!

One county in Delaware has 22,360 citizens, and another only 14,180, and yet they are represented by an equal number of members.

One city in Maryland, which sends two members to the house of delegates, has much more effective strength of population and pays nearly as much tax as ten counties which send forty members.

One county in Virginia, entitled to two members, contains a greater number of citizens than nine counties which send eighteen members.

One county in North Carolina, with two members, is equal in its number of citizens to seven counties sending fourteen members.

And yet we smile at the English system!   That has the plea of antiquity, the danger of "reform" in its favor; but what have we to plead for our equally ridiculous delegations of power?   We prate about liberty and declaim in favor of our just laws; we say that taxation without representation is tyranny!   How shall we be judged? — by that which we chatter about, or that which we suffer to be and sanction by our sufferance?

[1] The demand for equitable representation in Virginia was one of the chief causes for the holding of a constitutional convention in that State in 1829; yet this convention refused the equality sought.   Hezekiah Niles's editorial is an interesting expression of one of the impulses which lent strength to Jacksonian Democracy.

[THE MONROE DOCTRINE ENUNCIATED]

Niles's Register, December 6, 1823

The message of the President of the United States, delivered on Tuesday last, is remarkable for the amplitude and simplicity of its details, and suggests many subjects that will engage the serious attention of the representatives of the people, if they shall not be too much occupied with electioneering to attend to them. Instead of pointing out these things, or attempting to explain what the President means, the readers of this work are referred to the message itself, in a belief that the document may be understood without the aid of editorial interpretations. I would only invite a careful perusal of it.

There is one part of the message, however, that will attract particular attention. It is where the President suggests the possibility that the Allied Powers may attempt an extension of their "political system" to Mexico and the South American states; which, he declares, ought to be regarded as "dangerous to our peace and safety." Every thinking American will accord in this opinion. But the expression of it, on an occasion like the present, convinces us that there must be some special reason for putting it forth. It has been universally believed that the members of the Holy Alliance entertained the design of reducing all governments to their own standard of right, as Procrustes stretched or chopped off the limbs of persons that they might fit the measure of his bed; and we recollect also, that a work was published at Verona, dedicated by permission to the emperor of Austria, in which it was recommended, as necessary to the repose of Europe, that even England should be compelled to fall into their system. But we hardly thought that they had proceeded so far as we are now disposed to believe they have done. Be this as it may, the present is not a time to trifle or tamper with our means of defense. They should be cherished, as we love ourselves or our children. An increased power in them may not be necessary just now, but their *efficiency* should be kept up and increased.

[1] What has since become famous as the Monroe Doctrine was announced in President Monroe's annual message to Congress, December 2, 1823. Its main assertions were that the American continents " are henceforth not to be considered as subjects for future colonization by any European Powers," and that, as regards the Powers of the Holy Alliance, America "should consider any attempt on their part to extend their system to any portion of this hemisphere as dangerous to our peace and safety." The primary impulse in the announcement of this doctrine was furnished by the British Foreign Minister, Canning. In its final form it owed most to J. Q. Adams.

[ALBERT GALLATIN AS A "FOREIGNER"][1]

Niles's Register, April 17, 1824

I am not one of those who think all's fair in politics. "Jokes may be free in harvest," but truth is the same the whole year round. Nominated as Mr. Gallatin was by a *minority* of that political interest with which I have steadily acted from the year 1795 until the present day, no obligation whatever presents itself to my mind why, on account of that interest, I should support him for the Vice-Presidency of the United States; but an evident duty to principle urges me to reprove the practise of some who, whether friendly or unfriendly to the late caucus, speak of him as a *foreigner*. Indeed, judging from what I have seen on both sides, the nomination was an unfortunate one for the caucus party, for its design of operating on Pennsylvania has totally failed, as was predicted at the moment when it was made; and on every account it has rather taken from than added to the strength of the ticket. But Mr. Gallatin arrived in this country, not then the "United States," long before the present Constitution was formed, or even the war had ended; and, in the letter or spirit of that instrument, and in the fitness of things, he cannot be regarded any more as a foreigner than those of us who happened to be born in this land before the fourth of July, 1776, unless long enough before that period to have taken some part in ratifying the Declaration of Independence by the force of arms or otherwise. And in the very year that the government of the United States went into operation, Mr. Gallatin, as a member of the Pennsylvania convention, took an active part in the formation of the Constitution of that great State.

I escaped the honor of being a subject of his Britannic Majesty, but all the past Presidents were so; so was the present President, and all who are held up as candidates to succeed him. Were they or are they on that account to be suspected of having anti-American feelings? Or does the accident of birth under King George afford a better assurance that a person is more a friend of liberty than the accident of birth under the dominion of any other king? Is English royalty, that raised the tomahawk of the savage, that slaughtered our people, conflagrated our towns, and so on, in the Revolution, more deserving of respect than French royalty, which aided and assisted us in gaining our freedom? Is the much-esteemed and

---

[1] Gallatin's nomination for the Vice-Presidency in the spring of 1824, on the ticket of William H. Crawford, was the signal for bitter attacks upon him as a foreigner; he was born in Switzerland in 1761. Ultimately Martin Van Buren, who was one of the Crawford managers, decided that Gallatin weakened the ticket, and his retirement was arranged that autumn. Niles expresses the feeling of men of principle regarding the attacks.

venerable Colonel Paul Bentalou, now Federal marshal of the district of Maryland, less a citizen than I myself am, because he pronounces many English words with a French accent? No, no; he belongs to the small fragment of those who hewed out citizenship with their swords; he was a gallant captain in his youth in the celebrated legion of Pulaski, and there are few men living who saw more service in our country than he; and since the termination of the Revolutionary War, his home has been in the land that he helped to wrest from the hands of a tyrant. No one would have spoken of General Montgomery as a foreigner were he yet living among us; yet Col. Bentalou is frequently called a Frenchman, though many Englishmen or renegade Americans who actually fought against the republic are unhesitatingly accepted as citizens thereof. Nay, thousands lately imported seem willing to suspect the descendants of the original German and Dutch settlers of Pennsylvania and New York as foreigners, because perhaps they may use *und* for *and*, instead of saying *hand* for *and*, or *Hamos* for *Amos;* but the former is a language spoken by many millions of intelligent beings, and the other is local and not belonging to any language at all. Yes, and there are some of them, though possibly named Sheepshanks or Shufflebottom, "Clutterbuck or Higgenbottom," who laugh at the names of our German brethren and find others, native citizens, foolish enough to join in it with them!

The matters here spoken of come out of the host of miserable prejudices which have descended to us from our British ancestors; and concerning some of these I have often felt myself bound to speak freely. I will yet battle with them until a *national* feeling is established, that shall not regard imported doctrines and notions any more if received from England than from Japan.

[THE DEATH OF ADAMS AND JEFFERSON]

Niles's Register, July 15, 1826

We had hardly announced the decease of the patriot who drafted the Declaration of Independence than news arrived of the death of his venerable compatriot, who more than any other man, perhaps, urged the adoption of that famous measure, and supported it through every change of time and circumstance, himself unchanged. Thomas Jefferson departed this life between twelve and one o'clock on the fiftieth anniversary of the Declaration of Independence, and nearly if not precisely at the same hour of the day when it was first reading before Congress; and John Adams, who was also the committee who reported that Declaration, left us between five and six o'clock of the same jubilee-anniversary, at nearly if not precisely the very hour when the contents of that memorable paper were first proclaimed to the people in the State-House yard in Philadelphia, and when the United States were first saluted as "free, sovereign, and independent;" when the thunder of cannon and the loud huzza of the multitude first ratified the solemn and august act of representatives of the people, appealing to Heaven and resting confidently in the virtues of their fellow-citizens, for the accomplishment of the mighty work which had just then been planned.

It was a fearful time. But "there were giants in those days." And none were more conspicuous for ardent devotion and unlimited zeal, fixed resolution and steady perseverance, than John Adams of Massachusetts and Thomas Jefferson of Virginia. They both lived to grow old, if we may be allowed the expression, in the glories of the nation which they labored so faithfully to establish; they both died on the same day, and that was the jubilee-anniversary of the nation's existence! What a torrent of thought rushes on the mind when these things are mentioned — recollections of the past seemingly overwhelm us by the importance of events that have happened — we greatly wonder at what has taken place and endeavor to look into futurity; saying to ourselves, what will the next fifty years produce? — will anyone now living behold such mighty marches of mind and power as Adams and Jefferson witnessed? With what pleasure do we dwell on the past — with what pride do we look at the present and anticipate the future — with what delighted feeling we remember the services of these venerable and venerated friends, and of others who have long passed from works to rewards — and with what profound respect and grateful tenderness should we cherish the few, the very few oaks of the Revolution that remain, palsied by age, if not withered by neglect, and rendered helpless by former suffering and present privations!

ASPECTS OF AMERICAN SOCIAL HISTORY, 1827[1]

Washington *National Intelligencer*

General Washington's Works: January 29, 1827.

It is with great satisfaction that we have learnt that Mr. Jared Sparks, editor of the *North American Review*, has made arrangements with Judge Washington for publishing an entire edition of "General Washington's Works," to consist of his letters to the Governor of Virginia during the French War, his State Papers, Official Cor-

---

[1] No other newspaper in the country exhibited quite so fully the various phases of American life in its editorial columns, at this period, as the *National Intelligencer*. As the chief Washington newspaper, to which the whole press looked for full reports of Congressional debates, it was in large degree a national clearing-house of information.

respondence, both civil and military, and such of his private letters as may be deemed suited for publication; the whole to be comprised in a series of volumes, with notes and illustrations by the esteemed editor. It is well known that General Washington preserved, with scrupulous care, copies of his own letters, as well as the prodigious number of originals which he received from other persons. In addition to a full use of these papers, which are now at Mount Vernon, Mr. Sparks will profit by a mass of material for Revolutionary History, which he has gathered by a personal inspection of the several public offices in the old States, as well as from various private sources. The records, correspondence, and other papers of the old Congress are preserved in the Department of State, to which he will also have access. With these advantages and resources in aid of the editor, it may be expected that the work will possess a national interest, and constitute a most valuable addition to our political history.

A Railway Project: March 5, 1827.

A great Railway is spoken of in Baltimore, to extend from Baltimore to the Ohio, and many capitalists are said seriously to patronize the thought. They had better patronize the Ohio and Chesapeake Canal, which appears to us much more feasible than a railway *three hundred miles long*. We cannot conceive of the practicability of such work, as a regular everyday line of transportation. We shall, however, lay before our readers the arguments in favor of the measure, which we should be far from opposing from any mean motive of jealousy or envy, if the work be practicable. There would be trade enough leave the road, whenever it found a water communication — at Cumberland, for example — to make the part of the road which crosses the mountain ridge a very important work to this District.

Imprisonment for Debt: May 29, 1827.

. . . We need not cross the Atlantic for evidences of barbarity worthy of the ages from which it has descended. Imprisonment for debt yet exists by our laws — even by the laws of the United States, which exclusively govern this District. Yes, in sight of the splendid dome, the interior of which is adorned with the pictured story of the *triumph of Liberty*, and on the exterior of which proudly float the symbols of National Sovereignty, it is but a few months since a man was immured for *six months* for a debt of *three dollars!* It is almost incredible, but we arrive at the fact in a manner which leaves no doubt of it. Legislators of the Union, how long will you sanctify by your laws such outrages upon human rights? Let it not be said that it is the fault of our community that this man was suffered to lie so long in such durance. It is not *their* fault. The law must have its way; and it is one of the curses of the system that it shuts up its victim from the view of his fellow-men, and he might rot there for years without his situation being known, otherwise than by accident; and it is another of the worst features of the system that the more destitute and miserable a man is, the more so he is sure to become, under its operation.

Our Public Hotels: June 18, 1827.

There is no city in the Union, we believe, so well supplied with hotels of the first class, both in extent and style of keeping, as the city of Washington now is. The large number of these establishments, compared with the resident population of the place, is owing, of course, to the great influx of visitors for several months of every year, during the session of Congress, and the considerable number brought here at all seasons of public business, or by curiosity. The splendor of modern hotels has obtained for them the appellation of "the palaces of the public;" and really the elegance of some of them here and elsewhere almost justifies the phrase. A few years ago a casual visitor of this city, in winter, might think himself well off if he could squeeze himself into a comfortable lodging, and there was no little risk, some times, of getting none at all. Now, besides numerous genteel and excellent boarding-houses, there are three principal hotels that will vie with any others in the Union in extent, elegance, good keeping, and comfort. The Mansion Hotel of Mr. Williamson, and the Indian Queen of Mr. Brown, are long established and well known houses; both of them have lately been enlarged, particularly the latter, and highly improved. In addition to these commodious and excellent hotels, there has lately been erected a new establishment, of surpassing magnitude and elegance, the National Hotel . . . opened under the superintendence of our old friend Gadsby.

A Southern Lynching: July 23, 1827.

Some time during the last week one of those outrageous transactions — and we really think, disgraceful to the character of civilized man — took place near the northeast boundary line of Perry, adjoining Bibb and Autauga Counties, Georgia. The circumstances, we are informed by a gentleman from that county are, that a Mr. McNeily having lost some clothing or some other property of no great value, the slave of a neighboring planter was charged with the theft. McNeily in company with his brother found the negro driving his master's wagon; they seized him and either did or were about to chastize him, when the negro stabbed McNeily so that he died in an hour afterwards. The negro was taken before a justic of the peace, who after serious deliberation waived his authority — perhaps through fear, as the crowd of persons from the abov counties had collected to the number of seventy or eighty near Mr Peoples' (the justice) house. He acted as president of the mob an put the vote, when it was decided he should be immediately ex ecuted by *being burnt to death*. The sable culprit was led to a tre and tied to it, and a large quantity of pine knots collected and place around him, and the fatal torch was applied to the pile even agains the remonstrances of several gentlemen who were present: and th miserable being was in a short time burnt to ashes. An inquest wa held over the remains, and the sheriff of Perry County, with a com pany of about twenty men, repaired to the neighborhood where thi barbarous act took place, to secure those concerned, with wha success we have not heard: but we hope he will succeed in bringin the perpetrators of so high-handed a measure to account. . . .

New England Morals: August 8, 1827.

A theatre is about to be opened in Salem, and fifty dollars ar offered by the manager for the best poetic address. A theatre ir Salem! *Tempora Mutantur.*

The Evils of Drink: August 16, 1827.

Intemperance, with all its shocking consequences, seems to gair upon society, notwithstanding the laudable efforts made to arres its destructive march. Domestic wretchedness and ruin are its general, if not invariable, consequences; but to these are not in frequently added murder and suicide. In fact, it is heart-sickening to read the accounts which almost every day's mail brings us, o instances of these dreadful fruits of the prevalent vice. We do no often notice these occurrences in our paper, because if their ex hibition rouses public attention to the evil, it on the other hand tends to deaden the public horror and sensibility to the most re volting crimes, by rendering them familiar; but we really believe that there have been more murders committed in the United States within the last two years (most of them the effect of intemperance) than took place in all Great Britain during the same period.

[THE ARGUMENT AGAINST GENERAL JACKSON]

Washington *National Intelligencer*, August 4, 1827

Of the seductiveness of military fame in popular governments, if we had ever doubted it, the last Presidential election has given us instructive illustration. Mr. Adams, Mr. Crawford, Mr. Clay, and Mr. Calhoun, all distinguished civilians, were familiarly spoken of

s candidates for the Presidency before General Jackson was seri-
usly announced. The moment he was brought forward, the
oldiers whom he had led to battle rallied under his standard. · It
·as by them, in fact, that he was formally presented as a candidate.
`he military fervor, created by the arrival and triumphal progress
f the good Lafayette through the land, aided the spread of the con-
1gion; and in some populous districts of the interior, the militia,
xalted into enthusiasm by the militia victory at New Orleans,
1arched almost literally in embattled legions to the polls. Had the
lection taken place three months later, it is quite possible that the
xperiment would have been made, which we have been taught
y all history to deprecate, of a successful general arriving, by means
olely of a military achievement, at the highest station of the republic.
   Such an experiment we deprecate, not because we have any
pprehension for the form of our government from any leader,
1ilitary or civil. The Constitution will be found strong enough to
heck the boldest and most daring attempt at usurpation. But
·e object to placing a military man in the chief authority because,
aving once tasted of the pleasure of absolute command, as on the
.eld of battle, he may retain the relish for it, and is too likely, in
he exercise of public duties, to substitute for the injunctions of
1w, or the suggestions of policy, his own sovereign will and pleasure.
Ie cannot endanger the existence of the government, but he may
ndanger the public peace, at home as well as abroad. We object
o such elevation of a military man especially when his military
1me is the only argument in favor of it, and when his civil qualifi-
ations are either not inquired into, or not established.

[THE ARGUMENT AGAINST J. Q. ADAMS][1]

Natchez *Gazette*, November 1, 1827

John Quincy Adams has passed the principal part of his life in
:urope, amid the luxury and splendor of regal governments. Sur-
ounded by all that was enervating in manners, and seductive in
1leasure, by the glitter of dress and the fascination of voluptuousness,
t is not at all astonishing that he has contracted a few of the vices
vhich disgrace the age. Intercourse with a licentious nobility,
vhose profligacy of habit, insatiable avarice, and turpitude of heart
.re concealed by the "star, garters, and ribands" with which they
.re adorned, must exercise a deleterious influence upon a man who
1ows to every vicissitude, swims upon the tide of every revolution,

[1] This curious and absurd editorial represented a type of attack upon
ohn Quincy Adams which had immense potency throughout the South and West,
nd which was accepted by many rough voters of the Jackson following as gospel
·uth.

and is the acknowledged creature of circumstances. The courtly voluptuary, refined in all the stratagems of sensuality; the privileged libertine, at whose approach innocence trembles and the blushing cheek grows pale, who considers virtue as the *ignis fatuus* of imagination, and health and happiness as his lawful prey — the deceitful diplomatist, the fawning sycophant, the superannuated beggar, ecclesiastics without religion, and councillors without learning, are the characters who surround the thrones of Europe. These have been the associates of Mr. Adams, and those who idolize him add it to the catalogue of his qualifications. He went abroad, it is presumed, before his principles had been formed — in the immaturity of youth, when the mind is ductile and susceptible of impression. It was there that he learned the superiority of a monarchical over a democratic or federative government — that the people were not calculated to govern themselves — that republics wanted energy — that orders of nobility should be instituted, and Senators entrusted with their official functions for life.

PRESIDENT ADAMS'S REGARD FOR MERIT
Washington *National Intelligencer*, November 27, 1827

As for the madness of this Administration, we know wherein what is called its "madness" has consisted. What we have approved in this Administration — what convinced us of the political honesty and integrity of the President — has been this very thing; namely, that he has filled the great offices in his gift not with personal friends, or political parasites and office-seekers, but with high-minded and honorable men — with such men as Henry Clay, his associate in negotiating the Treaty of Ghent, and the fearless and free advocate of measures without regard to men; Richard Rush, the confidential friend and worthy pupil of the illustrious Madison during his Administration; James Barbour, the independent and enthusiastic supporter of the Madison Republican Administration, and of Mr. Monroe's, which followed it, and the true and conscientious friend of William H. Crawford; Rufus King, the venerable Federalist who stood forward for his country during the late war, and was for that reason placed by the Republicans of New York in the seat of honor; Albert Gallatin, a Republican of 1798 and a Republican now, whose talents, integrity, and valuable experience the President had the sense to appreciate and avail himself of . . . This loftiness of conduct of the President is the "madness" with which he is afflicted. We know, and probably he knows, how this imputation of madness might have been prevented; but, if the remedy were even now to be applied as a cure, having been neglected as a preventive, we should condemn the resort to it.

FANCIED SECURITY, OR THE RATS ON A BENDER.

JACKSON CLEARING THE KITCHEN.

(Two old campaign broadsides. The upper shows Fillmore, the Whig candidate, guarding the government crib against Frémont and Buchanan in 1856; the lower shows Jackson at the time of his Cabinet reorganization in 1830).

[THE BALTIMORE AND OHIO RAILROAD] [1]

Baltimore *Gazette*, April 30, 1828

When the Baltimore and Ohio Railroad Company first embarke in the undertaking of constructing the proposed road, it was the desire, if practicable, to procure the necessary iron in the Unite States; and they accordingly advertised extensively for proposa for the requisite supplies, in order to ascertain the quantities tha could be furnished and at what prices it would be delivered. Th result of this effort convinced them that it would be necessar to look abroad for this indispensable material, as but two offe: were made to the company, both of which were for very limite quantities and at prices above 100 per cent dearer than is paid b the Liverpool & Manchester Railroad Company.

From the best information that has been obtained, it appea that there is already a deficiency in the home supplies of iron, fc the ordinary purposes of this country, of twenty to thirty thousan tons annually. The lowest price at which iron rails could b obtained in the United States would be about $100 per ton; an should the company have to go into the market here for the quantit wanted, a considerable rise would unavoidably be the consequence to the serious prejudice of both the manufacturing and agricultura interests of the country.

Iron manufactured in England to suit the purposes of the rail road company . . . would cost delivered here, exclusive of duty upo it, about $57 per ton; and with a duty of twenty-five per cen ad valorem it would cost about $70 per ton. It is therefore obviou that the company must obtain their supplies from abroad, and th iron-masters of this country, under existing circumstances, can hav no interest whatever in the matter of a rebate of duty; the onl question being in fact whether the government will deem it judiciou to burden an undertaking, in the success of which the whole natior has a deep and vital interest, with a heavy and grievous incumbrance or will at once come forward and promote its accomplishment by the very reasonable and moderate encouragement its friends solicit No one who has reflected on the subject can fail to appreciate the importance of the great work before us, as it regards the political, commercial, and social relations of our country; and it is on all hands admitted that the enterprise has a strong claim upon the most liberal patronage of the nation. The mere amount of the duty

[1] Despite the doubts of the *National Intelligencer*, there was a heavy rush for shares in the Baltimore and Ohio Railroad as soon as the stock-books were opened, and ground was broken July 4, 1828, by Charles Carroll of Carrollton. The first division of the railroad was ready for use in 1830.

which the government would derive from the iron to be employed upon the road could be of no importance to the country, but at the same time it would be severely felt by the individuals who have so generously committed their fortunes in the undertaking.

[JOHN QUINCY ADAMS GIVES WAY TO JACKSON] [1]

New York *Evening Post*, March 5, 1829

"The long agony is over," as the *American* says, and the new Administration, the strongest ever seen in this country since the days of Washington, has entered upon its career. Of the past we will not say much, since we can say no good. The country has been rendered contemptible abroad and distracted at home. Of Mr. Adams himself we must be permitted to state that his acts have all shown that we were not wide of the truth when we said, as may be seen in our files, that although not deficient in literary acquirements, he has certain defects of character that unfitted him for directing the affairs of a great empire; and that his prejudices against that nation, with which it more behooves us to be on good and amicable terms than with all Europe besides, were so blind and so inveterate that we ventured to predict that no satisfactory settlement could ever be effected with it during his Administration. The event has proved that our fears were not chimerical. As to his Cabinet friends and advisers, we shall dismiss them from our consideration at this time by congratulating the country on its escape from what was once called by an eminent English statesman "the worst of evils that could predominate in our country: men without popular confidence, public opinion, or general trust, invested with all the powers of government."

A DECLARATION OF ANTI–MASONIC PRINCIPLES [2]

Albany *Evening Journal*, March 22, 1830

The public sentiment which spontaneously demanded the establishment of this journal is pregnant with interest and instruction. The "speck" which three years since appeared on the western horizon has magnified itself into a mighty cloud, overshadowing the whole State, and preparing to pour out healthful showers to refresh and vivify the civil and political institutions of our country.

[1] Probably one of the early editorials by William Cullen Bryant, who this year became editor-in-chief of the *Evening Post*.

[2] Written by Thurlow Weed, and taken from the first issue of this long-powerful newspaper. It began as an Anti-Masonic Organ, with the support of William H. Seward, Francis Granger, and other men just becoming prominent in New York State politics; it developed into one of the important newspapers of the Whig Party.

The abduction, imprisonment, and murder of a citizen, by an association of men sufficiently numerous and influential to hold our Tribunals of Justice at bay, naturally awakened a public investigation.[1] The offences were found to have been committed by Free Masons, for the protection of their order. Further investigation established the fearful fact that the laws were too feeble to vindicate themselves against Masonic aggression. Still further inquiry proved that the executive, legislative, judicial, and municipal departments of the government were in the hands of Free Masons and under the influence of their institutions. These startling disclosures provoked a searching investigation into the principles, tendency, and aims of the Masonic institution. They will soon be unfolded, and found to be utterly inconsistent with private rights, and fraught with manifold dangers to the public welfare. . . .

The mode adopted by the people to overthrow Free Masonry is at once the most effective and least exceptionable of any that could have been resorted to. It accomplishes a great public good, without inflicting any private wrongs. None suffer with Free Masonry except such as voluntarily elect to maintain her cause and abide its fate. The friends of the order generally admit that it is *useless* — while its opponents, having clearly proved it to be *dangerous*, call upon its thousand virtuous members to renounce it and place themselves upon an equality with their fellow-citizens. There is nothing of constraint in this. Those who prefer the swelling titles, the bauble sceptres, the mock majesty, and the mystic honors and emoluments of Free Masonry, to the simple, unostentatious duties of Republican citizens — who take and obey her unearthly oaths, certainly have no title to reproach the people for withdrawing *their* confidence from the sworn subjects of another government.

There is too much frankness in the character of our people, too little guile in the nature of our institutions, to tolerate the existence of secret societies. Studied secrecy always awakens doubts and distrust. The country has everything to apprehend and nothing to hope from formidable secret societies. Shame, vice, and treason are engendered by night, and woo concealment; but charity, science, and religion love the light, and seek to be reflected in its rays. The ancients aspired to a state of moral perfection which would enable them to walk with a window in their breasts. But from this test of heathen virtue the vaunting *"Hand-maid of Religion"* shrinks, toad-like, into her dark and loathsome lodge-room, from which the genial light and wholesome air are excluded.

[1] This is of course a reference to the disappearance of William Morgan, who had published a book on the secrets of Masonry. It was alleged that the Masons had murdered him. So stern became the indignation against him that the Anti-Masonic Party polled 128,000 votes in 1830.

This paper, while laboring to disrobe Free Masonry of its assumed vestments, and to exhibit it to the world in its assumed garb, will aim to disabuse the public mind in relation to the origins, progress, and purpose of anti-Masonry. The Masonic institution, when truly presented to the understandings of men, will be found to be barren and bald of all the virtues and wisdom with which it has been invested by fable and tradition.

[PRESIDENT JACKSON'S TOAST: A SOUTHERN INTERPRETATION [1]

Charleston *Mercury*, April 24, 1830

The President's toast at the late Jeffersonian banquet was, "The Federal Union — it must be preserved!" To this we respond, amen. But how preserved? There is but one mode, and that is by inducing the majority to respect the rights and feelings of the minority, or, in other words, by inducing the North and East to repeal or modify the iniquitous measures by which the South is impoverished and enslaved. And that the President alludes to this mode is too evident, we think, to admit the shadow of a doubt. His message to Congress distinctly recognizes the rights of the States, and solemnly cautions Congress to beware of encroachments on them. He is a disciple of Jefferson, whose whole life was devoted to State Rights doctrines, and who first pointed out the mode by which alone Federal usurpation can be resisted and repressed. He had met with numerous other disciples of the same great man, to do honor to his memory and to revive and perpetuate his political principles. When the President, therefore, under such circumstances says that "the Union must be preserved," it follows necessarily that he refers to the mode of preservation pointed out by Mr. Jefferson. And that is, by the exercise of the sovereignty of the States and by their interposing in their highest capacity, to arrest the progress of tyranny and injustice. The President's toast, we think, taken in connection with his well-known principles, and the peculiar circumstances under which it was announced, completely puts an end to whatever little doubt may heretofore have existed as to his feelings or opinions in relation to the momentous question, now at issue between the Federal government and the whole Southern section of the Union. Indeed, it is a distinct recognition of Jeffersonian principles, as contradistinguished from the consolidation doctrines advocated by Mr. Webster.

[1] This editorial, from the chief organ of the South Carolina Nullificationists, was a transparent misinterpretation for propagandist purposes; Jackson's famous toast at the Jefferson Day dinner this year, uttered as he looked John C. Calhoun, the Vice-President, straight in the eye, was a direct defiance of the Nullifiers.

PRESIDENT JACKSON AND INTERNAL
IMPROVEMENTS [1]

Richmond *Enquirer*, June 1, 1830

The President has negatived the Maysville road bill; and he has assigned the grounds of his objections in the eloquent and memorable message which we this day lay before our readers. We do not exactly agree with all its propositions; but we hail with pleasure the defeat of the bill which he has rejected — and we hail with gratitude the spirit he displays in favor of restoring the true principles of the Constitution. He assumes the construction of the Constitution set up by the old Republican party in 1798 as its "true reading in relation to the power under consideration." He wishes to bring us back to that reading through the agency of the people. He protests directly against the passage of any bill for works of internal improvement, which "bears upon the sovereignty of the States within whose limits their execution is contemplated, if *jurisdiction* of the territory which they occupy be claimed as necessary to their preservation and use." He disclaims especially such a work as the Maysville road, as being of a *local*, not *general*, of a *State*, not a *national*, character. He objects, on the strongest grounds of expediency, to the undertaking at this time of even "such works as are *authorized* by the States, and are *national* in their character." He insists, 1st, upon the propriety of paying off the national debt, leaving our resources unfettered, reducing the taxes and burdens of the people; and 2dly, after this grand event is consummated, he urges the expediency of embarking in no "system of internal improvements without a previous amendment of the Constitution, explaining and defining the precise powers of the Federal government over it."

Throughout the whole of this interesting document, we see the spirit of a man who is desirous of bringing back the Constitution to its true reading, and of limiting the Federal government to its specified powers — of arresting the rage of encroachment — of protecting the States against any further extension of Federal jurisdiction, and of saving as much of the money power as other Administrations have left — and thus arresting, as far as such precedents would permit, the alarming course of events which has set in to the augmentation and abuse of the Federal authority.

---

[1] By Thomas Ritchie, the founder of the *Enquirer*. Henry Clay, who favored internal improvements at Federal expense, had a bill passed in May, 1830, to build a turnpike from Maysville to Lexington, Ky. Jackson vetoed it, bringing the era of national internal improvements to an end.

THE ARGUMENT AGAINST FREE PUBLIC SCHOOLS
Philadelphia *National Gazette*, July 10, 1830

It is an old and a sound remark, that government cannot provide for the necessities of the People; it is they who maintain the government, and not the latter the People. Education may be among their necessities; but it is one of that description which the State or national councils cannot supply, except partially and in a limited degree. They may endow public schools for the indigent, and colleges for the most costly and comprehensive scheme of instruction. To create and sustain seminaries for the tuition of all classes — to digest and regulate systems; to adjust and manage details, to render a multitude of schools effective, is beyond their province and power. Education in general must be the work of the intelligence, need, and enterprise of individuals and associations. At present, in nearly all the most populous parts of the United States, it is attainable for nearly all the inhabitants; it is comparatively cheap, and if not the best possible, it is susceptible of improvememt and likely to be advanced. Its progress and wider diffusion will depend, not upon government, but on the public spirit, information liberality, and training of the citizens themselves, who may appreciate duly the value of the object as a national good, and as a personal benefit for their children. Some of the writers about universal public instruction and discipline, seem to forget the constitution of modern society, and declaim as if our communities could receive institutions or habits like those of Sparta. The dream embraces grand Republican female academies, to make Roman matrons!

Idem, August 19, 1830

We can readily pardon the editor of the *United States Gazette* for not perceiving that the scheme of Universal Equal Education at the expense of the State, is virtually "Agrarianism." It would be a compulsory application of the means of the richer, for the direct use of the poorer classes; and so far an arbitrary division of property among them. The declared object is, to procure the opportunity of instruction for the child or children of every citizen; to elevate the standard of the education of the working classes, or equalize the standard for all classes; which would, doubtless, be to lower or narrow that which the rich may now compass. But the most sensible and reflecting possessors of property sufficient to enable them to educate their children in the most liberal and efficacious way, and upon the broadest scale, would prefer to share their means for any other purpose, or in any other mode, than such as would injuriously affect or circumscribe the proficiency of their own offspring.

THE PROTECTIVE TARIFF AND THE SOUTH

Richmond *Enquirer*, March 15, 1831

It is impossible that the people of the oppressed sections of the United States *can submit much longer to so oppressive a system.* The extinguishment of the public debt is rapidly approaching. We tell our tariff brethren of the North in the frankest and most friendly spirit that it is impossible to remain in this durance vile for many years longer. When that debt is sponged away (and we go for that consummation even more anxiously than they do), the question must be settled — and we trust to heaven with the mutual consent of all the partners in the compact. Union, harmony, the most cordial fellowship with our brethren, are objects dear, very dear, to our hearts. But we cannot tolerate oppression — a subjection to a system so absurd, so much at war with every principle of our Federal system, the unfettering institutions of a young and a free people, and with the very spirit of the age itself.

TOKENS OF NATIONAL GROWTH

Philadelphia *Gazette*, February 23, 1832

The Centennial Anniversary (of Washington's Birth). — Yesterday will be ever memorable in the annals of our city. . . . The civic and military procession in honor of it, to which we particularly refer, was the most imposing, and altogether the most curious and respectable, that has taken place perhaps in modern times. If the remains of Washington had been the prize in a competition of effort throughout the land, to pay the most jealous and signal homage to his memory, they would, we think, have been allotted to this community. The procession embraced nearly 20,000 persons; it was between three and four miles in length; it consumed upwards of two hours in moving steadily past any particular spot; it must have marched about eight miles; it drew forth to the streets, or attracted to the windows, nearly the whole population of Philadelphia; and many thousands came in from the country to witness the extraordinary spectacle.

Washington *National Intelligencer*, April 19, 1832

Bustle at the Capital. — Crowds flock to the city as much as ever. There is no end to visitors. They are coming and going every hour in the day. All the lines between this city and Baltimore are full every day. We have several fresh beauties from the East; Philadelphia and New York parties are as frequent as ever. We had the other night three parties at the selfsame hour, and tonight two splendid ones. We don't know what the world is coming to. It is very evident it is not coming to an end, however.

A LEAF FROM MRS. TROLLOPE'S MEMORANDUM BOOK[1]

New York *Evening Post*, July 9, 1832

(Found among some loose papers accidentally left at her lodgings)

New York is rather a charming little city, containing from 100,000 to 150,000 inhabitants, mostly black. The streets are altogether monopolized by these sons and daughters of Africa, who take the wall of you on all occasions; and it would be entirely useless, as well as extremely dangerous, to notice any insult which they may offer you, as they all carry long daggers concealed in their bosoms, and use them, too, with utter impunity, under the very nose of the public authorities. Indeed, I once saw a little black boy carried to Bridewell for stealing, and that very afternoon the whole negro male population turned out in a procession, consisting of twenty thousand, with banners which bore the words "Wilberforce Philanthropic Society." From this I presume the boy's name was Wilberforce; at all events, the Court of Sessions (which, by the way, is here held in a little grocery store in William Street, called Harmony Hall) acquitted the culprit, in consequence of the sensation his imprisonment had produced.

This took place in the month of August, and so great was the alarm that immense numbers fled from the city, fearing another *insurrection*. Whole families departed at once. The steamboats (of which there are two tolerable good ones, one plying to Albany, the other to New Orleans on Long Island) were every day crowded with trembling passengers, who sought refuge from the bloody and atrocious scenes which yearly disgrace the streets, and retired to Saratoga, Communipaw, Brooklyn in New Jersey, Charleston in North Carolina, and Greenwich Village on Lake George. Scarcely a night passes without the negroes setting two or three of the houses

---

[1] Frances Trollope had come to the United States in 1827, and remained until 1831; a business venture — a small shop — of hers in Cincinnati failed, and her impressions of the country were colored by the fact. She published her "Domestic Manners of the Americans" in both England and America early in 1832, and its caustic and unfair picture of American life created great resentment. Bryant here satirizes its foolish exaggerations and inaccuracies. Not a single sentence in the memorandum "leaf" fails to include some wild absurdity. The names of the theatrical personages are ridiculously confused. At the same time, in other editorials the *Evening Post* admitted that Mrs. Trollope had hit some disagreeable facts squarely on the head. It credited her book with reforming a number of prevalent vulgarities; and declared that the mere cry "A Trollope! A Trollope!" would correct public misbehavior.

on fire with the view of destroying the inhabitants. As the best mansions are made of light pine wood, it may be easily imagined that they are universally combustible; but fortunately the city of New York has really a copious supply of water, which prevents much damage.

Their theatres are positively amusing, and I must say I laughed very heartily, although to confess the truth, it was only at their tragedies and their operas. The Park Theatre was originally an old barn; its outside is disgraceful, and its interior more so. It has been burnt down *fourteen times*, probably by the religious party, which form the majority, and have now elected Jackson to the Presidency. The establishment stands opposite the Roman Catholic Cathedral, and is under the management of Messrs. Pierson and Drurie. I am indebted to my kind friend for many of these particulars. He knows that I am writing a book of travels, and although himself only an American, has kindly volunteered his services to collect materials for me, giving me sketches of character and authentic anecdotes, and has corrected, with the most scrupulous care, all of my geographical and typographical illustrations, in which the reader may consequently repose the most implicit reliance. The theatres have, however, two or three decent performers. Mr. Barnes is the principal tragedian. I saw him one evening in Romeo to Mrs. Keppel's Juliet, and I must say I thought his conception of the character rather good. He is quite small, with large melancholy eyes, and features expressive of tenderness and passion. Mrs. Keppel, as Juliet, was not sufficiently poetic, but was nevertheless pretty well. This was, however, afterwards accounted for by the discovery that she was an English lady. I afterwards saw Mr. Hilson in Young Norval. The greatest attraction they have, however, is Mr. Povey, a distinguished vocalist. He plays the Prince in Cinderella, and Masaniello, quite delightfully; all the rest are not worth mentioning. A fellow by the name of H. Placide undertook to personate the Baron, but I was thoroughly disgusted.

There are some peculiar customs prevailing among the audience here, which are apt to provoke a smile on the lips of a rational stranger. All their ladies dress in the most tasteless and extravagant style, and yet betray the most incontrovertible evidences of vulgarity, sitting on the banisters with their backs to the stage, between the acts, eating Carolina potatoes, and drinking ginger pop. This is done every night at the Park Theatre, and some good society females smoke "long nines" with a degree of audacious ease and familiarity that are really shocking.

JACKSON'S VETO OF THE BANK RECHARTER[1]

New York *Evening Post*, July 30, 1832

We want words to express our sympathy with our worthy friends of the opposition at discovering that the veto message of the President is likely to increase his popularity, instead of destroying it as they had intended it should. That the opposition meant to give him a bill which should produce a veto, there is no question; but now they have got the veto, they are puzzled what to do with it; and the majority of them, we have no doubt, repent the haste they were in to get it. Their first manoeuvre was an attempt to excite the people against it by all sorts of opprobrious epithets bestowed upon the document, the President, and his Administration. Unluckily this had no effect. The great meeting at Pittsburgh — the great meeting at Philadelphia, in which the course of the President was approved in the warmest terms — the public rejoicings in various places in the State of Ohio — the general voice of the press in favor of this act of the President — these circumstances together soon convinced them how different is the effect of the veto from what they had expected with so much confidence.

Now take one of the leading opposition papers, and see what are its principal topics. They are full of railing against the Jackson party for supporting, indiscriminately, all the acts of the Administration; they are in a transport of indignation at the blindness of the people; and they abuse, in the bitterest terms, the presses which uphold the Chief Magistrate in refusing his signature, styling them "slavish" and "pensioned." Then they set their "ready and exact calculators" to work to ascertain how many people the area which contained the great Jackson meeting at Philadelphia could hold, with a view to reducing the supposed number of persons present. What is the fair inference from all this? Why, that the opposition are disappointed, and that the veto is popular.

THE CHOLERA IN NEW YORK

New York *Courier and Enquirer*, August 7, 1832

The cholera first made its appearance in this city about the 25th of June, in the family of a poor woman and her two children, said to be from Quebec, who lived in Cherry near James Street. It made

---

[1] Henry Clay, in an effort to provide his party with an issue, had a Senate bill introduced in the spring of 1832 for the recharter of the Bank of the United States. Passing both houses, this bill went to President Jackson on July 4, and six days later was returned with a veto. Clay had his issue, but it proved fatal to the hopes of his party. Bryant's editorial is characteristic of the Democratic rejoicings over the popularity of the veto message.

but little progress until the 3d of July, when the Board of Health first made their official report, announcing that several deaths had occurred of a disease resembling in some measure the cholera then prevailing in Canada. The disease lingered where it first broke out for several days, when it appeared in another section of the city, and on the opposite side of it, at the foot of Reed near Washington Street. In a few days after, it broke out in Lawrence Street, and the streets in that vicinity, and almost immediately afterwards at Greenwich Village, Orange, and other streets about the Five Points, and in the lower part of Manhattan Island. These different sections are distant from each other, some half a mile, and some one or two miles. They are all inhabited by a crowded population.

The cases have been by far the most numerous in Orange, Mulberry, and Lawrence Streets, each of which have had reported from one to two hundred cases. For instance, in Orange Street, No. 20 had ten; Nos. 27 seven, 33 ten, 61 twelve, 89 nine; and many other dwellings four and five each. Four houses in Little Water Street, Nos. 2, 4, 5, and 7, have thirty-six cases. The streets in the Sixth Ward at and near the Five Points furnished about eight hundred cases within the last four weeks; and if those taken to the various hospitals from that ward were added, it is probable that the number would amount to full twelve hundred. By the late census, the Sixth Ward contained 13,570 inhabitants. If we deduct those residing in the ward in high and respectable streets, and also the number that have left the city or ward, the number left in the crowded and filthy portions will probably be about 10,000. Of this number at least 1200 have had the disease, and fully half have died; a degree of mortality seldom equalled in any country. On an examination of the sections of the city where the disease has prevailed the most, it will be found that they are all principally made ground, or ground that has been filled in. Lawrence Street, the Five Points, and lower Manhattan Island are all of this description.

If the city authorities profit by past experience, they will, we think, make some law regulating the number of persons who may occupy a house. It is a notorious fact that a number of individuals, some of whom are wealthy, in this city employ their capital by covering their lots with tenements to shelter the greatest possible number of poor families, renting them by the month, week, or day, and compelling them to pay enormously for these miserable accommodations. We have the fact from an authentic source, that on two lots in a certain street in this city, 370 miserable poor persons were found at one time, being a population exceeding that of many country villages, who were crowded together on two lots of forty by one hundred feet, or a little more. We refer to the degraded population of St. Giles on London with no small degree of disgust, when we have sections of our city inhabited by equally debased and miserable blacks and whites, as deeply sunk in crime and filth as any that can be found within any of the parishes in London.

[A CITY EMPTIED BY THE CHOLERA PLAGUE]

New York *Evening Post*, August 20, 1832

The appearance which New York presents to one who views it at the present time from the midst of the Hudson or from the opposite shores of New Jersey is a spectacle scarcely less unusual and solemn than to one who visits what were two months since its crowded and noisy places of business. The number of persons who have left the city is estimated at upwards of one hundred thousand people, including all classes and occupations. So many domestic fires have been put out, and the furnaces of so many manufactories have been extinguished, that the dense cloud of smoke which always lay over the city, inclining in the direction of the wind, is now so thin as often to be scarcely discernible, and the buildings of the great metropolis appear with unusual clearness and distinctness. On a fair afternoon the corners of the houses, their eaves and roofs, appear as sharply defined as if the spectator stood close by their side, and from the walks of Hoboken you may count the dormer windows in any given block of buildings. The various colors of the edifices appear also with an astonishing vividness, while the usual murmur from the streets is scarcely heard.

THE UNITED STATES BANK AS THE ELECTION ISSUE

Washington *Globe*, August 30, 1832

A day or two since we spoke of the course taken by the opposition in making the Bank question the great engine of their party by which to eject the present Chief Magistrate and instal Mr. Clay in his place. Every mail brings a new confirmation of our remarks. The opposition relies on the Bank question to revolutionize the politics of Pennsylvania, to secure Kentucky to Mr. Clay, to remove all doubt of the vote of Ohio, and to alienate Maryland and Missouri from the Hero of New Orleans. It is impossible for one who does not daily look over the newspapers published in the various parts of the country to form an idea of the extent to which this devotion to the Bank is carried, and how completely the Clay party have identified their cause with that institution. All questions of public policy — all considerations relating to national character, public virtue, free institutions, taxation, commerce, foreign relations — all are forgotten in the zeal to perpetuate the privilege of a great and overshadowing association of money lenders. A whole party have put on the badge of mammon, and have taken his mark on their forehead. Let any candid man belonging to the National Republican Party pass in review the journals of his side, as we have done this morning, and it would be cruelty to ask him whether he did not feel ashamed of the position in which they have placed themselves — harnessed and toiling in the yoke of a monied institution — contending perpetually in that sordid cause, as if the things that make the true glory and happiness of a nation had no existence.

If the fate of the United States Bank has become a question between itself and the people, it is the Bank which has made it so. If that institution had refused to lend itself to the plans of the opposition, if it had contented itself with making the application for a new charter at a time favorable to impartial discussion, if it had followed the fair and usual course of business transactions, if it had kept itself clear of the suspicion of purchasing men and presses, it would have escaped an immense load of odium which now rests upon its cause, and which even the whole weight of the opposition party brought to its aid cannot counterbalance. The people will now demand that it shall come before them with clean hands. They will ask what is the meaning of this and that "ugly smutch" upon a palm which should be stainless, and they will not take long-winded, rhetorical explanations of the matters filling a whole newspaper; they will be satisfied only with direct plain answers, such as have not yet been given.

THE CORRUPTING INFLUENCE OF THE BANK

New York *Evening Post*, October 4, 1832

The election has now, we say it with feelings of the strongest regret, become little else than a battle between the United States Bank and the friends of the administration. Hitherto the warfare of elections has been carried on by the discussion of public measures and plans of policy, by the attack and defense of the characters and qualifications of the candidates, their acts, their opinions and their promises — by appeals to preconceived prejudices or partialities — but now, an element of a hitherto unknown and most dangerous nature is mingled with our party struggles. A monied institution, headed by an active, subtle and insinuating lender, has thrown itself with its capital of thirty millions, into the arena of political strife. What may be affected by such an institution, with such a means of influence, by the distribution of its favors among those from whom services are expected, of those whose enmity is feared, may be easily imagined. The Saviour of the world was betrayed for thirty pieces of silver. The influence of the "root of all evil" is not lessened by the lapse of eighteen hundred years, and the interests of the Union may be betrayed for thirty millions of dollars.

Sober and good men are alarmed at seeing the manner in which the Bank has intermeddled with the politics of the country. The regular organized system of corruption on which it has proceeded, the application it has made of pecuniary persuasion to men possessed of political influence — to members of Congress and conductors of the public press — while it has corrupted some enemies into friends, has caused hundreds of honest men who were its friends to become its enemies. We are yet, however, to see what will be the effect of all this upon public opinion. We are to see whether the detestation of corruption is strong enough among the mass of the people to cause them to rise in their might and prostrate, by a total and ignominious defeat, both the buyers and sellers engaged in the infamous traffic.

In the meantime, our readers may ask what the Bank is doing since the investigations of the Committee. We can assure them that it has intermitted none of its activity. The disgrace of exposure has had no influence upon its transactions. We take from the Washington *Globe* the following list of pecuniary favours distributed by it among those whose services are not to be undervalued. We have been assured from a respectable source that it is substantially correct. The accuracy of the statement that the Bank had *contracted* its loans may be judged of from this statement.

Innumerable *political* loans have been made by the principal Bank since the investigating Committee made their report.

To Gales and Seaton a new loan of $20,000 has been made, half covered up by a little indirection to give them a pretence for denial.

The faithless Senator from Mississippi has gotten at least $10,000, with mere nominal security.

About the sum of $14,000 was loaned to a member of the House of Representatives, supposed to be opposed to the Bank, who was not at his post to vote against the Bank.

Another member, always before opposed to the Bank, voted for the bill, and, with a friend who had taken care to be absent on the passage of the bill, went to Philadelphia shortly after, and the Bank loaned them on a mutual endorsement, $7,500.

After the veto, Daniel Webster, on his return home, got from the Bank about $10,000 — swelling his debt to about $40,000.

Other loans have been made, even *recently*, to members of Congress and public officers, to a considerable amount.

JACKSON'S VICTORY OVER HENRY CLAY

New York *Evening Post*, November 12, 1832

The question who is to be our President for the next four years is now universally allowed to be settled. Popular opinion has declared itself in a manner not to be misunderstood or explained away. The most obstinate and the most prejudiced of our adversaries no longer venture to question the fact that the present Chief Magistrate has, by some means or other, obtained a fast hold upon the affections and confidence of the people of the United States. They like his character, they like his manner of administrating the affairs of the nation, and they have made up their minds to have him for their President for another term. There has prevailed in the great mass of the people a deeply-rooted conviction that the principles of foreign and domestic policy adopted and avowed by him are essential to the peace and prosperity of the Union. This conviction did not manifest itself by any clamor, because there was no occasion for any; but when the time came for declaring itself through the ballot-boxes, it came forward with a strength which nothing could resist. The opposition were swept before it like stubble before the whirlwind. We look around us and wonder how so feeble a minority could have contrived to make so much noise, and by what means they could have inoculated themselves so universally — even to the shrewdest and most experienced in their ranks — with the delusion that they should prevail in the contest. . . .

For our own part, we rejoice at the result for manifold reasons independent of the ordinary pleasure attending the victory of one's own party. We rejoice because a man clear-minded, honest, and decided far beyond the majority of those who fill high political stations in the various States, is triumphantly sustained by the people against the malice of his enemies. We rejoice that the only man under whom there can exist a prospect of pacifying the discontents of the South, and of preserving the Union, is continued in power. We are glad that a pacific settlement of the Indian question is now certain, and that a civil war with Georgia, into which the declared policy of either of General Jackson's competitors would have inevitably plunged the nation, will be avoided. We congratulate the nation that so large a majority of its citizens have concurred with the President in placing the seal of reprobation on that folly which would have exhausted the resources of the nation in a series of wasteful and ill-considered projects of internal improvement, and which would have produced perhaps perpetual collisions between the national government and that of the States. We congratulate all honest men that the league between the opposition and the Bank, and the attempt to elect a President by pecuniary corruption, has been defeated in such a signal manner that it will serve as a fearful warning for the future. In the election of Mr. Van Buren to the Vice Presidency, we are gratified to see that the people have passed a solemn censure on that Senate which, listening only to the promptings of party hatred, endeavored to proscribe one of our ablest and most deserving citizens. Finally, we rejoice to witness with what an intelligent and fortunate unanimity the people have ratified the sound, wise, and healing principles of public policy adopted by the present Administration.

MR. VAN BUREN'S RETURN FROM ENGLAND [1]

New York *Evening Post*, November 22, 1832

The compliment paid by our city authorities to Mr. Van Buren has been consummated at a moment when, from every quarter of the land, every mail brings to him the most gratifying assurances that his private virtues and public services, the moderation of his temper, the integrity of his heart, the fortitude of his mind, and the zeal of his patriotism, are justly estimated by the people. At such a moment, an avowal of regard from a single city can hardly be supposed to produce the deep effect upon his feelings which, a short while since, such an expression from the metropolis of his native State could not but have occasioned. But let it be remembered, in justice to the Corporation, that they are not timeservers in this respect. They have not waited till the sentiments of other cities and other States could be ascertained. They have not hesitated to act until a land's united cry should speak, with an emphasis not to be misunderstood, the sense of the whole people as to the character of Van Buren, and as to that proceeding of the United States Senate by which, without cause, and on the most unfounded pretence that was ever alleged against a statesman, he was called from a diplomatic mission which his talents promised to render of great value to the nation. New York was not so tardy to do honor to her insulted son. As long ago as March, 1829, the compliment yesterday paid was determined upon, as will be seen by the resolution which will be found in its place in the account below of the proceedings upon this interesting occasion. Why this resolution was not carried into effect immediately upon Mr. Van Buren's return from Europe, all our readers will remember; and the conduct of that gentleman then, in declining the ceremonial of a public re-

[1] Martin Van Buren was appointed Minister to England on August 1, 1831; his enemies in the Senate, led by Vice-President Calhoun, and actuated by unworthy reasons of political enmity, rejected the nomination. Their act redounded to the political advantage of Van Buren, and Bryant's editorial recognizes the fact.

ception, and the various honors which were intended him, gratifying
as under the circumstances they must have been, was justly looked
upon as another instance, added to the many he had before given,
of his readiness at all times to sacrifice personal advantages to considerations of public good.

How significant, how beautiful, how fine a comment on the
character of our people and the nature of our institutions, is the
act of political retribution paid the Senate for their malignant
course to Mr. Van Buren! Who now are the rebuked? To the
same chair, lately occupied by the ambitious Lepidus when he
dared to throw his casting vote into the political balance against a
man his equal in acquirements, his superior in talents, and oh, how
greatly his superior in honesty, in singleness of motive, in elevation
of character, and in all those qualities which give the greatest value
to talents and learning — to that high seat the rejected is raised!
The rebuked of Clay and Calhoun is the honored of the people!
The very act that was intended to prostrate him forever, has made
him Vice-President of the United States! In contemplating such
an act of retributive justice, one might almost be excused for ex-
claiming, "Vox populi, vox Dei!"

THE UNION [1]

Washington *Globe*, November 29, 1832

Can there be a doubt of the purpose of the Nullifiers to carry it
to a civil war? Why the recent language of their leading partizans?
Why do we hear of pledges of life, fortune, and sacred honor, "to
carry into effect the resolves of the Convention"? Why has Governor
Hamilton been so assiduously courting and drilling the militia?
Why has he recently, by the most extraordinary means, procured
himself to be elevated to the military rank of a brigadier-general?
What is all this but preparation for war? What does Hamilton
mean, but to be the military hero of Nullification, while Hayne
shall hold the civil power, and Calhoun, the desperate author of
the whole scheme, watch to profit by their hazards and their perils?
This, then, is Nullification: — *It is* CIVIL WAR AND DISUNION!

Let each American now ask himself, *Shall the Federal Union be
preserved?* Shall these desperate men be permitted to entail on this
happy land, or on South Carolina itself, the miseries of Civil War
and the everlasting evils which will flow from the destruction of
this confederacy? Who is ready to have the blood of millions, the
oppression of this beautiful continent, and the slavery of its in-

---

[1] This long article is characteristic of the best editorial utterances of the *Globe*,
and is unquestionably one of those upon which the editors carefully consulted
President Jackson.

habitants, born and unborn, laid at his door? Let no man promise himself that these States can be riven asunder, and the fragments exist alongside each other in perpetual peace. Any anticipation of that sort is contradicted by all history, by the dispositions of men, and by the peculiar circumstances in which the new States or confederacies would be placed. As family quarrels are most bitter, so animosities as deep as can torture the human heart would actuate the disjointed remains of the confederacy, urging them into frequent conflicts, the most persevering and embittered. The North would rise up against the South, and the South against the North. The West would send her hordes over the mountains in search of glory and conquest. Instead of being a land of peace, plenty, and happiness, our country would present scenes of war, want, and wretchedness. From the points of millions of bayonets, liberty would fly to other lands, and leave us ages of blood, extortion, and misery, in the place of that Union whose blessings are now treated with derision.

Is it asked how the career of the Nullifiers is to be cut short and their fatal designs defeated? It may be done without the shedding of one drop of blood. Let the whole country rise up as one man and denounce them. Let the whole people out of the limits of South Carolina, and the true hearts within, form themselves at once into a great UNION PARTY, and say to them, in a language which they shall understand, THIS UNION SHALL NOT BE DISSOLVED. Let them resolve, one and all, that while they will make every concession to remove all just causes of complaint, they will rally round the government in support of the Union which *must be preserved at every hazard.* Let them tell the Nullifiers, it is not for you that we step forward in this crisis; it is for ourselves, for our children, for your children, for generations unborn, for the cause of freedom and the happiness of mankind.

A language like this from the other States, and especially from States in the South — from Virginia — from North Carolina — from Georgia — from Alabama — would make these men pause in their mad career, and suspend the hand of violence. Deprived of all hope from without, and resolutely opposed within, they would see only their own immediate ruin in a forward step, and would return to the path of duty and of moderation.

Will the States and the people in the South, the West, the North or the East, withhold the expression of their firm resolves not to permit the dissolution of the Union? Will they omit to do an act of peace, when they may prevent an act, or acts, which their country will mourn for ages to come? Will they not concentrate public opinion upon this horrible design with an intensity which shall make its projectors shrink appalled from their own imaginings before they are bodied forth in acts of violence?

Let no one say the expression of public opinion, through legislative bodies, public meetings, and the press, will not produce the desired result. It is *the hope of aid from abroad* which gives the Nullifiers courage. Deprived of that, they sink into despair and abandon designs which can end only in their own ruin.

No time is to be lost. The edict of Nullification has already appeared, as prepared by the conspirators for the adoption of the convention. With rapid pace, the attempt to execute it will follow. Unless public opinion do its work in a few weeks and awe the factious into submission, the mind cannot conceive the woes which these men may bring upon South Carolina and their own country. Let every legislature, every public meeting, every editor, and every American patriot, hasten to make his voice heard, that the warning may come in time to prevent the first act of violence.

SOUTH CAROLINA MUST YIELD

New York *Evening Post*, December 7, 1832

Letters from Washington assure us that notwithstanding the calm tone of the message in relation to South Carolina, the President, with his usual decision, is taking the *most efficient measures* to secure the due execution of the revenue laws in that State. No language has been employed the effect of which might be only to irritate, and it is not the manner of the President to bandy words with anyone. A course of legislation in relation to the tariff has been recommended which, if adopted, cannot fail to appease all discontentment in the South, and even to satisfy every man in South Carolina whose excitement on this question has not run away with his reason, or who has not suffered the views of a guilty ambition to make him forget his duty to the Federal Republic, and his regard to the welfare of his own State. This recommendation every true patriot must earnestly hope to see adopted — that it will be so, we cannot permit ourselves to doubt — if not by the present Congress, at least by the next. For our own part, we believe that the recommendation will of itself go a great way towards pacifying the excitement which exists in South Carolina, and that it will dispose the majority of her citizens to pause in the rash and violent career upon which they have entered. If it does not in a good degree operate as a sedative upon the inflamed feelings of that State — if many of the leaders of the Nullification party, worthy by their talents and their previous standing in the councils of the nation to take the lead in a better cause, are not influenced by it to use their exertions

in calming the storm they have raised, they will give the strongest
confirmation of what has been laid to their charge, that they are
guilty of a previous and deliberate design to dismember the Union.

In the meantime, however, while South Carolina remains a
member of the Union, she must expect to obey its laws and contribute to support its burdens. The utter confusion into which
the suspension of the revenue laws in one State, and that a State
possessing one of our most important ports, would throw the affairs
of the nation, the multiplied embarrassments in which it would
involve the trade and revenue, make it a matter of imperious duty
on the part of the government to see that those laws are strictly
enforced.

[SOUTH CAROLINA RISKING RUIN]

New York *Evening Post*, December 21, 1832

The Union party of South Carolina are no less ardent and determined in support of the execution of the laws of the Federal
government, than the dominant party in taking measures to resist
them. A letter from Columbia dated December 10, published in
the Charleston *Courier*, says that "if there is any difference between
the Unionists of Charleston and those of the interior, it is that the
latter exceed the former in warmth and violence." The people of
Greenville have raised the flag of the United States in the village,
and declare that it shall remain flying while they have lives to
defend it. Hamilton and Calhoun, it is said, have been hung and
burnt in effigy in Spartansburg District. A similar spirit prevails in
other quarters of the State, and the tyrannical decrees held over
their heads by the majority seem to have inflamed the excitement
which already existed into a feeling of fierce indignation. The
resolutions already before the Union Convention in that State
recognize most solemnly an undivided allegiance to the real government, and propose a military organization of the Union Party to
defend, if necessary, their rights by force.

Should a civil war break out in consequence of resistance to the
revenue laws, we have no doubt that it will first begin among the
citizens of South Carolina. Any feeling of jealousy, animosity, or
indignation with which the people of two portions of the Union may
regard each other is complacency itself to that which subsists between the two parties in South Carolina. An attempt to carry the
Ordinance of the convention into effect with the terrible array of
penalties by which it is accompanied, much as it might be regretted
for the sake of the Union at large, would be unutterably calamitous
for the State itself.

[NULLIFICATION AND THE TARIFF COMPROMISE]
Washington *Globe*, January 17, 1833

It is somewhat remarkable that Mr. Calhoun should feel himself called on to thrust his nullifying ordinance into Congress as a sort of firebrand at a moment when that body, from respect to the changed condition of the whole country, was temperately discussing the best means of accommodating the tariff to the various interests concerned. Did Mr. Calhoun imagine that, by waving the torch of civil war in the eyes of the Senate, and by giving intensity to its flame, he could drive that body into submission? We think not. It is probable rather that he took this course to arrest the progress of calm discussion, and to mar the spirit of conciliation which portended a sudden termination of the excitememt that gives him temporary importance — "a bad eminence!" It certainly required a good deal of hardihood in the former Vice-President to introduce into the Senate the snares which he has been preparing for two years to destroy its dignity — nay, its authority — its existence as the representative of a glorious confederacy of States. Catiline, we believe, although he held his seat in the Senate while without its walls he was conspiring its overthrow and that of the Republic, had not the hardihood to call on the body to sanction his designs and consent to self-immolation. Mr. Calhoun comes forth from the scene in which he has arrayed an armed force against the government, and has the audacity to present himself in the Senate chamber with the sword in one hand, and the nullification ordinance in the other, to demand submission — an acquiescence in the annihilation of the best government in the world; and this from the august assembly to which the States of the Union have most especially confided its preservation! We trust some Cicero will be found in that body, who will mark the assailant of our sacred institutions with more than the fire of the Consul's eloquence, and hand his own name and that of the public enemy down to posterity in the noblest strains of patriotic inspiration.

THE NULLIFICATION COMPROMISE OF 1833[1]
Washington *Globe*, March 22, 1833

The Nullifiers, for the sake of the political objects of their leaders, will conceal from the honest and deluded people the fact which Mr. Clay declared to be his strongest motive for entering into an

[1] Clay's compromise tariff bill, designed to allay the resentment of South Carolina, and providing for a gradual reduction of the tariff duties, extending over nine years, was passed by Congress on March 1, 1833, and signed by Jackson on March 2. The *Globe* here taunts Calhoun with having accepted a very bad bargain in order to save his face.

greement; that he foresaw that at the next session the South would
et all it asked.   Were the Nullifiers to confess that if they had
aited until the coming of the new Congress they would have ob-
.ined the same gradual reduction of the tariff, unclogged by the
ard conditions imposed by Mr. Clay in the cash duties, the home
aluation, and the increase of the duty on coarse woollens from five
▸ fifty per cent, what would the planters say to their Representa-
ves, who were in such haste to make sacrifices at the shrine of
political coalition?   And especially when they find themselves
. shackles to adhere to the terms, however willing a subsequent
ongress may be to make the adjustment more favorable;   and
hen the adjustment concluded is not to take effect in the way of
·duction till after the next Congress shall have been convened,
hereas the increase on the woollens begins, as we understand it,
∶fore any reduction takes place.   Thus Mr. Calhoun has bargained
·r an immediate increase of duties, and remote reductions coupled
ith hard conditions;   and all, as Mr. Clay says, to prevent the
∶xt Congress from granting a relief that would at once have been
tal to his system, for which he has obtained a reprieve of nine
∶ars.

ANDREW JACKSON VISITS NEW YORK

New York *Evening Post*, June 13, 1833

The reception of the President yesterday was one of the most
riking public ceremonies ever witnessed by the people of the city.
∶ did not derive its interest from any splendour of preparation,
.ough in this respect there was no deficiency, and the arrangements
·ere made generally in good taste, and executed with admirable
rder, but from the spirit of cordial good-will and the enthusiasm
f welcome which pervaded the vast population of the metropolis
nd the multitude of strangers assembled to witness his arrival, and
hich manifested itself in a thousand spontaneous demonstrations
f personal kindness and respect.   The inhabitants of the city seemed
▸ have deserted all the other quarters for the Battery and Broadway.
he approach of the steamboats and vessels in company made a
oble and picturesque appearance from the shore, proceeding as
.ey did, slowly and in beautiful order, decorated with coloured
.ags, and the decks covered so thickly with passengers that they
∶emed like vast animated masses, while the water around them
·as covered with smaller craft, which seemed with difficulty to
ıbdue their speed to the deliberate and majestic progress of the
·eamers.   The people stood waiting in the perfect silence on the
.attery and the neighboring wharves until the moment he landed,

when the salutes and the music were followed by deafening a
clamations from the multitude. But the most striking part of th
spectacle was the progress of the President through Broadway. Th
street from the Battery to the City Hall was thronged with spe
tators; the sidewalks were closely crowded; rows of carriages we
drawn up on each side, and the narrow passage in the midst wa
less densely filled with a shifting multitude. Every perch that coul
sustain a spectator was occupied, the lamp posts, the trees, th
awnings, the carriage tops, — every window showed a group of fa
faces, — the house tops were also crowded with spectators whereve
a footing could be obtained — men were seen sitting on the eav
and clinging to the chimneys. To those who looked from an elevate
position on this vast and crowded aggregate of human life, th
spectacle was inexpressibly imposing. The number of persons co
lected between the Park and the Battery has been estimated at
hundred thousand, but if we include those who occupied the wi
dows and the house tops, the number must have been scarcely le
than twice as great. As the President appeared, his white hea
uncovered, sitting easily on his horse and bowing gracefully o
either side, the recollection of his military and civic service, of h
manly virtues and chivalric character, rose in the minds of th
people, and their enthusiasm was not to be restrained. The
crowded about him so as often for a few minutes to impede h
progress, they broke through the circle of armed cavalry that su
rounded him, they rushed between the legs of his escorts' horses
touch his hand or some part of his person. The ladies waved the
handkerchiefs from the windows, and his course was attended wit
perpetual acclamations.

[THE BANK'S PROSTITUTION OF THE AMERICAN PRESS]

Washington *Globe*, July 4, 1833

The Bank of the United States has put out a new set of feeler
The Swiss Corps of Editors, who upon a search were taken with th
money of the people as well as of the private stockholders, picke
most dexterously from Mr. Biddle's breeches' pocket, have lost a
influence with the public. As *mere mercenaries*, it was soon perceive
that the patriotism of the enlisted body of editors was proportione
to the momentum derived from the Bank. Eighty thousand dolla
threw the *National Intelligencer* into ecstacies, and its zeal sparkle
out in thousands and tens of thousands of gratuitous extras. Fifty
two thousand dollars turned the *Courier and Enquirer* topsy-turv
and when fairly upon its legs again, it ran off in a direction directl

opposite to that which it had previously pursued. Those who supported the Bank (it had previously told us) were "bought as cattle in the market;" but the sum of $52,000, tendered to Mr. Webb, convinced him that the price given was quite too much for bullocks. It was found that the Bank was able and liberal enough to enter upon Sir Robert Walpole's traffic and buy *honorable men.* To get into such good company was always Webb's ambition, so he took the Bank's title and its pension; and a hard bargain the Bank has had of him.

Thirty thousand dollars metamorphosed the Pennsylvania *Inquirer,* and twenty thousand brought the *Telegraph* to renounce vows against the Bank more terrible than those of Hannibal against the Romans; and this, too, notwithstanding Mr. Biddle's written agreement that the money was not to be taken as a consideration for the abandonment of his principles. The notorious prostitution of the press to the Bank, although not yet half revealed, has brought its editorial corps into complete disgrace; and it has therefore fallen upon the expedient of setting its stipendiaries to work under disguises. One of its hirelings has disgraced the name of "Patrick Henry," another that of "Cato," and before all's over, we shall have every incorruptible patriot of antiquity and every illustrious name of our own times dishonored in the Bank's service.

THE UNITED STATES BANK

Cincinnati *Republican,* August 6, 1833

There remains not the least doubt that a desperate effort will be made by the Bank, at the ensuing session of Congress, to obtain a re-charter. Great hopes of success are founded upon the adhesion of the Nullifiers to the cause of the institution. In addition to the strength of this accession, it is well understood that her gold will be scattered with a liberal hand, on the theory of Horace Walpole, that *"every man has his price."* How many members she may be able to buy remains yet to be told. How many may yet yield up their principles and their honors to the graspings of avarice, and prostrate themselves before this modern temple of Plutus, cannot be conjectured now. History will inform posterity of the facts. Some of the honorable members may, Judas-like, betray their master, the people's will; but let not the fancied security arising from a secret sale of their conscience be relied upon to screen them from that punishment which will assuredly follow their crime.

The attempt will be made to carry the Bank bill over the head of the President by procuring its reconsideration by two-thirds of each house of Congress. The scheme is not even concealed. But it will not avail the Bank. However successful she may prove herself next winter, at the ensuing elections she will be compelled again to enter the field. The people who in 1832 decided this question by an overwhelming verdict, in the election of Andrew Jackson, are not to be trifled with by hollow-hearted agents. Those members of Congress who shall dare to become the purchased partisans of the Bank will meet with the full measure of that chastisement which the people can so effectually inflict. A new Congress, fresh from the fountain of power, will not hesitate to reverse an act that has been carried by corruption and political treachery.

Let the Bank, and the friends of the Bank, rest assured that if the veto of the people's President will not stay them in their attempts to obtain a renewal of their monopolies, the people, themselves, will pronounce that *veto*. They will pronounce it in a voice that cannot be misunderstood, and in a manner that will settle the question forever. Let the Bank and its mercenary tools look to it.

THE REMOVAL OF THE DEPOSITS [1]

New York *Evening Post*, September 23, 1833

Hung be the heavens with black! Yield day to night!
Comets, importing change of time and states,
Brandish your crystal tresses in the sky,
And with them scourge the bad revolting stars,
That let the public be removed
From Biddle's bank — too famous to live long!

Of this tenor are the jeremiads of the Bank journals. It is heart-rending to hear their doleful lamentations on the occasion of the removal of the deposits. They lift up their voices and weep aloud. From the depths of their affliction come sounds of sublime denunci-ation. They grieve with an exceeding great grief over the fallen glory of their temple, and refuse to be comforted. The tears which stream from their eyes seem to have cleared their mental vision, and they see future events as through a glass darkling. "A field of the dead rushes red on their sight." They foretell the ruin of their country, for "the Cabinet improper have triumphed!" and woe! woe! woe! is now the burden of their prediction. "The die is cast!" exclaims the *National Intelligencer;* "the evil counsellors by whom the President is surrounded have prevailed!" "The star of Olivier le Vain is in the ascendant!" "The evil consequences which we predicted *must* result from it to all the interests, public and private,

[1] The somewhat excessively literary tone of this editorial betrays Bryant's hand before he had learned restraint: but its description of the wailings of the Whig newspapers is hardly overdrawn.

of the country!" "If this be not tyranny — if this be not usurpation, what under heaven can constitute tyranny and usurpation?" "The law openly trampled on!" "its pernicious effects!" — "bankruptcy and ruin must result from it!" "Will the people stand by and calmly see their authority thus spurned? — We asked if the people will quietly witness the restraints of the law broken down, and trodden under feet by their own servants. Will the Secretary of the Treasury suffer the sanctity of the law to be violated in his person?"

The *National Gazette* is not less sublimely dolorous, nor less fearfully prophetic. But however great its patriotic grief for the evil that has befallen the country, the event does not excite its surprise. "It was to be expected," says that pure and single-minded journal, "that the scheme of profligate and rancorous hostility against the Bank would be implacably pursued;" and it added that "the case is fitted to awaken lively alarm and the gravest reflection." "To what does this lead? — to the result that the President of the United States will have usurped the command of the whole twenty-five millions of revenue! and the power of distributing that revenue to whomsoever he pleases, whether to Banks *or to individuals at Washington or elsewhere, as managers of a political game!*" "This affair is equal in fearful import to anything that has occurred in our country;" it is "outrageous law!" and is a "scheme of usurpation."

The rest of the purchased presses of the Bank are not less lachrymose and lugubrious, and all of them partake of a spirit of prescience. They all exclaim, almost in the words of Lord Byron,

> *The day of our destiny's over,*
> *The star of our fate has declined!*

— "the times are out of joint," they say — a disaster has befallen the country from which it can never recover — we are ruined, lost, utterly undone! — and like the misshapen dwarf in the "Lay of the Last Minstrel," they wave their lean arms on high and run to and fro, crying "lost! lost! lost!" Who can doubt the sincerity of their lamentations at the death-blow which has been given to the United States Bank, when it is remembered how munificent a patron that institution has been to them? Who can wonder that they appear at the head of the funeral train as chief mourners, and raise so loud their solemn wail, when he reflects how well their grief is paid for? No hired mourner at a New England funeral ever earned his wages by so energetic a wail, or so lachrymose an aspect. They seem as woe-begone as pilgrims from the Cave of Trophinious, when

> — *the sad sage, returning, smiled no more.*

But their wailing is in vain — "vainly they heap the ashes on their heads" — the fate of the Bank is sealed; and we, who are not paid to wet our cheeks with artificial tears, who have no cause to be a mourner, must be permitted to congratulate the country that a monopoly which, in the corrupt exercise of its dangerous power threatened to sap the foundation of American independence, has by this firm and timely act of the general government been reduced to a state of feebleness which, we trust, is only the precursor of its final dissolution.

THE PENNSYLVANIA PRISON SYSTEM[1]

American Quarterly Review, September, 1833

The idea of expiation does not belong to it. It is humane in all its operations, and the deprivation of liberty and of intercourse with others, is only to afford proper facilities for reflection and moral culture. It has no relation to society at large, further than the knowledge of the belief in the necessity of seclusion, to remove criminal propensities, may deter those whom the fear of the penalty, and not upright principles, keep in the path of honesty. What is the amount of atonement rendered to society by the confinement of the offender under discipline more or less rigorous? What gratification can the community derive from any amount of bodily pain which can be inflicted upon an individual? The prisoner in his cell is lost sight of by the world, and the whole operation of the system relates to himself. The causes which led to the crime are removed from him. The morbid influences of evil habits, associations, and passions are withdrawn — he is thrown back upon himself — he sees only those who are reputable, and learns to compare his present condition with theirs. When he leaves the prison, the finger of scorn is not pointed to him to throw him again into the paths of vice, and there is nothing to prevent the success of his exertions in the way of uprightness. . . .

After using language decidedly approbatory of the discipline in Pennsylvania, and stating it as that which offers the least embarrassment, the French commissioners are brought to speak of the discipline of the Auburn system. The infliction of stripes is the compulsory process of the plan last named. Stripes were once the punishment for offences committed in Pennsylvania. The whipping

[1] The Pennsylvania prison system was built upon solitary confinement with labor, and marked an epochal advance in American penal methods. The Auburn system in New York was based upon labor in common, but in silence, with corporal punishment for breaches of discipline. This semi-editorial article in a Pennsylvania review was called forth by De Tocqueville's report to the French Government, and defends the Pennsylvania system as the better.

post was once the great scandal of our humane community. Our old citizens advert to that period as that in which society had not emerged from barbarism. Humanity was outraged, and the system exploded as unworthy the age. It was almost the last remnant of the retributive system, but it was a material part of it. Our public men held the opinion that it degraded the moral sense, and that it was calculated to plunge men still deeper, who were already low enough in the moral estimate. They held that it produced vindictive feelings in the sufferer, and added malice and malignity to crime. The unhappy sufferer saw no means of regaining his station, after having undergone this degradation. He truly felt that the honest community was no community for him.

THREE OPPOSITION LEADERS: CLAY, CALHOUN, AND WEBSTER[1]

New York *Evening Post*, March 31, 1834

When an intelligent and rational people is called upon in a contest between two great political parties, it is proper for them to know who are their opponents and what they are fighting for; whether for something or nothing; principles or men. Although the question of restoring the deposits and perpetuating the monopoly of the Bank of the United States is inseparably associated with the result of the coming election, it is by no means the only point involved in the contest. The party we have to contend with is manifold; it is headed by the most discordant leaders, wielding the opposite weapons; each marching under his own banner, and each laboring in his own cause. Let us then pass in review their avowed principles and purposes, that the people may judge whether such discordant materials could possibly be kept together except by the strong cement of a common interest.

In the first place stands Henry Clay. He is the parent and champion of the tariff and internal improvements; of a system directly opposed to the interests and prosperity of every merchant in the United States, and devised for the purpose of organizing an extensive scheme through which the different portions of the United

[1] Bryant's hand is here plainly visible; these three characterizations represent the prevailing Democratic attitude, and that of Webster alone is excessively unfair and misleading. The essential disharmony of Calhoun and Clay was palpable. For a time after the settlement of the Nullification troubles Calhoun, acting with the Whigs though still independent, was as warmly opposed to Jackson as were Webster and Clay. But he shortly left the Whigs. When Van Buren proposed the sub-treasury scheme after the panic of 1837, Calhoun supported the President. Clay was much chagrined by his defection.

States might be bought up in detail. By assuming the power of dissipating the public revenue in local improvements, by which one portion of the community would be benefited at the expense of many others, Congress acquired the means of influencing and controlling the politics of every State in the Union, and of establishing a rigid, invincible consolidated government. By assuming the power of protecting any class or portion of the industry of this country, by bounties in the shape of high duties on foreign importations, they placed the labor and industry of the people entirely at their own disposal, and usurped the prerogative of dispensing all the blessings of Providence at pleasure. They could at any time decide what class of industry should be enriched, and what class impoverished; whether commerce should flourish or decay; whether the manufacturer of cotton, wool, or iron should become a king, while the common laborer sank into a pauper. Out of this system grew those great manufacturing establishments which have monopolized almost all the pursuits of simple mechanics, and converted them from independent men presiding over their own homes, masters of their own shops, and proprietors of their own earnings, into the pale, sickly, and half-starved slaves of companies and corporations.

It is against this great system of making the rich richer, the poor poorer, and thus creating those enormous disproportions of wealth which are always the forerunner of the loss of freedom; it is against this great plan of making the resources of the general government the means of obtaining the control of the States by an adroit specie of political bribery, that General Jackson has arrayed himself. He has arrested the one by his influence, the other by his veto.

In the second place stands John C. Calhoun. Reflecting and honest men may perhaps wonder to see this strange alliance between the man by whom the tariff was begotten, nurtured, and brought to a monstrous maturity, and him who carried his State to the verge of rebellion in opposition to that very system. By his means and influence, this great Union was all but dissolved, and in all probability would at this moment lie shattered into fragments had it not been for the energetic and prompt patriotism of the stern old man who then said, "The Union: it must be preserved!" Even at this moment Mr. Calhoun still threatens to separate South Carolina from the confederacy if she is not suffered to remain in it with the privilege of a *veto* on the laws of the Union. It is against these dangerous doctrines, which have been repudiated by every other State in the Union, which find no kindred or responsive feeling in the hearts of the people, that General Jackson stands arrayed, in behalf of the integrity of this great confederation. He appears as a champion of Union, and appeals to the people to support him in the struggle for their happiness.

The third of the triumvirate of this strange confederacy of contradictions is Daniel Webster. Without firmness, consistency, or political courage to be a leader, except in one small section of the Union, he seems to crow to any good purpose only on his own dunghill, and is a much greater fowl in his own barnyard than anywhere else. He is a good speaker at the bar and in the House; but he is a much greater lawyer than statesman, and far more expert in detailing old arguments than fruitful in inventing new ones. He is not what we should call a great man, much less a great politician; and we should go so far as to question the power of his intellect, did it not occasionally disclose itself in a rich exuberance of contradictory opinions. A man who can argue so well on both sides of a question cannot be totally destitute of genius.

And here these three gentlemen, who agree in no one single principle, who own no one single feeling in common, except that of hatred to the old hero of New Orleans, stand battling side by side. The author and champion of the tariff, and the man who on every occasion denounced it as a violation of the Constitution; the oracle of nullification and the oracle of consolidation; the trio of antipathies; the union of contradictions; the consistency of inconsistencies; the coalition of oil, vinegar, and mustard; the dressing in which the great political salad is to be served up to the people.

We must not deny, however, that these gentlemen have a sort of paternal, or maternal, influence watching over them and coöperating in the great cause of domestic industry and internal improvements; nullification and consolidation; State rights and Federal usurpations, thus inharmoniously jumbled together higgledy-piggledy. It is the Mother Bank, the Alma Mater, under whose petticoats they are fighting the great battle, every one for himself and Mother Bank for all. Nicholas Biddle, the paramour of the old lady, who has the sole management of her business, is connected with the partnership as a sort of Commissary-General of purchases. He holds the purse-strings, which are equivalent to both bridle and spur, arms and ammunition, in modern political warfare. To all these mighty powers and potentates the honest Democracy of this country have nothing to oppose but their ancient, invariable principles; their inflexible integrity of purpose; and their invincible old leader, Andrew Jackson. Is not this enough? We think it is, and await the issue without a single throb of apprehension.

PART TWO

THE AMERICAN PRESS AND PUBLIC OPINION
1835–1865

THE AMERICAN PRESS AND PUBLIC OPINION
1835–1865

A series of steps, each with a special significance, marked during the thirties — the decade of Jacksonian democracy — the advent of a new journalism. The first of these was the adaptation to American conditions of the English "penny paper," which was introduced to Boston and New York as a one-cent newspaper for the masses, filled with police court news, anecdotes, scraps of gossip, and other lively materials. The second was the establishment, under the leadership of the New York *Herald*, of the cheap newspaper appealing to a wide public not by sensational gossip, but rather through unprecedented enterprise in the publication of all news, political, mercantile, criminal, financial, and even religious, and through a new impudence and independence in editorial opinion. The third, partly a result of and partly a reaction against the two previous phenomena, was the emergence of newspapers which were as cheap as the *Sun* and the *Herald*, and as enterprising in securing news, but which were highly respectable in moral tone and serious in their attitude toward all current problems. The chief exemplar of this enterprising but moral journalism was Horace Greeley, who had begun editing the weekly *New Yorker* in 1834, had written editorials for the *Daily Whig*, and who in the spring of 1841 began the publication of the New York *Tribune*.

The first of the "penny papers," with Benjamin H. Day's New York *Sun* (launched on September 3, 1833) at their head, paid little attention to editorial utterance and influenced opinion only through their treatment of the news. They excluded from their columns all but a brief outline of the political happenings in Congress and the legislatures, and nearly all political discussions and events outside. What few editorials they did print commented briefly upon the latest sensation, upon municipal affairs, and upon questions of morals and manners. Thus the *Sun* loved to deal with drunkenness, duelling, gambling, reckless driving, and the relations between the sexes; it combined a frank portrayal of the vices and dissipations of the day in its news columns with a vigorous reprehension of them in its editorials — a combination always effective, and probably certain to live as long as journalism itself.

Nor was the *Herald*, either in its first struggling years before 1840, or in the later period when its wealth and energy gave it a measure of grudging respect, a newspaper of real editorial force. It attracted attention by its swagger, its cynicism, its recklessness, and its flippancy. It boasted of its independence upon all questions, political or otherwise, James Gordon Bennett declaring that he would avoid party commitments as if they were "steel traps." The founder loved himself to write brief editorials of an impudent nature, and astonished and scandalized the town by his pithy and Machiavellian paragraphs. Himself a Catholic, in writing of the Holy Roman Catholic Church he could add, "All we Catholics are devilish holy." Describing the commencement of an enterprise which ruined thousands, he remarked: "Ground was broken for the Erie Railroad yesterday; we hope it breaks nothing else." Again, his editorial columns contained the observation: "Great excitement among the Presbyterians just now. The question in dispute is, whether or not a man can do anything towards saving his own soul." He paraded his personality in the editorial columns after a manner which sometimes verged upon indecency, and which perhaps only the psychopath could fully explain. Thus he boasted of his intense industry; described his confidence in the paper's future — "Nothing can prevent its success but God Almighty, and he happens to be entirely on my side"; spoke of his contempt for speculators, pickpockets, and the sixpenny editors, "whose crimes and immoralities I have exposed, and shall continue to expose as long as the God of Heaven gives me a soul to think, and a hand to execute"; expatiated upon his joy in the prospect of marriage to "one of the most splendid women in intellect, in heart, in soul"; and dwelt upon his domestic felicity after the birth of his son.

Bennett knew that these materials helped to sell his newspaper; he knew that many readers were amused by the reckless levity of such editorials as that which James Parton quotes from an issue of 1836, in which he advocated the election of Jackson, Harrison, Martin Van Buren, Hugh White, or Anybody, as "the Emperor of this great Republic for life." At a later date Bennett, feeling himself firmly established, became somewhat more sober. He was also able to employ capable editorial writers, and one of his assistants, Isaac Pray, has left us a graphic account of how he used them:

The papers marked for Mr. Bennett are . . . taken to his own private room, where he is seated ready to receive them, as soon as he has finished reading the private correspondence and letters for publication which have been brought in from the post office. . .

In this way an hour is passed. The next hour will be devoted to the newspapers, and, perhaps, to a breakfast or luncheon or dry toast and tea, as an accompaniment. The editorials of the newspapers particularly are scrutinized, and every now and then dot, dot goes down a mysterious word as a peg to hang a thought or an article upon. If any political profligate or statesman has made a speech, or written a letter, the points in it are all seized with rapidity, and designated by a sign upon the memorandum. This work being done, and the tea and toast having been exhausted, the tray is removed by the boy who has been summoned for the purpose, and one of the gentlemen who phonographizes is requested to make his appearance. He arrives and takes his seat by Mr. Bennett's side, who passes the compliments of the day and asks if anything new has taken place worthy of notice. He then begins to talk; first giving the caption of the leading article. He speaks with some rapidity, making his points with effect, and sometimes smiling as he raps one of his dear political friends over the knuckles. Having concluded his article with, "that will do," he gives the head of another article and dictates it in a similar way, and then, perhaps, another and another, till the reporter sighs at the amount of the work he has before him, and he is told that that will be enough for "today."

The presence of another gentleman is now required. He may not be a phonographer, but one who is able to seize the points of a discourse, and fashion them with some force and elegance of expression, or even to illustrate them. Mr. Bennett invites him to a conversation on a particular topic upon which both have been thinking, and then gives his own view, which he desires to see written out. All the while his assistant editor takes notes, so as not to miss the points or spirit of the desired article, and thus having prepared himself with matter enough to fill two columns, he is permitted to withdraw.

Yet while the *Herald* prospered, printing early in 1840 some 17,000 copies of the daily and 19,000 of the weekly edition, and reaching during the Civil War a circulation of 100,000, its influence upon opinion remained slight. James Parton at the close of the Civil War declared that it was the chief newspaper of the metropolis. But, he added, it has singularly little power to sway the public view, as was demonstrated when its support of Lincoln against McClellan in the election of 1864 proved perfectly futile in New York city. "Influence over opinion no paper can have which has itself no opinion, and cares for none. It is not as a vehicle of opinion

that the *Herald* has importance, but solely as a vehicle of news."
This statement might well have been qualified, for at various junc-
tures and with various social groups the *Herald* really did exercise
some power. Having been consistently Democratic for years, its
support of John C. Frémont in 1856 was highly valuable to that
candidate. Soon afterward it became a vociferous mouthpiece for
the Southern slaveholders, and was read with much comfort and
satisfaction both by people of the Cotton Kingdom, and by the
commercial elements in New York which depended upon Southern
trade. During the Civil War the *Herald* made itself almost indispensable to close students of the conflict by its admirable field correspondence, upon which Bennett spent nearly half a million dollars.
As a result the *Herald* had genuine respect in England, where Goldwin Smith noted that it was regarded as *the* American newspaper;
while Lincoln was glad to placate it by offering Bennett the post of
Minister to France.

But it was the "respectable" new journalism of this period, and
not the disreputable *Herald*, which led in the formation of public
opinion. Above all, it was the New York *Tribune* and *Times* (join-
ing the older *Evening Post*), the Springfield *Republican*, and in the
fifties, the Chicago *Tribune* as well. To Horace Greeley's great
newspaper we may unhesitatingly ascribe the development of the
editorial page in its modern American character: that is, a page
treating a wide variety of topics in a variety of manners, though
pursuing a consistent policy; achieving a level of genuine literary
merit; produced by a body of editors, not by a single man, and
representing their united judgment and information; and earnestly
directed to the elevation and rectification of public opinion. The
editorial page of Bryant's *Post* answered, in the thirties, to some of
these requirements. It had a high purpose, and flashes of fine
literary quality. But Bryant's heart was not fully in it until he returned, in 1836, from a European tour which he had hoped might
last indefinitely, and he had but one editorial assistant; first that
fiery reformer William Leggett, and later Parke Godwin. Their
energies were largely consumed by tasks connected with the news
and the counting-room, and until after Greeley led the way the
Evening Post seldom contained more than one or two editorial articles
daily — these being almost exclusively political.

The New York *Tribune* for a whole generation, the fateful generation in which the struggle against slavery rose to a climax, stood
preëminent among the organs of opinion in the United States; it

was one of the great leaders of the nation, and its rôle in the particular drama which ended with the Emancipation Proclamation was as great as any statesman's save Lincoln. No free soil leader — not Chase, not Sumner, not Seward, and probably not all three combined — did as much to rally the North in unyielding opposition to the spread of slavery. Like all great newspapers, it became far greater than its editor. Indeed, the tragedy of Greeley's career is essentially that before 1861 he had created a magnificent instrument of democratic leadership which he proved quite unable to use wisely and safely in the four years of agony and effort which followed; and yet much of its greatness was drawn from Greeley. In his autobiography the editor writes that his leading idea in 1841 was "the establishment of a journal removed alike from servile partisanship on the one hand and from gagged, mincing neutrality on the other" — a journal which might heartily advocate the general principles of its own party, and yet "frankly dissent from its course on a particular question, and even denounce its candidates if they were shown to be deficient in capacity or (far worse) in integrity." But no mere idea would have carried the paper far without the qualities which he brought to it. These included a passionate moral earnestness; an ability to divine with marvelous clarity the deeper convictions of his readers; an unshakable faith in principles; and, as E. L. Godkin said, "an English style which, for vigor, terseness, clearness, and simplicity, has never been surpassed except perhaps by Cobbett."

Greeley quickly collected about him the ablest staff yet known in the history of American journalism. Early in 1847, when the combined daily and weekly circulation was 26,000, Charles A. Dana became city editor and shortly afterward managing editor, in which capacities he contributed to the editorial page. So did George Ripley, who in 1849 became literary editor, a post previously held by the gifted Margaret Fuller; so did Bayard Taylor, who in 1844 had begun to contribute travel sketches, and in 1848 became a regular member of the staff; and so did Solon Robinson, the agricultural editor and author of those remarkable "human interest" sketches of New York life which were collected into book form under the title of "Hot Corn." James S. Pike, the Washington correspondent, was frequently also invaluable. By 1854 there were, besides the editor and managing editor, ten so-called associate-editors, and fourteen reporters, while the regularly paid correspondents numbered no fewer than thirty-eight. In the years following the agitation of the Wilmot Proviso the *Tribune* came into the plenitude of its power. Its weekly edition penetrated to the remotest hamlets of the West, and in a day when popular magazines were few and costly, it was read from beginning to end and passed from household to household; with the result that Greeley and his staff spoke to all the free-soil States and Territories, as James Ford Rhodes states, "with a power never before or since known in this country." By 1853 the circulation of the weekly *Tribune* had risen to 51,000; by 1854 it was 112,000. Bayard Taylor, on a lecture trip in the fifties, could write that "The *Tribune* comes next to the Bible all through the West."

From the beginning, Greeley's conduct of the editorial page was characterized by the general absence of that autocracy which usually marks the strong editor. Having chosen associates in whose judgment he had confidence, he permitted them the utmost freedom in expressing their opinions. An examination of James S. Pike's "First Blows of the Civil War," a book which reprints many of the Washington articles, office letters, and editorials of the fifties, shows Greeley repeatedly expostulating with his sub-editors, especially Dana, for the way in which they ignored his views. He permitted one editorial writer, against his better judgment, to reiterate in 1861 the cry "On to Richmond!" At various times before or during the Civil War he explained to his readers that this or that article had been inserted despite his disapproval. Yet upon occasion he did exercise his dominant authority in a ruthless way. A wartime division of views between him and Dana led him, with some characteristic wabbling, to cut that lieutenant summarily from his staff.

We are fortunate in having from the pen of James Parton, himself a born journalist, a description of the methods of work pursued by the *Tribune's* editorial staff in the early fifties. The chief sub-editors — Bayard Taylor, Dana, Solon Robinson, Ripley — he says, arrived at eleven o'clock in the morning. For a time all was leisure. Taylor, "pale, delicate-featured, with a curling beard and subdued moustache," could be seen reading a newspaper; W. H. Fry, another editorial writer, slowly paced the carpet; Ripley took off his coat, and with deliberate care began examining the day's grist of twenty-four new books and nine magazines; and Dana, entering with quick, decided step, went to his desk in the central sanctum, and was soon reading Karl Marx. Between twelve and one Greeley came in, his pockets distended with papers, and after some chat in the outer rooms, seated himself at his desk to look over the letters, clippings, and newspapers which covered it, and to listen to a miscellaneous pack of visitors. Towards four o'clock, this preliminary business disposed of, he went out for dinner. When he came back the work of the day was taken up in earnest, and by nine o'clock in the evening it was in full swing:

> The editorial rooms . . . have become intense. Seven desks are occupied with silent writers, most of them in the *Tribune* uniform — shirt sleeves and moustache. The night-reader is looking over the papers last arrived, with scissors ready for any paragraph of news that catches his eye. An editor occasionally goes to the copy-box, places in it a page or two of the article he is writing, and rings the bell; the box slides up to the composing room, and the pages are in type and corrected before the article is finished. Such articles are those which are prompted by the event of the hour; others are more deliberately written; some are weeks in preparation; and of some the keel is laid months before they are launched upon the public mind. The Editor-in-Chief is at his desk writing in a singular attitude, the desk on a level with his nose, and the writer sitting bolt upright. He writes rapidly, with scarcely a pause for thought, and not once in a page makes an erasure. The foolscap leaves fly from under his pen at the rate of one in fifteen minutes. He does most of the *thinking* before he begins to write, and produces matter about as fast as a swift copyist can copy. Yet he leaves nothing for the compositor to guess at, and if he makes an alteration in the proof, he is careful to do it in such a way that the printer loses no time in "overrunning;" that is, he inserts as many words as he erases. Not infrequently he bounds up into the composing room, and makes a correction or adds a sentence with his own hand. He is not patient under the infliction of an error; and he expects men to understand his wishes by intuition; and when they do *not*, but interpret his half-expressed orders in a way exactly contrary to his intention, a scene is likely to ensue. . . .
>
> Midnight. The strain is off. Mr. Greeley finished his work about eleven, chatted a while with Mr. Dana, and went home. Mr. Dana has received from the foreman the list of the articles in type, the articles now in hand, and the articles expected; he has designated those which *must* go in; those which it is highly desirable *should* go in, and those which will keep. He has also marked the order in which the articles are to appear; and, having performed this last duty, he returns the list to the compositor, puts on his coat, and departs.

Three years after Greeley founded the *Tribune*, an eighteen-year-old lad in Springfield, Massachusetts, working on his father's weekly newspaper, became responsible for the founding and management of the daily *Republican* of that city. Within a decade Samuel Bowles had made it the best provincial journal in the country. It was enterprising, keen, independent, and soundly conservative. Like Bryant and Greeley, Bowles laid emphasis upon the moral, agricultural, and literary departments of his newspaper, and in the weekly edition particularly produced a sheet which was valued not merely in western Massachusetts, but by New Englanders scattered all over the Middle West. The young editor's chief assistant, Dr. J. G. Holland, who had been a preacher and a teacher, struck a rich vein when he began to contribute to the columns what he called lay-sermons, writing three series of "Timothy Titcomb's Letters to Young People." But more important than the wealth of New England news, the vigorous literary and religious departments, and the didactic and historical articles from Holland's pen, was the editorial page. Bowles made a specialty of brief, crisp, telling editorial paragraphs, printed alongside extended and careful articles which avoided all pedantry, but which emphasized principles dear to the anti-slavery party of the North. In 1848 he, like Bryant of the *Evening Post*, supported the Free Soil Party, and declaring immediately after the passage of the Kansas-Nebraska Act that the Whig Party was dead, he made the *Republican* one of the pillars of the new Republican party. His editorials never quite achieved the superb heights of ringing eloquence .reached by Bryant and John Bigelow in the *Evening Post* of the late fifties, nor did they have quite the Saxon strength of Greeley's best work; but clear, nervous, shrewd in their reasoning, and of unfailing elevation, they commanded respect throughout the North, and exercised a far wider influence than the circulation of the *Republican* (in 1860 some 5,700 for the daily edition, and 11,280 for the weekly) might have seemed to imply.

Henry Jarvis Raymond, who founded the New York *Times* on September 18, 1851, had begun his career in 1841 as assistant to Greeley at $8 a week. Late in life Greeley wrote of him that he had never known a person who "evinced so signal and such versatile ability in journalism," or who was "cleverer, readier, or more generally efficient." Raymond quickly saw that the expanding population of New York, and the fact that people had to choose between the highly moralistic Greeley and the highly cynical Bennett, furnished an opportunity for a fresh type of newspaper. His design, he announced, was to present all the news of the day from all parts of the world in the fairest manner, and to discuss public questions without "passion," in a just and good-tempered way. Unquestionably he had in mind not merely a middle line between the mental eccentricity of the *Tribune* and the moral eccentricity of the *Herald*, as Dana later put it, but an imitation of the London *Times* of Delane, trustworthy, authoritative, and complete. Founded with a capital of $100,000, a figure which contrasts strikingly with the $1,000 which Greeley had deemed to be all that he needed just a decade earlier, Raymond's *Times* quickly became a success. Its editor was a man of the world, who possessed strong political ambitions of his own, and who commanded valuable personal sources of information. He was well acquainted with Europe, and he shortly went far beyond his competitors in finding and publishing foreign news. His newspaper contained few innovations, but in its nice balance, its harmony of parts, its pervasive accuracy, and its abstention from coarseness and abuse, it was a model of journalism.

Editorially, Raymond exercised less power than his great contemporaries just named. The very fact of his temperance, of his constitutional inability not to see both sides of most questions, of his quietness and courtesy, made his editorial page seem to some readers laodicean and half-hearted. His writing was cautious, rational, and impersonal. He eschewed fervor as well as violence. But moderate men of his own bent of mind liked his freedom from bias, and respected his opinions as those of an editor devoted solely and broadmindedly to the truth.

Throughout the fifteen years before the Civil War newspapers in foreign tongues, with the German press most prominent, increased rapidly throughout the North and West. Journals championing special causes, the chief being William Lloyd Garrison's abolitionist *Liberator*, which was founded in 1831, gained a national hearing. Beyond the Alleghenies rose a series of powerful newspapers, such as the Chicago *Tribune*, which first appeared in 1847, and which became widely known after Joseph Medill purchased an interest in 1855, and the Louisville *Journal* (1830), which George D. Prentice made distinctive by his epigrammatic paragraphs, ironical or satirical — "stinging, hissing bolts of scorn," Bryant called them. News was being steadily broadened; the war correspondent had come in with the Mexican conflict; and we have only to turn to some of the travel letters of the time — Bayard Taylor's sketches of California in gold rush days for the *Tribune*, F. L. Olmsted's pictures of Southern slavery in the *Times*, and Bryant's letters from Europe in the *Evening Post* are salient examples — to see how excellent the general correspondence had become. If the telegraph after 1844 did much to kill such publications as *Niles's Weekly*, it contributed immensely to the improvement of journalism in general. It was against the background of these changes, and with the advantages which they afforded, that the editorial giants of the time spoke to the country.

[JAMES GORDON BENNETT'S SELF–EXPLOITATION][1]

New York *Herald*

May 10, 1836.

As I was leisurely pursuing my business yesterday, in Wall Street, collecting the information which is daily disseminated in the *Herald*, James Watson Webb came up to me, on the northern side of the street — said something which I could not hear distinctly, then pushed me down the stone steps, leading to one of the broker's offices, and commenced fighting with a species of brutal and demoniac desperation characteristic of a fury.

My damage is a scratch, about three quarters of an inch in length, on the third finger of my left hand, which I received from the iron railing I was forced against, and three buttons torn from my vest, which any tailor will reinstate for a sixpence. His loss is a rent from top to bottom of a very beautiful black coat, which cost the ruffian $40, and a blow in the face, which may have knocked down his throat some of his infernal teeth for anything I know. Balance in my favor, $39.94.

As to intimidating me or changing my course, the thing cannot be done. Neither Webb nor any other man shall, or can, intimidate me. I tell the honest truth in my paper, and leave the consequences to God. Could I leave them in better hands? I may be attacked, I may be assailed, I may be killed, I may be murdered, but I never will succumb. I never will abandon the cause of truth, morals, and virtue.

August 16, 1836.

We published yesterday the principal items of the foreign news, received by the *Sheffield*, being eight days later than our previous arrivals. Neither the *Sun* nor the *Transcript* had a single item on the subject. The *Sun* did not even know of its existence. The large papers in Wall Street had also the news, but as the editors are lazy, ignorant, indolent, blustering blockheads, one and all, they did not

---

[1] These are the three best-known of a long list of editorials in which Bennett advertised himself and his paper and catered to the public appetite for personal gossip. James Watson Webb, an explosive graduate of West Point, edited the six-penny *Courier and Enquirer*.

pick out the cream and serve it out as we did. The *Herald* alone knows how to dish up the foreign news, or indeed domestic events, in a readable style. Every reader, numbering *between thirty and forty thousand daily*, acknowledges this merit in the management of our paper. We do not, as the Wall Street lazy editors do, come down to our office about ten or twelve o'clock, pull out a Spanish cigar, take up a pair of scissors, puff and cut, cut and puff for a couple of hours, and then adjourn to Delmonico's to eat, drink, gormandize, and blow up our contemporaries. We rise in the morning at five o'clock, write our leading editorials, squibs, sketches, etc., before breakfast. From nine till one we read all our papers and original communications, the latter being more numerous than those of any other office in New York. From these we pick out facts, thoughts, hints, and incidents sufficient to make up a column of original spicy articles. We also give audiences to visitors, gentlemen on business, and some of the loveliest ladies in New York, who call to subscribe — Heaven bless them! At one we sally out among the gentlemen and *loafers* of Wall Street — find out the state of the money market, return, finish the next day's paper — close every piece of business requiring thought, sentiment, feeling, or philosophy, before four o'clock. We then dine moderately and temperately — read our proofs — take in cash and advertisements, which are increasing like smoke — and close the day always by going to bed at ten o'clock, seldom later. That's the way to conduct a paper with spirit and success.

June 1, 1840.

To The Readers of the Herald — Declaration of Love — Caught At Last — Going To Be Married — New Movement in Civilization. — I am going to be married in a few days. The weather is so beautiful; times are getting so good; the prospects of political and moral reform so auspicious, that I cannot resist the divine instinct of honest nature any longer; so I am going to be married to one of the most splendid women in intellect, in heart, in soul, in property, in person, in manner, that I have yet seen in the course of my interesting pilgrimage through human life.

. . . I cannot stop in my career. I must fulfill that awful destiny which the Almighty Father has written against my name, in the broad letters of life, against the wall of heaven. I must give the world a pattern of happy wedded life, with all the charities that spring from a nuptial love. In a few days I shall be married according to the holy rites of the most holy Christian church, to one of the most remarkable, accomplished, and beautiful young women of the age. She possesses a fortune. I sought and found a fortune — a large fortune.   She has no Stonington shares or Manhattan stock, but in purity and uprightness she is worth half a million of pure gold.   Can any swindling bank show as much?   In good sense and elegance another half a million; in soul, mind, and beauty, millions on millions, equal to the whole specie of all the rotten banks in the world.   Happily the patronage of the public to the *Herald* is nearly twenty-five thousand dollars per annum, almost equal to a President's salary.   But property in the world's goods was never my object.   Fame, public good, usefulness in my day and generation; the religious associations of female excellence;   the progress of true industry — these have been my dreams by night and my desires by day.

In the new and holy condition into which I am about to enter, and to enter with the same reverential feelings as I would enter heaven itself, I anticipate some signal changes in my feelings, in my views, in my purposes, in my pursuits.   What they may be I know not — time alone can tell.   My ardent desire has been through life, to reach the highest order of human intelligence, by the shortest possible cut.   Association, night and day, in sickness and in health, in war and in peace, with a woman of the highest order of excellence, must produce some curious results in my heart and feelings, and these results the future will develop in due time in the columns of the *Herald*.

THE SURPLUS AND THE TARIFF[1]

Washington *Globe*, March 2, 1836

The disposable fund of the nation, the surplus revenue, has now become a bone of contention in Congress.   Messrs. Clay and Calhoun, with their penchant for aristocratical abuses — the scheme of Hamilton to save the government from the dangers of democracy by corrupt influence — have seized with avidity upon the surplus as a fund to apply to such sinister purposes.   By the settlement for which they obtained the guarantee of Congress up to 1842, these politicians have provided against a reduction of the tariff to the ordinary wants of the government, and the fund to be accumulated under this arrangement they are anxious to scatter among the States from the hand of Congress.   The habit fostered by this system before 1842 will go to make Congress always collector, through its indirect taxation, of immense sums from the people generally, to be squandered by the leading men of the different States to promote their various objects of political ambition or pecuniary interest.   The

---

[1] Characteristic of the *Globe's* attacks upon the "American system" of Henry Clay, which called for a combination of high tariff and internal improvements.

MR. CLAY TAKING A NEW VIEW OF THE TEXAS QUESTION.

Now for one I certainly am not willing to involve this country in a foreign war for the object of acquiring Texas. Honor and good faith, and justice, are equally due from this country toward the weak as toward the strong.—*Mr. Clay's Raleigh Letter.*

FA, FE, FI, FO FUM: I SMELL THE BLOOD OF A MEXICUN! DEAD OR ALIVE I WILL HAVE SOME!

I feel as if I yet must go and slay a Mexican! *Mr. Clay's Speech at New Orleans.*

From *Yankee Doodle*, February 6, 1847.

power which has the responsibility of bringing in the immense tax will not have the responsibility of disposing of it; and the divided responsibility will in the end prove to be no responsibility. The State legislatures, like heirs inheriting property without encountering the difficulties of acquisition, will waste it prodigally. The Congress, plied on all sides by the members from the States to provide for the unchecked expenditure, will draw lavishly through its indirect channel of supply, the custom-house, upon the productive classes of the country, who make up the mass of consumers, to afford means to answer this new demand. The result will be an ever-enduring and increasing tariff, to feed the vices of aristocracy in all the shapes which it may assume among us.

TEXAS TRIUMPHANT[1]

Washington *Globe*, May 23, 1836

The gratifying confirmation of the defeat and capture of Santa Anna by General Houston has reached us under New Orleans dates of the 9th. Now the tone of the New York *American*, of the *National Gazette*, of the *National Intelligencer*, of the Richmond *Whig*, of the Louisiana *Advertiser*, the leading organs of the Webster, Harrison, and White combination, will be changed. They will now probably admit that to march out four hundred men to execution, after a solemn capitulation, was not altogether reconcilable to the laws of civilized nations, or even to the humanity of barbarians. They will cease to excuse the deliberate slaughter to which four columns, of one hundred victims each, were led, half famished but tantalized with hope, to unresisting destruction. Some were told that they were about to embark for their friends; others, that they were marched out to bring up beeves; others, that they were going to receive rations already prepared. This formal and coolly contrived butchery the Richmond *Whig* imputes (for Santa Anna's sake) to the uncontrollable fury of the Mexican soldiery!

The author of this monstrous cruelty is now in the hands of General Houston. Houston retains the Mexican Chief Magistrate and all his officers as hostages for the abandonment of the country by the Mexican troops, without shedding more blood. It would seem that he has made no pledges to Santa Anna; but we trust that whatever may be the determination as to the Mexican leader, no retribution will be allowed to fall upon the heads of such portions

[1] Samuel Houston surprised Santa Anna at San Jacinto on April 21, 1836, and crushed his army, capturing its leader. The *Globe* expresses the pleasure which the Jackson Administration, and the South generally, took in the now certain establishment of Texan independence. The massacre mentioned was that of Goliad.

of the officers and troops as had no participation in the councils which decided the fate of the brave and unfortunate men who suffered with the brave Fannin.

THE RIGHT OF WORKMEN TO STRIKE[1]

New York *Evening Post*, June 13, 1836

Sentence was passed on Saturday on the twenty "men who had determined not to work." — They have committed the crime of unanimously declining to go to work at the wages offered to them by their masters. They had said to one another, "Let us come out from the meanness and misery of our caste. Let us begin to do what every order more privileged and more honored is doing every day. By the means which we believe to be the best, let us raise ourselves and our families above the humbleness of our condition. We may be wrong, but we cannot help believing that we might do much if we were true brothers to each other, and would resolve not to sell the only thing which is our own, the cunning of our hands, for less than it is worth." What other things they may have done is nothing to the purpose: it was for this they were condemned; it is for this they are to endure the penalty of the law.

We call upon a candid and generous community to mark that the punishment inflicted upon these twenty "men who had determined not to work" is not directed against the offence of conspiring to prevent others by force from working at low wages, but expressly against the offence of settling by pre-concert the compensation which they thought they were entitled to obtain. It is certainly superfluous to repeat, that this journal would be the very last to oppose a law levelled at any attempt to molest the labourer who chooses to work for less than the prices settled by the union. We have said, and to cut off cavil, we say it now again, that a conspiracy to deter, by threats of violence, a fellow-workman from arranging his own terms with his employers, is a conspiracy to commit a felony — a conspiracy which, being a crime against liberty, we should be the first to condemn — a conspiracy which no strike should, for its own sake, countenance for a moment — a conspiracy already punishable by the statute, and far easier to reach than the one of which "the twenty" stood accused; but a conspiracy, we must add, that has not a single feature in common with the base and barbarous prohibition under which the offenders were indicted and condemned.

[1] Workmen in New York City and elsewhere had formed unions, and a number of journeymen tailors had commenced a strike. They were indicted under the laws against conspiracy and after a trial in the court of oyer and terminer, twenty-one of them were heavily fined. Bryant here expresses his indignation over this blow at the rights of workingmen.

They were condemned because they had determined not to work for the wages that were offered them! Can any thing be imagined more abhorrent to every sentiment of generosity or justice, than the law which arms the rich with the legal right to fix, by assize, the wages of the poor? If this is not SLAVERY, we have forgotten its definition. Strike the right of associating for the sale of labour from the privileges of a freeman, and you may as well at once bind him to a master, or ascribe him to the soil. If it be not in the colour of his skin, and in the poor franchise of naming his own terms in a contract for his work, what advantage has the labourer of the north over the bondsman of the south? Punish by human laws a "determination not to work," make it penal by any other penalty than idleness inflicts, and it matters little whether the task-masters be one or many, an individual or an order, the hateful scheme of slavery will have gained a foothold in the land.

"Self-created societies," says Judge Edwards, "are unknown to the constitution and laws, and will not be permitted to rear their crest and extend their baneful influence over any portion of the community." If there is any sense in this passage, it means that self-created societies are unlawful, and must be put down by the courts. Down then with every literary, every religious, and every charitable association not incorporated! — Gather up then and sweep to the penitentiary all those who are confederated to carry on any business or trade in concert, by fixed rules, and see how many you would leave at large in this city. The members of every partnership in the place will come under the penalties of the law, and not only these, but every person pursuing any occupation whatever, who governs himself by a mutual understanding with others that follow the same occupation.

THE SPECULATION IN WESTERN LANDS

Washington *Globe*, July 21, 1836

Within a very short time, notwithstanding the denunciations of the *Intelligencer* and the dismal croakings of the learned and lugubrious editor of the *National* (late United States Bank) *Gazette*, the salutary effects of the late Treasury regulation will be perceptible. The all grasping and monopolizing spirit of the speculators will be restrained; the public lands will be reserved for actual settlers, and purchasers, to a reasonable amount; gold and silver will become more abundant in the West, where in the natural course of events there must soon be a demand for it, and caution and economy will take the place of the recklessness and extravagance which have of late been but too common in some speculating communities.

Twenty years ago, we recollect there was a rush after the public lands very similar to the recent and present movements, except that it was not upon so great a scale. The money was obtained in the same way (from the banks), and made of the same material (rags), and the consequences were the same that we shall witness again, unless some check is given to this inordinate grasping after the public domain; thousands of individuals will be ruined, and millions of dollars will be lost to the United States.

Congress will, it is to be presumed, take up this subject and act upon it at the next session. It is one of vital importance to the community, and should not be lost sight of. The question is simply whether it is best to regulate the sales of public lands by the wants of the community, and the demands of emigration, or to let them fall, all at once, into the hands of speculators, who by a combination (which will certainly take place) may compel the purchaser who purchases to cultivate to pay four or five times the price fixed by the government.

[THE RIGHT TO FORM TRADE-UNIONS] [1]

New York *Plaindealer*, December 10, 1836

Some days ago we observed in one of the newspapers a paragraph stating that a meeting of mechanics and laborers was about to be held in this city for the purpose of adopting measures of concerted or combined action against the practise, which we have reason to believe exists to a very great extent, of paying them in the uncurrent notes of distant or suspected banks. No such meeting, however, as far as we can learn, has yet been held. We hope it soon will be; for the object is a good one, and there is no other way of resisting the rapacious and extortionate custom of employees paying their journeymen and laborers in depreciated paper, half so effectual as combination.

There are some journalists who affect to entertain great horror of combinations, considering them as utterly adverse to the principles of free trade; and it is frequently recommended to make them penal by law. Our notions of free trade were acquired in a different school, and dispose us to leave men entirely at liberty to effect a proper object either by concerted or individual action. The character of combinations, in our view, depends entirely upon the intrinsic character of the end which is aimed at. In the subject under consideration, the end proposed is good beyond all possibility of

[1] William Leggett, one of the leaders of the radical Loco-foco Democracy in New York City, and a passionate believer in greater social and political equality, was editor of the short-lived *Plaindealer*. Though the weekly lasted but ten months, he made it genuinely influential.

question. There is high warrant for saying that *the laborer is worthy of his hire;* but the employer who takes advantage of his necessities and defencelessness to pay him in a depreciated substitute for money, does not give him his hire; he does not perform his engagement with him; he filches from the poor man a part of his hard-earned wages and is guilty of a miserable fraud. Who shall say that this sneaking species of extortion ought not to be prevented? Who will say that separate individual action is adequate to that end? There is no one who will make so rash an assertion.

The only effectual mode of doing away the evil is by attacking it with the great instrument of the rights of the poor — *associated effort.* There is but one bulwark behind which mechanics and laborers may safely rally to oppose a common enemy, who, if they ventured singly into the field against him, would cut them to pieces: that bulwark is the *Principle of Combination.* We would advise them to take refuge behind it only in extreme cases, because in their collisions with their employers, as in those between nations, the manifold evils of a siege are experienced, more or less, by both parties, and are therefore to be incurred only in extreme emergencies. But the evil of being habitually paid in a depreciated currency; of being daily cheated out of a portion of the just fruits of honest toil; of having a slice continually clipped from the hard-earned crust, is one of great moment, and is worthy of such an effort as we propose.

THE EXPUNGING PROCESS [1]

Washington *National Intelligencer*, January 15, 1837

We believe that no question before Congress has ever been viewed with so solemn and painful a feeling by the thinking public, as the proposition which there is too much reason to fear is about to be adopted by the Senate. For our own part, we declare, in all sincerity, that we look upon it with more oppressed feelings than we should upon a proposition heedlessly to involve the nation in the calamities of war. We shall look upon its passage with a more painful emotion than we experienced when, many years ago, we saw the Capitol in flames, and our own individual property committed to the torch of an invading enemy. Time can obliterate the evils of war, and industry repair its ravages. But what time can heal a wound inflicted by the Senate on its own honor? It savors, we know, of arrogance, to interpose our humble voice in a question upon which the greatest minds of our country are exerting their

[1] Thomas Hart Benton's long fight to expunge from the Senate journals the censure of that body upon Andrew Jackson was successfully ended in the final days of the Jackson Administration, 1837.

powers. But in the fullness of the heart the mouth speaketh; and it is not without the hope of inducing some of those more considerate gentlemen who are conscientiously approaching this act as an act of duty, to pause and reflect whether there are not some sacrifices too fearful to be yielded to the vindictive exactions of party, or of vindictive party leaders, that we have said thus much. There is indeed scarcely a personal sacrifice which we would not cheerfully make to avert the impending calamity; and God knows that the sacrifice would be made by us with feelings untainted by party influence, and with the sole and only earthly motive of saving the Constitution of our country from a wound, and the Senate of that country from a dishonor, which we have no surety that the Senate itself would long survive.

THE BLESSINGS OF SLAVERY

New York *Plaindealer*, February 25, 1837

An extraordinary colloquy took place in the United States Senate some short time since between Mr. Rives and Mr. Calhoun, in which the latter Senator maintained with much vehemence that slavery is not an evil, but "a good, a great good," and reproached Mr. Rives, in sharp terms, for admitting the contrary. As his remarks were reported by the stenographers at the time, they contained some very insulting allusions to the free laborers of the Northern States, whom Mr. Calhoun spoke of in the most contemptuous terms as serfs and vassals, far beneath the negro bondmen of the South in moral degradation. An elaborate report was some days afterward published in the Washington papers, which probably had undergone the revision of the several speakers; and from that the offensive expressions relative to the free citizens of the North were wholly omitted. . . .

We have Mr. Calhoun's own warrant for attacking his positions with all the fervour which a high sense of duty can give; for we do hold from the bottom of our soul that slavery is an evil, a deep, detestable, damnable evil; an evil in all its aspects; an evil to the blacks and a greater evil to the whites; an evil, moral, social, and political; an evil which shows itself in the languishing condition of agriculture at the South, in its paralyzed commerce, and in the prostration of the mechanic arts; an evil that stares you in the face from uncultivated fields, and howls in your ears through the tangled recesses of the Southern swamps and morasses. Slavery is such an evil that it withers what it touches. Where it is once securely established, the land becomes desolate, as the tree inevitably perishes which the sea-hawk chooses for its nest; while freedom, on the contrary, flourishes like the tannen, on the loftiest and least sheltered rocks, and clothes with its refreshing verdure what without it would frown in naked and incurable sterility.

If anyone desires an illustration of the opposite influences of slavery and freedom, let him look at the two sister States of Kentucky and Ohio. Alike in soil and climate, and divided only by a river whose translucent waters reveal, through nearly the whole breadth, the sandy bottom over which they sparkle, how different are they in all the respects over which man has control! On the one hand, the air is vocal with the mingled tumult of a vast and prosperous population. Every hillside smiles with an abundant harvest; every valley shelters a thriving village; the click of a busy mill drowns the prattle of every rivulet, and all the multitudinous sound of business denote happy activity in every branch of social occupation.

This is the State which, but a few years ago, slept in the unbroken solitude of nature. The forest spread an interminable canopy of shade over the dark soil, on which the fat and useless vegetation rotted at ease, and through the dusky vistas of the wood only savage beasts and more savage men prowled in quest of prey. The whole land now blossoms like a garden. The tall and interlacing trees have unlocked their hold, and bowed before the woodman's axe. The soil is disencumbered of the mossy trunks which had reposed upon it for ages. The rivers flash in the sunlight and the fields smile with waving harvests. This is Ohio, and this what *freedom* has done for it.

Let us turn to Kentucky, and note the opposite influences of *slavery*. A narrow and unfrequented path through the close and sultry canebrake conducts us to a wretched hovel. It stands in the midst of an unweeded field, whose dilapidated enclosure scarcely protects it from the lowing and hungry kine. Children half-clad and squalid, and destitute of the buoyancy natural to their age, lounge in the sunshine, while their parent saunters apart to watch his languid slaves drive the ill-appointed team afield. This is not a fancy picture. It is a true copy of one of the features which make up the aspect of the State — and of every State where the moral leprosy of slavery covers the people with its noisome scales. A deadening lethargy benumbs the limbs of the body politic. A stupor settles on the arts of life. Agriculture reluctantly drags the plough and harrow to the field, only when scourged by necessity. The axe drops from the woodman's nerveless hand the moment his fire is scantily supplied with fuel; and the fen, undrained, sends up its noxious exhalations to rack with cramps and agues the frame already too much enervated by a moral epidemic, to creep beyond the sphere of the material miasma.

Heaven knows we have no disposition to exaggerate the deleterious influences of slavery. We would rather pause far within the truth, than transgress it ever so little. There are evils which it invariably generates a thousand times more pernicious than those we have faintly touched. There are evils which affect the moral character, and poison the social relations, of those who breathe the atmosphere of slavery, more to be deplored than its paralyzing influence on their physical condition. Whence comes the hot and imperious temper of Southern statesmen, but from their unlimited domination over their fellow-men? Whence comes it that "the church-going bell" so seldom fills the air with its pleasant music, inviting the population to religious worship? Whence comes it that Sabbath schools diffuse to so small a number of their children the inestimable benefits of education? Whence comes it that the knife and the pistol are so readily resorted to for the adjustment of private quarrel?

The answer to these and many kindred questions will sufficiently show that slavery is indeed an evil of the most hideous and destructive kind; and it therefore becomes the duty of every wise and virtuous man to exert himself to put it down.

THE SQUATTERS[1]

New York *Evening Post*, March, 1837

We see pretty frequently in the party prints, expressions of scorn concerning the squatters of the western country, and attempts to scout the notion of passing a general pre-emption law for their benefit. We know well what class of persons are designated by this title, for we have seen them amid the broad prairies, where they raise their harvests, and beside the noble woods where they hunt their game, and we have shared the hospitality of their cabins. They are our old friends and neighbors; men who have emigrated from the Atlantic States, men who are perhaps a little more adventurous and restless, but quite as moral and intelligent, as those they have left behind; nay, if we take into the estimate the inhabitants of the larger towns, more moral and intelligent. We have known among these squatters some of the best and purest men it has ever been our fortune to be acquainted with. No man who has once visited the West, scruples, if his convenience should lead him, to seat himself upon the unoccupied territory belonging to Government, the

[1] Of more than ordinary interest as embodying Bryant's personal reminiscences of a journey to visit his brother on the Illinois prairies.

sale of which is not yet permitted. Here he builds his log cabin, in the edge of a grove, splits his trees into rails, fences in a portion of the wide and rich prairie, turns up the virgin soil, which yields a hundred fold for the seeds which he casts upon it, and pastures his herd upon the vast, unenclosed, flowery champaign before his dwelling. One emigrant arrives after another, and in this way neighborhoods are formed, communities of honest, kind, and religious people, with their schools and places of worship, before a single inch is offered for sale. This is the universal and well understood custom of the West — not a custom of yesterday, but of a century's growth; a custom which dates back to the time when the first hunter raised his cabin in the rich natural meadows of Kentucky. It is a custom which the government itself has tolerated; we may use a still stronger term — it is a custom which the government has recognised and sanctioned, by passing from time to time pre-emption laws giving the settler the first right to purchase the soil he has occupied.

And these laws are consonant with natural equity. The cabin of the settler is the work of his own hands; and he has made the prairie valuable by surrounding it with fences, and breaking up the green sward. The neighborhoods formed by squatters give a value to the unclaimed lands around them which they otherwise would not have. The speculator and the newcomer both reap the benefit of a settlement already formed, instead of selling or settling upon lands in the midst of a wilderness. It is just that they who founded the colonies from which the lands derive their subsequent value should be compensated in some way or other for the hardships and inconveniences they have undergone.

If local and temporary pre-emption laws are just in principle, then is also a general pre-emption law. What is right in one case is right in all.

THE MASSACHUSETTS MADMAN[1]

New York *Plaindealer*, January 21, 1837

Though this be madness, yet there's method in it. — *Hamlet.*

The phrase which we make use of as a title for this article is furnished by the Albany *Argus:*

[1] The American Antislavery Society, Garrison's *Liberator*, and other Abolitionist activities had caused the presentation to Congress of numerous petitions praying for the destruction or restriction of slavery. Speaker James K. Polk of the House ruled that the constitutional right of petition did not oblige the House to *receive* a petition, and that it might be thrown into the wastebasket without being even referred to a committee for burial. John Quincy Adams at once took up the fight for the Anglo-Saxon right of petition in its full meaning, and rallied a great part of the North behind him. William Leggett's editorial shows how one Northern Democrat felt.

It will be seen, by the Congressional report, that Mr. Adams and the Abolition members of Congress have started the old game of agitation in the House of Representatives. No doubt the design is to waste as much as possible of the public time, at this short session, upon a question not less fruitless than mischievous. How discreditable it is to the country, that the *Massachusetts madman* is permitted, not only to outrage all order and decorum in the House, but to scatter incendiary evil and excitement throughout the country!

What an exquisite sense of "order and decorum" the Albany *Argus* displays! What dignity, what respect for the character which should distinguish the State paper, and what deference for a man who has filled the highest office in our republic, this modestly worded paragraph evinces! There is something in the circumstance of Mr. Adams being *permitted* to make a motion in the House of Representatives which, we must confess, deserves strong rebuke; and our only wonder is that the Albany *Argus* could so admirably command its temper, as to confine itself to so gentle a reprimand. "The Massachusetts Madman" merits harsher treatment. He should have been denounced, in the bitterest terms, as a baldheaded and paralytic dotard for the unparalleled audacity he has been guilty of in presenting a petition of his constituents to the House of Representatives, and asking that it might be appropriately referred.

That Mr. Adams is a madman there is medical authority for asserting. A physician being called on as a witness, not long since, in this city, in the case of a trial before one of our courts in which an attempt was made to prove one of the parties insane, defined madness to consist in conduct or opinions differing from those of the mass of mankind. Mr. Adams differs very widely, alas! from the mass of mankind, both in conduct and opinions, if we are to take the House of Representatives as a fair criterion of public sentiment. He strangely believes that slavery is an evil; that Congress has constitutional jurisdiction, in all respects, over the District of Columbia; that the right of petition is guaranteed to all citizens by the federal compact; and that the right of speech justifies him in expressing his sentiments, even on the tabooed question of abolishing involuntary servitude. To these crazy questions, he adds the crazy conduct of persisting in expressing them; and thus comes doubly within the category of madman. . . . The man who is so utterly frantic as to express unpopular opinions should be dealt with somewhat after the fashion that keepers of insane hospitals deal with their raving and delirious patients. Instead of ordinary habiliments, his limbs should be swathed in a species of straight waistcoat — an unguentous integument, composed of molasses and boiling tar; he should be placed on a diet of rotten eggs; and for exercise, ridden a few miles at a sharp trot on a wooden rail. This is the mode of treatment which the madness of uttering unpopular opinions is considered as calling for, and we faithfully copy the inscription from the latest edition of the Political Pharmacopœia, a chapter of which was transcribed from the Westchester *Spy* in the last number of our paper.

It has been discovered, we believe, of late years in Great Britain, that a free use of the *halter* is not the best possible mode of preventing petty crimes; and there are some who will probably question whether *tar and feathers* are a sovereign specific for the disease of abolitionism. Insanity, of the kind which the Massachusetts Madman displays, is certainly wonderfully on the increase. It has got to be an epidemic in the land; and what is most surprising, cases of the most aggravated description, and in the greatest numbers, occur in those neighborhoods where the remedial measures have been most energetically applied. We have our doubts even, if some patriotic practitioner should administer a dose of tar and molasses to Mr. Adams, whether the result would not be, not to effect a cure, but to spread the disease. The operation seems to be somewhat like that of the means adopted by the British Government to plant the Episcopal Church in Ireland, which, according to the London *Examiner*, have done more to advance the cause of Popery than could have been effected by a hundred *Colleges de Propaganda*. A hundred thousand undisturbed lecturers on abolition, at all events, could not have done half so much to spread their doctrines, as has been effected by the violence of those who sought to suppress them. They have but pricked the sides of their intent. They have but spurred them to more rapid progress. Their opposition has but inflamed the spirit which it could not vanquish.

THE INAUGURATION OF MR. VAN BUREN[1]

Washington *Globe*, March 5, 1837

All the concomitants which attended the inauguration were in happy keeping with the principal and attracting objects. A lovely day of brightest sunshine gladdened every heart — a soft spring snow, which had fallen two days before, in virgin purity reflected from the surrounding hills the cheering light and benignity of the heavens — the paved avenue, of more than a mile in extent, was thronged with citizens from every quarter of the Union, all dressed in holiday suits and cheering each other with eager salutations. At twelve o'clock the late venerable chief magistrate, with his successor by his side, took his seat in the beautiful phaeton built of the wood

[1] An excellent example of the common descriptive editorial of the period, combining news and comment. The *Globe* of course rejoiced in Van Buren's inaug-

of the frigate *Constitution*, and lately presented to him by the Democracy of the city of New York, and preceded by a splendid escort of cavalry and infantry, and a fine band of martial music, proceeded to the Capitol through the Pennsylvania Avenue. An immense crowd filled the square on the east front of the Capitol.

An opening was readily made for the late and present President, and the family of the former and of Chief Justice Taney (who are at present inmates of the President's mansion), and under the conduct of Messrs. Grundy, Parker, and Tallmadge, the committee appointed by the Senate, they proceeded to the Senate chamber. On ascending the steps of the eastern portico, cheers of unanimous greeting rose from the surrounding people, and were repeated with an effecting emphasis when the whitened head of the toil-worn general was seen, for the first time since his sickness, and probably for the last time, rising above the rest as he ascended the portico of the Capitol. After reaching the Senate, the procession was formed as set down in the published arrangements; and President Van Buren, attended by his predecessor, the members of the Senate, of the Cabinet, and of the diplomatic corps of foreign nations, led the way to the rostrum erected on the ascent to the eastern portico. He then delivered his inaugural address in clear and impressive tones, and in an easy and eloquent manner. At the close of it, the oath of office was administered by Chief Justice Taney.

There never was a more sublime spectacle presented to the reflecting mind than was exhibited in the fixed attention, the perfect order and quiet, which held the immense auditory in view of the rostrum as still as the sea in a perfect calm. Nothing disturbed the profound interest which those within the reach of the speaker's voice gave to the address. Those beyond it stood with a steady gaze on the objects elevated by the public confidence to the high station which the one was about to abandon, and the other to enter upon. So absorbing and riveting was the sense of the immediate transaction that many, we are told, did not even hear the peals of the cannon firing at the time a Federal salute at the navy yard, though it reverberated in the surrounding hills like the sounds of distant thunder. How beautifully this fact illustrates the feeling of our countrymen! The maxim that *inter arma leges silent* had its counterpart strongly displayed on the late occasion. While the organ of our civil institutions spoke in the gentlest tones, and was listened to with rapt attention, the thunder of the cannon which speaks the prowess of our country abroad rolled over the Capitol and was unheard.

uration. But the incoming New Yorker — whom some called the "Mistletoe Politician," nourished upon Old Hickory — attracted less attention than Jackson. The cheers both before and after the inaugural address were all an ovation for the retiring President.

THE PANIC OF 1837 [1]

New York *Journal of Commerce*, April 8, 1837

The past week will long be remembered by our merchants as a season of trial and difficulty, such as has not before been experienced for many years. It will be remembered also, we trust, as the crisis of the great financial troubles which have been gathering for more than a year past, from the combined influence of speculation, the surplus revenue, bad government, and so on. The first three days of the week were indeed gloomy: a number of failures occurred, chiefly however of houses essentially sound, but which were unable to sustain themselves under the tremendous money pressure which existed; and what was worse than all in some of its bearings, *confidence*, that essential element of credit, appeared to be entirely at an end. It was a glorious time for panic-makers, croakers, and assassins of credit, and well did they improve the opportunity afforded them. We could mention a dozen of our largest and best houses who were reported among the fallen, but who still survive unharmed. The temporary suspension of payments by Messrs. E. M. Morgan & Co. who were agents for twenty or thirty country banks, gave opportunity to the enemies of such institutions to propagate suspicion concerning them; and all these troubles were aggravated by a portion of the press.

Thus things were proceeding, when by a concerted movement between the United States Bank and our local institutions, measures were adopted for the relief of the community; and from that moment the state of the money market has been evidently improving. During the last three days of the week we did not hear of a single failure. Stocks which had been rapidly declining began to rally; and confidence, though still scarce, was perceptibly gaining ground. We feel assured that these encouraging indications will continue and increase, until the money market shall recover its usual healthy condition. Perfect restoration is not, however, to be expected in a day; the disease was too deeply seated, and some of the exciting causes still remain. But with prudence and moderation on the part of the patients, and careful management by the physicians, a complete recovery is certain, and cannot be far remote. To drop the figure, nothing could more fully prove the substantial basis on which our mercantile credit rests — the resources, even in the worst of times, which a vast proportion of our merchants are

[1] The cataclysmic panic of 1837 struck New York on March 17; by May the number of failures in the East was appalling, and in that month the bank stopped specie payments. The optimism of the *Journal of Commerce* was hollowly professional.

able to command — than the fiery ordeal through which they have passed.

The result of the whole matter, instead of destroying confidence, ought to increase it: — confidence, we mean, in the general soundness of the business community of New York, and their ability, under any supposable circumstances, to meet their engagements. We can say without fear of contradiction that there is no other mercantile body, equally numerous, in the world, which could have met such a storm with so few disasters. And as to the banks, there has not been a single failure, far or near. This speaks well for their condition, since to them also, as well as to the merchants, the ordeal has been severe.

We think it is now time for people to "thank God and take courage." Down with the panic-makers, and down with the prevalent mistrust! The resources of the country are vast, and no financial embarrassments, in time of peace, can be more than temporary. A bright sun will soon dispel the remaining darkness, and days of prosperity and glory will be ours. In the meantime we shall have learned lessons of wisdom which experience alone can teach, and which will tend greatly to restrain speculation in times to come. What we learn from our fathers we soon forget; but what we learn by experience, we are apt to remember. Nobody, says Dr. Johnson, ever forgot a man that kicked his shins.

[THE EFFECTS OF THE GREAT PANIC]

Salem (Mass.) *Gazette*, April 14, 1837

We regret to learn that the failure of several houses in New York, extensively engaged in the shoe business, has occasioned a great number of failures in Lynn, and has affected the other shoe-manufacturing towns in this county to some extent. In this city we have fortunately passed through the storm thus far unscathed, and we believe not a whisper or a doubt has been circulated in disparagement of the credit of any mercantile house. Retrenchment, both in business and expenditure, has been the order of the day for many months in Salem, and we regret to learn that one operation of this excellent system has been to occasion the suspension of labor on several whale-ships which are getting ready for sea. So far as this suspension extends to the employment of laboring men, it is a misfortune; but it is the only effectual way to meet the extraordinary crisis produced by Gen. Jackson's mad experiments upon the business of the country. The cessation of new expenditures and engagements is a great evil, but far less than the results of an opposite course.

Kennebec *Journal*, April 12, 1837

The prospects for the demand for lumber this year look rathe
blue. We shall have enough of it, though but little has been cu
the past winter. There will be but very little building in any of ou
Atlantic cities this season, and therefore small demand for lumbe
The price of wool will keep up as well as anything, for most of th
factories will probably continue in operation. But few if any ne
ones will be built, however, while the business of the country is i
its present condition, and especially while we are threatened with
repeal of the protecting duties. Hence it is that the waterpowe
which will be created this summer in this town will be of little us
until a new order of things is brought about. Last year near on
hundred buildings were erected in Augusta; this year all buildin
is nearly suspended. In Bangor it is much worse. We are told tha
there are at least sixty stores to let, which have been occupied. O
course with no new buildings being erected, our mechanics are go
ing away. Such are the fruits of the "golden experiment" — suc
the consequences of placing political mountebanks in power. An
the worst has not yet come.

New Orleans *True American*, April 14, 1837

Not a bale of cotton, not a hogshead of tobacco, was shippe
yesterday from this port. The failures still continue. On Wednes
day the largest cotton house in the Southern country went by th
board for fifteen millions of dollars. . . . The storm will have it
way, and as yet the patches of blue sky that now and then brea
upon us are but signs of increasing violence.

[THURLOW WEED PROTESTS AGAINST SLANDER][1]

Albany *Evening Journal*, May 9, 1838

A word in relation to the "grossness and unfairness of persona
assault that characterize the *Evening Journal*." When the *Evening
Journal* made its first appearance here eight years ago, the Albany
Argus commenced a series of gross and wanton "personal assaults'
upon its editor, such as has "characterized" few public journals.
Nothing in the shape of personal vituperation was too bitter for the
taste of the *Argus*. It was the daily habit of the State Printer to
represent us as a man of infamous character, unworthy even of the
ordinary courtesies of society. This system of personal reproach

[1] Between Thurlow Weed's Albany *Evening Journal* and the Albany *Argus* o
Edwin Croswell there long existed a bitter feud. Weed relates in his autobiography that the only time he ever stood plaintiff in a libel suit was against the *Argu*
and that he made Croswell retract.

nd assault was continued for years. We acted on the defensive.
f we indulged in personalities, it was only because we were person-
lly assailed.

Finally, about a year since, the *Argus* changed its course. The
ontroversy became, as the readers of both papers must have ob-
erved, divested of its unpleasant personal character. Our statement
hat we had not seen Mr. Biddle's letter was pronounced a false-
ood by the editor of the *Argus*. Unwilling to renew the personal
arfare, we repeated the statement, with the explanation that the
etter of Mr. Biddle only came to this city in the *National Gazette*, a
aper with which we do not exchange, and which we had not seen.
ut Mr. Croswell saw fit to reiterate his charge of falsehood against
s. The *Argus* has elected the terms upon which it chooses to stand
vith the *Evening Journal*. Let it not complain of us for "personal
ssaults" which were provoked by itself.

[THE DEFALCATION OF SAMUEL SWARTWOUT][1]

Albany *Evening Journal*, November 15, 1828

A strong sensation has been created in New York by the report
hat Samuel Swartwout, late Collector of the Port of New York, has
roved a defaulter to the government to the amount of a million
nd a quarter of dollars! We know nothing of the foundation of this
tory, but presume there is some truth in it. What can the government have been about, to let one man embezzle the public money
t this rate? Who has audited his accounts? Who has kept track of
hem? Has his own simple statement of the amount of money col-
ected at New York been deemed sufficient? Where has slept the
igilance of the Secretary of the Treasury? How long is it since
General Jackson assured Congress that his officers were performing
heir duties admirably, and resisted all attempts to investigate their
conduct as an impeachment of *his* veracity? Now, one of these
fficers, appointed by General Jackson and continued in office
hrough his entire eight years, proves a public defaulter and the
Tory organs not only "deny the responsibility," but turn him off
pon the Whigs!

But the *Evening Post* labors to twist this defalcation into an argument for the Sub-Treasury plan, and the *Argus* in its sneaking way
ollows in its footsteps. Let us look at this view of the case.

General Jackson appointed Mr. Swartwout Collector at New York
and exacted such securities as were deemed sufficient. His instructions were positive, to deposit every dollar of the public revenue in

[1] The horror created among all good Whigs by the enormous embezzlements of
Samuel Swartwout, who was appointed by Andrew Jackson over the protests of
Martin Van Buren, is best reflected in the pages of Philip Hone's Diary.

the deposit banks, thence to be drawn only on the deposit warrant
of the Treasurer of the United States. In point of fact, very little
of it should ever have come into the Collector's hands at all, but
should have been paid directly to the banks by the merchants as
their bonds fell due — an account of it only being kept by the
Collector. Now if the requisitions of law had been obeyed and the
money deposited in the banks, not a sixpence of it would ever have
been lost. But instead of this, Mr. Swartwout has constituted himself a sub-treasury, in advance of the passage of Mr. Cambreleng's
bill, and diverted the moneys to his own pockets, whence it has
been spent or lost. And this, say the *Post* and *Argus*, is an argument
against putting any money into banks and in favor of keeping it all
in the custody of public officers. We do not see the force of this —
does anyone?

THE FRUITS OF JACKSONIAN MISGOVERNMENT
Washington *National Intelligencer*, March 20, 1840

Had General Jackson been wisely distrustful of his own capacity,
he would have found in the example of his illustrious predecessors
the chart of safety. He had but to throw himself on the wave that
was carrying the whole country on to its proud and enviable destiny,
and all would have been well. But the infirmities of his character
prevailed over the dictates of reason. With daring courage, indeed,
but yet with presumption which ignorance alone could excuse, he
approached the most delicate and vital principles in the science of
government, and determined to reform them, though the wisdom of
nations had declared them good, and the experience of ages had
proclaimed them settled. He took hold of the currency and the
finances of the country, and in the absence of both information and
experience on the subject, resolved to change them from their settled
foundations. And this purpose he accomplished, in violation of the
sanctity of the Constitution, and in disregard of law. Without a
faltering step he pursued his determination, which has been the
prolific source of so much mischief. The warning of wise counsel,
the remonstrances of friends, and the predictions of evil, only made
his resolves the more inflexible, and his means of accomplishing
them the more desperate.

Thus was laid the foundation of all the evils which now scourge
the country; and our present Chief Magistrate, by following in the
footsteps of his illustrious predecessor, has consummated the work
of mischief and ruin.

From the beginning of General Jackson's crusade against the
currency, the finances, and the institutions upon which their suc-

cessful management essentially depended, must be dated the downfall of our national prosperity and happiness. And if the wit of mankind had been taxed to work out a scheme of the quickest and most successful ruin, none could have been devised more fatal and efficient than that whose success General Jackson's flatterers made him believe was to crown his fame with glory. We have but to cast our eyes over our continent, and we behold in all directions the sad memorials of a desperate and fatal maladministration of public affairs. Our commerce, that once floated on every sea, has dwindled down to a mere remnant. Our manufactures, which erewhile were enlivened with the busy movements of industry and profit, are lingering out an unprofitable existence. Our agriculture, that until lately was rewarded with a rich return, seeks in vain for a market. Our internal improvements, that recently stretched out their thousand arms to embrace the Union in one bond of fellowship and intercourse, are abandoned, and many millions of their cost are already lost to the country in consequence. The stream of capital that was flowing in from its capacious reservoir in the Old World to seek employment in the enterprises of the new is already cut off. Our credit, that once stood with proud respect in all the marts of the world, is now dishonored. Our enterprise, that was wont to explore every avenue for profit, is stricken down in hopeless despair. Labor, that brought its return of happiness and comfort to tens of thousands of families, now wanders about in rags begging for employment. The exchanges of our country, which ten years ago stood at less than one per cent between the extremes of the Union, are now ranging, between places only a hundred or two hundred miles apart, at from six and seven to fifteen and twenty per cent. In fine, a national paralysis, ruined fortunes, gloom, suffering, and a bankrupt treasury, are the prints of General Jackson's footsteps, in which Mr. Van Buren has faithfully followed.

[MAJOR JACK DOWNING'S LETTERS] [1]

New York *Express*, April 19, April 27, 1840

Washington, March 20, 1840.

To the Moderator of the Downingville Convention,

Respected Sir:

I don't mean to take things by hearsay, as some folks did a spell ago with tother Old Hero. Times have got so now, I am detarmined

[1] The original "Jack Downing" was Seba Smith, whose letters first attracted wide attention in the Portland *Courier* in 1830. They were extensively imitated, and Charles A. Davis published a series of "Jack Downing Letters" which in some respects surpassed those of Smith. It is from Davis's downright Whig series that the above extracts are taken. In intent, if not in form, they may be regarded as editorials.

to recommend no man for President till I have got a chance t
measure him. The People are entitled to a good man — one wh
will do justice by *all parties*, and go by the *Constitution and the Law.*
The country has had enuf of party Presidents, and as the party i
power have had it all their own way now for nigh twelve years, an
got things pretty considerable starn foremost (as any party wi
that goes more for *party* than the good of the hull country) I thin
it's about time to tack ship and see if we can't make things *go aheac*
Folks in office, I suppose, won't agree to this principle; and a
there are a good many on 'em, and all drawing good pay in har
currency, too, they will work like beavers to keep things as the
are — but I hope they will remember that they are not all creation

There is one thing, when I think on't, makes me crawl all over
and lifts my dander considerable: that a set of men filling all kind
of offices, from the highest to the lowest, with wages from $70
day down to $3 a day, all turn to and spend more time and labo
in working for the purpose of keeping in office than in performin
the duty of their office; and so, instead of being the people's sar
vents, claim to be the people's masters. This will never do; an
the longer things are left so, the worse it gits, till the President him
self don't dare to turn 'em out, for fear that they in turn will hitcl
teams and turn him out. This will never do; I for one can't stan
it any longer.

———

Log Cabin, North Bend, March 29, 1840 [1].
I got here yesterday and enquired for the Old Hero, and wa
told he was out attending to plowing up some bottom land, and
went off looking for him; and sure enuf I found him as busy as
bee in a tar-bucket, and twice as spry. I hadn't got my regimental
on and he took me for a settler. "Well, stranger," says he, "hov
do you do?" "Right smart," says I; "how is it with you?"
"From the East?" says he, "and goin' West?" "Yes and no,"
says I. "Well," says he, "that sounds right, and makes me hop
you will stop in these parts." I had never seen him afore, and a
I had come to measure him thru and thru, I got eyeing him, an
we had considerable conversation afore I let on who I was; an
when I did tell him I guess all Downingville, and especially ou
family and name, would like to see the right down hearty shake o

———

[1] William Henry Harrison, the "Old Hero" of the battles of Tippecanoe an
the Thames, lived at North Bend, Ohio, near Cincinnati. A part of his hom
here had formerly been a log cabin, but it was really a commodious and elegan
mansion. Harrison's political availability rested largely upon the fact that he wa
non-committal upon most political issues. It will be noted that Major Downin
deals in patriotic generalities. It will also be noted that he describes Harrison a
a hard-working farmer.

he hand the Old Hero gave me. "Why," says he, "Major, a rise
1 the Ohio arter a long dry spell was never more pleasing to me
han to see you." . . .

There are some things I like to see here in The Cabin, and which
ook about right. There are four pictures hanging up here, which
he Old Hero says ought to hang in every cabin in the country,
nd Congress ought to have printed and framed and sent round to
very cabin that can't affird to buy 'em (a leetle saving out o' the
ublic printing would pay the hull expense), and they be: 1st, *the
Declaration of Independence;* 2d, *the Constitution of the United States;*
d, *Gineral Washington's Farewell Address;* 4th, *the Map of the United
tates.* Now with these, the Gineral says many a good honest
Democrat — looking well to 'em — will straighten the crooks of
arty.

LOG CABINS [1]
Newark *Advertiser*, May 16, 1840

Log Cabins were the dwelling places of the founders of our re-
ublic. It was a Log Cabin that received the daring pioneers of
berty who exchanged the dangers of the half-sinking *Mayflower* for
he dangers and perils of an inhospitable clime. It was in view of
he Rock of Plymouth that the Puritans of New England first erected
heir Log Cabins. It was in Log Cabins that the pioneers of the
nighty West — the Boones, the Worthingtons, the McArthurs, the
helbys — of the vast region that stretches from the Appalachian
hain to and beyond the shores of the Mississippi, reared the race
f statesmen and heroes who have since civilized it. It was in a
Log Cabin that the illustrious Harrison, the governor of a territory
qual almost in extent to the dominions of the Russian Autocrat,
earned the lessons of wisdom, moderation, and courage which
ave placed him in the foremost rank of the great men of the nation,
nd are destined to invest him with the first honors of the republic.
Log Cabins were the early homes of the first settlers of every State
n the Union. Log Cabins were the garrisons of the frontiers
vhen every acre was won from the wilderness and the savage by
he sacrifice of a human life. Honored, then, through all time, be
hese memorials of the trials, the sufferings, the triumphs of our
orefathers. Thrice honored be he whom the splendid palaces, the
eduction of official station, the blaze of military and civic renown,
ould never allure from his attachment to the republican simplicity
vhich he learned between the unhewn rafters of his log cabin.

[1] Immediately after the Harrisburg convention of December, 1839, which nomi-
ated William Henry Harrison, a Baltimore newspaper quoted a friend of the
isappointed Henry Clay as saying that if Harrison were given a barrel of hard
ider and a pension of $2,000 a year, he would spend the rest of his days in his
og cabin by the side of the fire, studying moral philosophy. This editorial is typi-
al of the Whig response to the sneer.

[WHY HARRISON SHOULD NOT BE ELECTED PRESIDENT]

New York *Evening Post*, September 11, 1840

We promised yesterday to explain in what respect we differed from our correspondent Veto, when he said that "General Harrison has been all his life a brave, well-meaning, and honest man."

Animal courage we will not deny General Harrison to possess. He would probably at any time of his life, if engaged in a contest of physical force, stand his ground like most other men. This is a very common and not a very exalted kind of merit. So far Veto is right. The higher kind of courage, moral courage, we see no ground for ascribing to him. He is not the man who will boldly avow an unpopular opinion. He is too fond of being on good terms with everybody, too desirous of getting everybody's good word, and when he is a candidate, of obtaining every man's vote, to have any of that sort of boldness. His attempt to secure the votes of the Northern abolitionists, by writing letters representing himself favorable to their cause, while he was endeavoring to obtain the support of the Southern States by making different representations in that quarter, is an act of the grossest moral cowardice.

"Well-meaning" in certain respects Harrison may be. He is not, we believe, very select in his morals; it would not do to compile a code of ethics from his example. Yet he is hospitable, and probably in the main friendly in his dealings with mankind. He has good nature we doubt not, but his very good nature, being accompanied with a weak intellect, only makes him the easier tool of others. The most convenient and supple instruments of profligate politicians are often good natured. In a higher sense, that of governing his conduct by a steady and rigid conscientiousness, he is not well-meaning, as is evident from the course he has pursued towards Colonel Croghan, of which an account has already been published in this paper; and the same remark may be made on the course he has pursued in regard to the abolition question.

"Honest" in some respects, probably Harrison is. We hope he would not attempt to cheat anybody in driving a bargain, and that he punctually pays such debts as he contracts. He is probably a man who, if he had never been thought of for any place of honor or trust, might have passed through the world with the reputation of average honesty. But his conduct in the case of Croghan, to which we have alluded, and his concealment and double-dealing in regard to his political opinions since he was last nominated for the Presidency, are at variance with every principle of honesty. When his incapacity for places of high responsibility is threatened with exposure, as in Croghan's case, or when his popularity is concerned, as in the present canvass for the Presidency, he is neither brave enough nor well-meaning enough to be honest. His pliancy of temper and dullness of moral perception are such that when advised to play the knave by those who are about him, he does so without much hesitation.

We take no pleasure in discussing these matters. We have spoken of Harrison's personal character in this article in as mild terms as conscience would allow us to use, and we should not have written it had not the words of our correspondent been falsely imputed to us. The great objection, after all, to General Harrison is that he is set up by a party who are governed by pernicious maxims of government and who propose pernicious measures, and that his election is their victory. Another objection which certainly deserves great consideration is that made by Governor Tazewell, that even allowing him to be "brave, well-meaning and honest," he is "both physically and intellectually incompetent to the duties of the Presidency."

FEDERAL CENTRALIZATION UNDER THE DEMOCRATS

Kennebec *Journal*, October 1, 1840

We formerly held the opinion that the predictions of Patrick Henry and other Anti-Federalists, who opposed our present Federal Constitution, were visionary and not well considered. They apprehended that too much power was conferred on the general government and particularly upon the Executive. We could see no such danger, and looking at the doctrines of Nullification as eminently mischievous and dangerous, and many other State Rights doctrines which have been broached in our time as absurd, we rather apprehended that the centrifugal power was the greatest; that there was the most danger of the Union falling to pieces. These opinions were formed, however, when the Federal power was used under Monroe and Adams for beneficent purposes only. But the experience of the last ten years has entirely changed the face of things.

It has for several years been apparent to us, as we see by General Harrison's latest speech that it has been to him, and as it has been to thousands of others, that the principle of monarchy in our Federal Government, so much dreaded by Patrick Henry, Luther Martin, and others, has been steadily developing itself under the present Administration. The power and patronage of the Federal Government have been immeasurably extended within a few years. The patronage of the State governments has been brought in to swell that of the Federal Government. Governors and State officers are made obsequious partisans of the great Federal head at Washington. These State offices have become stepping stones to lucrative appointments under the President, and have, of course, been administered to meet the royal favor. There is nothing like State independence in any commonwealth which supports the Administration. The rulers of our own State, for instance, on the great question of our boundary, dare take no step which is not acceptable to Martin Van Buren.

The principle of Federalism, therefore, as it was understood by the old Democrats of 1798, has been expanding its proportions within the last few years far beyond all previous example, and this has been done altogether in the abused name of Democracy. Had it professed to be what it is — had it assumed no false disguise — it would not have been tolerated so long; more especially when connected with a ruinous administration of the finances of the country. But the people are now beginning to inquire more universally what Federalism really is, and what Democracy is, and whether the present Administration will stand a severe scrutiny. It will be found — it is found — that everything that was odious in ancient Federalism has been adopted ·and enlarged upon by the present dynasty, without any of its higher motives, its honorable purposes, or its pure integrity; and for that the true principles of Democracy have been disregarded to a most culpable extent.

THE PRESIDENTIAL ELECTION

New York *Courier and Enquirer*, November 7, 1840

The polls of our election closed last evening at sundown, and the result is a Van Buren majority, in this city, of about twelve thousand, being two thousand less than was claimed at Tammany Hall, and one thousand less than it was supposed the Democrats had received when the voting ceased. Although we have lost four members of Congress, and the results on the other nominations are the same as before, yet the anticipated majority of our opponents has been so greatly reduced that the Whigs may well regard the result as a substantial victory.

The defect of our registry law which allows the process of registration to be continued until the closing of the polls alone prevented the success of the entire Whig ticket. The great object of a registration of voters is to require that every voter should have "a local habitation and a name," at some given period before the opening of the polls. And by such registration only can an election be conducted in this city with an approach to fairness. Not a particle of doubt is now entertained but that the Whigs would have carried the city under the registration, large as it was, had not the doors been left open for the "certificate voters" who were yesterday manufactured to order for the occasion. We are informed that about two thousand of these voters were created in this way.

[HARRISON'S ELECTION IS BUT A TEMPORARY DEFEAT]

New York *Evening Post*, November 9, 1840

General Harrison is the President-elect of the United States; the returns from the western counties of New York have decided that question. The time for a "change" has at last arrived; the time when the people, in order to be convinced of the benefits of a Democratic policy, must try a taste of its opposite.

There is no teacher like experience. No man values the blessing of health like him who has just risen from a sick bed — no man enjoys the sweets of liberty like him who has tasted the bitterness of oppression. We suppose that it is just so with nations; to keep up their attachment to a wise and liberal government, which respects the rights and liberties of all alike, it may be necessary that now and then they should submit to see their affairs administered on principles which exalt the few at the expense of the many.

The Democratic party will watch the conduct of the new Administration, we hope, in a spirit of fairness, but with a determination to contest every inch of ground, in the attempt which will doubtless be made to revive exploded principles and pernicious measures. If they succeed in forcing a national bank upon us, we shall never cease to call for a repeal of its charter. If they return to the policy of internal improvements which prevailed under the younger Adams, we shall demand that they be abandoned the moment a Democratic party is again in the ascendency. If they revive a protective tariff, we shall claim that it be rescinded. Every step that is taken in violation of the Constitution and the principles of equal rights will be retraced the moment their brief hour of authority is past.

The first step will undoubtedly be to propose a national bank. They see that the commerce of the country is rapidly reviving, and the money market gradually recovering from the state of confusion into which it was thrown by the failure of our banking system, and they will be in haste to apply their grand remedy, in order that it may have the credit of bringing about the favorable results which must infallibly take place, and in fact, are now taking place without it. Let them create their national bank and let those subscribe in its stock who are willing to contribute their capital to an institution which has only four years at most to live! Its charter will scarcely outlive the period prescribed for filling up its stock.

We enter upon the contest which lies before us, not only with a firm resolution, but with the most cheerful hopes of the issue. Democratic principles have taken deep root in the hearts even of many who have been led, by a popular delusion, to assist in the overthrow of the present administration. The young men of the country, with no very numerous exceptions, are indoctrinated in democratic principles, friends to the freedom of trade, inclined to those plans of legislation which interfere least with men's employments, which create fewest offices, and which are founded on an honest and rigid construction of the Constitution. The moment the Whig party begin to move in those projects which their leaders have darkly hinted at, but which they dared not distinctly proclaim because they knew them to be unpopular, we shall have this class of young men instantly on our side.

SECTIONS AND VOTES IN 1840

Washington *National Intelligencer*, November 14, 1840

A view of the political complexion of the different States of the Union, as indicated by their votes at the recent election, will show how little is the influence which sectional prejudices exert in the formation of parties. For example, in the midst of New England stands New Hampshire, one State of the six, voting for the Democratic candidate which the other five reject. At the other extremity of the Union, South Carolina declines the sisterly association which her neighbors proffer on the north and south of her, and chooses her ally far away among the White Mountains. Louisiana prefers to go with Maine rather than with Arkansas; Ohio reaches out a long arm over Virginia and shakes hands with North Carolina.

But these results may show also the power of party discipline and of political alliances. In asking why South Carolina has adhered to the Administration, one need be at no loss for an answer. If there be one State in the Union which formerly displayed more than usual hostility against the men and the measures of the dominant party, that State was South Carolina. The language of the press, the speeches of her public men, abounding in denunciations and invective, fierce, bitter, unrelenting, demonstrated this. Whether Mr. Calhoun has abused the influence which his great abilities and personal authority gave him in his native State, in drawing her over to continue a coalition between herself and the Administration which he had so unsparingly condemned, is a question which the people of the State themselves must judge of. Perhaps the personal influence of a prominent citizen in Missouri, of another in New Hampshire, constituted the principal bond of coalescence which united those States also with the political fortunes of Mr. Van Buren rather than any natural affinity between their interests and the policy of his administration.

But if these individual instances show the force of party organization and of alliances among leaders, the grand result demonstrates how ineffectual are such devices to keep down or control the mighty power of the popular will. The cunning and the wise in their own conceit are confounded in the midst of their stratagems. They leave out in their calculations an item which proves large enough to overbalance the whole sum of their estimates, an item indeed which cannot be reckoned in figures — that spirit of independence in the people, the determination to vindicate their own power of rule when those to whom they entrust it have abused it. To this we are to look if we would ascertain the operative cause of the great and glorious revolution just accomplished.

THE CHANGES IN PRESIDENT TYLER'S CABINET[1]

New York *Tribune*, September 18, 1841

We heartily approved the course of Mr. Webster in remaining in the Cabinet after the retirement of his colleagues, believing that considerations of the highest national importance imperatively dictated the course he has taken. In saying this, we by no means imply that no other man is fully competent to the discharge of the duties of Secretary of State, under the most critical circumstances. But Mr. Webster has a standing as a statesman on both sides of the Atlantic which very few Americans enjoy; his character and talents command a respect and esteem in Europe which are of the highest consequence in the present state of our relations with England; he can proffer and obtain terms of adjustment which a new man could not, for the English will believe that he but asks what is right, while our people know that he will submit to nothing less than that; and even those who have spent the summer in foully reviling and libelling him as a truckler and traitor would at heart regret to see his de-

---

[1] The death of Harrison immediately after his inauguration gave the Presidency to John Tyler, who was far more nearly a Democrat than a Whig, and who fell once under the influence of a coterie of fellow-Virginians led by Henry A. Wise. In consequence he refused to promote the principal Whig measures, and vetoed the bill for a third United States Bank, upon which the Whigs had set their hearts. Nearly all the Whig members of his Cabinet, feeling personally affronted by this veto, resigned; but Daniel Webster remained, declaring that he did so in order to carry through the negotiations with Great Britain over the northeastern boundary line. Most of the Whig press stood by him in this decision, and so did Horace Greeley.

partment now confided to any other man. If he were to resign and any other man but Henry Clay be appointed in his stead, the nation would feel that it had sustained a serious loss at a moment least opportune — that, from some cause or other, the public interest had been put at hazard by personal differences on points of comparatively no moment. We have rejoiced, therefore, that Mr. Webster has remained at his post, and we doubt not that he will be found fully competent to the guardianship of the national rights and his own honor.

But we are not well pleased with the tenor of his letter of Monday to the editor of the *National Intelligencer*. His letter states that he has "seen no sufficient reasons for the dissolution of the late Cabinet," and that "if I had seen reason to resign my office, I should not have done so without giving the President reasonable notice," etc., etc. We think all this better unsaid by Mr. Webster. What *he* has seen, we cannot positively say; but we have seen, among other things, the following:

> We have seen the obnoxious Jacksonian claim of exclusive executive power in the President asserted in behalf of President Tyler by the journal most devoted to him in Washington, with the corollary that his Cabinet Ministers ought to reflect and sustain his views or resign. . . .
>
> We have seen a disreputable journal, which has notoriously been honored with too large a share of the President's consideration, clamoring for the resignation of the Cabinet (Mr. Webster included), accusing them of meanness in clinging to their places, and threatening that they would soon be kicked out if they did not resign.
>
> We have seen a "Tyler" Congressman from Virginia, elected as a Whig but opposing every Whig measure of the session, submit to the House approvingly the resolutions of a Loco-foco meeting in Louisa County declaring that they accorded in opinion with the Administration proper (to wit, John Tyler), at the other end of the Avenue (the White House), but not with the Administration improper (the representatives of the people) at this end (the Capitol). The Cabinet were known to sympathize with the Administration improper — we had before hoped Mr. Webster did also. . . .

One word now of Mr. Webster's position. There are very many clamoring for his resignation. But to what end? To resign *now* is to sacrifice himself irredeemably, and to no good purpose whatever. Mr. Webster occupies a position of fearful responsibility and peril. He stands virtually pledged to the country that the Administration of John Tyler shall, in spite of seductions, jealousies, and abstractions, be a Whig Administration, and that a satisfactory plan of adjustment of the currency question shall be proposed, or at least approved, by the President at the approaching session. Should he prove to have been deceived in this, his position is lamentable. What lover of his country, what lover of fairness, can considerately seek to embarrass him in his position or his course?

A DEFENCE OF PRESIDENT TYLER [1]

Philadelphia *American Sentinel*, June, 1843

No President has been more fiercely denounced by the rancor of party hatred than John Tyler. Professing Democratic principles, it is his misfortune to have been indebted for his election to "Federal Whigs" — to have been the head of a party whose measures he was forced to negative, and he in turn be denounced as guilty of inconsistency, vacillation, ingratitude, and treachery.

And yet, notwithstanding this denunciation, few statesmen of any distinction in this country have been guilty of less political tergiversation than Mr. Tyler. The very acts for which he is now condemned by his former Whig friends are the best proofs of the general consistency of his political conduct.

When selected by the Whigs as their candidate for the Vice-Presidency he was, like Mr. Rives, a prominent member of the conservative Democratic party; his uniform hostility to the great leading doctrines of Federal Whiggery was matter of history. He was selected by the Whigs *as a Democrat* — because they believed his nomination would secure the defeat of the regular Democratic candidates.

They knew that Mr. Tyler, as governor of Virginia, was a faithful Democrat who had never wavered from the creed of Jefferson; that in 1819, as one of the Congressional committee of investigation into the abuses of the United States Bank, he joined in Mr. Spencer's able report convicting the Bank of a forfeiture of charter, and took an active part in the subsequent discussions, which finally resulted in placing Mr. Cheves at the head of its reform direction.

They knew that in the succeeding ten years, Mr. Tyler's conduct was marked by the same consistent support of Democratic doctrines; that from 1830 to 1834 he occupied a seat in the United States Senate as a State Rights Jackson man, where his votes were generally recorded for the measures of the Administration; that his consistent attachment to State Rights principles led him to oppose the famous proclamation of General Jackson against South Carolina, and finally

[1] By 1843 Tyler had no friends in the Whig party, and few who really respected him in the Democratic ranks, though the Democrats were willing to make use of him. This defence is from a Democratic newspaper. The Whigs united in regarding him as a traitor of particularly low sort.

occasioned the resignation of his seat in 1836, when the legislature of Virginia instructed him to vote for the "expunging resolutions."

The Whigs knew all this when in 1840 they drew him from his retirement, and with the assistance of the conservative Democrats elected him to the Vice-Presidency of the United States. By the death of General Harrison he became President, and since that event has continued to manifest the same consistent attachment to the Democratic State Rights principles which marked his career in Congress up to the time of his resignation.

The Whigs, we have said, when they nominated Mr. Tyler well knew the principles by which he had been uniformly guided in his long public career. His nomination was intended for political effect; it was shrewdly calculated that his known hostility to a United States Bank would secure a vast increase of political capital. But they never dreamed that he might be called to exercise the duties of chief magistrate. His nomination was the result of a factious combination, willing to compromise principles to obtain power — one of those alliances which look only to "expediency" — and the profligacy of the spirit which impelled the policy has been well rebuked.

We are by no means certain, from the aspect of things, that a change in 1844 is desirable. The policy of Mr. Tyler's administration is developed and generally approved. That his leading measures have been essentially Democratic is universally admitted. His appointments have been the worst feature of his Administration; for by the appointment of Whigs to office, that party seemed to have a conceded right to demand that he should sanction Whig measures. Political principles apply as much to men as to measures, and a Democratic President can be well served only by Democratic officers.

[MR. TYLER'S POLITICS: A REPLY]

The Pennsylvanian, June, 1843

The *Sentinel* insists upon it that at the time of his nomination to the Vice Presidency, Mr. Tyler was a conservative Democrat of the Rives school, hostile to the doctrines of Federal Whiggery, and that he was on this account selected to strengthen the Whig ticket, "without a why or a wherefore." Even if all this were true, we do not regard it as being much to the credit of the same John Tyler, to have been thus a trimmer between parties, and to allow his name to be used to operate against the party which he regarded as soundest in principles. Taking it for granted that the *Sentinel's* assertions are correct, Mr. Tyler is made out, on the showing of his friends, to be a very paltry politician. But the *United States Gazette* denies the statements of the *Sentinel* in toto, and in the following terms declares that John Tyler received the nomination as a professor of Clay Whiggism.

"He was selected by the Whigs. He declared himself to be a Whig, and a Clay man, and he was selected or rather nominated on these professions, as a compliment to the Clay men, who, though a *majority*, had given up their candidate — had given up against their better sense, and the *tears* of John Tyler.

"Mr. Tyler's uniform hostility to the doctrines of Federal Whiggery is, we suppose, to be inferred from his Pittsburgh letter."

THE WEBSTER–ASHBURTON SETTLEMENT [1]

Niles's Register, June 10, 1843

That a war of blood and devastation would speedily ensue between Great Britain and the United States, in consequence of any of the difficulties which lately existed, many of which have been happily settled by the treaty of Washington, our readers must well remember we have never conceded as probable. At every recurrence of dispute we have maintained that between two nations whose people were as intelligent, who had as much influence in controlling their own governments through the force of public sentiment, and who had such manifest inducements to remain at peace and such reason to apprehend direful results in case of resorting to "the unpleasant alternative of trying which could do the other the most harm," there was too much *good sense* to allow their governments to get into a war with each other for any considerations so comparatively trifling as they were to war about. Kings as well as people have learned within the last half century that war is a dangerous and expensive game to play at. Mr. Webster and Lord Ashburton were entitled to and have received the thanks of their countrymen for most faithfully representing and carrying out the public disposition in their negotiations and adjustments of difficulties, so far as they have succeeded in adjusting them. None could have better done that which the occasion required — few if any could have done it as handsomely — yet it would be injustice to the great body of the people of both England and America to insinuate that the restoration of harmony in the case was dependent upon any two men. When peace was so manifestly the interest of both countries, and was so desired by the people of both, agents could surely be found qualified to carry the desires into effect.

---

[1] The Webster-Ashburton Treaty settling the Maine boundary and questions of extradition and the slave trade was ratified by the Senate in the late summer of 1842. *Niles's Register* reflects the relief of conservative and thoughtful men over the disappearance of a dangerous crisis.

THE INCONSISTENCIES OF JOHN C. CALHOUN[1]

Macon *Messenger*, July, 1843

In 1816, the godfather of a protective tariff; in 1833, the advocate of nullification to overthrow it — in 1832, the supporter of the compromise act; in 1841, the violent opponent of it — in 1816, the advocate of a national bank; in 1834, proposing to extend its charter twelve years; in 1838 and 1841, denouncing it as unconstitutional — in 1816, the advocate of a system of internal improvements; in 1819, the moving spirit that breathed life into it; in 1832 the denouncer of it as entailing all the evils of the tariff; in 1843, again its advocate — in 1836, the advocate of distributing the proceeds of the sales of public lands among the States, and the author of the scheme; in 1841, the reviler of the scheme as unconstitutional; in 1842, the advocate of the proceeds of the public lands being continued in the Treasury, as the only constitutional mode of application; in 1834, the author of the proposition to take them from the old States, and to cede them to the States in which they lie — in 1816, the author of the proposition to appropriate the bonus of the United States Bank to works of internal improvement; in 1840, the reviler of those who voted for his proposition — in 1825, the proud boaster of his great services in giving being to the "American system"; now the traducer of those who acted with him and followed his lead — the author of the system of internal improvements, which has squandered so many millions of dollars for no good end, and now the prosecuting reviler of those who attempt to carry out the schemes he planned — the opponent of the sub-treasury in 1834, and the great advocate of it now — the advocate of every measure hated by the South, and the bold Senator who declared in 1842 that he had not changed any of these principles, and yet the suppliant for their votes. The blustering advocate now of "free trade," in his whole Congressional career before his connection with Mr. Monroe's cabinet, he was the ultra advocate of protection both by his votes and speeches. A member of the Senate since 1832, amidst all the excitement of the tariff question he has never yet presented to the American people the first free trade proposition.

This is the politician who never yet raised a party around him, and this is the political weathercock whose friends have established a press at Macon to persuade the people of Georgia to follow him. This is the Presidential aspirant who cannot get the vote of any two States in the Union. What an imposition upon common sense!

[1] Calhoun in 1843, and indeed throughout his life, coveted the Presidency as ardently as did Henry Clay. In details, his policy was often inconsistent. But he never wavered in his central aim — the welding of a solid South. He sought to unite the Southern people behind the great sectional interest of slavery.

THE TRADE OF THE MISSISSIPPI VALLEY

Baltimore *American*, August 19, 1843

The increase of trade on the Mississippi waters in the last thirty years furnishes a most striking indication of the astonishing progress of the country in wealth and prosperity. The July number of *Hunt's Merchant's Magazine*, in an article on this subject, sets forth a series of facts which are truly wonderful.

In 1817, less than thirty years ago, the entire tonnage on all the waters of the Mississippi was only 6,500 tons. Steamers were then newly in use; they were heavy and slow — almost as far behind the steamers of the present day in construction and rapidity as the keel boat was inferior to the early steamer. A Louisville paper quotes the *Commercial Chronicle* for May, 1818, of the port of Louisville, from which it appears that the steamboat *Etna* arrived at Shippingport at the falls of the Ohio, a few miles below Louisville, in thirty-two days from New Orleans. The steamboat *Governor Shelby* arrived at Shippingport from New Orleans in twenty-two days running-time. On the first of May, 1818, a hermaphrodite-rigged barge arrived at Shippingport in seventy-one days from New Orleans. A keel boat arrived there on the same day in one hundred and one days from New Orleans. The time now occupied in making a trip from New Orleans to Louisville is between five and six days.

In 1834 there were two hundred and fifty steamboats afloat on the Mississippi waters with an aggregate tonnage of thirty-nine thousand tons. In the eight years following this tonnage was more than doubled; for in 1842 there were on the western waters four hundred and fifty steamers, averaging two hundred tons each, and making an aggregate of ninety thousand tons, built at a cost of seven millions of dollars. To this vast amount of steamboat tonnage there must be added, in the great account of the Mississippi trade for that year, four thousand flatboats of some seventy-five tons each. The whole amount for 1842 shows an increase of 130 per cent over the tonnage of 1834; an increase in eight years most remarkable.

When it is recollected that the great west is yet in its infancy — that millions of acres traversed by its mighty rivers are yet unproductive, awaiting the hand of culture — that vast works of internal improvement in that fertile region are but just beginning to aid in the development of its exhaustless resources — how immense is the swelling aggregate of future trade which rises to the mind's eye! Let the view extend to the Western tributaries of the Mississippi, and to the fertile countries watered by them; and in contemplation of the results which succeeding years must bring to pass on the banks of the Missouri, the Arkansas, the Red and other great rivers, all pouring their rich freights into the Mississippi, it is not in the power of imagination to take in the incalculable and ever-increasing mass of trade which is destined to give wealth, splendor, and magnificence to that portion of the republic and to all other parts also as participants in its diffusion.

[THE DEMOCRATS SHOULD NOMINATE MR. VAN BUREN]

Richmond *Enquirer*, August, 1843

We have no selfish ends in view. We shall gain not a feather's weight by the election of Mr. Van Buren. As for a glass of wine which he would give us when we visited Washington, it is no more than Mr. Calhoun, or Mr. Buchanan, would give us. As to Mr. Van Buren's declining the office, we frankly express the sentiment we entertain, that he is less anxious to obtain it than any of the other candidates. He will bear his defeat with as much philosophy as any of them. He might gain some credit for magnanimity by the act of withdrawing; but would not Messrs. Calhoun, Buchanan, and others gain honor by it also? and would not their biding time give them a higher claim upon the democracy than either of them now possesses? We repeat our impression, that Mr. Van Buren is among the least anxious for his personal elevation, and that rather than endanger his party, he would magnanimously decline the nomination.

But can he do so? His numerous friends throughout the country would consider him bound to act as the instrument for restoring those principles which were struck down with him, and would they consent to his withdrawal? Mr. Van Buren has, it is true, been covered with honors, and he has worn them well; but there is one other and last reward which the Democracy wish to bestow upon him for his fidelity. They desire to rescue his name from the stains so unjustly cast upon it in 1840, and to restore him to that elevation from which he was overturned on account of his steady devotion to republican principles. Say rather, what is more strictly the truth, they wish the true principles of the government, cloven down with him in 1840, to be restored in 1844. They wish the cloud which was thrown over the capacity of the people for self-government through the tricks of the Whigs to be now dispersed by their signal defeat.

Though Mr. Van Buren be kept before the people twelve years, did not the same thing occur with Jefferson and Jackson; and can the Democracy ever regret that the public mind was engaged so long in the elevation of these true patriots? There were peculiar circumstances in each case; and in the present instance, it would be far from an "injustice."

THE DEFAULT OF STATES ON THEIR DEBTS

Niles's Register, August 5, 1843

Two of the States and one of the territories have officially equivocated as to their obligations. Mississippi disputes paying five millions which was obtained for banking purposes, as her governor alleges, in violation of the Constitution of the State; Michigan disputes $2,200,000 which was negotiated for purposes of internal improvement through the United States Bank. And Florida has repudiated three millions which she obtained for banking purposes; making a total, in disputed debts, of $11,200,000.

Without referring to the pretexts alleged for disowning their obligations in these cases, it is sufficient for the present that we recognize the seal and signature of the constituted authorities, as the act of the States respectively. And we have no doubt that the people of the States, without exception, will compel their own governments to redeem those evidences of indebtedness. Disputing a claim is always injurious to the credit of the debtor, but can never invalidate a debt; neither refusing payment, "repudiating," nor any act of "limitation," can invalidate a just claim upon a government. The binding obligation of *contract* is more sacredly insured by the moral obligation in such a case than even by the letter and spirit of a constitutional provision.

There is no form of government which is more likely to retrace an error than the form under which Americans are now reposing. Florida, one of the disputing three named above, is not yet one of the States of this Union. She is still in her minority, and Uncle Sam is her guardian. Is there a sensible man in this Union that doubts either the *disposition* or the *authority* of the guardian to have justice done in the case of her debtors? Michigan is the youngest sister in the Union. Her people assumed the power of self-government at the unfortunate instant when speculation was at its acme, and the first exercise of her sovereignty was to make an imprudent adventure for such a moment. She was for the moment overwhelmed by the crash which ensued. But the circumstances of Michigan are most rapidly improving. What will two millions of debt be to such a State as Michigan will be seven years hence? What are her resources even now? Look at the teeming products of her soil that are already seeking every market!

Mississippi was the first to contest her liability for her bonds. What Mississippi has *suffered*, instead of gained by that act, let her melancholy condition answer. How long she will continue in an attitude so unenviable, we can only conjecture. That a change will speedily be wrought looks probable from the fact that whilst one of the political parties there in unbroken column is exerting every nerve to have the State redeem their bonds, the party heretofore in majority were so far divided upon the subject at their State convention held a few days since that those who insisted upon the State paying, actually seceded and withdrew from the convention. Whether the change is at hand, or is to be yet delayed, it will eventually come. We do not mean a change of party, but a change of the State policy. Mississippi can and will redeem her character, and we verily believe that no party will continue long in power there that neglects the means of retrieving it. See, in another part of this number, Governor Hamilton's admirable speech upon repudiation in that State.

So much for the two States and one territory which dispute paying their debts. Six other of the States, though admitting their indebtedness, have for some time past been unable to pay regularly the whole of the interest accruing thereon. Each one of them, however, has evinced more than anxiety to do so, and most of them have resorted to measures that in a short time will insure their future punctuality.

Most of the debtor States have the improvements for which the debts were contracted. These will in a few years be able to relieve the States of any charge on their account, and many of them will in process of time no doubt pay off the principal, and then remain a source of profit to the State, as well as of convenience to their communities. . . . Maryland, our own State, is in this dilemma, and according to her means as deeply involved as any State in the Union, yet even if her vast public works, in constructing which the debt was incurred, and which are yet incomplete, should fail to produce anything — even in that case an annual tax of one per cent upon the assessable property in the State would redeem the whole of her obligations in a few years. Who believes that her people would not rather endure such a tax than endure the opprobrium themselves, and bequeath to their descendants the disgrace of dishonoring the faith of the State? Whoever so judges of Maryland has mistaken her character, and forgotten her history.

THE ANNEXATION OF TEXAS[1]

Washington *National Intelligencer*, April 4, 1844

Our objections at the threshold of the project of annexation, that that question has been sprung upon us without any regard whatever to the wishes of the country; that its present agitation is the result

---

[1] At the time this editorial appeared, the treaty annexing Texas to the United States was about to be signed. John C. Calhoun, an ardent annexationist, had become Secretary of State in February, 1844. He at once entered upon negotiations

of the mere individual will of the President, independent of any expression of the national will, such as ought to have preceded it, or of the President's constitutional advisers, whom he did not deign to consult on the subject; that it is, in short, an act of the President *per se*, have lost none of their force by further reflection upon them. The President, entering upon this negotiation, appears to us to have acted upon a misconception of the nature and extent of the executive authority in reference to the treaty-making power. Reasoning from analogy, probably, the President appears to have considered the treaty-making power to be in his hands an independent self-existent power, for the exercise of which, so far as the President is concerned, he is responsible only to his own will and pleasure; instead of its being a representative power, in the exercise of which he is bound to obey the national will when ascertained, and for that purpose, before he embarks in any new adventure, to take all proper means to ascertain that will. Much more is he bound, in all practicable cases, if not under all possible circumstances, before undertaking negotiations of such possible consequence as the annexation to the United States of a foreign country, or even the mere purchase of territory from a foreign power, to consult the Senate, that body without whose consent and coöperation in such matters the Presidential office is a mere pageant. For such purposes the President has the power to convene the Senate if the public service requires it. He could have obtained the advice of the Senate on this subject in the recess of Congress, in less time than it took to make his first ineffectual overture to the President of Texas. But when the last overture was made, the Senate was in session, and nothing could have been easier than for the President to have taken the sense of the Senate before proceeding to extremities which, he knew, involved the question of war — a question which he had not the shadow of a right to determine.

We object to the institution of this negotiation, further, because the public opinion, so far as there had been any expression of it, was decidedly more against it than for it; because there was no public necessity, nor any plausible excuse, for this forced march in diplomacy; and because it was against the national dignity to depart, in such strange haste as characterized the opening of this negotiation, from the ground heretofore solemnly and wisely taken by this government in relation to it.

What sort of a moral spectacle should we exhibit to the gaze of

---

with the Texas government, and signed the treaty April 12. The *Intelligencer's* editorial is a very moderate expression of the opposition sentiment. Old J. Q. Adams wrote in his Diary on April 22 that "The treaty for the annexation of Texas to the Union was this day sent to the Senate, and with it went the freedom of the human race."

the world in possessing ourselves of the territory of Texas (putting its government and population out of the question) under the circumstances, which the world understands as well as we? Here is a territory wrested from Mexico — so far as it is actually severed from that republic — by citizens of the United States, who emigrated to it in military array against the laws and in defiance of instructions by the Executive of the United States to its law-officers to "prosecute, without respect to persons, all who might attempt to violate the obligations of our neutrality;" Mexico, our sister republic, being then in perfect peace and amity with us. With what face can this government — now that the emigrants above-mentioned have possessed themselves, in defiance of the civil authority of the United States, of the territory of Texas — turn round and buy from these very persons the territory which they wrested from the republic of Mexico, we being still in the same relations of perfect amity with that republic that we were at the date of the message of President Jackson referred to? What would the world say of us were we, under existing circumstances, to do this thing?

[TEXAS SHOULD BE ANNEXED AT ONCE]

Washington *Globe*, April 20, 1844

Texas will come in at the right door, for she will be cordially received by the family to which she belongs. We have said before that we looked upon Texas, in right, as a territory of the Union. The guardian who once had the disposal of this fair patrimony in his hands made way with it wrongfully by throwing it into the arms of the Spanish potentate. A revolution made it the possession of another power on this continent — Mexico; another revolution makes it the appanage of a young branch of our own family. These children of the American Union now come forward and say: "The inheritance which was divorced from us by unworthy management has been honestly regained. It is ours and we are yours. We ask the annexation of Texas 'on a footing in all respects equal with the other States of the Union.'" Is there a State in the Union prepared to repel this fair proposal? — a proposal which brings to us innumerable benefits, and confers on them all the blessings of our glorious nation.

It is said that President Houston and the patriotic men who have redeemed Texas will, in yielding their acquisitions to us, make a conquest of the United States for themselves. This is a proud achievement, worthy of their ambition. The Roman citizens who gave new States to their country were indulged with a triumph at the

seat of their empire.   We should be glad to welcome, in the same
way, the conquerors of Texas in the capital of the United States.
And who will object, if they thus receive back their own country by
winning for it again the fine regions dissevered by faithlessness?
But we think the people of Texas will deserve more than a triumphant welcome for the services they have rendered.   We would be
glad to see an ample, nay a noble dowry put at the disposal of the
State;   one not only commensurate with its sacrifices and its sufferings, its expenditure of money and of blood, but sufficient to requite
her for the full value of the lands she brings into the common stock,
and to make some advance for the rich contributions which must
be derived from imposts upon the consumption of her people.

[MR. VAN BUREN'S CANDIDACY LOSING STRENGTH] [1]

Niles's Register, May 11, 1844

The Democratic national convention for nominating candidates
for the Presidency and Vice-Presidency is to meet at Baltimore on
the 27th instant, and notwithstanding the apparent certainty three
weeks ago that Mr. Van Buren would be the nominee of that convention, there is now great uncertainty of the result.   The defeat
of his party in the Virginia elections seems to have convinced many
of his warmest friends in Congress and elsewhere that there remains
little hope of success with him as their candidate for the Presidency.
If we may judge by the language of the *Globe*, the *Pennsylvanian*,
and other leading journals in favor of Mr. Van Buren, there must
be at this moment a warm contest in the ranks of the party as to
the course best for them to adopt.   A Congressional caucus is spoken
of as having been held, at which it was proposed and we rather think
must have been carried, to induce the reconsideration of instructions
which have been given to the delegates to the national convention to
vote for Mr. Van Buren as the candidate.   This is indicated by a
movement made where we should have least expected to see it;
we mean at Richmond, and made too by Mr. Ritchie himself, who
has been regarded on all hands as the senior field marshal of Mr.
Van Buren's party — the first and the warmest of his advocates,
and with whom, if we mistake not, he had proposed to "sink or
swim."

Mr. Ritchie's sincere devotion to Mr. Van Buren has been too
well established throughout many a well-fought campaign to admit

---

[1] This editorial struck a fatal blow at Van Buren's already tottering candidacy
for the Democratic nomination; see G. P. Garrison's "Westward Extension,"
page 129.   James K. Polk, the first "dark horse," was named instead.

of doubt. He led in the late severe electioneering contest in Vir ginia, and sustained the banner of his party with all his accustome tact and untiring vigilance, nor once wavered in regard to Mr. Van Buren as the Democratic nominee. He could not command suc cess, however his efforts may have deserved it. He was fairl beaten. He has been beaten before and few politicians ever evince more skill than Mr. Ritchie has in rallying from a defeat, musterin munitions, and supplying magazines for renewed operations. Hi present movement has been influenced, no doubt, by what he nov deems a certainty that Mr. Van Buren stands no chance of bein elected, if nominated, and he thinks it better for the party to be a liberty to look for a more available candidate.

A letter from Mr. Dromgoole of the House of Representative addressed to Mr. Ritchie, was published in the *Globe* of the fourt instant, full of remonstrances and complaints at the course whicl Mr. Ritchie has thought proper to pursue. Mr. Dromgoole say that "if Mr. Van Buren, who has evidently been preferred, must b withdrawn because he cannot be elected by the party, then it i manifest that no one, with an inferior share of the confidence an favor of the party, can be elected by it as at present constituted an organized." These demonstrations have quickened all kinds o political fermentation at Washington. The Tyler Committee have put out an address in which this appeal is sounded:

> Democrats! arouse to a sense of your danger. Listen not to the siren song of those who would delude you with assurances o security. Behold the precipice on the brink of which you ar standing. Calculate calmly and soberly the awful stakes in thi unequal game. Consider well what you are doing. Think before you act. Do not suffer yourselves by any unworthy prejudice to be betrayed into self-destruction. Consider well that the in terests involved in the struggle of 1840 are as nothing compared to those of 1844. What were the questions then agitated, com pared to the readmission of Texas into the Union, to the settle ment of the Oregon question, to our last and final independence of Great Britain, and the expulsion of English influence and English intrigue from our soil?

The address recommends to the Democracy to carry a banner in scribed with "Tyler, Texas, America, and the Vetoes, against Clay, the Bank, Van Buren, and England."

The *Spectator*, Mr. Calhoun's organ at Washington, says: "We have, for six months, looked to Mr. Van Buren as the candidate o the Democratic party for the Presidency, and expected as such to support him, as we had done at the last election. Mr. Calhoun's friends in Virginia coöperated with all their zeal with his friends

1 the late elections. But Texas has destroyed him; and considering
im as beside the Presidential canvass, we shall hereafter say but
ttle concerning him in connection with this high office. We thank
ne Richmond *Enquirer* for its frank acknowledgment of the course
f Mr. Calhoun's friends in Virginia."

The Washington *Globe* preserves a bold and determined front in
he midst of the confusion which this movement produces in the
anks of the party. Its language is, "If the Richmond movement
s persisted in, the Democratic party in that State is separated from
he body of the party and disbanded." But the Washington corre-
pondent of the New York *American*, dated on Saturday last, says:
'Pandemonium is in deep conclave at the moment that I write, and
he destinies of Locofocoism form the subject of the deep debate.
The proceedings of the Whig convention at Baltimore, the letter
f Van Buren against annexation, and generally the signs of the
imes have struck dismay to the hearts of the party here. There
s such absolute confusion and fear of coming events, that the leaders
now not what to do."

A NEW PUBLIC PARK [1]

New York *Evening Post*, July 3, 1844

The heats of summer are upon us, and while some are leaving
he town for shady retreats in the country, others refresh themselves
with short excursions to Hoboken and New Brighton, or other places
among the beautiful environs of our city. If the public authorities
who spend so much of our money in laying out the city would do
what is in their power, they might give our vast population an
extensive pleasure ground for shade and recreation in these sultry
afternoons, which we might reach without going out of town.

On the road to Harlem, between Sixty-eighth Street on the south
and Seventy-seventh on the north, and extending from Third
Avenue to the East River, is a tract of beautiful woodland, com-
prising sixty or seventy acres, thickly covered with old trees, intermingled with a variety of shrubs. The surface is varied in a very
striking and picturesque manner, with craggy eminences and hol-
lows, and a little stream runs through the midst. The swift tides of
the East River sweep its rocky shores, and the fresh breeze of the
bay comes in, on every warm summer afternoon, over the restless
waters. The trees are of almost every species that grows in our
woods — the different varieties of ash, the birch, the beech, the
linden, the mulberry, the tulip tree and others; the azalea, the

[1] To this editorial, the first important demand for an uptown park in New York
is to be traced the inception of the movement which led to the creation of Central
Park. It was written by William Cullen Bryant.

kalmia, and other flowering shrubs are in bloom here in their season and the ground in spring is gay with flowers. There never was a finer situation for the public garden of a great city. Nothing is wanting but to cut winding paths through it, leaving the woods as they now are, and introducing here and there a jet from the Croton aqueduct, the streams from which would make their own waterfalls over the rocks, and keep the brooks running through the place always fresh and full.

As we are now going on, we are making a belt of muddy docks all round the island. We should be glad to see one small part of the shore without them, one place at least where the tides may be allowed to flow pure, and the ancient brim of rocks which borders the waters left in its original picturesqueness and beauty. Commerce is devouring inch by inch the coast of the island, and if we would rescue any part of it for health and recreation, it must be done now.

All large cities have their extensive public grounds and gardens; Madrid and Mexico City their Alamedas, London its Regent's Park, Paris its Champs Elysees, and Vienna its Prater. There are none of them, we believe, which have the same natural advantages of the picturesque and beautiful which belong to this spot. It would be of easy access to the citizens, and the public carriages which now rattle in almost every street of this city would take them to its gates. The only objection which we can see to the plan would be the difficulty of persuading the owners of the soil to part with it — and this rich city can easily raise the means.

THE ANNEXATION OF TEXAS CARRIED! [1]

New York *Tribune*, March 1, 1845

By the midnight mail, we have the astounding intelligence of the passage of annexation through the Senate by a vote of 27 to 25; every Locofoco voting in the affirmative, with just the three necessary Whigs: Johnson of Louisiana, Henderson of Mississippi, and Merrick, the purchased traitor of Maryland. The two former were constrained by the popular sentiment of constituents, but Merrick knew that *his* constituents thought as he did when he seemed to be an honest man, and had just been told so by the legislature. So black a perfidy as his has not been known since Tyler's.

Yes, the mischief is done and we are now involved in war! We have adopted a war ready made, and taken upon ourselves its prosecution to the end. We are to furnish the bodies to fill trenches

[1] Texas was annexed by joint resolution; this resolution passing the Senate by a vote of 27 to 25, and the House (February 28, 1845) by a vote of 132 to 76. The anguish of the Whigs opposed to the expansion of slavery was intense, and Greeley gave it its best expression.

and the cash to defray its enormous expense. Mexico, despoiled of one of her fairest provinces by our rapacity and hypocrisy, has no choice but to resist, however ineffectively, the consummation of our flagitious designs. If she should not resist now on the Rio Del Norte, she will soon be forced to struggle against our marauders in Sonora and California. Already it is openly declared at Washington that we must and will have all North America in due season; that the question is one of time only. If therefore Great Britain should see fit to stand up for the feeble and unoffending people upon whom we are making war, she will be but obeying the instinct of self-preservation. By our proceedings in getting possession of Texas, we have declared ourselves the enemies of the civilized world, or are only constrained from becoming such by the lowest considerations of self-interest. Surely there must come a reckoning for this. If those who are driving us on to untold expenditure and carnage were themselves to pay the taxes and stop the bullets, it would be a different matter.

People of the United States! what shall yet be done to turn aside this storm of unjust war from our borders? Say not that Mexico is feeble; the God of justice is with her, and we have proved how powerful is a just cause against the greatest disparity of physical force. Ought we not to hold public meetings to consider and determine what is incumbent on us in this crisis?

CITY EMBELLISHMENTS [1]

New York *Mirror*, April 26, 1845

You may remember the marble mantelpieces in the Verandah parlors in New Orleans. They are of the color of snow, with the soft semi-transparency of alabaster, covered all over with sculptured ornaments — vines, with trunks, leaves, and fruits, wrought in full relief with the cunning skill peculiar to the Italian! Each piece cost $1,000 in Florence.

Not long ago, we saw a respectable sugar planter from St. Landry, whilst discussing the general question of "protection," raise a heavy, metal-heeled boot to a level with the lowest button of his waistcoat, and place it firmly against a cluster of these leaves, bracing back his chair upon two of its legs! We ran up an estimate in our own minds, directly, of the probable damage, fixing it at one hundred and twenty-five dollars. Presently a leaf crumbled, and the bits of white marble fell upon the carpet. It was just as we had anticipated.

[1] This Jefferson Brick editorial was by either G. P. Morris or N. P. Willis; probably the latter. The Fountain Mirabeau was an exceptionally massive and ugly fountain temporarily placed in Battery Park, New York City.

Feeling his footing give way, the gentleman brought his foot to the floor. Our estimate, we thought a remarkably close one. But to our surprise, and in the face of all probability, whilst the gentleman grew warm upon the "sugar duty," he replaced his boot higher up the column, and let it down by hitches over the delicate sculpture. We were obliged to admit that the damages were, in the end, about two hundred and fifty dollars!

We are afraid the "ten thousand" will speak harshly of the St. Landry planter. Softly, my friends! This much you may say of the planter of the parish St. Landry: — In matters of art, he has an indifferent taste. You may go further. You may say the same thing of the mass of his countrymen. You may go further. You may say the same thing of the mass of Englishmen. But, of the St. Landry planter, it is to be observed that he is educated. He possesses a vigorous judgment, general intelligence, and a spirit of independence and courage that becomes him well. There is about the St. Landry man a certain noble peculiarity. He has the *bearing of an American.* I will venture a small wager he cannot fiddle. But I will wager again that he has made a thousand acres of wild forest blossom like the rose. *Like the fountain Mirabeau is your American.* In the little, nothing. In the great, incomparable.

THE ASTOR CATACOMBS[1]

New York *Mirror*, May 17, 1845

These mysterious caverns under the portico and vast vestibule of our great granite caravanserai have been conjured, during the last week, into a garden pavilion looking out upon flowers and a fountain. Herein, hereafter, the Astorians will gossip and smoke — as luxuriously quartered as a Turk in a kiosk of Constantinople. The large inner court of the Astor was, till lately, a place for house-rubbish, clothes to dry, and unhappy dogs — unsightly to look into, and devoted to the establishment's inevitable lumber. Strangers wished for the rooms which *look outward*, for the *look inward* was a wet blanket to the spirits. Now — all this is felicitously changed. The quadrangle court is made into a garden — balsam firs planted in the green sward — a beautiful fountain sending up its sparkling uselessness in the centre, and the low windows of a pillar'd saloon looking *inward* upon all. It is a hotel built around a garden — the most desirable windows looking *inward*. The guest in his solitary room sits and dreams pleasantly of his home, beguiled by the restless upgush and music of the fountain, and the thoughtful smoker goes down into the catacombs, when weary of Broadway and out-of-

[1] By N. P. Willis.

doors, and puffs away with his eyes on green grass and bright water.

These changes in the Astor have been, to our thinking, a most significant sign of American progress. It is the defect in our national character — a defect we are just now ready to remedy — to make all our culture look *outward*. Away from business and away from friends, the American is as vacant as a monomaniac in a lucid interval, and the interior of his mind is a place for unsightly lumber which he has no pleasure in returning inwards to contemplate. The education of a gentleman makes the same improvement in a man that this garden and fountain have made in the Astor — making *his windows that look inward the most desirable*. A city is a vastly pleasanter place when it is only an accessory to a mind that is pleasantest when the city is shut out, and New York is a tiresome place (as any other would be) when the gloom and rubbish of a *man's inner court* compel his attention to be only occupied out of doors.

We did not think we should preach such a sermon when we began, however!

TEXAN ANNEXATION AND ITS CONSEQUENCES

New York *Tribune*, March 3, 1846

The thunder of cannon, the shouts of exhilarated thousands, no less than the silence of anxious, thoughtful tens of thousands, apprise us that so far as the preliminary action of Congress is concerned, the cause of annexation is triumphant, and Texas is in a fair way to be incorporated with our country. The evil which the illustrious, pure-minded, philanthropic Channing foresaw and so eloquently reprehended years ago — which was more widely proclaimed by some faithful members of the Twenty-seventh Congress — which had been in a hundred ways most lucidly exposed to all who were not resolved to be blind — has been put in train of consummation. We have seen the beginning, but who shall show us the end?

Disguise it as we may under the cant of extending the area of freedom and the like phrases wherein gigantic crime and rapacity have in all ages invested themselves, this drama of annexation, taking into view all its acts and scenes from the migration to Texas of Houston and his confederates with the purpose which they have at length so nearly effected, cannot fail to startle the civilized world. We had before been seen to break faith with and practise hideous cruelties upon the poor aboriginal tribes within our geographical limits, but we haughtily repelled all foreign inquiry into their treatment, as a matter of purely domestic concern. Soon our border adventurers cross our well-ascertained, solemnly-established national boundary, rifle and bowie-knife in hand, drive out the national authorities, and establish their own dominion. Our government is appealed to and pretends to discountenance and frown upon the irruption, while pleading inability to act more effectively. But at length the mask is thrown off; our Executive first shows his hand in a treaty of annexation, next in a diplomatic declaration that for twenty years we have been intent on acquiring Texas, and at last, by the use of fraudulent disguises in a Presidential election and a most unconstitutional appliance of Presidential power and patronage in aid of party discipline after it, we have the measure barely screwed through the Senate by the smallest possible majority. In a most unconstitutional manner, we have an acquiescence put in for the Union to the accession of Texas to the confederacy. *She* will consent — no fear of that. She is at war and will gladly see us taxed and shot, if need be, to finish her war. The resolutions of annexation leave her in absolute possession of her public lands.

DISPOSITION OF THE PUBLIC LANDS[1]

New York *Weekly Tribune*, March 6, 1847

What we would have done by legislation with regard to lands may be summed up as follows: 1. Let the Public Lands, whether of the Union or of any State, be disposed of to actual settlers only. 2. Let each man who needs land be permitted to take without price so much as he actually needs. 3. Let no man be authorized to acquire and hold more than a fixed maximum of arable land, say 160,320 feet, or 540 acres. 4. Take from no man that which is lawfully his; but let him who falls heir to lands above the legal maximum be required to sell the excess to someone who has less, within a year after coming into possession. 5. Let the Homestead of a family, to the extent of forty acres, not including more than one dwelling, be rendered inalienable by mortgage, execution, or otherwise than by the voluntary deed of the occupying owner and his wife, if such there be. These measures, though various, are parts of one system, of which the end is to enable every industrious man to sit under his own vine and fig-tree, with none to molest nor make him afraid. That the idea will encounter vehement hostility and misrepresentation was inevitable from the outset, but the day of its triumph "Is coming yet for a' that." It needs but to be discussed and understood to secure it an overwhelming approval and support.

[1] The demand for free homesteads, of which Thomas Hart Benton was the first great champion, and which was to prove victorious in 1862, was vigorously supported by Greeley, who added some curious ideas of his own.

THE PHILOSOPHY OF FERRIES [1]

Brooklyn *Eagle*, August 13, 1847

Our Brooklyn ferries teach some sage lessons in philosophy, gentle reader (we like that time-honored phrase), whether you ever knew it or not. There is the *Fulton*, now, which takes precedence by age, and by a sort of aristocratic seniority of wealth and business, too. It moves on like iron-willed destiny. Passionless and fixed, at the six-stroke the boats come in; and at the three-stroke, succeeded by a single tap, they depart again, with the steadiness of nature herself. Perhaps a man, prompted by the hell-like delirium tremens, has jumped overboard and been drowned; still the trips go on as before. Perhaps some one has been crushed between the landing and the prow (ah, that most horrible thing of all!); still no matter, for the great business of the mass must be helped forward as before. A moment's pause — the quick gathering of a curious crowd (how strange that they can look so unshudderingly on the scene) — the paleness of the more chicken-hearted — and all subsides, and the current sweeps as it did the moment previously. How it deadens one's sympathies, this living in a city!

But the "most moral" part of the ferry sights is to see the conduct of the people, old and young, fat and lean, gentle and simple, when the bell sounds three taps. Then follows a spectacle indeed — particularly on the Brooklyn side, at from seven o'clock to nine in the morning. At the very first moment of the sound, perhaps some sixty or eighty gentlemen are plodding along the sidewalks, adjacent to the ferry boat — likewise some score or so of ladies — with that brisk pace which bespeaks the "business individual." Now see them as the said three-tap is heard! Apparently moved by an electric impulse, two thirds of the whole number start off on the wings of the wind! Coat-tails fly high and wide. You get a swift view of the phantom-like semblance of humanity as it is sometimes seen in dreams — but nothing more — unless it be you are on the walk yourself, when the chances are in favor of a breath-destroying punch in the stomach. In their insane fury, the rushing crowd spare neither age nor sex. Then the single stroke of the bell is heard; and straightway what was rage before comes to be a sort of ecstatic fury! Aware of his danger, the man that takes the toll has ensconced himself behind a stout oaken partition, which seems only to be entered through a little window-looking place; but we think he must have more than ordinary courage to stand even there. We seriously recommend the ferry superintendent to have this place as strong as iron bars can make it.

[1] By Walt Whitman; a characteristic subject, characteristically treated.

This rushing and raging, however, is not inconsistent with oth
items of the American character.   Perhaps it is a part of th
"indomitable energy" and "chainless enterprise" which we get
much praise for.   But it is a very ludicrous thing, nevertheless.
the trait is remembered down to posterity, and put in the annal
it will be a bad thing for us.   Posterity surely cannot attach an
thing of the dignified and august to a people who run after stear
boats with their hats flying off, and shirts streaming behind!   Thir
of any of the Roman senators, or the worthies of Greece, in such
predicament. — (The esteem which we had for a certain acquain
ance went up at least a hundred per cent, one day, when we four
that, though a daily passenger over the ferry, he never accelerate
his pace in the slightest manner, even when by so doing he coul
"save a boat.")

A similar indecorum and folly are exhibited when a boat aj
proaches the wharf.   As if some avenging fate were behind then
and the devil was going to "take the hindmost," the passenge
crowd to the very verge of the forward parts, and wait with frigh
ful eagerness till they are within three or four yards of the landir
— when the front row prepare themselves for desperate spring
Among many there is a rivalry as to who shall leap on shore over tl
widest stretch of water!   The boat gets some three or four feet fror
the wharf, and then the springing begins — hop! hop! hop! -
those who are in the greatest hurry generally stopping for sever
minutes when they get on the dock to look at their companior
behind on the boat, and how *they* come ashore!   Well: there is
great deal of inconsistency in this world.

THE MEXICAN WAR: HOW END IT?[1]

Springfield *Republican*, October 14, 1847

The point at which the war with Mexico has now arrived is or
which ought to call out the unbiassed and patriotic judgment (
every citizen who is unwilling to see the national character dimme
in the light of national glory — the glory of arms.   To maintai
our claims to a vast desert, we have carried our victorious eagl
round nearly the whole circuit of Mexico.   At the threshold of h
proud and ancient capital we stopped to talk of peace; we demande
of her the surrender of half her territory;   but she determined not

---

[1] When this editorial was written General Scott had won the victories of Moli
del Ray and Chapultepec, had occupied Mexico City on September 14, 1847, an
had compelled the abdication of Santa Anna.   A new Mexican government w
about to reopen negotiations with Nicholas Trist, the American commissioner.   B
by this time many Americans, including Secretaries Buchanan and Walker of th
Polk Cabinet and some prominent Democratic Senators, wished to annex the whc
of Mexico.

ield even the desert. She did propose to abandon all claim to
Texas, and to give us a strip of territory equal to five such States as
Virginia, and containing on the Pacific a jewel which we had long
coveted to place in our casket. Now hostilities are resumed; and
from our own capital goes forth the proclamation that we will no
longer ask for half the territory of Mexico; let us proceed forthwith
to take the whole. "We must talk less," says the Administration
organ at Washington, "of the exercise of humanity!"

Has it indeed come to this? In the land of Washington, Franklin
and Jefferson, all of whom deeply deplored the influence of a love
of war on our institutions, are we now officially told that "the exercise
of humanity" is not to be talked of, and must be abandoned?
"The inhabitants of her towns," says the Administration organ,
"must be laid under stringent contributions." And for what?
Simply because she refuses to surrender one-half of her territory.
And who are the inhabitants upon whom these contributions are
to be laid? Are they a bold, spirited, intelligent, enlightened body
of freemen? Are they a flourishing, thriving, wealthy population?
Are they a class of inhabitants who are worthy to meet the foe that
calls upon them for contributions? Nothing like it; nothing like it.
They are like the Sikhs, upon whom England in the plenitude of her
warrior-fame levied contributions in the East — debased, ignorant,
idolatrous, unthrifty. Is this worthy of a nation that lays claim to
so lofty a position as the American Union? We are strong and
powerful; Mexico is weak and distracted. We have a population of
twenty millions; Mexico, not more than one-third of that number.
We are the giant; Mexico the dwarf. We stand high — Mexico!
gone so low to do her reverence.

What then is the dictate of generosity; what the voice of humanity? What is due from us to the sentiment of the world? What is
due to our own great principles? What is due to liberty? What is
to be the influence of our example on the progress which free institutions are making? Is there nothing in all this? Are we, on
the other hand, to stifle the pleadings of humanity and forego its
exercise? Are we, with barbaric ambition, to seek for barbaric
conquest, and thus to cover ourselves with barbaric fame? All this
can easily be done; we can easily blot out Mexico from the list of
republics — easily, because we have the power.

But what is to be the issue then? The "exercise of humanity"
laid aside and Mexico conquered! — all this will be but the prelude
to scenes upon which no thoughtful mind can dwell without anguish. How is the country thus gained to be governed, disposed
of, parcelled out? In the "Instructions of the Ministerial Council to
the Mexican Commissioners," appointed to negotiate for peace,

the thirteenth article of the instructions was: "The United State
shall engage not to permit slavery in any part of the territor
acquired from Mexico." But suppose the result to be that th
United States conquer and appropriate to their own use the whol
territory of Mexico; what will the engagement then be on the pa
of the United States with regard to slavery? Who can look unmove
at the prospect spread before us by such an inquiry?

ZACHARY TAYLOR AND THE PRESIDENCY[1]

Springfield *Republican*, December 29, 1847

Since General Taylor's return to the United States, the fervc
seems to have increased in his behalf as a candidate for the Pres
dency. Nobody can doubt the strength of the popular feelin
towards him; and he certainly seems destined to be a stumblin
block in the way of politicians. Those wary agents in the Keyston
State, Mr. Vice President Dallas and Mr. Secretary Buchanan, ar
pushing themselves forward, through the instrumentality of thei
friends, for the favor of the next Baltimore convention of the Locc
foco Party. What progress these gentlemen make out of their ow
peculiar precincts, we do not know; enough only is known t
render it certain that they are striving each for the mastery. O
the score of subserviency to the slave power, it would be difficult t
say which has the advantage. They are both without any con
scientious or constitutional scruples on that head; they seem perfectl
willing to toe the mark indicated by the "patriarchal" dictators
and under their auspices slavery would flourish in all its greenness
Their worthy compeers, Cass in the West and Woodbury in th
East, are equally pliable and docile.

The South, *per se*, manifests no indications of its usual forth
putting. It names no candidate; but as far as appearances go, wil
be very willing to come under the rule of a Northern man with
Southern principles. Yet at the same time General Taylor has un
questionably the hearts of the Southern people; and the Southwes
and most of the Western States are equally devoted to him. Th
hero of Buena Vista has declared, since his arrival at New Orleans
that he is and means to be a candidate for the highest *civil* post in
the country. But he eschews all conventions. He says the peopl
have taken him up, and he will not consent to be put down by th
politicians; none but the people shall make him budge an inch

So far as political or party caste is concerned, it is beyond disput
that General Taylor is, as he always has been, a Whig. This h
makes avowal of himself; and that, too, since the speculations on

[1] By the first Samuel Bowles.

hat point have ceased to bother the public mind. He has made the tatement very deliberately. What all this may amount to everyone will say for himself. At all events, it does not augur very avorably for the continued ascendancy of those schemes of party lespotism of which the party in power have always been singularly namored, and of which the Baltimore Convention that nominated Mr. Polk is a pregnant example. We are free to say that we shall regard it as a great point gained if by means of General Taylor the despotic practises of such a convention and of the party which upholds it can be shattered. But this is not all that is to be kept in view in the movements toward a right result at the next Presidential election. The continued ascendancy of the slave power is a greater evil than the domineering rule of party. If both can be put down, happy, happy indeed will it be for the country!

The power of slavery is to be overturned only by a steadfast, perhaps long-continued conflict — a conflict already begun, and to be most vigilantly maintained, in order that it may be gloriously ended. The contest against slavery will not cease or be relaxed until slavery itself shall be extinguished; of this we may feel perfectly assured. Is General Taylor identified with the slave power? If not, will he identify himself with it? These are questions which will agitate the free States during the coming Presidential campaign. He is known to be a slaveholder; how does he stand as to the power which slavery gives, and how as to slavery itself?

MR. WEBSTER'S SPEECH[1]

New York *Evening Post*, March 30, 1848

The speech lately delivered by Mr. Webster in the Senate on the Ten Regiment bill is mainly, as it appears to us, a defence of his vote for rejecting the Mexican treaty. Mr. Webster, it appears, is an enemy to all further acquisitions of territory in the Southwestern quarter. His objection is two-fold. In the first place, he urges that the States which will be formed out of this territory will possess but a small population, and will therefore be represented in the Senate by two members, while they will not send any more, or perhaps not so many, members to the House of Representatives, which, he says, "will inevitably break up the relation existing between the two branches of the legislature and destroy its balance." In the second place, he objects that the character of the inhabitants, whom

[1] The Ten Regiment bill was a bill to increase the army engaged in Mexico by ten new regiments; and it gave Webster an opportunity to declare himself opposed to the enlargement of the Union in any direction. In this he was largely actuated by his perception that the new territories would involve the question of slavery extension, and that this would endanger the nation's harmony.

the annexation of New Mexico and California will introduce in
the Union, is so degraded, that their morals are so depraved, an
their ignorance so gross, that we shall debase our national charact
by admitting them as citizens.

The first of these objections certainly has very little force.
what Mr. Webster calls a balance between the two branches of th
national legislature be what is wanted, it is what we never hav
had. There has never been a time, since the adoption of the Cor
stitution, when there was anything like an equality of representatio
in the Senate. In 1790 Virginia had eight times as many inhab
tants as Georgia, and Pennsylvania seven times as many as Rhod
Island, yet the Constitution which gave each of these States tw
members, and two only, in the Senate, was adopted in spite of thes
differences. . . .

We do not get rid of the inequality concerning which he declain
so loudly by refusing to receive New Mexico and California into th
Union. It is an inequality which was born with us as a nation;
congenital distemper, which was with us at first, has been with u
till now, and which will not be done away with till the Constitutio
is essentially changed. Mr. Webster's argument is therefore, if i
be worth anything, an argument against the Constitution, and nc
an argument against the acquisition of new territory. It is as goo
a reason for a dissolution of the present Union as it is against ex
tending that Union to new States.

To alarm us by the prospect of the future, Mr. Webster affirms tha
California and New Mexico can never sustain a considerable popu
lation. New Mexico, he says, contains sixty thousand inhabitants –
an exaggerated estimate doubtless — and cannot contain any more
Let us see how this is. New Mexico, it is admitted, abounds ir
mines; it is known also that Mexican agriculture is the most slovenl
and superficial in the world. When emigrants from the North worl
the mines will there be no essential addition to the population? I
there be not, the result will be contrary to all former experience
When our modes of agriculture are introduced, under the directior
of our industry, will the soil be able to support no more inhabitant
than now? Mr. Webster, we think, would be obliged to answer thi
question in the affirmative. New Mexico, says Mr. Webster, is ar
old settlement, and therefore must have nearly all the inhabitant
it can well contain. We remind him that Florida is as old a settle
ment as that, and has just begun to be peopled.

Mr. Webster takes it for granted that the soil of California is
barren and incapable of affording sustenance to a large population
He is mistaken in this, so far at least as relates to a tract of land one
hundred and fifty or two hundred miles in width, running the whole

ength of the coast. Here a population as large, if not larger, than
that of all New England, might be supported in comfort from the
produce of a fertile soil which only requires occasional irrigation
to make it as fertile as the valley of the Mississippi. We speak from
the information of intelligent persons who have seen the country.

The morals of the people who are to be taken into the Union, if
the treaty with Mexico goes into effect, occasion Mr. Webster much
anxiety. The Boston Cato certainly does well to be vigilant in this
matter, and we applaud the zealous severity with which he exercises
his censorship. We do not think much of the authority he has
quoted, the book of the traveller Ruxton, but we are willing to
admit that the morals of the people of that country are not what
they ought to be. Under better institutions they will doubtless
improve — those of the whites at least — while for the Indian portion of the population, we see nothing to prevent the gradual waste
and early extinction of their race, a fate which has fallen upon the
Northern tribes. Both New Mexico and California will shortly be
as fully Americanized as Florida has been.

Thus it will appear that two objections raised by the great Eastern
champion of the Whig party against the treaty, even if we admit
that they have any present application, are but objections which the
lapse of a few years will remove. They are not of sufficient per-
manence to form the elements from which the statesman of large
views, "looking before and after," estimates the unfolding of that
destiny which lies wrapped up in the present as the leaf lies sheathed
in the bud. We recollect that when Mr. Webster made his treaty
with Great Britain concerning the Maine boundary, he endured
many attacks on account of his concessions to that Power. The
time for retaliation has arrived; his political adversary of that day
has made a treaty, and he is paying off the old debt. We cannot
congratulate him upon having added anything to his reputation as
a statesman by the choice he has made of the grounds for his attack.

[THE NOMINATION OF LEWIS CASS][1]

Springfield *Republican*, June 1, 1848

At first blush, the nominations of the Loco-foco national convention — General Lewis Cass for President, and General William
O. Butler for Vice-President — appear the weakest that could
possibly be made; but reflection and experience will prove that it
could have settled upon no stronger candidates. Their strength

[1] The nomination of Lewis Cass by the Democratic national convention in 1848
was the signal for a revolt by those Democrats who were unalterably opposed to the
extension of slavery, and who gave their votes to Táylor or to the Free Soil candidate, Martin Van Buren.

lies not so much in the personal ability of the men themselves, as in the power of the party which nominated them. General Cass is a thorough party man; he is in close fellowship with the Administration in all its acts and purposes; his Administration if chosen would be but a continuation of Mr. Polk's. It was the power of the Administration, undoubtedly, that secured his selection by the convention in preference to his competitors.

General Cass, moreover, is a base intriguer, an unprincipled demagogue; he sacrifices means to the ends. These are strong terms, but they are deserved; they are such as men of his own party apply to him — such as we have heard them apply to him since his nomination. And yet these men will probably vote for him, so overpowering to their subservient souls, is the strength of party discipline and fealty. General Cass is a "Northern man with Southern principles." None have played the sycophant, none have bended in abject submission to the South, more basely than he; none have more completely turned the back upon their former professions, and deserted the interests of the section in which they live and which they represent, for the purpose of gaining favor and strength with the enemies of those they so meanly betray, than has he. A year or two since, the Michigan Legislature adopted resolutions in favor of the Wilmot Proviso, which were dictated and strengthened by him; within the past few months he has written a crouching, slavish epistle, denouncing the Proviso as unconstitutional, inoperative, improper, and inadvisable. He stands forth, therefore, as the representative of the pro-slavery party — the defender of the war — the friend of territorial acquisition — the opponent of true freedom — and in every thing prepared to be the successor of the present Executive in all his objects, purposes and wishes, his weakness and his political deformity.

On the river and harbor question, although a Western man, he has wrongly betrayed the interests of the West in apologizing for and defending the President's vetoes, and thus aiding in the defeat of all efforts during the present administration to improve the great inland seas of the Union, on which in so immense a degree depend the individual and public prosperity and wealth of the country. His non-committal six-line letter to the Chicago Convention on this subject excited unmeasured contempt and ridicule among all friends of internal improvements. One would think that this would be almost a death-blow to his prospects at the West, yet there his main strength is said to lie. What he has done to secure the affections of the Western people, we are not able to perceive, and must doubt the truth of his boasted personal popularity among them, till we have better evidence of it. He is a Western man, it is true, has long lived in that section, and held responsible offices, and was an officer in the army in the War of 1812, without, however distinguishing himself by any remarkable deeds; farther than this, what claims he can urge for their especial support it is not in us to see. Certain it is that he has betrayed their highest interests on the river and harbor and free-Territory questions. If they can forgive him for this, their charity must be unbounded.

General Butler of Kentucky, the candidate for the second office, is a less objectionable person, and within his own State, at least, will add strength to the ticket. He served in the War of 1812, as aid to General Jackson, and was an early volunteer in the war with Mexico, where he has served with distinction, been rapidly pushed forward by Executive power, and now, in the recall of General Scott, occupies the post of Commander-in-Chief of the United States forces in that country. He was the candidate of his party for Governor of Kentucky a year or two since, and pressed Judge Owsley, the Whig candidate, who was unpopular, quite hard, but did not secure an election. We cannot conceive of a nomination by the Whigs against which he can carry the State for Cass and himself.

Out of New York, we do not perceive that there is any reason to expect that these candidates will not get the main strength of their party. New York is irrecoverably lost to the ticket. The Barnburners utterly repudiate the convention and its deeds; most especially and most pointedly the nomination of General Cass, who is scouted by all the Barnburning papers in the State, of which there is at least one in every large city, and their number is increasing rather than diminishing. We doubt whether the convention could have made any nomination that would have carried New York; certainly none, which in so doing, would not have endangered a far greater number of electoral votes in other States.

THE RESULT OF THE ELECTION[1]

New York *Evening Post*, November 8, 1848

The electoral ticket nominated by the friends of General Taylor has carried the city of New York by a large majority over all the other candidates. The preference for this ticket has secured the success of the other Whig candidates in the city; members of Congress, members of the Assembly, and county officers, including the recorders, though by smaller majorities. The returns from different

---

[1] Bryant had taken a leading part in the Free Soil nomination of Van Buren, and the *Evening Post* energetically supported the Free Soil ticket. The Van Buren candidacy threw New York State to the Whig nominee, Taylor; while the Free Soilers elected thirteen Congressmen, who held the balance of power in the House between the Democrats and Whigs.

parts of the State show also that the Taylor electoral ticket has been chosen, and the vote of this State is certain for Taylor by a huge majority.

The causes of this result lie upon the surface; everybody who attended yesterday at the polls, whether in the city or in the country, saw and felt that Taylor had carried the State, not on account of any high personal popularity, not on account of any strong confidence which the people have in the ability or wisdom with which his Administration will be conducted, but because they believe the contest to be between Cass and Taylor, and they preferred the latter. Cass had declared himself against the prohibition of slavery in the territories. Taylor had said nothing on the subject, with the exception of some general declarations concerning his veto power, from which, however, numbers, with little ground in our opinion, drew the inference that he would not apply the veto power to any future edition of the Wilmot Proviso.

With those who regarded the matter in this light, the desire to express their disapprobation of the nomination of General Cass overbalanced every other motive. Hundreds of Whigs, known to be free soil men, appeared yesterday at the polls with votes for Taylor in their hands. "We know that your principles are right," said they in answer to the remonstrances of other Whigs who had heartily espoused the Free Soil party. "We esteem your cause to be just, and we prefer your candidate for the Presidency. We should be glad to vote for Van Buren, but we do not believe that he can possibly be elected. We regard this as a struggle between Cass and Taylor; the choice lies between these two, and we cannot afford to take a course which will in any way increase the chance that Cass will be elected."

To secure the votes of the two parties for Taylor and Polk, the friends of these candidates found it necessary to make the most profuse expressions of their zeal for the cause of free soil. We believe it will be found that not a single member of Congress has been elected in this State who has not probably pledged himself to resist the extension of slavery. John A. King, who is elected as the Taylor candidate to Congress from Queens County by a thousand majority, came out in the papers with a declaration of his devotion to the cause of free soil just before the election. Such declarations made by the Whig candidates no doubt had the effect of confirming the vague idea which numbers of both parties entertained that Taylor was not personally hostile to the Wilmot Proviso.

In spite of all these influences, in spite of the newness of our party, a party yet in its cradle, in spite of the difficulty of creating a large vote for any party at the very first election after it makes its appearance, we have, according to all indications, polled a large vote in the State, unprecedentedly large, considering the short time allowed us to organize and to employ the means of influencing public opinion. We have laid the foundation of a mighty party, with a great principle for its basis. The establishment of this party has already effected great results.

It has determined, indirectly but most effectually, the Presidential election between the two candidates of the Baltimore and the Philadelphia conventions.

It has compelled both parties to do homage to the principle of freedom in the Territories, and to acknowledge it as an established maxim of political conduct.

It has emancipated the Democratic party from the control of the slave power.

It has so disturbed the torn position of the Democratic party of the North, that it will compel it to reorganize with the principle of free soil in its creed as a settled doctrine.

It has taught an emphatic lesson to all politicians who are disposed to sell themselves to the South. That trade is broken up and Mr. Cass is the last adventurer in it.

Lastly, it has in all probability decided the question of freedom or slavery in the Territories. The agitation of that question by the Free Soil party, has, we believe, made the success of the slaveholders in this controversy impossible.

A WASHINGTON MONUMENT[1]

National Anti-Slavery Standard, December 28, 1848

If one must needs have something to remember our great men by, statues would be better than anything else. For not only is there a natural desire in men to see how a famous person looked, but this kind of remembrance has also the farther advantage that we have a great and original sculptor of our own to make them for us. Probably the world has never had five such sculptors as Powers, and we ought to see to it that he has enough to do. Our present statues of Washington are poor. There is not one of them which we can look at with so much pleasure as upon that of Penn in front of the hospital in Philadelphia. However wanting in other respects, that figure has a simplicity and integrity about it which we miss in all the stone that has been chiselled in honor of Washington. The statue by Houdon has a vulgar swagger. That by Chantrey has a certain English dignity and solidity about it well befitting the subject, but the sculptor was afraid to make an American without

[1] By James Russell Lowell; for seven years, 1844–1850, Lowell was associated with Abolitionism. The Washington Monument was actually begun in 1848.

a kind of apology to ancient art in the drapery. Greenough's we
have never seen, but we should consider the size as sufficient objection to it. Great men do not require to be represented as giants.
The costume also is bad. The clothes that were good enough for
the man are good enough for the marble. The objection of familiarity has no force, for it is merely one of time — a transient consideration of which a fine work of art is entirely independent. Nothing
could be uglier than court-dress of the time of Charles the First,
nothing more unbecoming than a suit of armor. Yet in Van
Dyke's pictures they seemed natural, graceful, and dignified.

After all, Washington is not our representative American man.
He is rather English than American. Daniel Boone is more like
it — adventurous, forever pushing westward, annexing by dint of
long rifle and longer head, yet carrying with him a kind of law,
and planting the seed of a commonwealth. Our art is likely to do
better things with such a man than with Washington. But the
monument at present proposed to be built to Washington is an
obelisk five hundred feet high, springing from a square base presenting on every side a columned front. The Anglo-Saxon race have
never shown much aptitude for any kind of architecture except that
of colonies and states. With stone and mortar they have done
little, and that meagre and imitative. Not sentimental nor eminently imbued with religious feeling, they have housed their religion
worse than any other race. The cathedrals and abbeys of England
and Scotland sprang from Norman brains. Use and not sentiment
has been the Saxon characteristic. Accordingly their dwellings
have been the most comfortable, their ideas of government the
most practical, and their criticism (till inoculated from Germany)
the coldest and most meagre in the world.

The Pilgrims who came to New England in 1620 represented in
tolerable completeness the Saxon element of English life. They
built up a state and a commerce forthwith. Ere long they began to
send out colonies. They could not have elbow-room enough on
the continent while the French were seated to the north of them.
They made a religion hard, square, and unyielding, and then con-
structed square boxes to hold it where they might be sure to find
it once a week. For religion was a job of downright hard work,
which they went at with their coats off. Organization, trade, and
the sending out of new colonies — these were their play. From
such a race architecture for architecture's sake was not to be looked
for. They have built best what was useful and practical, as ships,
railroads, and aqueducts. In all the United States there is not a
beautiful church — or, if beautiful, it is not in any sense American.
But we have handsome shops enough.

No nation should be more cautious in undertaking to erect a monument. The drawing of the one now proposed for Washington does not strike us favorably. We can perceive no peculiar appropriateness in it, and consequently no peculiar beauty. On the other hand, we find many incongruities. What is the meaning, for example, of the figure in front of the obelisk driving four horses abreast? There are such figures on some other monuments, perhaps, borrowed from the antique, and there is something like it in Guido's Aurora, but where is its fitness? Sensible people do not drive horses in this manner, nor did we ever see anything like the chariot to which they are attached, except an ox cart or a dray. Then, too, the inscription is in Latin. Why? Because it is more generally understood? Then why not in French, which is more generally understood still? Or perhaps it is Classic? In that case, why did not the Romans use Greek in their inscriptions — a language more classic than their own, and which was the French of the ancient world beside?

But we do not see the need of any monument at all, least of all in such an out of the way place as the city of Washington. . . We would not forget that he held slaves, but neither would we forget that he was Washington, and, even if we were anxious that a pile of stones should be heaped up to his memory, we could never consent to give any the least aid toward building it in the District of Columbia. Let no shaft rise for so great and good a man in a market-place for human flesh! If our Whig friends must keep reminding us that Washington held his fellow-men in bondage, they cannot, at least, say that he was a slave-trader. Let no man, Abolitionist or not, contribute to rear an obelisk within hearing of the man-seller's hammer, and in front of which the wretched slave-coffle shall be driven to the hopeless South!

THE FUTURE OF THE SOUTH

Boston *Atlas*, May, 1849

We fully agree with the statement which is often made that so far as natural advantages are concerned, the South altogether leads the North in facilities for manufacturing, especially in the manufacture of cotton. She has waterpower in abundance. She has coal and iron in inexhaustible supplies, of which the New England States have none; and more than all, she possesses the soil and climate on which to grow the raw material, and which no law, no capital, no enterprise, can take from her. In this last particular, the cotton-growing States need fear no competition. Not all the free trade laws in the world, or all the protective tariffs that ever filled the

PROGRESSIVE DEMOCRACY—PROSPECT OF A SMASH UP.

(An old campaign broadside, picturing the Lincoln-Hamlin triumph of 1860.)

pages of a statute book, can transfer the immense business of cotton growing from the South to the North. It remains there, fixed by the immutable laws of Providence. Possessing all these advantages, what is to hinder the South from outstripping the North in the manufacture of cotton? Nothing but the very thing which our South Carolina friend is so anxious to preserve and perpetuate, slavery.

[THE FUTURE OF THE SOUTH: A REJOINDER]

Augusta [Georgia] *Sentinel*, May, 1849

The holders of slaves owe it to themselves to demonstrate, in a large way, that cotton can be picked, carded, spun, and woven, as well as grown at the South. Nothing short of this will stop the ceaseless reproaches and unjust imputations cast upon the relation of master and servant, as it exists in this quarter of the Union. It is the duty of all cotton planters to take hold of this great question of manufacturing and mechanical industry in good earnest. Of all men, you are most deeply interested in creating a steady home market for your great staple. Of all men, you are most to be benefited by proving that slave labor in Georgia is as profitable to you, and as useful to the world, as free labor is at the North or can be at the South. The whole matter will turn in the end on the one pivot of dollars and cents. Slavery was abolished in New York because experience proved that the relation of master and slave was not profitable to the master. The people of the non-slaveholding States firmly believe that institution is unprofitable at the South; that every planting State would be much better off if its citizens would emancipate their servants. This is also the deliberate opinion of ninety-nine in every one hundred of the hundreds of thousands of emigrants from Europe, who annually flock to this country, remain permanently, and become a portion of its sovereign rulers.

We must show by visible results that slavery is not incompatible with improvement of the soil; is not inimical to common schools and a high standard of general intelligence; and is not hostile to the most successful manufacturing, mechanical, and commercial industry. We can influence and control public opinion on all these points if we will only set ourselves properly and steadily at work to attain the objects indicated. Our sectional movements, our empty resolutions and "committees of safety," are taken by the civilized world as a confession of weakness; a consciousness of wrong which cannot endure the searching light of truth and a free discussion.

So far is slavery from being naturally opposed to all progress and improvement in rural and mechanical arts, in internal trade and foreign commerce, in popular education and moral instruction, that it can easily be made auxiliary to all these important ends. It is the perfection of human wisdom to make the best possible use of all the means which a good Providence has placed at our disposal. To whom much is given, much will also be required. Because God has given us much, it will not do to say in practise that we need do nothing for ourselves. Our abundant means for labor, our great advantages of climate, soil, and waterpower, demand the most skilful use, the most profitable employment.

[FIRST STEPS TOWARDS THE INDUSTRIAL FUTURE]

Baltimore *American*, May, 1849

It is not generally known that within the last year or two steps have been taken at the South to supply the home market with domestic flour. Several large flouring establishments have been put in operation in the States of Georgia and Alabama, by which good merchantable flour is produced from Southern grain. The "Mobile City Mills," of Messrs. Anderson & Company, are capable of turning out six hundred barrels a week, and the papers state that they find a ready sale for all the flour they can make. These mills are supplied with wheat from New Orleans, but during the past year they consumed about 3,000 bushels of Alabama wheat, bought at $1 to $1.25 a bushel. There are at present in Georgia several extensive mills producing flour, which finds a ready home market and is rapidly reducing the amount of importations from the Northern markets. In addition to those now in operation, it is contemplated to erect one or more large flouring mills at Augusta, on the immense waterpower which has been recently introduced there for manufacturing purposes.

MR. WEBSTER'S SPEECH [1]

New York *Evening Post*, March 8, 1850

The *Journal of Commerce* exults at Mr. Webster's declaration that he will not support any measure to prohibit slavery in the territories.

We did not suppose that he would. We knew that the Administration had been generous to the family of the Massachusetts Senator, and that he is, by temperament, grateful, and sensible of the obligations which those who receive benefits are under to those by whom they are bestowed. It was for that, among other reasons, that we so confidently assured our readers, the other day, that he would

[1] Webster's Seventh of March speech in favor of the Compromise of 1850 brought down upon his head a storm of abuse from anti-slavery newspapers and leaders.

not fail to support the Administration in its recommendation not to apply the proviso of 1787 to the new territories. It was as natural to suppose that he would do this, as that he could abandon, in the manner he has done, the doctrines of free trade, once maintained by him in their fullest extent, and taking the money of the eastern mill-owners, enroll himself as the champion of protection for the rest of his life.

We take no pleasure in making these animadversions, but they are forced upon us. Mr. Webster stands before the public as a man who has deserted the cause which he lately defended, deserted it under circumstances which force upon him the imputation of a sordid motive, deserted it when his apostasy was desired by the Administration, and immediately after an office had been conferred upon his son, to say nothing of what has been done by the Administration for his other relatives. It is but a little more than two years since that he declared himself the firmest of friends to the Wilmot Proviso, professing himself its original and unvarying champion, and claiming its principles as a Whig doctrine. In a speech which he made at a Whig convention held at Springfield in Massachusetts, in the year 1847, he said:

> There is not a man in this hall who holds to the principles of the Wilmot Proviso more firmly than I do, no one who adheres to it more than another. I feel some little interest in this matter, sir. Did I not commit myself in 1838 to the whole doctrine, fully, entirely? And I must be permitted to say that I cannot quite consent that more recent discoverers should claim the merit and take out a patent. I deny the priority of their invention. Allow me to say, sir, that it is not their thunder.

But now, in the speech delivered yesterday on the floor of the Senate, in reply to Mr. Calhoun, of which our readers will find the telegraphic report in our columns, he ridicules the Wilmot Proviso as the invention of Northern Democracy, and declares that he "will not vote for the insertion, into any bill giving territorial government to the new Territory, of any provision prohibiting slavery."

Of course there is a pretext for this shameful renunciation of a principle once so zealously professed; no apostasy is ever without its pretext. Mr. Webster now pretends that it is impossible that slavery should exist in the new Territories, and says that the adoption of the Wilmot Proviso would be "a re-enactment of the law of God."

What would he have? Would he have an enactment contrary to the law of God? But what are his reasons for supposing that slavery cannot be transplanted to New Mexico and the portions of California not included in the new State? He states none; he *can* state none: there are none. Let it be once understood that Congress will not interpose to forbid the introduction of slavery into the new Territory, and it will migrate thither as readily as it did into Missouri. Any man who has passed much time at Washington during the sessions of Congress knows that such is the opinion of the Southern members, and that they express it freely in private conversations. "Sugar and cotton," they say, "can be raised in the new Territories, and we mean to go thither with our slaves." In a speech, delivered last February in the Senate, Mr. Foote said that, were slaves to be introduced into California and employed in mining, their owners would derive from their labors "pecuniary profits not heretofore realized by the most successful cotton and sugar planters of the South." . . .

But the catalogue of Mr. Webster's concessions to the slave interest is not yet closed. He offers up all Texas, if his speech is fairly reported. We quote the words:

> Texas had been admitted with all her territory, with the institution of slavery, and an irrepealable law by which, if new States are erected out of any portion of her territory, they shall be slave States, and he wished it to be distinctly understood, that he considered this government solemnly bound by law to create new slave States out of Texas, when her territory shall contain a sufficient population.

For aught we see, Mr. Webster is prepared to accept Mr. Bell's scheme of a compromise by balancing the introduction of California into the Union with the immediate admission of a slave State from the domain of Texas. It is singular, however, that he should have paid no heed to the resolution of Congress under which Texas was admitted, pretending to provide that slavery should not be lawful above 36° 30' north latitude.

We leave Mr. Webster's speech here. It is sordidly timorous and temporizing in spirit, and if the report we have of it be not a perfect caricature, deplorably feeble in argument. He had an opportunity of replying nobly to Mr. Calhoun, and of taking ground upon which he might stand with the port and attitude of a leader in this great battle of opinion. He prefers to stand by the baggage wagons.

[FUGITIVE SLAVES AND THE OMNIBUS BILL]

New York *Tribune*, May 17, 1850

"But the passage of the Omnibus Bill will not settle the slavery agitation." You never said a truer thing than that! Neither Mr. Clay's, the President's, nor any other plan can stop the slavery

agitation so long as slavery shall not merely exist but insist on extending its dominion.   With Cuban invasions, Haytian conquests,
and New Mexican subjugations imminent, he must be green indeed
who expects any abatement even of the slavery excitement.   On the
contrary, it is morally certain to swell and spread until it overrrides
and overrules everything else.   If the South were as wise now as
were its great statesmen in 1787, when they joined heartily in
excluding slavery forever from the territory northwest of the Ohio,
there might be a lull in the tempest; but the Ruler of Nations
would seem to have other designs, and they will be accomplished.
This slave-catching bill now pressed upon Congress will make a
hundred Abolitionists oftener than it catches one slave.   But is there
any use in throwing up rockets to warn the wilfully blind?

THE SOUTH AND THE COMPROMISE

De Bow's Review, July, 1850

The Union is the source of our greatness and strength; its dismemberment will probably be of our impotence and ruin, whilst
all the world will look on, with amazement, upon the dissolution of
a fabric so fair and beautiful in its proportions.

Thus we should feel and think.   Yet there must be an end, some-
where, of concessions.   If not a *voluntary* end, a *necessary* one, when
everything to be conceded is gone.   It becomes the South to determine how far its safety will admit of concession.   The stand should
be made there.   None can mistake the *anti-slavery* growth — it has
no resting place.   The cry is onward!   When was there ever a step
backward in its history?   It will sweep over Mr. Webster as the
whirlwind sweeps over the reed.   Every concession made to it will
induce a more imperious tone — every success will embolden and
pave the way for a new and higher triumph.   "Will you interpose
the Constitution?"   There is a voice higher than the Constitution!
Will you make a compromise and hold up its sacred assurances?
Majorities rule — numbers have assumed the sway — the edict of
Congress goes out upon the land, backed by its fleets and its armies,
potent as the nod of the autocrat of Russia, and unalterable as the
law of the Medes and the Persians.   The path is clear, the end
undisputed.   The protection of the national flag will be withheld
from the slave, in his passage from one port to another in the Union.
His arrest in a free State impossible.   Slavery will go by the board
in the District of Columbia — in the forts and navy yards.   The
trade between the States will be prohibited.   The final act is not
yet, but soon.   There is a precedent in the British Parliament and
the West Indies.   *They will use the precedent*.   We know the rest

[THE DELIVERANCE OF THE SLAVE SHADRACH IN BOSTON] [1]

The Liberator, February, 1851

"The head and front of the offending," in this instance — what is it? A sudden rush of a score or two of unarmed friends of equal liberty — an uninjurious deliverance of the oppressed out of the hands of the oppressor — the quiet transportation of a slave out of this slavery-ruled land to the free soil of Upper Canada! Nobody injured, nobody wronged, but simply a chattel transformed into a man, and conducted to a spot whereon he can glorify God in his body and spirit, which are his!

And yet, how all the fiends of the pit are writhing and yelling! Not tormented before their time, but just at the right time. Truly, "devils with devils damned firm concord hold!" The President of the United States is out with his Proclamation of Terror, conveying it to us in tones of thunder and on the wings of the lightning; even as though in the old Bay State chaos had come again, and a million of foreign myrmidons were invading our shores! A poor, hunted, entrapped fugitive slave is dexterously removed from the courtroom, and the whole land is shaken! A hundred free white citizens of the North may be thrown into prison, or tarred and feathered, or compelled to flee for their lives at the South, on suspicion of being morally averse to the slave system; but who cares? A thousand colored seamen of the North may be incarcerated in loathsome cells, and compelled to pay for their imprisonment, though guiltless of crime, and even sold into slavery on the auction-block at the South; but whose breast burns with indignation, or what voice calls for redress? Official State Commissioners, venerable for their years and esteemed for their worth, sent to the South to test the constitutionality of such acts, are driven away by lawless violence, and not allowed to remain on the soil; but where is the Presidential proclamation calling on the people to obey the laws and observe their Constitutional obligations? But a solitary slave in Boston is plucked as a brand from the burning, and forthwith a Cabinet council is held, and behold a menacing proclamation, bearing the signature of Millard Fillmore, President of the United States! Henry Clay — with one foot in the grave, and just ready to have both body and soul cast into hell — as if eager to make his damnation doubly sure, rises in the United

---

[1] The fugitive slave, Shadrach, was rescued in Boston from the United States deputy marshal on March 16, 1851, this being the first important Northern defiance of the new Fugitive Slave Act. The incident showed that in Massachusetts and other Northern states the law would be enforced with difficulty if at all. Congress took up the affair, and President Fillmore issued a proclamation demanding obedience to the Act. William Lloyd Garrison here angrily replies to it.

States Senate and proposes an inquiry into the expediency of passing yet another law, by which everyone who shall dare peep or mutter against the execution of the Fugitive Slave Bill shall have his life crushed out!

UNCLE TOM'S CABIN[1]

The Liberator, March 26, 1852

In the execution of her very difficult task, Mrs. Stowe has displayed rare descriptive powers, a familiar acquaintance with slavery under its best and its worst phases, uncommon moral and philosophical acumen, great facility of thought and expression, and feelings and emotions of the strongest character. Intimate as we have been, for a score of years, with the features and operations of the slave system, and often as we have listened to the recitals of its horrors from the lips of the poor hunted fugitives, we confess to the frequent moistening of our eyes, the making of our heart grow liquid as water, and the trembling of every nerve within us, in the perusal of the incidents and scenes so vividly depicted in her pages. The effect of such a work upon all intelligent and humane minds coming in contact with it, and especially upon the rising generation in its plastic condition, to awaken the strongest compassion for the oppressed and the utmost abhorrence of the system which grinds them to dust, cannot be estimated; it must be prodigious, and therefore eminently serviceable in the tremendous conflict now waged for the immediate and entire suppression of slavery upon American soil.

The appalling liabilities which constantly impend over such slaves as have "kind and indulgent masters," are thrillingly illustrated in various personal narratives; especially in that of "Uncle Tom," over whose fate every reader will drop the scalding tear, and for whose character the highest reverence will be felt. No insult, no outrage, no suffering, could ruffle the Christlike meekness of his spirit, or shake the steadfastness of his faith. Towards his merciless oppressors he cherished no animosity, and breathed nothing of retaliation. Like his Lord and Master, he was willing to be "led as a lamb to the slaughter," returning blessing for cursing and anxious only for the salvation of his enemies. His character is sketched with great power and rare religious perception. It triumphantly exemplifies the nature, tendency, and results of Christian non-resistance.

[1] Following serial publication in the Washington *National Era,* "Uncle Tom's Cabin" was issued in book form in March, 1852. William Lloyd Garrison's editorial is an expression not only of his admiration for it, but of his strong pacifist convictions.

We are curious to know whether Mrs. Stowe is a believer in the duty of non-resistance for the white man, under all possible outrage and peril, as well as for the black man; whether she is for self-defence on her own part, or that of her husband or friends or country, in case of malignant assault, or whether she impartially disarms all mankind in the name of Christ, be the danger or suffering what it may. We are curious to know this, because our opinion of her as a religious teacher would be greatly strengthened or lessened as the inquiry might terminate. That the slaves of the South ought, "if smitten on the one cheek, to turn the other also," — to repudiate all carnal weapons, shed no blood, "be obedient to their masters," wait for a peaceful deliverance, and abstain from all insurrectionary movements — is everywhere taken for granted because the victims are black. *They* cannot be animated by a Christian spirit and yet return blow for blow, or conspire for the destruction of their oppressors. *They* are required by the Bible to put away all wrath, to submit to every conceivable outrage without resistance, to suffer with Christ if they would reign with Him. None of *their* advocates may seek to inspire *them* to imitate the example of the Greeks, the Poles, the Hungarians, our Revolutionary sires. . . . But for those whose skin is of a different complexion, the case is materially altered. When they are spit upon and buffeted, outraged, and oppressed, talk not to them of a non-resisting Saviour — it is fanaticism! Talk not of overcoming evil with goodness — it is madness! Talk not of peacefully submitting to chains and stripes — it is base servility! Talk not of servants being obedient to their masters — let the blood of tyrants flow! How is this to be explained or reconciled? Is there one law of submission and non-resistance for the black man, and another law of rebellion and conflict for the white man? When it is the whites who are trodden in the dust, does Christ justify them in taking up arms to vindicate their rights? And when it is the blacks who are thus treated, does Christ require them to be patient, harmless, long-suffering, and forgiving? Are there two Christs?

[MRS. STOWE'S PERNICIOUS SENTIMENTALITY][1]

De Bow's Review, March, 1853

It is useless for us to tell the benevolent ladies and gentlemen who have undertaken to instruct us in our catechism of humanity that they are entirely ignorant of the condition of the negro. "Uncle Tom's Cabin" tells them differently. It is useless for us to tell them

[1] While this utterance may be regarded as editorial, and was accompanied by an explicit endorsement by the editor himself, it was written by an anonymous woman contributor to the *Review*, and not by James D. B. De Bow himself.

that our slaves are not "interdicted education in the truths of the gospel and the ordinances of Christianity;" it is useless for us to repeat that their family ties and social affections are respected and indulged in a greater degree than those of any laboring class in the world. "Uncle Tom's Cabin" says differently; and the negrophilists have very nearly reached the point of pronouncing sentence of excommunication, on the ground of infidelity, against all who dispute the authenticity of so high an authority. It is useless for us to point to the comparative census of the nations of the earth; it is useless for us to show that in none are the tables of crime, of deformity, and insanity so low as in our slave population. Mrs. Stowe and Uncle Tom! Mrs. Stowe and Uncle Tom! Mrs. Stowe and Uncle Tom! ding, ding, dong. What is the use of reasoning, what is the use of facts, when those who should hear us deafen themselves with this eternal "ding, dong" of superstitious prejudice and pharisaical cant? As regards the condition of our slaves, compared with that of the white population of our own free States (than which, avowedly, no population in the world enjoys greater advantages), ten minutes' investigation of our late census returns, with about so much arithmetical knowledge as any boy of ten years old can command, will suffice to show that, for every insane slave, there are from eight to ten insane whites; and that this is not an exception resulting from any physical peculiarity of the negro, is proved by the fact that among the *free* blacks the proportion of insane is, within a very small fraction, equal to that among the whites. This fact alone speaks volumes. The number of deaf mutes and of blind, though the disproportion is not so great, shows largely in favor of the slave, and are worth dwelling upon as indicating the comforts of his position; but, would men consent to open their eyes and hearts to the truth, volumes of argument and cartloads of Uncle Tom's Cabins would not weigh a feather against the indisputable fact which we have just noted of the disparity in the numbers of the insane presented in the different positions referred to.

A GREAT OLD SUNSET[1]

The *Ohio Statesman*, 1853

What a stormful sunset was that of last night! How glorious the storm and how splendid the setting of the sun! We do not remember ever to have seen the like on our round globe.

[1] Reprinted all over the country, this long-famous editorial by S. S. Cox gave him his sobriquet of "Sunset" Cox. It is a fair example of the tawdry rhetoric which innumerable readers of the time thought really admirable. The *Ohio Statesman* was published in Columbus. Cox, after retiring from the editorship, served for many years as a Democratic Representative in Congress, first from Ohio and later from New York.

The scene opened in the West, with a whole horizon full of golden interpenetrating luster, which colored the foliage and brightened every object into its own rich dyes. The colors grew deeper and deeper until the golden luster was transfused into a storm cloud full of the finest lightnings, which leaped into dazzling zigzags all around over the city.

The wind arose with fury, the slender shrubs and giant trees made obeisance to its majesty. Some even snapped before its force. The strawberry beds and grass plots turned up their whites to see Zephirus march by. As the rain came and the pools formed and the gutters hurried away, thunder rolled grandly and the firebells caught the excitement and rang with hearty chorus.

The south and the east received the copious showers, and the west all at once brightened up in a long polished belt of azure, worthy of a Sicilian sky. Presently a cloud appeared in the azure belt in the form of a castellated city. It became more vivid, revealing strange forms of peerless fanes and alabaster temples and glories rare and grand in this mundane sphere. It reminded us of Wordsworth's splendid verse in his "Excursion":

> *The appearance, instantly disclosed,*
> *Was of a mighty city — boldly say*
> *A wilderness of building, sinking far*
> *And self-withdrawn into a boundless depth,*
> *Far sinking into splendour — without end!*

But the city vanished, only to give place to another isle, where the most beautiful forms of foliage appear, imaging a paradise in the distant and purified air. The sun, wearied of the elemental commotion, sank behind the green plains of the West. The "great eye in heaven," however, went not down without a dark brow hanging over its departed light. The rich flush of the unearthly light had passed, and the rain had ceased when the solemn church bells pealed, the laughter of children rang out loud, and, joyous after the storm, was heard with the carol of birds; while the forked and purple weapon of the skies still darted illumination around the Starling College, trying to rival its angles and leap into its dark windows.

Candles were lighted. The piano strikes up. We feel it good to have a home, good to be on earth where such revelations of beauty and power may be made.

THE RASCALS AT WASHINGTON[1]

New York *Tribune*, January 26, 1854

If the traitorous men at Washington who are plotting the surrender to slavery of the free territory west of the Mississippi believed that a majority of the North would fail to sustain the movement, they would instantly cease their clamor and skulk back and we should hear no more about it.

But they have adopted the belief that the passage of the compromise measures of 1850, and the triumphant election of Frank Pierce, have taken all the spirit out of the North, and that the mass of the voters are now ready to wink at any party iniquity, and sustain any party measure, whatever its iniquity. . . .

There has been no time during the last seven years when the Whig and Freesoil parties have not been in a clear majority in nearly all the Northern States. The only ground upon which any doubt can be thrown on this presumption is the result of the last presidential election. But the vote of the Freesoil party in that contest was only partial, being but the ineffectual remonstrance (and so felt to be) of the more earnest of the Freesoilers against the settlement of the Compromise measures. And the vote of the Whigs in the North was notoriously the vote of a party divided against itself. It was a contest utterly balked by cross purposes. The presidential election of 1848, and the congressional elections of 1850, furnish the only grounds of any just judgment as to the real strength of the anti-slavery sentiment in the country; and these elections justify the statement that in every Free State that sentiment, whenever it could be fairly reached, would prove to be predominant.

Assuming this to be so, the only question to be answered is, whether that sentiment can be aroused and consolidated and brought to bear in solid phalanx against the atrocious proposition in consequence. The fools in Washington believe it cannot. We believe it can. And we further believe that this is by no means the whole strength of the North that will be brought into the field against this infamous project. We shall have the whole conservative force of the Free States of all parties against it. We shall have all the men who do not believe in violating contracts nor in repudiating solemn engagements on the side of earnest opposition. The moral stamina of the Free States will be set against the measure. Fair dealing and honest purposes will everywhere frown upon such faithlessness and

[1] Stephen A. Douglas's Kansas-Nebraska Bill, repealing the Missouri Compromise, was introduced into the Senate on January 4, 1854. Throwing open all the Territories to slaves, and leaving the question of their ultimate exclusion to "squatter sovereignty," or the vote of the actual settlers, it intensely angered all Free Soilers. Greeley's editorial is a scorching expression of that anger.

fraud. Sober-minded men who have leaned to the side of the South in the late contests, on the ground that the Abolitionists were the aggressors, will turn and resist this movement as a gross outrage and aggression on the part of the South.

IS IT A FRAUD?[1]

New York *Tribune*, February 15, 1854

We are charged by some of the active and open promoters of as well as by the more cowardly and timid connivers at, Douglas' meditated repudiation of the Missouri Compromise, with using harsh and uncharitable language with reference to that scheme and its abettors. Our answer to the charge is, that no other language than that we use would faithfully express our sentiments or do justice to our convictions. Were it simply a bad measure, we might speak of it calmly and measuredly; but as an act of deliberate bad faith, impelled by the most sordid motives and threatening the most calamitous results, we must treat it as we do other gigantic perfidies and crimes. The conflagration it threatens is not to be extinguished by jets of rosewater.

Is it a fraud? That is the first question to be considered. Did the country, did Congress, did Mr. Douglas, understand when the Adjustment of 1850 was under consideration, that its success would repeal the Missouri Compromise and open the Territories from Missouri, Iowa, and Minnesota, westward to the Rocky Mountains, to the introduction of human slavery? That is a question which certainly admits of a definitive answer. If that *were* the understanding, then there *must* remain some contemporaneous evidence of the fact. It cannot be that this tremendous consequence was involved in the Adjustment of 1850, and yet that no Southern advocate thereof, though sorely pressed to justify his course against the assaults of Jeff Davis, Soule, Mason, Hunter, Butler, the Richmond *Examiner*, and so on, ever deemed it worth his while to mention this virtual repeal of the Missouri Restriction as among the advantages gained for slavery by the Compromise, and that no Northern Seward, Hale, Dayton, Beecher, or other anti-compromiser, ever enumerated it among the losses to Freedom by that settlement. In view of the notorious, acknowledged, unbroken silence in 1850 of all parties upon this point, is not the fundamental assumption of Douglas & Co. not only a fraud, but one most impudent, shameless, audacious?

[1] As the historian Rhodes says, this editorial bears in its autobiographical passages plain evidences of Greeley's authorship; and it is an unanswerable exposure of the hollowness of Douglas's claim that the Compromise of 1850 had been really a repeal of the Missouri Compromise, and that his own bill merely underlined that repeal. Greeley utterly destroys this argument.

Consider how sternly this Compromise was resisted by Calhoun, Butler, and every Representative from South Carolina — by the two Senators and most of the Democratic Representatives from Virginia — by the delegations from Arkansas and Mississippi (Senator Foote only, we believe, excepted) — by Venable and Yulee, and nearly every extreme pro-Slavery man in Congress. What did they all mean, what *could* they mean, if the adjustment they sought so savagely was to have the effect which Mr. Douglas now ascribes to it?

We were among the first, after it became evident that no bill affirming the Wilmot Proviso could be carried through the Senate, to suggest and advocate the devising of some practicable middle ground whereon moderate men of the North and South might unite in effecting an organization of the newly acquired Territories. Though we did not approve the connection therewith of topics palpably extraneous, such as the rendition of Fugitives and the District Slave-Trade, we did support Mr. Clay's Omnibus Bill defining the boundary of Texas, admitting California as a Free State, and organizing New Mexico and Utah as Territories without restriction as to slavery. We know Henry Clay did not deceive us with regard to *his* views and purposes in urging that Compromise; we are morally sure that no idea of repealing or "superseding" the Missouri Compromise entered into *his* mind. Others may have been deeper in his confidence; but he deceived no man, and he discussed the whole subject freely with us, and ever regarded it as one wherein the Territories were to enure to Free Labor, and that the practical business was to save the South from all needless and wanton humiliation. And so Senator Butler of South Carolina, when the Senate adjourned after defeating the Omnibus, said to us as he passed exultingly from the chamber, "I don't wonder at *your* support of this bill, for it would give you all you seek" — that is, the practical exclusion of slavery from the new Territories. How would he have been astounded by the information that the passage of that bill would repeal the Missouri Restriction, and open all the remaining Louisiana Territory to slavery!

But look at the Douglas proposition in another aspect — that of the numerous and serious transformations to which it has been subjected by its author since he first introduced it. First, it was a mere organization of Nebraska which quietly and ambiguously ignored the Missouri Restriction; next, it declared that Restriction "superseded" by the Adjustment of 1850 — which if true need not have been thrust into an act of Congress; and so it has been worked over and over, until at last we have a pointblank proposal to repeal the Restriction — but a proposal with a glaring falsehood appended by

way of apology — or as Truman Smith forcibly terms it, "an enact
ment with a peroration." Is this the way honest and straightforward
enactments are urged?

Suppose you were standing in your garden, and a rough and
ready half-acquaintance should stalk in, make himself extra familiar
and meanwhile busy himself with eating up half of some rare and
precious fruit which you had just brought to maturity, then cram
the residue into his capacious pockets and bid you a cordial good
day; you would have your own opinion of his breeding, but you
could not consider him a thief. But suppose you were sitting out of
sight in an arbor, and should see such a customer crawling and
sidling up to your rear garden wall, dodging from the shelter of one
shrub to another, and worming himself along the sinuosities of a
Virginia fence, until he finally got within reach of your Seckels or
Apricots — you might let him have a stone or a charge of peas with
a moral certainty of hitting nothing short of a scoundrel.

It is our earnest conviction that the bill of Douglas, in so far as
it proposes to disturb the Missouri Compromise, involves gross
perfidy, and is bolstered up by the most audacious false pretenses
and frauds. If we are wrong in this conviction, let it be shown, and
we stand condemned; but if we are right in our view of it, who can
truly say that we speak of the plot and its contrivers more harshly
than they deserve?

[STEPHEN A. DOUGLAS AS THE VOLUNTEER EXECUTIONER]

New York *Tribune*, February 22, 1854

Some years ago, several localities of the South were terribly
agitated on the subject of Abolitionism. It was at the time that
Mr. Van Buren sanctioned the opening of private letters and pack-
ages by postmasters in their search for "incendiary documents."
In a place we care not to name the opposition to the anti-slavery
sentiment ran so high that a Committee of Safety was appointed,
and before this dread and irresponsible tribunal were arraigned all
who could in any way be suspected of entertaining anti-slavery
sentiments. Our soul sickens at the scenes of brutality that were
witnessed there; but the reign of terror was for the moment triumphant. . . . A poor, miserable, half-witted and degraded wretch,
who consorted with the negroes because he found no other willing
associates, and what is most singular, a native born citizen of the
very place we write about, was arrested and tried for using inflammatory expressions before the negroes. The poor creature could
not comprehend his situation; born and reared in the place, he had

no idea that any harm was intended him; and he listened to the charges on the trial with a silly laugh, and heard himself condemned to be hanged as if it were a joke.

The moment that sentence was pronounced, there went up a clamor for the execution, and from the tribunal the prisoner was hurried to the fatal tree. In a few moments a limb was selected, the rope adjusted, and the cart was driven beneath it. So far, all had been action, and consequently there was a want of time for reflection; but the moment that an executioner was needed, the moment that the fearful responsibility of taking life could not be distributed out among the multitude, there was a holding back, an irresolution, a fear that the act was not right.

In the meanwhile the victim sat on the edge of the cart, his hands tied behind his back, almost able to see the miserable cabin in which he was born, silent — speechless with terror. His life was trembling in the balance. A moment more and there would have gone up in the crowd a cry, "Let him go," "Let him go;" but at this critical moment a person unknown to the crowd was seen to move toward the cart. Springing upon it and rudely seizing the dangling rope, he turned round to the astonished spectators and said: "If none of you will act as hangman, I will. Damn the Abolitionists!" In another instant the fatal cord was adjusted, the cart driven off, and there was seen suspended between heaven and earth the trembling— the dead — form of an innocent man. The body in due time was cut down and hastily buried beneath the fatal tree, and the crowd dispersed with horror depicted upon their faces, and dark and before unknown passions of destruction awakened in their hearts.

Now who was this hangman? Who was this fierce defender of the peculiar institution? Was he a Southern man? No. Was he a citizen identified with the South? No. It was on the contrary a Northern man, from a free State — in fact, one who had been but two days in the place. It seemed as if, suspecting his own principles, revolting in his heart at slavery and afraid that in the excitement of the hour he might next be arraigned, he took this fearful and terrible office of executioner in order to place himself, as he supposed, on "high Southern ground." Thus, by one glaring act, wherein he violated his conscience — his early education — every law, in fact, of God and man — he thought to identify himself as a defender of slavery, and have his soundness placed above suspicion.

And here is to be seen reflected the true picture of Mr. Douglas's turpitude. Southern men may have in the madness of the hour conceived such iniquity as is embodied in the Nebraska bill. They may have prepared the halter for the neck of the Missouri Compromise — but the last fatal act would never have been undertaken had not the Senator from Illinois volunteered to act as executioner, been willing to mount the scaffold, and call down the infamy of murdering liberty upon his own head.

Thus it has ever been in Congress whenever the rights of man have been violated. Southerners, from the necessity of defending their local interests, are compelled to advocate principles repugnant to their consciences, but they would never press them upon the people of the North if there had not always been volunteers, like Douglas, willing to do the foul work that Southern men themselves revolt at, while feeling toward these ready tools of tyranny a contempt that is ever extended toward the traitor, whatever may be the advantages they reap from the treason enacted.

[THE INTOLERABLE KANSAS-NEBRASKA ACT]

New York *Tribune*, May 18, 1854

"We are in the midst of a revolution," said Mr. Clay on a memorable occasion. We are in the midst of a revolution, is our response to the proceedings at Washington on the Nebraska bill. The attempted passage of this measure is the first great effort of slavery to take American freedom directly by the throat. Hitherto it has but asked to be allowed to grow and expand side by side with that freedom, until now, at what is believed a favorable moment, it springs from its lair and clutches at the life of its political associate in the government. It engages in a *coup d'état*, and by the aid of Northern traitors to liberty attempts the most intolerable usurpation.

Should success attend the movement, it is tantamount to a civil revolution and an open declaration of war between freedom and slavery on the North American continent, to be ceaselessly waged until one or the other party finally and absolutely triumphs.

If Nebraska passes, the two parties must immediately marshal themselves in hostile array. The North will go on as it has done, to oppose every step toward making the Northwest pasture-ground for African slavery. It will oppose the introduction of slavery into Kansas and Nebraska as much after the passage of the bill as before, and should it gain foothold there, it will make open and direct war upon the institution within their limits now and henceforth. It will fight against the admission into the Union of either as a slave State, and in doing this it will necessarily be compelled to carry the war into Africa, and will fight against the admission of new slave States from any quarter whatever. Soundness upon this question will be made a test in the election of every Northern Representative. The popular branch of the government must be speedily purified, and no man elected thereto from the North who is not firmly committed against the admission of more slave States. A President must be elected by the Free States who will cordially support and earnestly respond to these views. There will be no other course but this open to the Free States, excepting one of abject, slavish submission to the iron rod of the Southern slave-drivers, and the more despicable domination of Northern flunkeyism. The passage of the Nebraska bill will arouse and consolidate the most gigantic, determined, and overwhelming party for freedom that the world ever saw. We may already see in the future its gathering groups on every hill side, in every valley, and on every prairie in the free States. We hear the deep and ominous murmur of the earnest voices of its myriad slowly-moving masses. We behold in their faces the unalterable determination of their purposes in behalf of freedom. We see the gigantic array gradually approach, closing its thick ranks, and moving onward with a force that no merely human power or human institution can resist. It sweeps along with the force of the tempest or the tornado. The spirit of liberty animates, the spirit of progress impels, and a spirit of solemn religious duty inspires and leavens the whole mass. This invincible army bears aloft the motto, "God with us!" Its immediate duties are plain. We have indicated them in the gross. Details will adjust themselves. What ulterior duties may be in store for this great party of Liberty time only can discover. The decisive events of history come but slowly. They have their source, as the great rivers have theirs, in the little rills that trickle in the hidden recesses of the plain and the mountain. But we cannot hide from our vision the vital fact that this party, once aroused, and consolidated on a platform sufficiently wide and substantial to afford a sure basis for its operation, such as the passage of the Kansas-Nebraska bill will furnish, will not hesitate in its course, or fail in its duties, however radical and sweeping those duties may become.

For the mole-eyed squad of little Northern men of Washington who are accidentally the controlling political force of the government at this junction of public affairs, lighting the torches of civil discord and vainly dreaming that no conflagration is to ensue, we have but pity for their blindness and fatuity. They are under the lead of men of gross and grovelling purposes, base instincts, and narrow vision. They are but blind followers of the blind.

To avert the throes and convulsions which must inevitably follow this infamous act, we have labored and shall labor, and as a last resort to this end, if there shall prove to be a majority of the House in favor of the final consummation of this scheme, we advocate the determined resistance of the minority to that consummation.

This bold and astounding assault upon the cause of liberty and of progress should be met by Northern representatives in Congress in the spirit with which freedom in its most lofty mood has ever resisted oppression. It is a solemn duty which devolves upon them, without agency of theirs, to bring about the crisis that enjoins their action. We know that it is easier to shirk it than to discharge it. But in so clear a case it were culpable to refuse to engage in the only procedure which gives any hope of arresting the infamous measure. For whatever results shall follow such a course we cheerfully court our share of the responsibility. Whatever that result shall be, we unhesitatingly say, Let it come. There are greater evils than a conflict between two parties in the legislative branch of the government — greater evils than temporarily blocking the wheels of public affairs, or than producing a shock which shall precipitately send the members of Congress home to their constituents. And clearly among them, in our estimation, are the fatal and far-reaching consequences of the passage of the Nebraska bill.

SLAVE–CATCHER'S TRIUMPH[1]

New York *Tribune*, June 3, 1854

The fugitive Burns is delivered into slavery. A man as much entitled to his freedom as any other man on the soil of Massachusetts has been seized in that State by other men, manacled, and consigned to hopeless bondage. The people of that great Commonwealth, containing a million of inhabitants, every one of them knowing the act to be a gross and unpardonable exercise of tyrannical power, a criminal outrage upon the inalienable rights of man, have suffered it to be done without interposing force to prevent it. That there was opposition to the act is seen, however, in the means employed for its consummation. Burns was not torn from the soil of freedom and consigned to slavery by any ordinary methods of imprisoning malefactors. He was not taken by a constable or sheriff, or even a whole police force of a great city. All these were insufficient. It took all the police of Boston, three companies of United States troops, one company of cavalry, and an entire battalion of militia, together

---

[1] Anthony Burns, a fugitive slave, was arrested in Boston on May 24, 1854; and a futile attempt at rescue, led by Theodore Parker, Wendell Phillips, and Thomas Wentworth Higginson, was made on the night of the 26th. On June 2 the slave was marched to the wharf through a crowd of fifty thousand jeering and groaning people, and placed on board a Federal revenue cutter to be taken back to the South. To guard the streets that day the authorities used the Boston police, twenty-two companies of Massachusetts soldiers, a battalion of Federal artillery, four platoons of marines, and a large civil posse. The cost of remanding the prisoner southward was nearly $40,000. The episode was an impressive demonstration of the revolt of the North against the Fugitive Slave Act.

with several pieces of artillery, to secure the capture of this citizen and remand him to slavery. It is said that this was an experimental case of slave-catching, got up especially for the purpose of showing how readily the North would acquiesce in the Nebraska bill, and succumb to the aggressions of the slave power. We trust the managers of the performance are satisfied. What do they think of the prospect of performing the same feat over again?

This cowardly capture of an innocent man, and consigning him to the horrors of a servile bondage, necessarily provokes some reflection. We desire to ask the principals in the affair, the leading Nebraska conspirators, and the Executive Government at Washington, what was the use of the ostentatious display of artillery charged with grape-shot that were planted in Court Square on the occasion? Do they not know that the discharge of that cannon upon the Boston multitude there assembled would have been the signal for fifty thousand men of Massachusetts to fly to arms? Do they not know that they did not dare discharge that artillery upon the friends of freedom in that commonwealth? Why, then, did they indulge in this piece of intimidation? Was it for the luxury of an unmeaning taunt? It may be that they cannot see that through all this Burns trial the public peace has been slumbering upon the edge of a volcano. If they cannot, perhaps they had better devote themselves to a closer scrutiny of the existing state of the popular pulse.

There has been the most imminent danger of a violent and armed outbreak during this late tragedy. And suppose it had taken place? Who would have quelled it? Who would have restored the public peace when once broken? Burns has been taken away, but let us tell the slave power that nothing has been accomplished by that capture but to deepen the resolution that slaves shall not be taken on the soil of the Free States. Nothing has been accomplished by it but to arouse the Northern mind to a determination to resistance to such scenes in the future. This time men have been unarmed. Another time it may be otherwise. We are but at the beginning of the resistance to the arrogant domination of the slave power. Things are but in the bud, in the gristle. Nothing has been done in this case but to declare against the proceeding. Not an arrangement to rescue the fugitive has been made. Nothing which savored of earnest resistance has been attempted. But it will not be so always. Some such event as a forcible rescue will yet take place, and when that takes place in Massachusetts, the fugitive will not be sent to Canada. He will be held upon her soil, and a note of defiance sounded to let them come and take him who dare.

The future is big with events such as these unless something is done to allay the public excitement produced by the proceedings of the slave power, backed by our rulers. The fugitive slave law, as it now stands, can no longer be enforced without jeopardizing the public tranquillity to an alarming extent. We again call upon Congress to give their earnest and immediate attention to this grave subject. If there can be no repeal of the law at this session, which we think is quite certain, let us at least have the trial by jury. A modification of this sort is absolutely demanded unless the country is to be precipitated upon insurrection, and perchance civil war.

[THE ERROR OF ARMING THE KANSAS FREE–SOILERS][1]

The Liberator, April 4, 1856.

What are the facts respecting Kansas? Briefly these: "squatter sovereignty" has turned out to be repeated invasions of the Territory by armed bandits from Missouri, who have successfully made it a conquered province, manufactured a Territorial Government, enacted a code of laws worthy of pandemonium, and trampled the civil and political rights of the *bona-fide* settlers under their feet; and for one sole object — to make Kansas a slave State. Hence the appeal, in self-defence, to the people of the free States for men, money, and arms; hence the justification for the employment of Sharp's rifles against the "border ruffians." It is said to be a struggle for liberty; and earnest appeals are made to the hearts and the pockets of all who desire to see liberty victorious.

We burn with indignation at the insults and outrages to which the settlers have thus been subjected, and acknowledge their position to be a most trying and perilous one. But we deny, in the first place, that they are acting upon principle, or contending for equal rights. They resent as a foul slander the charge of being abolitionists; they proclaim a truce on their part with slavery where it now exists; they are pro-slavery in spirit and position, with regard to the millions who are now grinding in the Southern house of bondage; they have meanly and wickedly proscribed every man of color, and made it illegal for him to be a resident in the Territory; they do not object to slave-hunting on their soil, but recognize it as a constitutional obligation which they have no disposition to annul; they go for *all* the pro-slavery compromises of the American Constitution; they are contending for their own rights *as white men*, not for the rights of all, without distinction of caste or color; they have pursued a shuffling and compromising policy throughout;

[1] William Lloyd Garrison wanted to see Kansas free soil; but he did not believe in fighting to make it so.

hey have consented to make the existence of liberty or slavery in
he Territory dependent upon the will of the majority, fairly expressed, and *to abide by the result.* The retribution now meted out to
hem is divinely ordered: having sown the wind, they are reaping
he whirlwind. It is for them to say to one another, as did the
treacherous brethren of Joseph: "We are verily guilty concerning
ur brother, in that we saw the anguish of his soul when he be-
ought us, and we would not hear; therefore is this distress come
pon us." And while they are yet standing, in common with the
reat body of the American people, with their feet upon the necks
f four millions of chattel slaves — and while, to propitiate the pro-
lavery spirit, they have banished from their presence all free colored
migrants, at the very time they are complaining of having their
wn rights wrested from them — with what face can they ask for
he sympathy and coöperation of those who are battling for the
ause of freedom on a worldwide basis? "Let the dead bury their
ead."

Again, if such men are deserving of generous sympathy, and ought
o be supplied with arms, are not the crushed and bleeding slaves
t the South a million times more deserving of pity and succor?
Vhy not, first of all, take measures to furnish them with Sharp's
ifles? Their wrongs are beyond description; in comparison with
vhich, those of the people of Kansas are utterly insignificant. Why
train at a gnat, and swallow a camel? If every "border ruffian"
nvading Kansas deserves to be shot, much more does every slave-
nolder, by the same rule; for the former is guilty only of attempting
oolitical subjection to his will, while the latter is the destroyer of
ll human rights, and there is none to deliver. Who will go for
rming our slave population?

[THE ABOLITIONISTS AND THE FRÉMONT CANDIDACY]

The Liberator, November 4, 1856

To these inquiries [Horace Greeley's question "whether you will
oersonally vote, and advise those who agree with you to vote, for
Col. Frémont"] we shall make categorical replies. 1. Personally,
ve shall not vote for Frémont. 2. We do not advise those who agree
vith us to vote for him, because he goes for perpetuating "the
Jnion as it is" — we for its immediate dissolution as "a covenant
vith death." 3. The language attributed to us by such lying
ournals as the *Pennsylvanian* and the Boston *Post,* being torn from
ts connection and basely garbled, does not truly represent our views.
Ve said: "If there were no moral barrier to our voting" (but there

is), "and we had a million of votes to bestow, we should cast them all for Frémont as against Buchanan and Fillmore" — not because he is an abolitionist or a disunionist (for he is neither, any more than was Washington, Jefferson, Webster, Clay, or Jackson, occupying precisely their ground), but because he is for the non-extension of slavery, in common with the great body of the people of the North, whose attachment to the Union amounts to idolatry.

Well, the Presidential struggle will terminate on Tuesday next with all its forgeries, tricks, shams, lies, and slanders. *Laus Deo!* Whatever may be the result, upon our banner will still be inscribed in ineffaceable characters the motto: "No Union with Slaveholders!"

IMMIGRATION — POSITION OF THE DEMOCRATIC PARTY[1]

Richmond *Enquirer*, April, 1855

Not to arrest immigration by absolute prohibition, but to suffer foreigners to come hither and then to deny them the privileges of citizenship, is so foolish and fatal a policy that it is difficult to understand · how any man of ordinary intelligence can assent to it. A repeal of the laws of naturalization will not sensibly diminish the flow of immigration. By so harsh and illiberal a policy, we may repel some of the prouder, brighter, and more aspiring spirits, who might seek freedom and distinction in this country; but as the vast mass of immigrants come here only in quest of peace and bread, they would not be driven away by exclusion from office or the polls. The tide would continue to flow with undiminished impetuosity, but the character of the immigration would be sadly deteriorated. And the effect of the Know-Nothing policy would be such that in a few years the community would be divided into two distinct and aristocratic classes of privileged patricians and disfranchised plebeians. The native would be haughty and overbearing, from a sense of personal consequence and the distinction of caste. The foreign-born population, detached and dissociated from the community; exasperated by consciousness of wrong and degradation; bound by no interest to the state; driven into compact array by the blows of oppression, and animated by exclusive sympathies and hopes, would be indeed an alien people in a foreign country, and instead of being, as they are now, an element of wealth in peace and of strength in war, they would become a source of distrac-

[1] During 1855 the Whig Party and the Know-Nothing Party seemed drawing closer in the North, and in 1856 they nominated the same Presidential candidate, Millard Fillmore. The Democratic Party was at pains to make its hospitable attitude toward newcomers from Europe clear. The *Enquirer's* editorial is a good Southern expression of this attitude, and an attack on Know Nothing policy.

tion, disease, confusion, and inconceivable calamity. If, therefore, our foreign population be a pest, let us not strengthen them for evil, while we inflame their passions and exasperate revolt. The true policy is either to mitigate the evil, or else eradicate it by some sweeping and efficient remedy. Rather than pursue the insane policy of Know-Nothingism, it would be better by arbitrary enactment to expel our foreign-born fellow-citizens from the country, and to prohibit further immigration.

But the Democratic party denies that the foreign population is a pest. Without regard to the accidental abuses of immigration or naturalization, we contend that our foreign-born fellow-citizens have contributed incalculably to the power and glory of the country — that they have imparted a prodigious impulse to the development of its resources and to its progress in wealth and refinement. On the other hand, they have done nothing to retard the growth or to dishonor the name of America. Why, then, the proposition to proscribe and degrade them? Is it from the apprehension that they would ultimately subvert the liberties of the country? To this suggestion the Democratic party responds, "Sufficient unto the day is the evil thereof." When our foreign-born fellow-citizens manifest a disposition to overthrow the government and destroy the country, it will be time enough to fetter them with disabilities and to treat them as traitors. Meanwhile we maintain that any tendency to excessive immigration will be corrected by the irresistible laws of nature, or rather by the kind care of Providence. So long as the tide of immigration flows hither, it shows that the country is in want of labor — and when that is not the case, the current will turn without an artificial impulse, and run in another direction. The law of supply and demand, which is, in political economy, what the principle of gravitation is in the physical universe, will correct the evils of immigration. Indeed, we may already perceive that the tide of immigration is ebbing, and beginning to flow in the contrary direction.

THE PROSPECT FOR KANSAS [1]

New York *Tribune*, April 18, 1855

The unmitigated villains who have just overrun Kansas aim to gain the support of the more moderate and sensible men of the South by laying before them calculations showing that slavery

---

[1] During 1855 the Kansas struggle grew rapidly in intensity. Both the slavery forces and the Free Soilers formed governments; Emigrant Aid Societies in the North did everything in their power to promote the flow of settlers. When Greeley wrote his editorial, a legislative election had just been held (March 30), to which about 5,000 Missourians crowded from across the boundary, casting illegal ballots and carrying everything before them. The Northern press was naturally filled with indigation by this high-handed outrage.

there must be profitable. These calculations are not, however, of character very speedily to captivate men who are looking to their private interests, or likely to induce any very sudden rush, or indeed any rush at all, into that Territory by the slaveholders with their chattels. The calculations are that slaves can be made very productive in raising hemp, wheat, corn, oats, and tobacco. Now in ordinary times, the raising of these commodities in the latitude of Kansas is a starving business for the masters. The estimated profit in the raising of these articles are based upon the fictitious price which hemp has borne under the recent unparalleled stimulation of the shipping interest, and upon the past and present famine price of breadstuffs. All of these prices must sooner or later recede, and be followed, through an inevitable law, by a corresponding depression below the average rate. The business of slave-breeding alone saves them. But a new State cannot be a slave-breeding State. A virgin country revolts, through an instinctive rigor of nature, against all attempts to devote it to such loathsome uses. The infamous occupation of breeding men and women for sale, flourishes only in the feculent muck accumulated from the corruptions of whole generations of squalid servitude and incompetence and slothful cupidity; such, for example, as the foul currents of slavery have deposited over the moral and physical wastes of Maryland and Virginia. Their principal trade cannot be rivalled by Kansas. We do not, therefore, fear for Kansas so much because slavery can be made so very profitable there as to induce a speedy slave immigration as we do from the efforts of slavery, as a political power, aiming at universal control on this continent.

The slaveholders of Missouri and of other States are determined to secure Kansas to their uses. They will occupy it to as great an extent as they are able — not for money-making, but for political purposes. They have rushed upon the Territory in the most outrageous manner in the late election. They stand ready to do the same thing at every step of its political organization, till a Constitution establishing slavery is secured. But these efforts, it should be remembered, are but fitful, from the nature of the case, and may be overborne and successfully resisted by the steady, natural current of immigration, if the flow of that current does not suffer itself to be hindered by the clamorous threats of the slaveholders to establish slavery. Kansas is to be saved to freedom by a steady, persevering emigration thither from the Free States. What we need now is time to get a foothold. We require a great mass of free emigrants there — too great to be outvoted by a few thousand ruffians from Missouri, who at a given signal intend to rush in and extemporize a State Constitution, as they have extemporized a Legislature. Give

ıs the masses there before slavery shall be allowed to affix its black
,eal to the fundamental law of the State.   Kansas without slavery
s our motto; and she must wait for admission as a State until this
s her established condition.

THE TEMPER OF THE SOUTH

Montgomery Mail, *July, 1855*

Concerning the slavery question, the South has not been for many
years in so quiet a mood.   There is a perfect placidity of sentiment
throughout the slave States.   We have no indignation meetings, no
torrents of declamation and denunciation, no fiery threatening
resolutions.   For all these there is a deep, deep calm.   And the
reason is that at length, after decades of bickerings, the whole section is agreed that the day is at hand.   At length — at length, and
for the first time in many a long year — the South occupies her
true position, untrammeled by thrice accursed "compromises,"
and looking only to the Constitution for the measure of her rights.
For the first time, too, she sees her fanatical enemies clothed with
full power to do their will, in the House of Representatives of the
United States.   And thus there is made, for the first time, the true
issue between the North and the South.   How it will be decided is
another question, but it is glorious that it is to be decided; that a
few short months will give the conflict its culmination; and that
whether the hordes of Free-Soilers and abolitionists are driven back
impotent, overpowered by the innate conservatism of the whole
people, or the South is compelled to withdraw from a government
which is fast becoming her greatest enemy — in either event, our
real relations with the antagonist section will be brought out in
bold relief.   The day of hypocrisy and duplicity will be over; our
friends will be our friends and our enemies our enemies.

SOUTHERN RETALIATION AGAINST
MASSACHUSETTS

New Orleans Bulletin, *July, 1855*

Under the Massachusetts "personal liberty law" no open action
as yet has taken place.   Even the public gazettes have scarcely
noticed the subject, so far as I can ascertain.   Our people are
scattered for the summer, hundreds spending their money in pleasure
excursions or purchases in Massachusetts.   No, my good friends
of Bunker Hill and Lexington (and long may I be permitted to
address you as such), there has been as yet no open action.   Some
of our bees and butterflies have fluttered off among you, but we

who are toiling here at home consult together about your "liberty law," and other movements, and I have leave to tell you some things which are more than hinted at if such laws are to be enforced.

First. — Excluding your ships.

Second. — Excluding your manufactures.

Third. — Ceasing our visits to your borders, already unsafe and more or less unpleasant.

Fourth. — Requiring your citizens trading here at least to take out licenses, perhaps to furnish bond for good behavior.

How will such laws suit you? Of course not at all. They trench on that provision of the Constitution which declares that the citizens of each State shall be entitled to all the privileges and immunities of citizens in the several States. They certainly do, my conscientious friends, and such laws operate against all other rights the people of the several States have in other States under the Federal Constitution. We know it! but we also know that this is precisely our objection to this "liberty law," which has made all the trouble, and that its unconstitutionality has been pronounced by our highest tribunals.

All your reasoning would have done very well, so long as you held to your bargain — so long as you yourselves submitted to the paramount law, and recognized our rights under its guarantees — so long as Massachusetts held to her obligations and place in the great American family. But now you have repudiated a right of vital importance to us, and passed a law to fine and imprison as felons our citizens who may claim their rights under that Constitution. Why wait for a formal rupture and separation from you? You have not done so. Our compact is broken by *you*. There is little obligation on us to respect the rights of your citizens or their property, when you openly trample on ours. There is as little to restrain a mob from taking possession of one or more of your ships, as there was to restrain your mob in the case of the negro Burns from their assaults on the court and its officers, and from murdering the marshal Batchelder.

THE BLESSINGS OF SLAVERY[1]

De Bow's Review, July, 1855

Divine Providence, for its own high and inscrutable purposes, has rescued more than three millions of human beings from the hardships of a savage state, and placed them in a condition of greater comfort than any other laboring class in the world; it has delivered them from the barbarous idolatries of Africa, and brought them

---

[1] An excellent illustration of that new doctrine of the beneficial nature of slavery of which Calhoun was the most distinguished exponent.

within the blessings covenanted to believers in Christ. At the same time it has provided the whites of the Anglo-Norman race in the Southern States with the necessary means of unexampled prosperity, with that slave labor, without which, as a general rule, no colonization in a new country has ever or ever will thrive and grow rapidly; it has given them a distinct and inferior race to fill a position equal to their highest capacity, which in less fortunate countries is occupied by the whites themselves. A large class — often the largest class — living from day to day by the labor of their hands, exists and must exist in every country; and it is impossible, as a general thing, for the persons of that class to have time or even inclination for much mental improvement. The force of peculiar genius may raise one in ten thousand to a higher place in society, but such cases become more and more infrequent as wages diminish with the progress of population, and the care of providing food grows more engrossing.

The whole question therefore resolves itself into this: Shall the laboring class be of an inferior race, so controlled and directed by the superior minds of the whites as continually to progress in material and moral well-being, far beyond any point it has ever shown a power of attaining in freedom? Or shall that laboring class be of whites and equals, capable of becoming "gods, as one of us," and yet condemned to a slow but sure increase of want and poverty — the slaves of society instead of individuals — isolated from their employers by the invisible but impassable barriers of customs, alien from their hearts, and utterly separated in manners, information, opinions, and tastes? Between the Southern master and his slave there is a fellow-feeling in sorrow and in joy, a mutual dependence and affection, which calls into play all the finer feelings of man's nature. What of all this is there between the Northern capitalist and his day-laborer? They have not known each other from infancy, nor been partners through good and evil fortune. Perhaps the tide of emigration brought them together yesterday and will hurry them apart tomorrow. The laborer does not look to his employer as his natural protector against the injustice of the powerful, or as his refuge in sickness or in old age. He must find that in the almshouse. If the laborer is a factory operative — perhaps a girl, or even a child, for in manufacturing societies the children of the poor never know the plays or freedom of childhood — he is regarded as but a part of the loom he attends to. Factory labor becomes more and more divided, the employments more and more monotonous, with each improvement in machinery. There is none of that variety of occupation and those frequent calls upon the discretion and intelligence of the laborer, which make the work upon a plantation in the South at once the most improving, the healthiest, and the most delightful species of manual labor. The factory operative, on the contrary, is chained to some single minute employment, which must be repeated thousands of times without the least variation. Nothing worse for the intellect can be imagined.

Idiocy and insanity multiply under their influences. In 1840, while the proportion of idiots and insane to the whole population was only 1 in 1,100 in the slave States, it was 1 to 900 in all the free States, and as much as 1 in 630 in New England alone. The effects of factory life on health are quite as bad. The cotton factories, the dyeing and bleaching factories, are hotbeds of consumption and disease of the lungs. At Sheffield a dry-grinder, no matter how vigorous his constitution, is never known to live beyond the fated age of thirty-five. In Massachusetts, according to her own statistics, factories shorten the life of the operative one-third! According to the evidence taken before the committee of the House of Commons it has taken but thirty-two years to change the operatives of Manchester from a race more vigorous than those of New England now are — a well-fed, well-clothed, moral population — into demoralized, enervated, feeble beings. As one of the witnesses says, "their life has been passed in turning the mule-jenny; their minds have been weakened and withered like a tree." How many years will it require to produce these effects in the North, when the span of man's life is already so much shortened? The very severity of the labor undermines the constitution. What wears out the human body is not the greatness of any exertion, but its duration. But the spinner has to move silently from one machine to another for twelve or fourteen hours a day, the attention never to flag, the mules never to rest. It has been calculated that the factory girl walks in this way twenty miles a day! The system is equally pernicious for the morals. We always find, first, illegitimate births and then prostitution, as well as drunkenness and crime, increase in great manufacturing districts. How should it be otherwise, when the family is broken up and the factory boarding-house substituted in its place; when children and girls are separated from their parents at the most critical period of life, crowded in heated work-rooms with a promiscuous herd of strangers, lost to all the conservative influences of home?

In what regard is such a condition of labor superior to Southern slavery? Let the free States begin within their own borders; let them place their white slaves in as good a condition, moral and physical, as the negroes, and then they may talk to us. The increasing hosts who live by toil in factories, the paupers who belong to the State, and the still greater number who drag out a wretched existence in the crowded haunts of want and vice in their great cities, form more than an offset to anything that can be said of negro slavery. We have no patience with this meddling philanthropy, which does not take the beam out of its own eye before it takes the mote out of its brother's, at the imminent risk of his eyesight; whose charity is all for show, and never grows warm except for objects at a distance; which overlooks want and misery at its own gate, in its eagerness to reform countries it has never seen, and institutions it cannot understand. It is the crying vice of our age; this desire to attend to everybody's business but our own, to perform any duties but those that lie immediately before us. Instead of making the most of our opportunities, we waste our time in vain wishes that the opportunities were greater.

THE OUTRAGE ON MR. SUMNER [1]

New York *Evening Post*, May 23, 1856

The friends of slavery at Washington are attempting to silence the members of Congress from the free States by the same modes of discipline which make the slaves unite on their plantations. Two ruffians from the House of Representatives, named Brooks and Keith, both from South Carolina, yesterday made the Senate Chamber the scene of their cowardly brutality. They had armed themselves with heavy canes, and approaching Mr. Sumner, while sitting in his chair engaged in writing, Brooks struck him with his cane a violent blow on the head, which brought him stunned to the floor, and Keith with his weapon kept off the by-standers, while the other ruffian repeated the blows upon the head of the apparently lifeless victim till his cane was shattered to fragments. Mr. Sumner was conveyed from the Senate chamber bleeding and senseless, so severely wounded that the physician attending did not think it prudent to allow his friends to have access to him.

The excuse for this base assault is, that Mr. Sumner, on the Senate floor, in the course of a debate had spoken disrespectfully of Mr. Butler, a relative of Preston S. Brooks, one of the authors of this outrage. No possible indecorum of language on the part of Mr. Sumner could excuse, much less justify an attack like this; but we have carefully examined his speech to see if it contains any matter which could even extenuate such an act of violence, and find none. He had ridiculed Mr. Butler's devotion to slavery, it is true, but the weapon of ridicule in debate is by common consent as fair and

[1] The famous assault by Preston S. Brooks, a member of the House of Representatives from South Carolina, upon Senator Sumner of Massachusetts, raised a cry of Northern execration. This editorial is unmistakably Bryant's.

allowable a weapon as argument. The *Journal of Commerce* of this morning apologizes for the brutality of Brooks and his confederate, by saying that Mr. Sumner was guilty of "wholesale denunciation and bitter personalities;" and quotes what the Washington *Star* says of the character of Mr. Sumner's speech. What the Washington *Star* may say is nothing to the purpose; the question is what Mr. Sumner said, and as this has been published, the *Journal* should have placed it before its readers, that they might judge for themselves. It prudently, however, keeps the provocation, whatever it might be, out of sight. Our readers have already had the speech, and we leave it to them to say whether there is any wholesale denunciation or bitter personality in it; whether it contains anything which goes beyond the fair decorum of debate. There is surely, no wholesale denunciation — for Mr. Butler is assailed on one point only, his insane devotion to slavery; there is no bitter personality in it, for his character as a man in the ordinary relations of life is left unquestioned. We agree fully with Mr. Sumner that Mr. Butler is a monomaniac in the respect of which we speak; we certainly should place no confidence in any representation he might make which concerned the subject of slavery, and we say this without any expectation of an attempt being made upon our lives, or even of having our heads broken, for our boldness.

Has it come to this that we must speak with bated breath in the presence of our Southern masters; that even their follies are too sacred a subject for ridicule; that we must not deny the consistency of their principles or the accuracy of their statements? If we venture to laugh at them or question their logic, or dispute their facts, are we to be chastised as they chastise their slaves? Are we too, slaves, slaves for life, a target for their brutal blows, when we do not comport ourselves to please them? If this be so, it is time that the people of the free States knew it, and prepared themselves to acquiesce in their fate. They have labored under the delusion hitherto that they were their own masters.

Even if it were true, as it is not, that there were "wholesale denunciation and bitter personalities" against Mr. Butler in Mr. Sumner's speech, the denunciation should have been repelled and personalities rebuked by some of the fluent speakers of the powerful majority to which Mr. Butler belongs, and the matter should have ended there. The sudden attack made with deadly weapons upon an unarmed man in the Senate Chamber, where he could not expect it or have been prepared for it, was the act of men who must be poltroons as well as ruffians. It was as indecent, also, as it was cowardly; the Senate floor should be sacred from such outrages; or if they are common, if at all, it should only be by Senatorial blackguards. It is true that the Senate had just adjourned, but the members were still there, many of them in their places; it was their chamber, and this violence committed in their presence was an insult to their body. Yet we have no expectation that the Senate will do anything to vindicate the sacredness and peace of their chamber, or the right of their members not to be called to account for words spoken in debate. There will be a little discussion; some will denounce and some will defend the assault, and then the matter will end.

The truth is, that the pro-slavery party, which rules in the Senate, looks upon violence as the proper instrument of its designs. Violence reigns in the streets of Washington; violence has now found its way into the Senate chamber. Violence lies in wait on all the navigable rivers and all the railways of Missouri, to obstruct those who pass from the free States into Kansas. Violence overhangs the frontiers of that territory like a storm-cloud charged with hail and lightning. Violence has carried election after election in that territory. In short, violence is the order of the day; the North is to be pushed to the wall by it, and this plot will succeed if the people of the free States are as apathetic as the slaveholders are insolent.

SLAVERY AN ECONOMIC NECESSITY

Richmond *Dispatch*, May, 1856

The whole commerce of the world turns upon the product of slave labor. What would commerce be without cotton, sugar, tobacco, rice, and naval stores? All these are the product of slave labor. It is a settled fact that free labor cannot produce them in sufficient quantities to supply the demands of mankind. It has been said that one free laborer is equal to five slaves. If this be so, why has not free labor been employed in the production of the above staples? It has been attempted, and in every case in which it has been introduced has failed. The world follows its interests, and if free labor was more valuable than slave, it would be employed at this moment in the United States, Cuba, and Brazil, which are all open to free labor. And herein note the greater liberality and self-reliant strength of the slave States over the free States. The former freely permit the Northern capitalist to come in with his free labor and compete with slave labor. The latter pass laws prohibiting the Southern capitalist from coming in with his slaves to compete with Northern labor. Their prohibitory laws are passed because they are afraid of slave competition; whereas the South, in the face of the pretence which has been handed down from Wilberforce to these times, that one white laborer is equal in value to five slaves, throws her door wide open and invites free labor to walk in and try its hand, and it dare not come. What would become of England, the arch-agitator of abolitionism, but for cotton, by the manufacture of which she has waxed fat and strong, while she curses the system by which it is produced? By the way, will someone inform us why the English conscience has never suffered as much from slavery in Brazil as slavery in the United States?

SOUTHERN THREATS OF DISUNION[1]

New York *Evening Post*, October 6, 1856

It will be seen in looking over Mr. Botts's letter to the editor of the *National American*, which we give today, that he imputes the threats of disunion contained in the speech which Governor Wise delivered the other day at Richmond to a disordered mind. That Wise is not perfectly sane may be true enough — a more well-balanced mind than his might be overset by the excitement and want of sleep of which he complained so pathetically at Richmond; but all this blustering about disunion is simply a deliberately laid plot to frighten the North. If any votes for Buchanan can be obtained by it, if Frémont can be deprived by it of any votes, its object will be effected; if not, no harm will be done, and the politicians of the slave states will submit as quietly as they did when General Jackson enforced the laws of the Union in spite of the nullifiers, and as when Mr. Banks was elected Speaker of the House of Representatives.

Our readers may rely upon it, therefore, that Mr. Botts is too charitable. They who make this threat of disunion are more knaves than madmen. Mr. Forsyth and Governor Wise, and the men who speak through the Washington *Union*, if they were absolutely mad, might make a serious attempt to carry their project into effect; but not one of them all, at present, has any more thought of attempting a dissolution of the Union than of attempting a dissolution of the solar system. With the election of Colonel Frémont impending over them, not the slightest preparation has been made on their part for the event which they so studiously with one voice represent as inevitable.

---

[1] In an effort to frighten Northern voters into casting their ballots for either Buchanan or Millard Fillmore in 1856, numerous Southern leaders declared during the campaign that if Frémont were elected by the Republicans, the South would secede. Governor Henry A. Wise of Virginia and John Forsyth of Alabama were two of those who made the fiercest threats; and John Minor Botts of Richmond was a Virginian who defended the idea of an indissoluble Union. Though Bryant scoffed at these threats, they led many men to vote for Buchanan. This was particularly true in Pennsylvania, a pivotal state.

[THE GROWING DEMAND FOR SECESSION]

New Orleans *Bulletin*, August, 1856

Secession is a foul and rank weed which finds no culture or sustenance in this uncongenial soil.   Such being the universal sentiment predominant in this community, our people have always been slow to credit the fact of the existence of an opposite feeling in any part of the country.   The wild and irrational ravings of the abolition press proper were supposed to be confined to a few fanatics, small in number and despicable in character, and by no means representing the opinions of the Northern people in the aggregate.   Most unfortunately, different impressions begin to prevail.   We cannot beguile ourselves any longer with such delusive hopes.   The fact cannot be disguised or circumvented that this feeling of hostility to the institution of slavery, and to the section of country where it exists, is getting to be widespread, bitter and insatiable.   The most discreet, conservative, and patriotic men of the North are openly taking sides on the sectional issue, which if it be their design to agitate until it is disposed of, can be terminated in no other way than by a dissolution of the Union.   This is the only *finality* of the vexatious and embarrassing question which the factious disputants who persist in agitating it expect or hope for.

De Bow's *Review*, November, 1856

But, it is said, the South will not dare to leave the Union;   that the sentiments of anti-slavery will pursue them into whatever political connection they may seek a refuge, and that the only ark of their political safety is in association with the North.   This we doubt, and will give a brief consideration to this aspect of the subject.

It is said that anti-slavery will war upon us more than ever, but we doubt it.   Under the forms of a political connection they can now disturb us with impunity.   Tied by the ligaments of a common government, with a preponderance of legislative power against us, they can treat us as they please and laugh at our indignation.   They can vote away the common fund;   they can impose whatever impost duties upon foreign fabrics may be best calculated to build up interests among themselves, and while outraging every feeling of affection, can determine for us what discrimination in reference to our own interests will best subserve their ends.   Possessed of this security, it is a cheap oppression to war upon the South — to disturb our social institutions — to circumscribe us in extent — to set the world against us and exercise the common incidents of merely vulgar despotism.   But possessed of the functions of political sovereignty;   at liberty to treat the North, not as it may please them but as it may please us; to hold them strictly responsible for their conduct, and cause them to feel that for every unwarrantable act we will make them pay the penalty in such discriminations as we shall have the power to use against them, and it is by no means certain that aggression will continue.

THE CONSPIRACY AGAINST THE WORKING CLASS[1]

New York *Evening Post*, October 29, 1856

That those who are attached to the party of Mr. Buchanan by official ties should give him their support does not surprise us; it is the infirmity of human nature to cheat itself with the idea that what is for our present interest must be right. That those who own slaves at the South, and those at the North who are connected in any way with the slave-holding class by interest or other affinities, should support him, is quite natural; he is the slave-holders' candidate. But that any man who depends on the labor of his own hands for subsistence, who wishes that honest labor should be honored, and that the great West should be open to him and the class to which he belongs, and to their children, as a region in which they may exercise their calling without social degradation — that any such man should stand ready to give his vote for Buchanan, is what we cannot account for.

There are, we believe, very few farmers and mechanics at the North who are not fully aware that if slavery goes into the Territories, free labor must go out. When they look at the map of the United States, they perceive that the slave States are one-fourth larger in their areas than the free States. When they look at the census of the United States, they perceive that the number of white inhabitants in the free States, though their area is so much less, is more than twice the white population of the slave States. They perceive that slavery is an engrossing, encroaching institution, a greedy devourer of land, requiring three or four times as much space as free labor. They perceive also another important fact, that the less wealthy part of the Southern population are constantly migrating to free territory or to the western free States, where labor is held in honor, and where they can till the soil, or toil in other callings requiring bodily exertion, without being regarded as an inferior class. We published the other day a letter from Professor Hendrick, of North Carolina, in which he spoke feelingly of this constant necessity of removal to free territory, a necessity which forces his old friends and neighbors to leave their homes, and keeps down the natural

[1] Typical of the appeal by the Republicans in 1856 for the votes of Northern workingmen and of newly arrived immigrants.

increase of population in his native State. The census shows that a large proportion of those who settle the free States of the west come from slave States. Go where you will in the new settlements, you meet the emigrant from Virginia, from Kentucky, from Tennessee, from North Carolina. We have ourselves frequently partaken of the hospitality of those sons of the South in their cabins on the prairies. Southern Ohio, Illinois and Indiana are peopled by them and their descendants; they follow up the rivers to Iowa, to Wisconsin, to Minnesota, to Nebraska; they help to swell the population of Cincinnati, Chicago, Madison, and the other flourishing towns of the free West. Thus it is the South casts out her offspring; she keeps slavery, and parts with her children, who should make her strength and her honor. Free labor cannot live by the side of the oligarchy which tills the soil by the hands of its bondmen, and sells carpenters, blacksmiths, and masons under the hammer. The free white laborer of the South finds that in a thin population, public schools cannot be supported. The planter, with a domain of from three to ten thousand acres, can send his children to some private school or keep a tutor; but the poor man must see his children grow up in ignorance. No wonder that he should remove to a place where education is brought to his door, and where labor is no longer a badge of degradation.

If, therefore, slavery is introduced into the Territories, as the Southern politicians, with the co-operation of all that party at the North now supporting Buchanan, are attempting to introduce it, we see what the effect must be. We of the free States may enter those Territories with the purpose of settling there, but if we do not become slaveholders we must go out again. The farmers who go thither to work with their own hands must consent to be looked down upon by the planters, with their domains of thousands of acres and their hundreds of work-people whose muscles and bones are their property. The white farmer will take his place by the negro field-hand; the white carpenter will be looked upon as a proper companion for the black carpenter who is sold at auction. In going to such a community the farmer from the free States must renounce the advantage of schools; he must see his children brought up as the poor population of Missouri are brought up, in utter ignorance, and with the propensity to debauchery which is nourished in those who have no intellectual resources.

They cannot live in such a community. They will come thronging back to the new free States, as they now come from Virginia and North Carolina, driven out by the stinging sense of degradation which at the South is connected with poverty, and by the frightful dearth of the means of education, which makes this degradation more complete. They will come back to us with their families, all the worse in mind and morals for their sojourn in a land which to them and their children will have been like the land of Egypt to the Israelites.

[THE REAL ISSUE OF 1856]

Springfield *Republican*, November 4, 1856

The real abstract question between the two parties is, whether Congress shall control the destinies of the territories, and dedicate them as of old to freedom, or whether they shall be left for bitter and bloody struggles between the settlers, like those which in Kansas now shock the moral sense of civilization everywhere. Practically the question is whether the influence of the national government shall be used to extend slavery, and aggregate its political power, or to limit its bounds and weaken its hold over the politics, the business, and the religion of the nation. Were the issue thus plainly known of all men, there would be no dispute of the result. The American party stepped in at an inopportune moment, overwhelmed the true issue before the country, and turned aside the minds of many men by the glittering success which it momentarily won. And if the Republican party fails today to inaugurate that revolution in the national government which must come ere this generation passes away, or the government itself perishes, the responsibility cannot be escaped by the American organization. To its door must the defeat of John C. Frémont and the election of James Buchanan be laid. By implanting in many minds a weak substitution for the strongest issue, and by keeping temporarily in the Democratic ranks many who but for their opposition to Americanism would have rallied around the Republican standard, it has given fresh strength to the Democracy, and enabled them to contest this election with a fair prospect of success. . . .

The result of the struggle is in grave doubt, and the eagles of victory are as likely, perhaps, to perch on the one side as on the other, tomorrow morning. Of the two contestants, the Republicans can alone afford to be beaten. With the Democracy, defeat is destruction. The party is only held together by its alliance with the national treasury and the slaveholder. Separated from one, it becomes useless to the other, and its power is gone. But a reverse cannot break the Republican column. It has an enduring vitality in its principles, and a glorious destiny, as sure as the Republic has an existence. Whether it enters upon the affirmative exercise of its mission now, or four years hence, is to all seeming the only question of today. Time will only vindicate its truthfulness, its necessity, and its strength. It can afford to wait, if the country and the world can afford to have it.   But the country cannot afford to wait for its healing, peaceful mission, and though we look not upon the day's struggle with confidence of victory, we await its result with a buoyant hope that the day and the hour of redemption have come.

THE ELECTIONS OF YESTERDAY

New York *Evening Post*, November 5, 1856

The battle is over, and we are all waiting for the smoke to clear away that we may see the exact position of the armies which have been engaged in the conflict.   The present aspect of the field is disastrous for the cause which we have supported.   We will not undertake to say at present that all hope is lost; we will not affirm that it is impossible that the reports we are yet to hear from Pennsylvania may change the apparent defeat into a victory; we will not yet affirm that there is no chance that the election may be carried into the House of Representatives.   The chances for Fillmore in Kentucky and Louisiana were thought a week since to be as good as in Maryland, which it is said has been carried for the Fillmore electoral ticket.

But taking it for granted that Buchanan has succeeded, we confess that there are considerations which, with us, mitigate the pain of disappointment.   If we have not carried the United States, we have obtained heavy majorities in a part of the Union which stands high in the confederacy for intelligence and prosperity, and which, through these characteristics, exercises a powerful influence on public opinion.   We have at least laid the basis of a formidable and well-organized party, in opposition to the spread of slavery — that scheme which is the scandal of the country and of the age.   In those states of the Union which have now given such large majorities for Frémont, public opinion, which till lately has been undecided and shuffling in regard to the slavery question, is now clear, fixed and resolute.   If we look back to 1848, when we conducted a Presidential election on this very ground of opposition to the extension of slavery, we shall see that we have made immense strides towards the ascendancy which, if there be any grounds to hope for the perpetuity of free institutions, is yet to be ours.   We were then comparatively weak, we are now strong; we then counted our thousands, we now count our millions; we could then point to our respectable minorities in a few States, we now point to State after State — to powerful old States on the Atlantic, and flourishing young States in the West — which rally with us under the banner of resistance to the extension of slavery.   The cause is not going back — it is rapidly going forward; the Freesoil party of 1848 is the nucleus of the Republican party of 1856; but with what accessions of numbers, of strength, of illustrious names, of moral power, of influence, not merely in public assemblies, but at the domestic fireside!

MR. DELAVAN'S PROHIBITION LETTERS[1]

Albany *Atlas and Argus*, March 10, 1857

The day has gone by when individuals or parties are to be denounced as the enemies of temperance because they resist unconstitutional legislation. That game has been played out. When Governor Seymour was in the gubernatorial chair, the Whigs (so called at that day) sent to him for approval, a prohibitory law, which even the advocates of prohibition, in nine months afterwards, admitted violated the Constitution. Of course he vetoed it, as his duty and his official oath required. Straightway a howl was set up against him and the party which sustained him, charging both with hostility to the cause of temperance. The Chambers, the Burleighs, the Raymonds, the Greeleys, and the whole tribe of Whig politicians, suddenly became zealous reformers, and many of them over their cups drank success to prohibition and Sewardism. Governor Clark, a quiet and respectable citizen of Canandaigua, solely for the purpose of securing temperance votes, was taken up and set astride the prohibitory hobby. Raymond, giving a pledge to the temperance people which he violated before the ink was fairly dry, submitted to the humiliation of mounting behind and riding on the crupper. The coalition was successful. Mock philanthropy and corruption rioted at the capitol. To preserve a decent appearance of faith, a prohibitory law was passed in direct violation of the Constitution, which in less than a year fell before the judgment of the Court of Appeals.

The Democratic party opposed all this — the sham benevolence, the corruption, the violation of the Constitution — and now all disinterested men, even many of the actors in the shameful farce, concede the correctness of its action.

[1] In several Northern States during the fifties, including Massachusetts, Michigan, and New York, prohibitory laws were enacted but declared unconstitutional by the courts. The slavery excitement and Civil War arrested the spread of prohibition. Horatio Seymour, who was elected Governor in 1852, vetoed a prohibition bill on the Maine model. The result was the election, by a majority of a few hundred votes, of an ardent prohibitionist, Myron H. Clark, as Governor on the Whig ticket. This was in 1854. In 1855 a new prohibition bill was passed. As the *Argus* states, the Court of Appeals promptly declared it unconstitutional. This disposed of the issue in New York.

PRENTICEIANA[1]

Louisville *Journal*, 1830–1859

The editor of the *Ohio Statesman* says more villainy is on foot. We suppose the editor has lost his horse.

James Ray and John Parr have started a Locofoco paper in Maine, called the *Democrat*. Parr, in all that pertains to decency, is below zero; and Ray is below Parr.

Whatever Midas touched was turned into gold; in these days, touch a man with gold and he'll turn into anything.

Have I changed? exclaims Governor P——. We don't know. That depends on whether you were ever an honest man.

The Washington *Globe* says that such patriotism as Mr. Clay's will not answer. True enough, for it can't be questioned.

The editor of the —— speaks of his "lying curled up in bed these cold mornings." This verifies what we said of him some time ago — "he lies like a dog."

Wild rye and wild wheat grow in some regions spontaneously. We believe that wild oats are always sown.

The *Globe* says that Mr. Clay is a sharp politician. No doubt of it, but the editor of the *Globe* is a sharper.

Men are deserters in adversity; when the sun sets, and all is dark, our very shadows refuse to follow us.

A well known writer says that a fine coat covers a multitude of sins. It is still truer that such coats cover a multitude of sinners.

Messrs. Bell and Topp, of the North Carolina *Gazette*, say that "Prentices were made to serve masters." Well, Bells were made to be hung, and Topps to be whipped.

THE NEW FEDERAL CONSTITUTION[2]

New York *Evening Post*, March 9, 1857

Some of the journalists who support the cause of the Administration are pleasing themselves with the fancy that the decision of the Supreme bench of the United States in the Dred Scott case will put an end to the agitation of the slavery question. They will soon find their mistake. The feeling in favor of liberty is not so easily smothered; discussion is not so readily silenced. One specific after another has been tried, with the same view and with the same suc-

[1] George D. Prentice, who founded the Louisville *Journal* as an organ of Clay and the nascent Whig Party in 1830, became famous for his brief editorial paragraphs, a collection of which was issued under the title "Prenticeana" in 1859. Prentice died in 1870.

[2] Bryant's fiery editorial is typical of the refusal of Northern newspapers to accept any of the main implications of the Dred Scott decision, and to hold it null and void.

cess. The Fugitive Slave Law, we are told, was to quiet all agitation, but it did not; the Nebraska bill was to stop all controversy
on the slavery question, but it proved to be oil poured on the flames.
The usurpation of the government of Kansas by the inroad from
Missouri was thought for a time to be a blow to the friends of liberty
which they could not survive, but it only roused them to greater
activity. The election of Mr. Buchanan as President in November
was to put an end to the dispute, but since November the dispute
has waxed warmer and warmer. It will never end till the cause of
liberty has finally triumphed. Heap statute upon statute, follow
up one act of executive interference with another, add usurpation
to usurpation, and judicial decision to judicial decision, the spirit
against which they are levelled is indestructible. As long as the
press and speech are free, the warfare will be continued, and every
attempt to suppress it, by directing against it any part of the
machinery of the government, will only cause it to rage the more
fiercely.

This has been the case hitherto. The more our Presidents have
meddled with the matter, the more the majority in Congress have
sought to stifle the discussion, the more force has been employed
on the side of slavery — whether under the pretext of legal authority,
as when Mr. Pierce called out the New Jersey troops to enforce the
pretended laws of Kansas, or without that pretext, as when armed
men crossed the border of that territory to make laws for the inhabitants — the more determined is the zeal by which the rights of
freemen are asserted and upheld against the oligarchy. It will
not cool the fiery temper of this zeal to know that slavery has enlisted
the bench on its side; it will rather blow it into a stronger and more
formidable flame.

Here are five slaveholding judges on the bench, disciples of this
neologism of slavery — men who have espoused the doctrines lately
invented by the Southern politicians, and who seek to graft them
upon our code of constitutional law — men who alter our Constitution for us, who find in it what no man of common sense, reading
for himself, could ever find, what its framers never thought of putting
into it, what no man discerned in it until a very few days since it
was seen with the aid of optics sharpened by the eager desire to
preserve the political ascendency of the slave States. We feel, in
reading the opinions of these men, that local political prejudices
have gained the mastery of that bench, and tainted beyond recovery
the minds of the majority of the judges. The Constitution which
they now profess to administer, is not the Constitution under which
this country has lived for seventy years; it is not the Constitution
which Washington, Franklin, and Jefferson, and the abler jurists

who filled the seat of justice in the calmer days of our republic, recognized; this is not the Constitution to which we have so long looked with admiration and reverence; it is a new Constitution, of which we never heard until it was invented by Mr. Calhoun, and which we cannot see adopted by the judges of our Federal court without shame and indignation.

Hereafter, if this decision shall stand for law, slavery, instead of being what the people of the slave States have hitherto called it, their peculiar institution, is a Federal institution, the common patrimony and shame of all the States, those which flaunt the title of free as well as those which accept the stigma of being the Land of Bondage; hereafter, wherever our jurisdiction extends, it carries with it the chain and the scourge, — wherever our flag floats, it is the flag of slavery. If so, that flag should have the light of the stars and the streaks of running red erased from it; it should be dyed black, and its device should be the ship and the fetter.

Are we to accept, without question, these new readings of the Constitution — to sit down contentedly under this disgrace — to admit that the Constitution was never before rightly understood, even by those who framed it — to consent that hereafter it shall be the slaveholders' instead of the freemen's Constitution? Never! Never! We hold that the provisions of the Constitution, so far as they regard slavery, are now just what they were when it was framed, and that no trick of interpretation can change them. The people of the free States will insist on the old impartial construction of the Constitution, adopted in calmer times — the construction given it by Washington and his contemporaries, instead of that invented by modern politicians in Congress and adopted by modern politicians on the bench.

IMMIGRATION AND SLAVERY [1]

Albany *Atlas and Argus*, January 28, 1857

(Official immigration figures of the Port of New York for the year 1856 show that a total of 141,625 immigrants entered then, bearing $9,642,104 in cash means. Of these 56,055 with $2,150,656 named New York as their destination; 13,327 with $1,984,126 Wisconsin. — *News Item*).

The portion of these new-comers who went to the old States were doubtless to a great extent laborers of both sexes, and show a less average amount of means per head. But it does not follow that they are less valuable, or perform less important functions in the great body politic. They fill a place in society which must be filled by a population of some description, either bond or free. They are

[1] A prominent place among the "doughface" newspapers — Northern newspapers with Southern views or principles — was long occupied by the Albany *Argus,* which here appears in the role of apologist for slavery.

the laborers of our nation. Their hands dig our canals, build our railroads, furnish the muscle in the erection of our houses, stores and various structures, aid the movements of commerce upon our docks, till our fields and gather our harvests, do the domestic service of our houses, and in brief, perform the great mass of the mere manual labor and physical service in all these Northern and Western States. The effect is to elevate our native population above the mere drudgery of physical labor, and give them a higher position in the scale of society, to make them the employers instead of the employed, to give them the position in the social and economical structure which depends more upon the exercise of mind than of muscle.

The speculation as to what would have been the condition in the present free States without the introduction of this vast mass of foreign labor, opens an interesting field of thought and inquiry. Without this foreign supply, who would now be our laborers and our domestic servants? Would all these places be filled by our own native population? Would they have discharged and continued to discharge all the various offices and duties which this foreign element has met? We doubt it. At the South the black population has supplied precisely the want which we should have experienced without the aid of immigration. The blacks are the laborers and the domestic servants of the South. Will it do for us to boast so much upon our superior philanthropy and humanity as to be quite certain that we should have released our hold upon the African race, had not this press of foreign bone and muscle been at our doors, soliciting employment and ready to do for us all that a system of compulsory service supplied and to do it better and cheaper? The motives of our action are not always quite apparent to ourselves. The human heart can easily persuade itself that it yields to the promptings of humanity or the stern demands of duty, when in fact it only follows the lead of self-interest. Radical changes in the social and political condition of a people are much more commonly conceded to the latter, than to the former. Without intending to depreciate or undervalue the influences of the former, we think the latter must be set down in any sound system of political economy as a far more controlling principle of human action.

[HOW SLAVERY IMPOVERISHES THE SOUTH]

New York *Tribune*, March 15, 1858

Senator Hammond occupied the greater part of his speech on Lecompton with an exposition of the capacity of the slave States to establish and maintain what he called "a separate political organization." This is a common topic of abstract inquiry with South Carolinians, and we do not object to it, though its special relevancy to the question of admitting Kansas into the Union under a fraudulent Constitution we do not perceive. In this review Mr. Hammond went over the old ground of Southern theorists, and reproduced with little change and no novelty the various considerations going to show how admirably a Southern slave-holding government would work in practise. For our part, as a general proposition, we have no hesitation in admitting that the Southern States are able to maintain, in one way or another, an independent government of their own. How powerful it would be or how prosperous is a question upon which there will be diversity of opinion. Governor Hammond has the good sense to admit that its strength would not consist in its fighting power. He gives it a high prospective rank among the nations, however, on the ground that, as he declares, "Cotton is king," and a king with whom none can afford to go to war. The reign of this monarch will thus, as Governor Hammond thinks, be not only eternal but eternally pacific.

But we cannot allow one fallacy of Governor Hammond to go unreproved and unexposed, especially as it is one that the slave-holding statesmen are forever putting forward. We mean the notion that foreign exports are the measure of a country's wealth and power. We cannot understand how it is that gentlemen of intelligence can so tenaciously insist on this dismal fallacy. What can be plainer than that it is the aggregate production of a country that constitutes its wealth, and is the real measure of its power? Exports are nothing but the exchange of products that are produced, for products that are not produced by the exporting country. Diversify production in any country, and no exports or exchanges with foreign countries are necessary. Simplify production by confining it to one or two staples, and exchanges for foreign productions or exports must be proportionally large. But is this to be taken as any evidence that the country that has a varied production is poor, and the country that has not is rich? Yet such is substantially the deduction of economists who count exports as evidence of wealth. If they were right, then an island in the ocean whose entire population was engaged in the oyster or whale fishery, and who by dint of hard work and poor fare were able to make both ends meet at the end of a year, could point to the exports wherewith they bought their pork, and hard bread, and tarpaulins, as an evidence of their abundant prosperity, because their earnings were comparatively so large. This is just the kind of prosperity the South exhibits in her reported surplus. She raises cotton, but she can neither eat nor spin it, and hence it goes abroad to buy what she wants to eat and to wear.

But this is not all. A country where industry is not diversified, but where production is confined to one or two, or a very few staples, is constantly in a precarious condition. A failure of its chief crop for a single year spreads bankruptcy and famine. A threatened war fills it with dismay; an actual one with ruin. The country of large exports in proportion to its production is thus the weakest of countries rather than the strongest. The country whose products are the most varied, and the gross result of whose industry is the largest, is that which has the greatest amount of all the elements which constitute wealth, even though its exports may be comparatively small.[1] But if the Southern economists reject so sound a test of the wealth and resources of a people, they surely cannot object to estimate them by the earned surplus on hand in the form of taxable property. If this be done, how stand the slave and free States in a comparative estimate? The State of Massachusetts, with a population of 994,514 in 1850, possessed personal and real estate to the amount of $573,342,000. The valuation of the State of Virginia, with a population of 1,421,661, at the same period, was $391,646,000; and this comparison can be almost indefinitely extended between the free and the slave States.

What then becomes of the labored attempt of Governor Hammond and his coadjutors to show the comparative wealth and power of the slave States, by exhibiting their exports as contrasted with the free? And when we can demonstrate, as we did lately, that the aggregate production of the largest of the slave States is not equal to its annual expenses of living by $14,000,000 per annum? This one fact exhibits the wastefulness, weakness, and poverty inherent in the system of slavery in a more striking light than volumes of theoretical illustration. It shows, too, why it is that commercial capital does not accumulate in the South as it has done in the older free States, and why a never-ending succession of bankruptcies seem always necessary to extinguish the indebtedness which the South is constantly incurring at the North. It shows why it is that the banks of the South are so long in showing recuperative power after their suspension. If Virginia is any evidence, and even Maryland any evidence, of the working of the system of slave labor, none of the slave States are paying the expenses of their own living. They do not support themselves, they do not pay their own way, but live, to a greater or less extent, according to situation and circumstances, off the industry of the rest of the country. In fact, the slavery of the South is a positive pecuniary burden upon the free States — an absolute tax upon the free labor of the country.

[1] It is unquestionably true that a great part of the annual surplus produced by the South went to the North. It was used there to pay for tools, clothing, household wares, and food bought by the South.

[ASPECTS OF AMERICAN SOCIAL HISTORY, 1858][1]
Harper's Weekly

What Will You Do With Her?: January 30.

In the little neighboring town of Orange, Mrs. Lucy Stone, a woman of intelligence, sense, and spirit, declines to pay her taxes. Why?

Because, she says, there should be no taxes without representation. That was good doctrine on Bunker Hill and in Boston Harbor some eighty-four or five years ago. It remains to see how it will work in Orange.

She is undoubtedly a woman — but the tax-gatherer can hardly push that argument very far — for she is also a peaceable, useful citizen; and it must be a very eloquent tax-gatherer indeed who could persuade sensible people in Orange that so good a citizen ought to be taxed without representation.

It is, in fact, a brave little *coup d'état* in favor of Woman's Rights; and its success would hardly peril the prosperity of Jersey: for even if the Lords of Creation should graciously allow their female slaves to vote, there are very few of them who would take the trouble to exercise the right.

Prohibitive Legislation: February 13.

A *bona fide* attempt has recently been made, by the Mayor of New York, to put down gambling houses. Policemen, duly armed with authority and prepared to execute the laws, have made descents upon well-known gambling establishments; they have not, in any single instance, found anything to justify a seizure. When they made their appearance the most notorious dens of gamblers presented an aspect of primeval innocence. After heroic exertions they have been compelled to confess themselves beaten, and the Mayor's aim has, for the time, been defeated. It is needless to add that, after a convenient delay, the gambling houses will resume operations without let or hindrance.

The last Mayor of New York, Fernando Wood, began his career with a like display of virtuous vigilance. He, too, undertook to execute the laws and abate nuisances. But the desire did not last long. He soon abandoned a hopeless and thankless contest with the vices and propensities of the people. We are doing no injustice to Mayor Tiemann when we say he will follow the example. He will discover, before a fourth of his term has elapsed, that the evils

---

[1] By 1858 *Harper's Weekly,* now a year old, was popular and influential; the best of these editorials are from the pen of George W. Curtis, already a regular contributor.

against which the laws we have enumerated are directed are beyond the reach of law and police to eradicate. And, like a sensible man, he will confine his efforts to the pursuit of objects and reforms which are humanly feasible. . . . We have, in large cities, certain habits and modes of thought and action; these can not be altered or modified by any act or statute. The only effect of prohibitive legislation in reference to these settled and inherent vices is, first, to induce concealment with its obvious concomitant evils, and secondly, to engender a contempt for the law. There is no instance where a rooted habit among the people of a large city has been eradicated by legislation.

Reopening of the Slave Trade: March 13.

It seems that while the eyes of Northern politicians have been steadily fixed on Kansas, the practical men of the South have been quietly increasing their stock of negroes by vigorous importations from Africa. At least such is the statement of the New Orleans *Delta*, which journal avers that the plantations of Mississippi and other Southern sea-board States are plentifully supplied with negroes fresh from Africa. The story derives a plausibility from the bill which has just passed the Legislature of Louisiana for the importation of negro apprentices from Africa, and from the agitation which has existed for two or three years in South Carolina, Tennessee, and one or two other Southern States, in favor of the reopening of the slave trade. It is a pity that some one does not suggest some practical means by which the difficulties which now impede the acquisition of labor by the South could be overcome. All admit, and the steady increase in the value of negroes proves, that the great want of the South is labor. If in the North our supply of foreign labor were suddenly cut off, the country would receive a shock in comparison with which the late revulsion would seem utterly insignificant. Yet the natural increase of our laboring population is greater than that of the negroes.

Physical Decay in the United States: February 27.

There seems to exist among the people of the United States a decided aversion for field sports and open air exercise. Among the people of the large cities physical exercise is never considered for a moment. No athletics, exercises, or sports are popular. We have cricket clubs, at which the bulk of the players are Englishmen. We have no hunts, with horses and dogs; a few enthusiastic persons shoot a little in the season, but the sport can not be said to be general. As a general rule the New Yorker never takes a gun in his hand except when he goes out on those doleful processions called target excursions, which are usually equal parts of dullness and drink. New Yorkers do not ride. Their idea of horse exercise is sitting in an uncomfortable wagon behind a fast trotting horse, and swallowing several pounds of dust on a road covered with flash men and flash teams. There are several gymnasia in the large cities. They are frequented by very few acolytes, and after a few months' patronage these generally desert them. In fine, it may be said broadly that, after our people reach manhood, they never seem to think that it is necessary to exercise their muscles.

Lastly, the first and ruling consideration of every American is business. Walk up Broadway and listen to the conversation of the people whom you pass — ninety-nine out of a hundred are talking of dollars, percentages, and premiums. The same is true of the groups of men assembled in drawing-rooms, hotel parlors, and bar-rooms. Wherever two or three Americans are gathered together there you may be sure that business and dollars are on the tapis. There are a few boys whose prime aim in life is billiards, cigars, gloves, and drink; but they are an exception. The bulk of our people have no time to be vicious. They are too busy to sin. As Dr. Watts teaches, they shame the Evil One by the intensity of their application to the serious things of life. An English merchant works seven hours a day, goes home, eats a hearty dinner, and plays with his children till bedtime. A Frenchman drops into his office before breakfast, returns home at eleven, goes back to work at two, and dines at five, after which he may be seen at an opera or in a ball-room. An American begins work before he is dressed in the morning, and never stops till he goes to bed.

Effects of the Atlantic Telegraph: August 14.

That ocean steam navigation has tended to enlarge the social mind of the peoples of Great Britain and of the United States no one will be inclined to dispute. It has helped the two nations to know each other better, to get rid of ignorant prejudices, to share each other's progress. A volume would be required to describe the benefits which each nation has conferred on the other — through the agency of steam navigation — in respect of new inventions alone. This mutually improving process will be further developed by the telegraph. Hourly intercourse with Europe will familiarize us with the progress of the European mind, and efface the last remains of provincialism here. Regular morning and evening bulletins from the United States will open the eyes of Europe to the real state of society here, and will dispell that ignorance and prejudice which to this day disgrace so many enlightened Europeans. It is said that one of the most sagacious statesmen of continental Europe has been

from the first opposed to the telegraph; he foresaw that regular
announcements of the working of our system of self-government
would exercise no small effect on the popular mind of Germany and
France.

The Great Prize-Fight: October 30.

Without doubt the leading event of last week — to a large mass
of the people of New York and the other large cities — was the
prize-fight which took place between Morrissey and Heenan not
far from the city of Buffalo.   Other events there were, of no small
import — Congressional nominations, speeches of political aspirants,
début of Mlle. Piccolimini, the success of "Miles Standish," arrival
of steamers from Europe, departure of war vessels from Paraguay —
but all of these were overshadowed and swallowed up by the great
boxing-match at Long Point.   On Thursday, especially, there was
nothing heard of — uptown, downtown, and in the country — but
the great prize-fight and the wonderful skill and science, and luck
and pluck, and gentleness and behavior generally, of Morrissey and
his antagonist, the Benicia Boy. . . . The rush for the paper which
happened to contain the only report of the fight was frantic.   Copies
were in demand at a shilling apiece, and at 10 A.M., in some parts,
as the financial reporters would say, the market for *Heralds* was
buoyant at a quarter.   The prize-fight was, we venture to assert, the
only topic discussed that morning in bank parlors, counting rooms,
and offices generally throughout the city — to say nothing of bar-
rooms, and places of like character.   What are we to infer?   That
the brutal element in our nature is simply vailed over by social
habits, but that it will tear away the vail under adequate provocation?

Coffee Displacing Tea in the United States: October 30.

For the past six or eight months at least, the sales of imported
teas at this port (which is the type of all the ports) have been un-
usually small, and the prices ruinous to the importer.   Just before
the revulsion of last year teas — having been imported in excess —
were selling at a severe loss.   The war with China suddenly imparted
vitality to the market.   There was a possibility that our supply of
tea might be cut off for years, and the price rose, in a very short
space of time, to a point which left a profit on the importation.   But
what happened?   People throughout the country were poor, and
sought to retrench.   As if by concert with each other, families
throughout the North and West began to dispense with tea — at
the advance in price — and in many cases to adopt coffee as a substitute.   This was only discovered when the great tea-houses, which

had been holding their cargoes throughout the long depression of 1856–7, attempted to realize on them at the advance in price. They found it impossible. Nobody wanted tea. . . . The spring and summer of 1858 passed. From time to time the pulse of the market was felt by auction sales. No advance worth mentioning was realized. The stock of tea in the interior must have been exhausted long since, and yet at the present moment the demand is so small that teas are actually selling in this market at 40 and 50 per cent loss on the cost of importation. In a word, a people who are in the habit of importing and consuming annually over 20,000,000 pounds of tea, have been content this year with one-fourth of that amount. Tea-drinking for the present has almost ceased.

On the other hand, coffee has been in steady demand throughout the year. It soon recovered from the depression caused by the financial crisis, and has been active, at a fair price, almost ever since.

DEATH OF BENTON[1]

New York *Tribune*, April 12, 1858

In the death of Mr. Benton the country loses one of its marked public characters. He was a man of great force, but that force was of a personal rather than of an intellectual nature. An intense individuality characterized all that he said and did. His frame was large, his health robust, his nature burly. He was truculent, energetic, intrepid, wilful, and indomitable. He always wore a resolute and determined air, and, simply viewed as an animal, possessed a very commanding aspect. He strode into public life with these qualities all prominent and bristling. Whenever he shone he shone in the exhibition of them. His intellectual powers always appeared as subsidiary; they never took the lead, never appeared to be the propelling force in any of the marked epochs of his life. The leading points of his career were his land-reform measure; his opposition to the old United States Bank; his expunging resolution; his war on Mr. Calhoun after his disappointment in the succession to the Presidency; and his hostility to the Compromise measures of 1850. In all these contests, at least in all but that for the reform of the land system, he bore himself as a fighting man. He carried this so far as to allude, in one of his later senatorial exhibitions, to a pair of pistols, which he said had never been used but a funeral followed.

Mr. Benton had been ten years in the Senate before he was known to the country as a prominent debater. The discussion on the United States Bank question brought him out fully, and was of a

[1] This admirable characterization is typical of Greeley's style at its best.

character to exhibit his powers to the greatest possible advantage.
It was a question that touched the feelings and the private interests
of individuals deeply, and roused the intensest ardor of all partisan
politicians. The debates were heated and fiercely personal. A
hand-to-hand political encounter overspread the country. This contest suited Benton exactly. He loved the turmoil and the war, and
he rose with each successive exigency until he became, par excellence, the champion of General Jackson's Administration in its contest with the Bank. On one occasion, in 1830–31, he made a speech
of four days. At the close of the fourth day Mr. Calhoun sarcasti-
cally remarked that Mr. Benton had taken one day longer in his
assault on the Bank than it had taken to accomplish the revolution
in France.

The intellectual strength of Mr. Benton's efforts never impressed
his great adversaries, Clay, Calhoun, and Webster. They never
regarded him as belonging to their class intellectually. Yet they
always appreciated and dreaded his great personal force. In no case
did this peculiar Bentonian ability manifest itself more clearly or
more offensively than in the passage of the expunging resolution.
General Jackson had been censured by the Senate in a resolution
drawn by Mr. Clay for acting "in derogation of the Constitution."
Mr. Benton set about to remove the censure by expunging it from
the records. He has told how he accomplished this in his "Thirty
Years' View." The story is fairly told and illustrates the man perfectly. The whole transaction bears the marks of a haughty,
domineering, and repulsive spirit. The reader, as he peruses Mr.
Benton's account of it, feels the triumph to be of a coarse and vulgar
character, the work of ill-temper and passion, with not a single flash
of intellectual or moral elevation in the whole proceeding.

In his political career Mr. Benton often showed himself a fierce
and malignant, but never, we think, a generous adversary. It is
said that on his deathbed he has done full justice to Mr. Clay in
finishing his abridgement of the debates of 1850, and it is pleasant
to hear it. We do not doubt that his temper was mollified in later
years, as he found himself rapidly approaching the termination of
his life. In that debate he came directly in collision with Mr. Clay,
and was the only man, indeed, who offered or was able to offer
anything like real practical resistance to the impetuous and overbearing march of that great parliamentary leader. In the great
debate of 1850 in the Senate, Mr. Clay crushed at will all effective
opposition but that of Mr. Benton. On that occasion Benton did
not, however, furnish the brains of the debate any more than on
previous occasions. Mr. Seward and others of the opposition had
done that much more strikingly. But in parliamentary tactics, in

the exhibition of personal intrepidity, and in individuality and manner — which in every legislative contest are important elements —
Mr. Benton rose superior to every ally. His temper was roused, and
he hurled wrath and defiance at his enemies. On a question of
parliamentary law he came in immediate conflict with Mr. Clay,
who had the majority of the Senate with him and was determined
to carry his point. Mr. Benton met him with equal resolution, and
with a bulldog ferocity that caused his antagonist to recede and
yield the point from considerations of expediency. Mr. Benton was
allowed his way after hours of violent struggle and a night's deliberation of the majority. It was, to a very great extent, a triumph of
his fighting qualities. Foote, of Mississippi, entered very largely
into that debate, and persisted in dogging and attacking Benton.
Benton at last bade him stop, he would bear no more of his insults.
Foote continued in the same strain. Benton rose from his seat and
strode directly toward Foote, as if to throttle him on the spot. Foote
fled, and Benton was checked; but Foote never referred to Benton
afterward in the Senate. On another occasion Mr. Benton laid
himself out to attack Mr. Calhoun. He did it with ability, but his
bad blood, his ill-temper, his violence of manner and gross personalities were the predominant characteristics of the attack. There
was no pleasure to be derived from it merely as an intellectual
demonstration. On the contrary, it only impressed the hearer as
repulsive and disgusting.

In all these examples we see where Mr. Benton's power lay as a
parliamentarian, a debater, and a man. He never carried his point
by winning or convincing, or by pure mental effort. He never
reached his objects nor accomplished his successes by mere force of
oratory or intellect. He never impressed his audience or the public
by sheer strength of mind. It was his intense individuality and
animal force, acting upon an intellect of common scope and character, that gave him all his triumphs. His industry was great and his
memory remarkable. His knowledge was large, but it was in the
domain of facts. He never rose to the consideration of scientific
principles, and perhaps never even to the commoner field of philo-
sophic generalization. For himself he claimed to be a man of
"measures" rather than of principles or ideas. We should further
qualify this claim by saying he was chiefly a man of "facts." His
ideas of currency and the "gold" reform, which occupied him for
many years, were very crude; and so far as we know, were never
improved by after-study or reflection. They found expression in
the existing sub-treasury system. Another favorite measure of his
was a road to the Pacific, across the continent. His services in
establishing the preëmption system in the disposition of the public

lands were conspicuous, and their results have been eminently be-neficent, but we think the record of his principal "measures" must stop here. . . .

Mr. Benton's moral character as a public man is deserving of very high praise. In his public acts we believe he always followed the dictates of an honest purpose. He did not legislate for popularity nor for pay, nor for any individual advantage in any way. He advocated and opposed public measures on the ground of what he considered to be their merits. His judgments may have been clouded by passion or partisan feeling, as no doubt at times they were, but we believe he was always true to his convictions. Of venality and corruption in legislation he had an instinctive abhor-rence, and during the thirty years of his senatorial life we do not think the perfect integrity of his votes on all subjects, whether of a public or private character, was ever impugned. In this respect his ex-ample is worthy of the attention of all our rising public men, who, in these budding years of corruption, are likely to be tested by severer temptations than the statesmen of the past. Whatever else is unattainable in reputation to a legislator, the proud distinction of integrity is beyond no man's reach, and it is a virtue that is not likely to lose any of its lustre by being too common.

MR. POLLARD'S "MAMMY"[1]

New York *Tribune*, May 18, 1859

There are many instances of filial piety recorded, and very properly recorded, in history. The reader will please recall that which has most warmly touched his sensibilities, or most closely captivated his memory — of some Athenian son or Roman daughter, illustrious for obedience or devotion — and when contemplation has warmed him into an admiration of the Ancients and an inclination to depreciate the Moderns, we shall triumphantly bring forward Edward Pollard, of Washington, in the District of Columbia, Esq., as the champion, in this behalf, of the present day. Mr. Pollard has printed a pamphlet in defence of the proposition to re-open what may be most properly called the African Man-trade. Of Mr. Pol-lard's arguments in this production we cannot speak, for many reasons, the chief of which is that we have not seen them. But what Mr. Pollard may think of the slave-trade is of small consequence when compared with his filial devotion; and the expression of that feeling we have seen, for it has been disintegrated, if we may say so, from the main work, and, in the highly respectable character

[1] By C. T. Congdon, who wrote many of the most pungent and exasperating of the editorials which helped to provoke the Civil War.

of an Elegant Extract, is now making a fashionable tour through the newspapers.

We trust that the Reverend Doctor Adams has seen this wandering small paragraph; that it has rendered moist his venerable eyes, and warmed the cockles of his ancient heart. For it appears that when Mr. Edward Pollard was a boy, his father had not merely the happiness to possess such a son, but in addition to this blessing in tunics, Mr. Edward Pollard's father — not to put too fine a point upon it — owned niggers. As Mr. Edward Pollard lives in Washington, and is therefore, *prima facie*, an impoverished office-holder, the presumption is that the black diamonds are no longer retained as their-looms in the Pollard family, but have been sold by papa Pollard, and sent to enjoy themselves upon the sugar-plantations, or to paddle and splash in the rice-swamps. Edward Pollard, Esq., has therefore the inestimable privilege of indulging in the Pleasures of Memory, and the way in which he does it is creditable to his heart. He sighs not for the stalwart field-hands, worth one thousand dollars apiece; he mourns not for the yellow hand-maidens with taper waists and languishing eyes; he weeps not for the coachman who guided his father's chariot; the laundress who got up his infant linen; the cook who prepared the domestic hominy; or the scullion who scrubbed the ancestral floor.

From these treasures, worth, in the aggregate, a very handsome sum of money, Edward Pollard, Esq., turns to drop a tear upon the grave of his "mammy." "Mammy" was Edward Pollard's nurse. From the sable heart of "mammy" he first drew his snowy sustenance. In the dark arms of "mammy" he tasted the titillation of his first dandle. From the black hand of "mammy" he received his initial corn-cake. Her voice chanted his vesper lullaby and summoned him to his matin ablutions. Mr. Pollard "confesses" — although, under the circumstances, we do not see the necessity of the qualification — that he is not ashamed of his affection for his "mammy." She died; for all "mammies" — even the "mammy" of Mr. Pollard — were or are mortal. Then came her sepulchral honors. Wiping the copious tears from his eyes, Mr. Pollard informs us that "in his younger days" he made "little monuments over the grave of his mammy." How many he made he does not inform us. What material he used, we are not told; but we know that infant architects have a partiality for mud.

And now Mr. Pollard, discarding the sentimental, waxes savage. Standing over the grave of his "mammy," and suddenly getting angry without any apparent occasion, he cries: "Do you think I could ever have borne to see her consigned to the demon abolitionists?" There is really no need of all this vehemence. We perfectly understand the case. We appreciate Mr. Pollard's feelings. We know that he could not have borne it. For who then would have ministered to his necessities? Who would have darned his juvenile hose? Who would have rocked his cradle? Who would have "run to catch him when he fell and kissed the place to make it well?" And, moreover, had "the demon abolitionists" caught Mr. Pollard's "mammy," he is perfectly certain that they would have "consigned her lean, starved corpse to a pauper grave." From which we infer that in addition to the mud memorials heretofore mentioned, as erected by Mr. Pollard, in the first gush of childhood's sorrow, he has since placed over the grave of "Mammy" something very splendid in the way of a mausoleum. For, as we have already noticed, "mammy" is no more; and Edward Pollard, Esq., to use his own most charming language, can "only look at her through the mist of long years." She died without the aid, assistance or cruel commerce of "the demon abolitionists," and Mr. Pollard, who appears to be an elderly gentleman, has to pay a washing-bill every Saturday, and as he d—ns the laundress in respect of buttons, remembers "mammy" and conjures up the image of "the dear old slave." He recalls how, when his mother scolded him, his "mammy" protected and humored him; and seems, in his desolation to have come to the conclusion that this is rather a weary world. There appears nothing to do but to put Edward Pollard, Esq., out to nurse — dry-nurse or wet-nurse, according to circumstances — and to strive by every tender art to divert his mind from the distracting memory of the original "mammy." Of all the poor white people in Washington, he seems to be in the lowest spirits — if we except Mr. James Buchanan.

Whether the result of Mr. Edward Pollard's grief for his "mammy" will re-open the African Man-trade, is more than we can determine. The connection between his bereavement and that branch of commerce we have been somewhat at a loss to discover. We have been able to conclude only that there now exists at the South a dearth of "mammies," and that Mr. Pollard, having felt through long years the want of that useful article, seeks to replenish the market by the importation of what we may call the raw material. Left himself an orphan in respect of "mammy," at a tender age, with his locks unkempt, with his face dirty, with his mouth pitifully gaping for gruel, and with his trousers torn, he looks forward to future Pollards — still, if we may use the figure, mere shrubs in a like condition of emptiness and squalor. He seeks, like a true philanthropist, to provide for this great want; and when the importation commences, "mammies" will, we suppose, be regularly quoted in the Prices Current. Meanwhile, Mr. Pollard's case must be attended to by the charitable. A pair of "mammies" — one for him and one for the White House — should be purchased at once by subscription.

THE DEFENSIVE SQUARE OF AUSTRIAN ITALY[1]

New York *Times*, July 16, 1859

The main merit of Peschiera is that this fortress lies on an island, and was captured by the Duke of Genoa in 1848. At this time the Sardinians crossed the Mincio after several hours' hard fighting; and if we follow the windings of the Mincio we shall find countless elbows formed in the elbows of the regular army, at places like Salianza, Molini, and Borghette. These places make up the base of the allied army. The line of the Mincio is the base of the new campaign we are about to open.

Almost at the southern end of the river Mincio lies the strong fortress of Mantua, the only Gibraltar of Austria in Italy guaranteed by the treaties of 1815. Mantua, as we have said, lies on a lake of the river Mincio. In spite of the labors spent on it, Mantua still holds the next rank to Verona. It is a post of danger for the army shut between its walls, rather than for the enemy without. After a battle of several hours' duration, the Sardinians at Goito gave way; and, if we follow up the course of the Mincio, we shall find innumerable elbows formed by the sympathy of youth. Defended by Wurmser in 1797, Austria surrendered to Napoleon III in 1859. Notwithstanding the toil spent by Austria on the spot, we should have learned that we are protected by a foreign fleet coming up suddenly on our question of citizenship. A canal cuts Mantua in two; but we may rely on the most cordial Cabinet Minister of the new power in England.

CORRECTION

New York *Times*, July 18, 1859

We owe it to our readers to say that, by a confusion of manuscripts, sent up at a late hour on Friday night, our leading article of Saturday on the "Austrian Defensive Square" was rendered perfectly unintelligible. The article appeared correctly in our second edition, but we reprint it today in another column. As our extremely ridiculous blunder afforded matter for much legitimate and good-natured merriment to our contemporaries of the Sunday press, and a happy occasion for airing a little envy, malice, and uncharitableness to the less respectable among the daily journals, the newspaper world is indebted to us for making it, and our apology is addressed to the world of readers alone.

[1] By W. H. Hurlburt, a brilliant if dissipated writer long with the *Times* and later with Manton Marble on the *World*. This editorial was written after a somewhat too gay evening party in honor of a friend departing for Europe.

JOHN BROWN AND A SLAVE INSURRECTION[1]

New York *Evening Post*, October 18, 1859

The stories connecting the name of "old Brown of Ossawatomie,' as he is called, with the leadership of this fanatical enterprise are we are induced to think, well-founded; and in that event the whole affair might be regarded as a late fruit of the violence which the slaveholders introduced into Kansas. Brown was one of the early settlers in that territory; he was a conspicuous object of persecution all through the troubles; his property was destroyed; he and his family were cruelly treated on several occasions; three or four of his sons were killed by Southern desperadoes; and these many exasperations drove him to madness. He has not been regarded since, we are told, as a perfectly sane man. He has been known to vow vengeance against the whole class of slaveholders for the outrages perpetrated by their representatives in Kansas, and this insurrection if he is at the head of it, is the manner in which he gluts his resentments. Frenzied by the remembrance of his wrongs, his whole nature turned into gall by the bitter hatreds stirred up in Kansas, and reckless of consequences, he has plunged into the work of blood.

Passion does not reason; but if Brown reasoned and desired to give a public motive to his personal rancors, he probably said to himself that "the slave drivers had tried to put down freedom in Kansas by force of arms, and he would try to put down slavery in the same means." Thus the bloody instructions which they taught return to plague the inventors. They gave, for the first time in the history of the United States, an example of the resort to arms to carry out their political schemes, and dreadful as the retaliation is which Brown has initiated, must take their share of the responsibility. They must remember that they accustomed men, in their Kansas forays, to the idea of using arms against their political opponents, that by their crimes and outrages they drove hundreds to madness, and that the feelings of bitterness and revenge thus generated have since rankled in the heart. Brown has made himself an organ of these in a fearfully significant way.

No one can think of the possible results of an outbreak of this kind, should it become general, without shuddering; without calling up to his imagination the most terrible scenes of incendiarism, carnage, and rape. In nearly all the Southern States the negroes greatly preponderate in number. Many of them, it is true, are too ignorant and stupid to take any effective part in an insurrection;

[1] John Brown began his famous raid into Virginia to free the slaves and excite an insurrection on October 16, 1859; he was captured on the 18th, severely wounded, and after trial in the Virginia courts, he was found guilty of treason and publicly hanged on December 2.

AMINADAB SLEEK AT JONES' WOOD.

"My friends, there is no patriotic duty on earth more gratifying to my feelings than to make a speech over Mr. Lincoln's political grave. [Loud cheers.] I do not make this remark out of any unkindness to Mr. Lincoln, but I believe that the good of his own country requires it."—*Douglas's Speech, Wednesday, September 12th, 1860.*

From *Vanity Fair*, October 13, 1860.

others, too, are profoundly attached to their masters or their families; but these excepted, there are yet thousands able and willing to strike for their emancipation. It has been impossible to keep them in entire ignorance of the blessings of freedom, and of the possibility of attaining it by force of arms; the fugitive slaves of the North have found means of communicating with their old comrades; the Abolitionists have spoken to them by pictures, if not by language; Democratic orators have told them falsely that the entire North was engaged in a crusade against the South for the sake of the slaves; and as servants in the cities they have heard the talk of the parlor and barrooms, and in innumerable other ways have been made to think and to desire. When the hour comes, therefore, they will not be found either so incapable or so docile as the slaveholders seem to suppose.

But what a condition of society is that in which half the population constantly menaces the other half with civil war and murder; in which the leading classes go to sleep every night, carelessly, it may be, over the crater of a volcano; and in which the dangers do not lessen, as in other societies, with time, but grow with its growth until an explosion becomes as inevitable as the eruptions of Etna or Vesuvius! What a condition of society, to be extended over the virgin territories of the West, the seat of our future empire, and for which politicians should clamor and sear their consciences, and desperadoes should fight!

How insane the policy which would recruit and extend this form of social existence, even while it is becoming unmanageable as it is! Open the gates to the slave trade, cry the Southerners, who are as great fanatics as Brown; tap the copious resources of Africa, let new millions of blacks be added to the enormous number that now cultivate our fields, let the alarming disproportion between them and the whites be increased; it is a blessed institution, and we cannot have too much of it! But while they speak the tocsin sounds, the blacks are in arms, their houses are in flames, their wives and children driven into exile or killed, and a furious servile war stretches its horrors over years. That is the blessed institution you ask us to foster and spread and worship, and for the sake of which you even spout your impotent threats against the grand edifice of the Union!

[JOHN BROWN OF OSSAWATOMIE]

Springfield *Republican*, 1859

Brown's Character: Oct. 19, 1859.

He is so constituted that when he gets possessed of an idea he carries it out with unflinching fidelity to all its original consequences, as they seem to him, hesitating at no absurdity, and deterred by no unpleasant consequences to him personally. He is a Presbyterian in his faith and feels that it is for this very purpose that God has reared him up. This is evident in the answers given in his catechism, as he lay chained and bloody, with fierce eyes against him and hearts thirsting for his blood. His perfect coolness and self-possession, his evident truthfulness and transparent sincerity, and the utter absence of fear in his manner, commanded the respect of all about him. The universal feeling is that John Brown is a hero — a misguided and insane man, but nevertheless inspired with a genuine heroism. He has a large infusion of the stern old Puritan element in him.

An Unfair Trial: Oct. 24.

The whole manner in which the trial is conducted shows that the Virginians have not recovered from their original fright. They scent a rescue in the air, surround their poor wounded and worn prisoners with bayonets, and promise to bring them to the gallows within thirty days. Let them go ahead in their crazy cowardice and see if their "ain roof-trees" are any firmer for it.

Brown's Speech on Receiving Sentence: Nov. 4.

In calm dignity, in the conscious rectitude of good intentions, in an honest and hearty faith in Christianity, it has in it heroic elements that elevate it toward the sublime. . . . If he had been a weak man or a wicked man, a felon in the common acceptation of that word, when the sentence was pronounced upon him there would have been a general and tumultuous demonstration of satisfaction in the Charlestown court-room. Instead of that, the impressive silence was broken only by the clapping of a single pair of hands, and the people were shocked and mortified that even one man should have been found in Virginia who appreciated so poorly the character of the prisoner and the nature of his condemnation. This scene shows the wonderful impression made by Brown upon those about him. It is this great sincerity and heroic self-sacrifice to what he believed to be right that gave him such influence over the men who enlisted in his scheme, and that has so impressed the Virginians with respect, from Governor Wise down, and that will make it a difficult thing to hang him.

Awaiting Death: Nov. 12.

We can conceive of no event that could so deepen the moral hostility of the people of the free States to slavery as this execution. This not because the acts of Brown are generally approved, for they are not. It is because the nature and spirit of the man are seen to be great and noble, and everybody feels that he acted from feelings that do honor to human nature, and that are to be condemned only because they were not directed by wisdom and soundness of mind. John Brown is neither a traitor nor a murderer in intention. His death will be a result of his own folly, to be sure, but that will not prevent his being considered a martyr to his hatred of oppression, and all who sympathize with him in that sentiment will find their hatred grow stronger and deeper as they contemplate his death. Nobody can respect an institution to the safety of which the death of the too ardent lover of liberty is essential. If Virginia were wise she would see this and be magnanimous; but she is neither wise nor magnanimous in anything that concerns her property in human brains and bones, and so we suppose the appointed hanging will occur.

The Day After the Execution: Dec. 3.

John Brown still lives. The great State of Virginia has hung his venerable body upon the ignominious gallows, and released John Brown himself to join the "noble army of martyrs." There need be no tears for him. Few men die so happily, so satisfied with time, place, and circumstance, as did he. . . . A Christian man, hung by Christians for acting upon his convictions of duty — a brave man hung for a chivalrous and self-sacrificing deed of humanity — a philanthropist hung for seeking the liberty of oppressed men. No outcry about violated law can cover up the essential enormity of a deed like this.

THE HELPER BOOK [1]

New York *Tribune*, January 12, 1860

"The stars in their courses fought against Sisera." The slavery question cannot be discussed, even in the most commendatory manner, without inuring to the advancement of the cause of truth and righteousness. The Congressional denunciations of Helper's book are producing the most astonishing effect in promoting its circulation. The orders flow in for it from all quarters, in all quantities, from a single copy up to three hundred in a bunch. We do not know how many copies have been ordered, but we have reason to believe the number already exceeds one hundred thousand. The price is now reduced to about eighteen dollars a hundred in conse-

[1] Hinton Rowan Helper, a "poor white" of North Carolina, published "The Impending Crisis of the South, and How to Meet It," in 1857, and by 1859 it attained an enormous circulation. It attacked the oligarchy of the wealthy slaveholders in the South as a fatal impediment to the advancement and happiness of the millions of whites who had little or no property. Slavery, Helper argued, would have to be abolished in order to give the whites a proper economic and social position, to stimulate industry and commerce, and to encourage cities and schools.

quence of the extensive sale. The work goes everywhere, through all sorts of channels, to the North, East, South, and West. Old fogy Union-saving merchants in the Southern trade stand aghast at the sly requests slipped in all over the South, in the shape of notes and postscripts for goods, for "that Helper book that is making such a fuss in Congress." Innocent bales, bags, boxes, and barrels bound for the South, looking for all the world as though they contained nothing more inflammatory than coffee, calico, hardware, and other similar commodities, have each a copy of Helper tucked furtively away in the hidden centre of their contents. In this way the work is penetrating the whole South in a manner that no hunter for incendiary pamphlets would suppose or can possibly arrest. If we go about the streets of this most conservative city, ten to one we are delayed at the first crossing by a hand-cart or wheelbarrow load of Helper. It is Helper on the counter, Helper at the stand, Helper in the shop and out of the shop, Helper here, Helper there, Helper everywhere. It looks now as though every man, woman, and child in the United States was bound to have a Helper before the year is out. There never was a political pamphlet that had such a rushing demand and sale before, with the exception, perhaps, of the Life of Scott issued in the Presidential campaign of 1852. For the extraordinary impetus thus given to the sale of this highly valuable and interesting work we renewedly tender our heartfelt acknowledgments to the "Gulf Squadron" of members of the Federal House of Representatives at Washington. We certainly never expected them to do so much for the cause of their country, and we dare say they are equally astounded and sorry to have aided it so essentially. Let them be thankful that they have been the means of public enlightenment on an important topic, and that they have widely contributed to the spread of anti-slavery sentiment. It shall be gratefully remembered by the children of oppression, and be chiselled on their tombstones.

> *The meanest reed that trembles in the wind,*
> *If Heaven select it for its instrument,*
> *May shed celestial music on the breeze,*
> *As clearly as the pipe whose notes*
> *Befit the lip of Phœbus.*

[SLAVE LIFE PREFERRED BY NEGROES]

De Bow's Review, April, 1860

A few days ago, Ben H. Baker, Esq., says the Montgomery *Mail*, visited the city and caused to be introduced a bill in the legislature by which twelve free negroes are allowed to become slaves. The bill passed both houses and was signed by the Governor; the speedy transaction of the affair being caused mainly by the entire confidence which members of both houses have in the personal integrity and fine intelligence of Mr. Baker. The facts are briefly these: These negroes, men, women, and children, have been reared by Mr. Young Edwards, of Russell County, and have always lived with him as servants. Lately someone informed these negroes that, being free, the sheriff would be required to expel them, under a provision of the code, within thirty days. At this they were greatly alarmed, and protested that they were unwilling to leave their master, and were perfectly willing to remain his slaves, and in fact preferred it. Mr. Baker visited the negroes, and explained to them their position and rights fully; and the upshot was, they induced him to come and lay their case before the Legislature, asking it to allow them to become the slaves of Mr. Edwards. The bill was accordingly passed. It provides that the probate court of Russell shall have the negroes brought before it, and diligently take testimony to ascertain if any undue influence has been used to obtain their consent to become slaves; and upon being satisfied that they, wittingly and with full knowledge of their rights, desire to enter a state of servitude, shall decree them to be the slaves of the person they may choose to be their owner.

These negroes know what their own best interest is. They will be better fed and clothed than ever Horace Greeley or Lucy Stone was, before these worthies made money by shovelling the filth of fanaticism; they will be better rewarded for their labor than any operative in any cotton mill in all Lawrence; and in sickness and old age, forever, will be tended carefully and surrounded with all necessary comforts. And so they don't choose to go into the wretchedness, privation, and squalor of free negro life in the North.

THE ISSUES OF THIS CAMPAIGN

Springfield *Republican*, August 25, 1860

The South, through the mouth of many of its leading politicians and journals, defies the North to elect Abraham Lincoln to the presidency. It threatens secession in case he shall be elected. It arrogantly declares that he shall never take his seat. It passes resolutions of the most outrageous and insolent character, insulting every man who dares to vote for what they call a "Black Republican." To make a long matter very short and plain, they claim the privilege of conducting the government in all the future, as they have in all the past, for their own benefit and in their own way, with the alternative of dissolving the Union of the States. Now, if the non-slaveholding people have any spirit at all, they will settle this question at once and forever. Look at the history of the last two administrations, in which the slave interest has had undisputed sway. This sway, the most disgraceful and shameless of anything in the history of the government, must not be thrown off or else the Union will be dissolved. Let's try it! Are we forever to be governed by a slaveholding minority? Will the passage of four years more of misrule make it any easier for the majority to assume its functions?

There are many reasons why we desire to see this experiment tried this fall. If the majority cannot rule the country without the secession of the minority, it is time the country knew it. If the country can only exist under the rule of an oligarchy, let the fact be demonstrated at once, and let us change our institutions. We desire to see the experiment tried, because we wish to have the Southern people, who have been blinded and cheated by the politicians, learn that a "Black Republican" respects the requirements of the Constitution and will protect their interests. Harmony between the two sections of this country can never be secured until the South has learned that the North is not its enemy, but its best friend. We desire to see it tried, that the whole horde of corrupt officials at Washington may be swept by the board, and something of decency and purity introduced there. We desire to see it, that the government may be restored to its original integrity. And any Northern man who has not pluck enough to stand up and help do this thing is a poltroon. It will be tried, and our minority friends may make up their mind to it.

THE HOME OF JOHN C. CALHOUN

De Bow's Review, September, 1860

We saw Mr. Calhoun first in Greenville District, South Carolina, in 1838, and heard him, in the presence of an assembled multitude, discourse of the independent treasury, and meet in debate the Hon. Waddy Thompson, who had then the hardihood to splinter a lance with him. How the eyes of the old man flashed and his form towered, and how the welkin rang with the loud plaudits! He was a guest that night at the simple farmhouse where we resided. Next we saw him in the old theatre at Charleston, which was thronged from pit to dome. "If ever," said he in opening, and the multitude stood without a pulsation, "if ever a representative had just reason to be proud of his constituents, I am that representative and you are those constituents." Again, and this time we were companions on that memorable trip to the West (it was our first trip, from which we did not return, and hence the *Review*), it was our never-to-be-forgotten privilege of witnessing the ovations which, all along the banks of the great river, from New Orleans to Memphis, were paid to him by assembled hosts. At Vicksburg, Jefferson Davis addressed the great statesman, who, embarrassed by the compliment, said in reply that he was "unaccustomed to speak without a subject," which caused some merriment. On the part of the beautiful ladies who came on board, it was remarked that it was a custom established on the river by Mr. Clay that they had the right to kiss any great man who chanced to be passing by. "I dare not pretend," said Mr. Calhoun, "to vie with Mr. Clay in gallantry." Hereupon his son, a chivalrous young army officer, peace to his ashes, remarked to us aside, provoked by his father's austerity, "the old gentleman would do better to make me his deputy in the matter." A plain homespun countryman exclaimed on approaching, quite audibly, "Great God! It is old Jackson!" and another, somewhat inebriated, in attempting rather roughly to approach, was struck aback by the imposing presence, but rallying himself, at last found words, which the reader, we trust, will forgive us for repeating — "Mr. Calhoun, I have sworn by you all my life, and next to the Almighty, you are the greatest man in the world." But now the great Memphis convention is in session, and its president has risen from the chair to speak upon the questions at issue. Not a breath stirred the vast auditory. Oratory such as this, which spellbinds and yet deals not in the lightning and the thunderbolt, is a new revelation at the West; but when the words come, in speaking of the old Mississippi, that it is "an inland sea," there goes up a shout which is like the roar of Niagara, and rising from their seats, and waving their hats in wild enthusiasm, these men of the West give cheer after cheer to the Palmetto Chief. Not soon did the turmoil cease. In 1847, we took tea with him at Washington, and heard him speak of his intended treatise upon government, which, he said, would not be appreciated for twenty-five years; and when the smoke of Buena Vista had cleared away, and men began to agitate the nomination of its hero for the Presidency, there came to us at New Orleans, through the mail, one of those laconic dispatches which Mr. Calhoun only could indite, and which we remember nearly word for word, and will give, in remarkable illustration of his capacity for condensation:

> I see that General Taylor's arrival among you is announced, and it is said he will run for the Presidency. How stands the fact, and what are understood to be his opinions in regard to party nominations for the Presidency, the "Wilmot Proviso," and the Tariff of 1846?

But space compels me to pause in these, to us, interesting reminiscences. They are recalled by everything around us. We are on
classical ground. We tread the halls which so long answered only
to *his* step. We are in his library, and here are the books which he
read, and this is his writing desk, and his lamp, and his chair, and
his walking-cane, as he left them. Here is a portrait, which shows
him worn by the grim advances of age and disease, and another, a
glorious picture, new to us at every point, showing him in those proud
days of early manhood, when he was the very master-spirit of the
Monroe Cabinet! Near by hangs the portrait, the first we have seen
taken in his prime, of his friend and almost twin-brother in fame,
George McDuffie.

Fit abode for such a man! — from its grand scenery and as grand
historic associations. Just here was the site of Fort Rutledge (hence
the name which Mr. Calhoun changed from "Fort Place" to "Fort
Hill"), a relic of which we find in an old, now filled-up well. Tradition has it that this well was dug by the white inhabitants who
were besieged and cut off from the river by innumerable savage
hordes, and in their attempt afterward to escape, were surprised
and ruthlessly put to death. One alone of the whole party remained
to tell the tale. Tradition has it also, and Mr. Calhoun was wont
to tell it himself, on the authority of his father-in-law, the story being
confirmed to him by a well-informed Indian historian, that in the
far remote past, ere yet the white man had been anywhere seen, a
giant struggle took place at this very point between the Cherokees,
who inhabited the country, and a tribe of Northern Senecas, who,
victorious over every tribe in the Southern marches, were first
brought to a stand here on the banks of the stream which thence
took the name of Seneca, and were driven back with fearful slaughter.
May not future history have in store a like record of other *Northern*
tribes?

THE PERIL OF THE SOUTH [1]

Charleston *Courier*, November, 1860

Immediate danger will be brought to slavery in all the frontier
States. When a party is enthronged at Washington, in the executive
and legislative departments of the government, whose creed is to
repeal the fugitive slave law, the underground railroad will become
an overground railroad. The tenure of slave property will be felt
to be weakened; and the slave will be sent down to the cotton
States for sale, and the frontier States enter on the policy of making
themselves free States.

[1] The *Courier* was the mouthpiece of Robert Barnwell Rhett and the extreme
secessionists of South Carolina.

With the control of the government of the United States, and an organized and triumphant North to sustain them, the abolitionists will renew their operations upon the South with increased courage. The thousands in every country who look up to power and make gain out of the future will come out in support of the abolition government. They will organize; and from being a Union party to support an abolition government, they will become like the government they support, abolitionists. They will have an abolitionist party in the South of Southern men. The contest for slavery will no longer be one between the North and the South. It will be in the South, between the people of the South.

If in our present position of power and unitedness we have the raid of John Brown, and twenty towns burned down in Texas in one year by abolitionists, what will be the measures of insurrection and incendiarism which must follow our notorious and abject prostration to abolition rule in Washington, with all the patronage of the Federal government and a Union organization in the South to support it? Secret conspiracy and its attendant horrors, with rumors of more horrors, will hover over every portion of the South; while in the language of the Black Republican patriarch, Giddings, they will "laugh at your calamities, and mock when your fear cometh."

Already there is uneasiness throughout the South as to the stability of its institution of slavery. But with a submission to the rule of abolitionists at Washington, thousands of slaveholders will despair of the institution. While the condition of things in the frontier States will force the slaves on the market of the cotton States, the timid in the cotton States will sell their slaves. The general distrust must affect purchasers. The consequence must be that slave property will be greatly depreciated. We see advertisements for the sale of slaves in some of the cotton States for the simple object of getting rid of them; and we know that standing orders for the purchase of slaves in this market have been withdrawn, on account of an anticipated decline of value from the political condition of the country.

We suppose that, taking in view all these things, it is not extravagant to estimate that the submission of the South to the administration of the Federal government under Messrs. Lincoln and Hamlin must reduce the value of slaves in the South $100 each. It is computed that there are 4,300,000 slaves in the United States. Here, therefore, is a loss to the Southern people of $430,000,000 on their slaves alone. Of course real estate of all kinds must also partake in the depreciation of slaves. Slave property is the foundation of all property in the South. When security in this is shaken, all other property partakes of its instability. Banks, stocks, bonds, must be influenced. Timid men will sell out and leave the South. Confusion, distrust, and pressure must reign.

The ruin of the South, by the emancipation of her slaves, is not like the ruin of any other people. It is not a mere loss of liberty, like the Italians under the Bourbons. It is not heavy taxation, which must still leave the means of living or otherwise taxation defeats itself. But it is the loss of liberty, property, home, country — everything that makes life worth having. And this loss will probably take place under circumstances of suffering and horror unparalleled in the history of nations. We must preserve our liberties and institutions under penalties greater than those which impend over any people in the world.

THE CRISIS AND THE REMEDY [1]

New York *Herald*, January 5, 1861

Let the people, therefore, speak. Of the five millions of voters in the United States, it is within bounds to say that four million three hundred thousand are conservative in sentiment and prepared to concede to the South their reasonable demands. A constituent convention of the Southern States is already impending. The effervescence which has resulted in mob rule, violence, the seizure of national fortresses, custom houses, postoffices, and arsenals in South Carolina is generally disapproved of, even in slaveholding communities. If similar acts are committed elsewhere they will be isolated and irresponsible, and the popular voice will fail to sanction them. The general idea at the South, as is apparent from a study of the advices from the separate States, is that each aggrieved member of the confederation should secede, but that, once having passed acts of secession, they should leave relations with the Federal government as they are, and have recourse to a constituent convention of the Southern States to decide upon future definite action.

It is from such a Southern constituent convention that welfare to the Union may yet proceed. It will be assembled, necessarily, to the comparative exclusion of the small fry of mere sectional politicians, and the guarantees which it asks will be sensible, reasonable, and such as must commend themselves to the common sense of the masses of the people in the Central and Western States. They will insist upon the recognition of the property rights of their citizens everywhere; upon the needful stipulations which intolerance

---

[1] A number of the New York newspapers, including the *Day Book*, *Daily News*, and the *Journal of Commerce*, were opposed to any coercion of the seceding States; but none went to the length reached by James Gordon Bennett's *Herald*.

has hitherto denied; upon full liberty to carry slaves into the common territory, and upon the recognition of universal toleration of opinion respecting slavery as a social institution in the several States of the Union. They will submit these different conditions, as amendments to the Constitution, to the Northern States, earnestly inviting acceptance of them, and assigning a period, similar in principle to that which was appointed for the ratification of the Constitution in 1787, when all States which shall have agreed to them shall be considered as forming thenceforth the future United States of America.

It cannot be doubted for an instant, by those who have carefully analyzed the vote at the last Presidential election, and considered the reaction in the Republican ranks which has since taken place, that the people of the North and West will respond at once to the rational requirements of their Southern fellow-citizens. They will not pause in choosing between the happiness and prosperity which will flash upon the country out of concord, and the misery which perseverance in the chaotic byways of Abolition would produce. But, in order to be prepared to act with the promptitude which the occasion demands, the voice of the Northern States ought to be raised now, without the procrastination of an instant, in calling for constituent State conventions by legislatures north of the Potomac. The propositions of the South must be submitted to the non-slaveholding States separately, and these States should hold themselves ready to consider them. It is not an issue of parties. It is the people only who, "like the voice of many waters," must overpower and drown beneath a deluge of patriotism the anti-Union heresies which infect the republic. Let massmeetings everywhere call upon our Northern State Legislatures to summon together constituent State conventions. If New York begins, Pennsylvania, New Jersey, Michigan, Illinois, Indiana, will speedily follow their example, and a contagion of those sentiments which lighted the fires of Bunker Hill, and stained with blood the ice-blocks of the Delaware, will spread from the Atlantic shore to the log-cabin of the most distant squatter in Nebraska. "The Union must and shall be preserved" will be echoed and reëchoed far and near, and may even produce its rebound in the frozen consciences of Massachusetts and Vermont.

In a constituent Southern convention, and in constituent State conventions, assembled at the call of massmeetings everywhere by our Northern State Legislatures, to consider the amendments to the Constitution which the exigency of the times demands, is to be found the remedy of every evil. It is possible that States east of the Connecticut River may reject the propositions which the South presents; but if they do so let them act upon their own peril. Let them elect Garrison, Greeley, or Wendell Phillips as the president of a rigid Abolitionist republic; let them annex themselves to Canada; let them feed upon their own provincial self-conceit, love for isms, hatred for everybody but themselves, and console themselves in the enjoyment of a petty, intolerant, hard-bargaining, lawless, clergy-beridden nationality, with the reflection that not only the Southern, but the Middle States, are glad to get rid of them, and have regarded them as an incubus upon the Union for over a quarter of a century.   Meanwhile, let the action of the Union-loving States be prompt.   There is no time to be lost.   With proper diligence massmeetings may initiate action on the part of all our Northern legislatures within the present month.   In February the South will be ready to present its propositions, and before the period has arrived for the inauguration of Mr. Lincoln the tempest that now threatens so menacingly may have been entirely dispelled from our political horizon.

THE INAUGURAL ADDRESS OF MR. LINCOLN

New York *Herald*, March 5, 1861

It would have been almost as instructive if President Lincoln had contented himself with telling his audience yesterday a funny story and let them go.   His inaugural is but a paraphrase of the vague generalities contained in his pilgrimage speeches, and shows clearly either that he has not made up his mind respecting his future course, or else that he desires, for the present, to keep his intentions to himself.   The stupendous questions of the last month have been whether the incoming Administration would adopt a coercive or a conciliatory policy towards the Southern States; whether it would propose satisfactory amendments to the Constitution, convening an extra session of Congress for the purpose of considering them; and whether, with the spirit of the statesmen who laid the cornerstone of the institutions of the republic, it would rise to the dignity of the occasion, and meet as was fitting the terrible crisis through which the country is passing.   The inaugural gives no satisfaction on any of these points.   Parts of it contradict those that precede them, and where the adoption of any course is hinted at, a studious disavowal of its being a recommendation is appended.   Not a small portion of the columns of our paper, in which the document is amplified, look as though they were thrown in as a mere make-weight.   A resolve to procrastinate, before committing himself, is apparent throughout.   Indeed, Mr. Lincoln closes by saying that "there is no object in being in a hurry," and that "nothing valuable can be lost by taking time."   Filled with careless *bonhomie* as this first proclamation to the country of the new President, is, it will give but small contentment to those who believe that not only its prosperity, but its very existence is at stake.

The inaugural opens by deliberately ignoring the true issue between the Southern and Northern States. It declares that the slaveholding members of the confederation have no grievances; that "nobody is hurt," or will have a right to imagine himself hurt, until the peculiar institution is actively invaded when it exists. "Apprehension," he says, "seems to exist among the people of the Southern States, that their property, and their peace and personal security, are to be endangered. There has never been any reasonable cause for apprehension. Indeed, the most ample evidence to the contrary has all the while existed, and been open to their inspection." The same spirit runs through the whole speech. He quotes the Chicago platform resolution against John Brown, as though that were an all-sufficient reply to his objections, and elsewhere exclaims: — "Is it true that any right written in the Constitution has been denied? I think not." Yet, in the line and a half which is all that he thinks proper to devote to the momentous question of the common Territories, out of which has grown the sectional strife which convulses the Union, he virtually kicks to pieces the whole groundwork of Republican aggressions, and confesses the untenableness of their past claims. "Must Congress," he says, "protect slavery in the Territories? The Constitution does not expressly say."

A couple of paragraphs devoted to the Fugitive Slave law contain acknowledgment of his duty to enforce it, but while emphatically promising to do so, the President quibbles respecting the manner of carrying out the law, and interpolates for the benefit of his abolitionist friends a query respecting free negroes which is completely out of place. "Might it not be well," he asks, in their behalf, "to provide by law for the enforcement of that clause in the Constitution which 'guarantees that the citizens of each State shall be entitled to all the privileges and immunities of citizens in the several States?'" This is a covert fling, of course, at South Carolina, whose recent legislation on the subject of free negroes is thus held up for reprobation. . . .

In a word, the inaugural is not a crude performance — it abounds in traits of craft and cunning. It bears marks of indecision, and yet of strong coercive proclivities, with serious doubts whether the government will be able to gratify them. It is so clearly intended to admit of a double, or even of any possible interpretation, that many will content themselves with waiting for the progress of events, in the meanwhile seeking in it for no meaning at all. It is neither candid nor statesmanlike; nor does it possess any essential of dignity or patriotism. It would have caused a Washington to mourn and would have inspired Jefferson, Madison, or Jackson with contempt. With regard to the ultimate projects of Mr. Lincoln, the public is no wiser than before. It is sincerely to be trusted that he is yet ignorant of them himself.

THE POLICY OF THE ADMINISTRATION DEVELOPED

New York *Herald*, April 9, 1861

It is becoming too evident that, so far as a vicious, imbecile, demoralized Administration possesses power, the hideous horrors of civil war are about to be forced upon the country. The deliberations of Mr. Lincoln and his advisers have been shrouded in mystery; but the very concealment they have affected has betrayed their iniquitous purposes. Amid the contradictory reports that have lately prevailed, unmistakable facts have compelled a tardy and reluctant acquiescence in the conviction that aggressive measures are contemplated against the seceding States, and that hostile demonstrations, upon an extensive scale, have for many weeks formed part of the design of the government. Ominous and painful uncertainty has, at length, given place to the fearful prospect of an internecine strife between the North and the South, which is inevitable unless the troops that are being sent southward, more patriotic than their leaders, shall emulate the example of French soldiers when ordered to fire upon the people, and refuse to imbrue their hands in the blood of their fellow-citizens. The factious pressure upon the President for the adoption of a definite coercive policy has been crowned with success. The doors of the temple of Janus have been thrown open, and if, which is doubtful, proclivities for peace ever existed, they have been buried out of sight. Mr. Lincoln has fallen back upon the war doctrines of his inaugural, or his still less ambiguous utterances during the memorable journey from Springfield to Harrisburg.

"Irrepressible conflict" has thus succeeded in developing the outlines of a fearful shadow over the land; but it is to be hoped that the very armies which are soon to be brought face to face will shrink from permitting it to acquire a bloody substance. Far better that the Union should be dismembered forever than that fraternal hands should be turned against one another, to disfigure the land by slaughter and carnage. The masses of the population reprobate the blood-thirsty imbecility of the Washington government. They are forewarned, by the gigantic footsteps with which anarchy has been progressing, that a military despotism is imminent, which may reduce the country to the lowest place in the scale of nations. In the annals of history there would be found no parallel of a people, from such a height of prosperity as the United States have attained, so recklessly plunging its future destiny into an abyss of ruin, if the present mismanagement of affairs is allowed to continue. The popular sentiment is everywhere peaceful, and the time cannot be distant when the shameful manner in which Mr. Lincoln and his Cabinet are sacrificing the welfare of the land, and betraying its most sacred interests, will call forth an outbreak of indignation before which even Republican fanaticism and intolerance will tremble.

THE WAR AGAINST THE GOVERNMENT OF THE UNITED STATES[1]

New York *Times*, April 13, 1861

The Disunion conspiracy, which has for the last twenty years been gnawing at the heart-strings of the great American republic, has at last culminated in open war upon its glittering and resplendent flag. For the first time in the history of the United States, an organized attempt is made to destroy, by force of arms, the government which the American people have formed for themselves — to overthrow the glorious Constitution which has made us the envy of the world. The history of the world does not show so causeless an outrage. Amid all the rebellions against government which have stained the annals of civilized and Christian nations, not one can be found which had not more provocation than that which yesterday opened a war at Charleston upon the government and the forces of the United States. Not a solitary act of oppression — not a single act of wrong — not the faintest possible trespass upon Southern rights can be urged in extenuation of this infamous rebellion. Whatever may be the result of the war which the South has now begun, it will stand on the pages of history, for all time to come, as the blackest and most dishonoring outbreak of irrational and ferocious passion which has ever marked the checkered annals of national progress. Whatever the leaders of this conspiracy may believe, the civilized world will have but one opinion of their conduct; they will be greeted with the indignant scorn and execration of the world. . . .

One thing is certain. Now that the rebels have opened the war, the people will expect the government to defend itself with vigor and determination. There is no room for half-way measures now.

[1] The bombardment of Fort Sumter began on the morning of April 12; the garrison surrendered the following day.

There can be no further talk of a pacific policy — of measures of conciliation — of fears of exasperating the people of the Southern States. The day for that has passed. *The South has chosen war, and it must have all the war it wants.* The issue is not made by the United States government. It is made by the South. The Administration has gone to the very verge of pusillanimity in its forbearance. It has endured wrongs and tamely submitted to outrages which no other government on the face of the earth would have endured for an hour. It has done everything consistent with honor, and many things which it is very hard to reconcile with a proper feeling of national self-respect, to avert this horrible alternative which is at last thrust upon them. For no other offence than that of trying to relieve its soldiers from starvation, the batteries of the Southern Confederacy have been opened upon the government of the United States. The flag of the republic is to be lowered in disgrace — or the issue of war is to be met.

The President of the United States must not hesitate an instant as to the policy he will pursue, nor must he spare anything of vigor and energy in the manner of putting it into execution.

[ON TO WASHINGTON!][1]

Richmond *Examiner*, April 28, 1861

Washington is the weak point with our enemies — their fears and their preparations prove that they feel and know it. It is to Washington that the Northern rabble is summoned. Cannot Virginians and other Southerners reach Washington before this multitudinous and disorderly rabble arrives? Let not individuals, or companies, or regiments wait for orders, but proceed to Alexandria, where they are sure of a hearty welcome; nor wait for arms; *furor arma ministral* — brave men will always find something to fight with, or, that failing, find useful occupation in aiding those who are properly equipped for fight. If companies, and regiments, and individuals, from Richmond and Petersburg and Charlottesville and Warrenton, and from the counties between the James River and the Blue Ridge and Potomac, will hurry on to Alexandria, they will soon be joined by large forces from the Southern Confederacy. Soon, very soon, Davis and Beauregard, and Lee of Virginia, will be there to lead them on. And Scott, too, with his towering form and worldwide fame, unless the report be true that Scott has been arrested and imprisoned by the base and treacherous powers at Washington.

[1] The Confederate army was organized with great rapidity. Jefferson Davis called out 100,000 volunteers as early as March 6. They poured in with such celerity that some had to be turned back because arms were not available. Full of confidence, many Confederates felt in April that the war was in their hands.

[ON TO RICHMOND!]

New York *Tribune*, June 3, 1861

Next to Charleston, there is no city in the rebel States whose occupancy by the Union forces would strike more dread to the hearts of the traitors, and so encourage the loyal citizens of the South, and so elate the masses of the loyal States, as that of Richmond. For years it has been a den of conspirators, plotting the destruction of the Republic. Affecting to act with more calmness and candor, with more deliberation and judgment, with more dignity and discretion, than its impulsive, fiery Palmetto sister, it has really been more guilty and far more despicable than she, because while committing the same offences against the public weal, it has assumed an air of virtue and innocence, attempting to cloak insidious treason under the guise of patriotic devotion to the doctrines of the fathers of the republic. In a word, and not to put too fine a point upon it, Richmond has been striving to do the dirtiest and most degrading work of the conspiracy, in a dignified and courtly manner. She has been the Robert Macaire of the plot, putting on mock airs and a shabby-genteel costume, and affecting to despise the Jacques Strops of the Gulf States, while in fact being the real leader of the conspirators.

Mr. Jeff. Davis has summoned his Congress of Confederate rebels to meet in Richmond on some day in July. Ere that time, we trust its capital will be the headquarters of the commander-in-chief of the Federal forces.

THE NATION'S WAR–CRY[1]

New York *Tribune*, June 28, 1861

Forward to Richmond! Forward to Richmond! The Rebel Congress must not be allowed to meet there on the 20th of July! BY THAT DATE THE PLACE MUST BE HELD BY THE NATIONAL ARMY!

BEATEN FOR A DAY — NOW TO CONQUER FOR ALL TIMES

New York *Tribune*, July 23, 1861

We have fought and been beaten. God forgive our rulers that this is so; but it is true and cannot be disguised. The Cabinet, recently expressing in rhetoric better adapted to a love-letter a fear

---

[1] Charles A. Dana, and not Greeley, was responsible for this foolish war-cry of the *Tribune*, and it was actually written by one of the editorial staff, Fitz-Henry Warren, who later joined Dana on the *Sun*. Bull Run was lost on July 21.

of being drowned in its own honey, is now nearly drowned in gore; while our honor on the high seas has only been saved by one daring and desperate negro, and he belonging to the merchant marine. The sacred soil of Virginia is crimson and wet with the blood of thousands of Northern men, needlessly shed. The great and universal question pervading the public mind is, "Shall this condition of things continue?"

A decimated and indignant people will demand the immediate retirement of the present Cabinet from the high places of power which, for one reason or another, they have shown themselves incompetent to fill. Give us for the President capable advisers, who comprehend the requirements of the crisis, and are equal to them; and for the army, leaders worthy of the rank and file, and our banner, now drooping, will soon float once more in triumph over the whole land. With the right men to lead, our people will show themselves unconquerable.

Onward, then, to victory and glory! But let not those who hold places of responsibility disregard for a day longer the means requisite for success. Our government is instituted and intended for the general good; and no private interest or personal ambition should be permitted to remain an obstacle to the achievement of that great object. The people will insist upon new heads of Executive Departments; and then upon a half million troops and the best qualified and ablest captains, colonels, and generals whom the country can furnish. All these must be had, and without delay.

JUST ONCE[1]

New York *Tribune*, July 25, 1861

I wish to be distinctly understood as not seeking to be relieved of any personal responsibility for urging the advance of the Union Grand Army into Virginia, though the precise phrase "Forward to Richmond" is not mine, and I would have preferred not to iterate it. I thought that that army, one hundred thousand strong, might have been in the rebel capital on or before the 20th inst., while I felt that there were urgent reasons why it should be there if possible. And now, if anyone imagines that I, or anyone connected with the *Tribune*, ever commended or imagined such strategy as the launching of barely thirty thousand of the one hundred thousand Union volunteers within fifty miles of Washington against ninety thousand rebels enveloped in a labyrinth of strong intrenchments and unreconnoitred masked batteries, then demonstration would be lost

---

[1] The shock of Bull Run, and his own sense of personal responsibility, were so great that Greeley fell under a severe attack of brain fever, and was confined to his bed for several weeks.

on his closed ear. But I will not dwell on this. If I am needed as a scapegoat for all the military blunders of the last month, so be it! Individuals must die that the nation may live. If I can serve her best in that capacity, I do not shrink from the ordeal.

Henceforth, I bar all criticism in these columns on army movements past and future, unless somebody should undertake to prove that General Patterson is a wise and brave commander. He seems to have none to speak his praises; so if there is anything to be said in his behalf, I will make an exception in his favor. Other than this, the subject is closed and sealed. Correspondents and reporters may state facts, but must forbear comments. I know that there is truth that yet needs to be uttered on this subject, but this paper has done its full share — all that it ought, and perhaps more than it could afford to — and henceforth stands back for others. Only I beg it to be understood — once for all — that if less than half the Union armies directly at hand are hurled against *all* the rebel forces that could be concentrated — more than double their number — on ground specially chosen and strongly fortified by the traitors, the *Tribune* does not approve and should not be held responsible for such madness. Say what you will of the past, but remember this for the future, though we keep silence.

Henceforth, it shall be the *Tribune's* sole vocation to rouse and animate the American people for the terrible ordeal which has befallen them. The Great Republic imminently needs the utmost exertions of every loyal heart and hand. We have tried to save her by exposing breakers ahead and around her; henceforth be it ours to strengthen, by all possible ways, the hands of those whose unenviable duty it is to pilot her through them. If more good is thus to be done, let us not repine that some truth must be withheld for a calmer moment, and for less troubled ears.

The journal which is made the conduit of the most violent of these personal assaults upon me attributes the course of the *Tribune* to resentment

> "against those who have ever committed the inexpiable offence of thwarting Mr. Greeley's raging and unsatisfied thirst for office."

I think this justifies me in saying that there is no office in the gift of the government or of the people which I either hope, wish, or expect ever to hold. I certainly shall not parade myself as declining places that are not offered for my acceptance; but I am sure that the President has always known that I desired no office at *his* hands; and this not through any violation of the rule above stated, but through the report of mutual and influential friends, who at various times volunteered to ask me if I would take any place whatever under the government, and were uniformly and conclusively assured that I would not.

Now let the wolves howl on! I do not believe they can goad me into another personal notice of their ravings.

HORACE GREELEY.

July 24, 1861.

[BULL RUN: WHO IS RESPONSIBLE?]

New York *Times*, July 25, 1861

The great blunder of Sunday lay in fighting the battle which ended so disastrously. Under no circumstances is it ever justifiable, in a military sense, for an inferior force to attack a superior when the latter has his own choice of position and is strongly intrenched. The chances are fifty to one against success. In this instance General McDowell was perfectly aware that the rebel forces either outnumbered his own, or could easily be made to do so by reinforcements which they had every facility for bringing forward. To use his own expression, the night before the battle, it was with them simply a question of rolling stock and provisions. He knew, too, that they had labored zealously for three months, under skilful engineers, in a country adapted admirably to defence, to fortify their position.

General McDowell is not at all likely to have fought this battle on his own responsibility. General Scott is known to have been opposed to the whole scheme from the beginning, and his own declaration, repeated by Mr. Richardson in Congress yesterday, proves that he was utterly hostile to attacking the rebels at that time, and that he was overruled in this matter by his only superior, President Lincoln himself. No one who knows Mr. Lincoln will believe for a moment that he put his own judgment against that of General Scott in so important a matter as this. But there is not the slightest doubt that he yielded to the urgent and almost imperative representatives of that portion of his Cabinet whose views have been reflected by the *Tribune*, and who asserted from the beginning that 10,000 men could march from Washington to Richmond with the greatest ease. It is these men who have constrained the President for the moment to override the opinion and the wish of General Scott, and to order the battle which has resulted in so much of shame to the national arms.

It is known, and need not be longer concealed, that there is in the Cabinet an element of intense hatred of General Scott. Perhaps Mr. Montgomery Blair embodies and represents it more thoroughly than any other member. He has made no secret of it, but has often, in spite of the gross breach of official propriety which such an act involved, denounced the general in public places as utterly unfit for his high position. It seems to us quite time that the President should make his choice between General Scott and those members of his Cabinet who would substitute for his experience and military skill their own resentments and ignorant pretence. His Cabinet has been distracted and his own action weakened long enough by these presumptuous and disastrous counsels.

THE BATTLE OF WILSON'S CREEK[1]

New Orleans *Picayune*, August 17, 1861

The victory in Missouri is gloriously confirmed; Lyon is killed and Siegel in flight and believed to be captured; Sweeney is killed, and Southwestern Missouri cleared of the national scum of invaders. All honor and gratitude to Ben. McCulloch and the gallant men with him, who met and scourged the minions of national tyranny.

The brave sons of Louisiana were there and foremost in the fight, as at Manassas. There was a panic, it seems, of the untried and probably half-armed troops of Missouri, but the steady discipline and dashing courage of the Arkansas and Louisiana regiments retrieved the day, and after a stubborn fight with the United States regulars, under their most vaunted generals, made a clean sweep of the field. The flying enemy, intercepted by Hardee, have laid down their arms, and the day of the deliverance of Missouri is nigh. These were the best soldiers which the United States had in the State and in the West. They were well drilled by veteran officers and confident of an easy victory in Missouri. They were the nucleus of the great Western army which was to hold Missouri in bondage as the basis of a grand movement for the subjugation of the States on the lower Mississippi. They have been broken and dispersed. Southwestern Missouri is free already. The southeast cannot long stand before the advancing armies of Pillow and Hardee, joined to those of McCulloch, and the next word will be: On to St. Louis! That taken, the power of Lincolnism is broken in the whole West; and instead of shouting, Ho! for Richmond! and for New Orleans! there will be hurryings to and fro among the frightened magnates at Washington, and anxious inquiries of what they shall do to save themselves from the vengeance to come. Good tidings reach us from the North and the West. Heaven smiles on the arms of the Confederate States; through the brightly beaming vistas of these battles we see golden promises of the speedy triumph of a righteous cause — in the firm establishment of Southern independence.

[1] The battle of Wilson's Creek, Missouri, was fought on August 9, 1861, between the Union forces under Nathaniel Lyon, and the Confederates under Price and McCulloch. The Confederates won a brilliant victory.

[THE EFFECTS OF THE BLOCKADE ON THE SOUTH][1]

Richmond *Examiner*, September, 1861

Starch, soap, ink, paper, leather, cotton goods, yarn, and a hundred other commodities scarce, used up, or outrageously dear, in a country of "abundant resources" — among a people who "want nothing from abroad" and intend in future to "depend upon themselves"! We are often hearing the remark, "if the blockade outlasts three years, we shall be one of the greatest nations in the world"; and yet again, "the war may last three years, and while it lasts we are engaged in meeting its demands," is pleaded by many as an excuse for slowness. But are we to wait until the war is over before we begin to supply the demands of such attainable articles as cotton goods, soap, starch, and yarn? The truth is, we must become a more practical people before the above results are reached. We must pocket our pride, and if we cannot be lawyers and professors, give our attention to those occupations that *will* pay, and not leave it to successful though less aspiring Yankees to creep in and establish themselves in this or that craft, and pocket our money because we are too genteel to supply our own needs.

We as a people have been blessed with plenty, and our land is teeming with wealth; as yet we have not learned to economize. Our children have been reared in habits of wastefulness and extravagance. Our very servants despise saving, and have no notion of collecting scraps. Rags, sheets of paper, bits of twine, pens, pins, needles, bottles, are daily swept away, burned up, or cast on rubbish heaps, which they are too lazy to pick up, even to "sell for cash," and which in such times as these ought never to be on the floor at all. . . . And you, our gentlemanly Micawber cousins, rouse your inventive faculties and dip into your encyclopaedias for practical knowledge. "Necessity is the mother of invention," and how can you display your patriotism to better purpose, if not fighting, than by contriving, suggesting, and assisting to establish and improve the many manufactories which have been already, and must be still further, set on foot to meet the demands of the nation, who need neither watch for the raising of the blockade, nor wait till the war is over, before they begin to become "a great and independent people."

[1] President Lincoln at once proclaimed a blockade of Southern ports. By the fall of 1861 its pressure had begun to be felt painfully. Dry goods had become very scarce. The best women of the South were wearing homespun. Medicines were running low. Salt, bacon, butter, coffee, tea, and soap had advanced enormously in price. Surgeons felt severely the scarcity of lint and plasters. This appeal is typical of many addressed to Confederate citizens; but under the circumstances economy could avail but little.

SLAVERY AND THE WAR: A BLOW THAT WILL BE FELT[1]

New York *Times*, September 2, 1861

There is no victory so complete as that which solves a great political dilemma which has rested like a pall upon the public mind, destroying all life and spirit, paralyzing all enterprise and action, and producing all the consequences of a disastrous defeat. It is a happy stroke of genius that can overstep the bounds of tradition or conventional rule, and show a clear path in a direction supposed to be beset with insuperable difficulties. Such is the service rendered the nation by General Frémont's proclamation, placing Missouri under martial law and visiting upon traitors the penalties due to treason, with all the celerity of military dispatch. The traitor is to be divested of property as well as life; and further, a blow is struck where it has long been seen it might fall, upon the institution which is both the cause and support of the rebellion. Self-preservation renders no other course longer possible. If we would save ourselves, we must take from treason every weapon by which it can strike the deadly blow. We must maintain the rights of loyal men intact, but take from those in arms against us the means of keeping them in the field.

It has long been the boast of the South, in contrasting its strength with that of the North, that its whole white population could be made available for the war, for the reason that all its industries were carried on by the slaves, in peace as well as war; while those of the North rested upon the very men who, in case of hostilities, must be sent into the field. For the North, consequently, to fight, would be the destruction of all its material interests; for the South, only a pleasant pastime for hundreds of thousands of men, who without war would have no occupation. The South was another Sparta, the Helots of which, a degraded caste, performed all the useful labor, leaving to the privileged one only the honorable occupation of arms. The vast host which the South has put into the field has, to a great extent, made good these words. With the enemy at our throat, we must strike from under him the prop upon which his strength rests. It is our duty to save every life and every dollar of expense in our power. By seeking to put down the rebellion only by meeting the enemy in the open field, is uselessly to sacrifice hundreds of thousands of lives, and hundreds if not thousands

---

[1] Frémont's proclamation, freeing the slaves of all Missouri rebels taken in arms, and issued on August 30, 1861, met the approval of nearly the whole Northern press and of many public men, but was disapproved by Lincoln because of his fear of its effect upon the border States.

of millions of money, and perhaps after all accept a disastrous defeat as the result.

In this crisis General Frémont has sounded the keynote of the campaign that will be echoed wherever we have a soldier in arms. He has taken a step which cannot fail to produce a very marked effect throughout the South. He has declared that every slave who may be employed or permitted by his master to aid in the rebellion against the United States, shall be *free*. This, it will be seen, is no general act of emancipation. It has nothing to do with that general crusade against slavery which many have urged as the proper means of carrying on the war. It simply confiscates the property of rebels employed against the government. It does not touch the slaves of loyal citizens, nor affect the institution in any way, except as those responsible for it may choose to identify its fate with that of the rebellion itself. But just so far as slavery actively supports the rebellion must it become the object of attack. . . . It is very clear that Frémont's proclamation is, up to this time, by far the most important event of the war.

[DISENTHRALMENT OF SOUTHERN LITERATURE]

De Bow's Review, October, 1861

While much has been gained by the withdrawal of Southern youth from the colleges of the North, still more good might be accomplished by raising those of the South to the position of universities in the proper acceptation of the term. Many of the latter are already universities in name, but in name only — being really inferior, in many respects, to the best high schools of which England can boast. Perhaps the only exception to this remark is afforded in the University of Virginia; and its success has shown that the lack of institutions of the highest order, in the South, has not been owing to a want of ability to sustain them. We have had, within the last two years, some cheering prospects in other quarters, which we sincerely hope may not be blighted by the existing war; for, with the establishment of Southern universities of equal grade with those of Europe, we may anticipate the dawn of a new era in Southern literature.

In the next place, we must rid ourselves of Yankee newspapers and periodicals. How is this to be accomplished? We cannot, by expostulation or command, prevent booksellers from selling, or the thoughtless among us from buying, this ephemeral trash of the North. We must resort, if possible, to the method of supplanting it by superior publications of our own. This, we think, can be readily accomplished by the proper action on the part of the reading men

and women of the South.   It is apparent that if our best Southern
journals be inferior to the Northern, the inferiority consists not in
tone, authenticity, or editorial ability; for, in the first two particulars, our journals have decidedly the advantage, while in the last
they are at least the equals of their Northern contemporaries. . . .
What, but the persistent efforts of Yankee periodicals, could have
given the prosaic Longfellow a wider circle of readers on this side
of the Atlantic than Tennyson, Campbell, or Burns?   What, but
they, could have convinced anybody out of New England, and in
his senses, that John Greenleaf Whittier — that most uninspired of
fanatics — was capable of aught in metre but the veriest doggerel?
or that the stuff manufactured from the brain of James Russell
Lowell was any more like genuine poetry than the taste of wooden
nutmegs resembles that of the real article?

THE CONFEDERACY: PRESENT AND FUTURE

De Bow's Review, December, 1861

There will be peace; will they offer to negotiate for it? We can
propose no terms, but we must demand them. We desire nothing
that is not right and just, and we shall submit to nothing that is
wrong. But no peace will be acceptable to the people that permits
the Lincoln Government to hold its abolition orgies, and fulminate
its vile edicts upon slave territory. Much valuable property of our
citizens has been destroyed, or stolen and carried off by the invaders;
this should be accounted for, and paid. The Yankees were shrewd
enough to cheat us out of the navy, but we must have half of the
war vessels and naval armaments in possession of the North at the
commencement of this war. We should enter into no commercial
alliances or complications with them, but assume the entire control
of our commercial policy and regulations with them, to be modified
at our own discretion and pleasure. They have closed against us
all navigation and trade on the Mississippi, Missouri, and other
rivers; it is our right and duty hereafter so to regulate the navigation
of these streams as may best conform to our own interests. It
cannot be expected that we should permit the free navigation of the
lower Mississippi to the West after they have closed it against us
above, without the most stringent regulations. There is no palliation in the pretence that the blockade above was a war measure;
they cannot so claim it unless we had been acknowledged as belliger-
ents, and hence they have forfeited all right to free navigation as a
peace measure. If, then, permission be given to the free States of the
West to navigate the lower Mississippi, it should be under such
restrictions as to afford a commensurate revenue to the Confederacy,

and the strictest rules regulating the ingress and egress of passengers, officers, and hands. . . .

We have conquered an outlet to the Pacific which must be maintained, though we can desire no dominion on the Pacific coast but such as may be sufficient to secure the terminus of our great Pacific railroad through Texas and Arizona. Toward the north and east, the Maryland and Pennslyvania line, including Delaware, is our true landmark. Kansas, on the other side, must be conquered and confiscated to pay for the negroes stolen from us, abolitionism expelled from its borders, and transformed into a slave State of the Confederacy. Perhaps, after we have done with Lincoln, this arrangement may be very acceptable to a majority in Kansas, without force. We will have no desire to disturb Mexico so long as she conducts herself peaceably toward us, and as a neighbor, maintains good faith in her dealings with us. Central America must remain as a future consideration; and instead of the acquisition of Cuba, she becomes our *friendly ally*, identified with us in interests and institutions, and so long as she continues to hold slaves, connected to us by the closest ties.

EMANCIPATION: THE QUESTION OF THE DAY

New York *Tribune*, December 13, 1861

It is utterly idle to talk of ignoring questions affecting slavery while providing for the prosecution of the War for the Union. They *will not* be ignored; indeed, they *can not* be. We should be willing to refrain from discussing them; but we are not allowed our choice. Those who openly sympathized with and justified secession last spring, and who now loudly proclaim themselves the only hearty supporters of the government and the war, keep up a deafening clamor against any interference with slavery which they mean to have mistaken for public opinion. Silence on our part is acquiescence in gross misrepresentation under circumstances which stamp such acquiescence as cowardice. We propose once more to elucidate the position and vindicate the sagacity of those who maintain that it will not be possible to uphold both slavery and the Union.

I. We insist, that, in the present crisis, neither slavery nor abolition, per se, has any right to consideration at the hands of the government. One loyalist thinks slavery a good thing; another deems it entitled to legal protection so long as the slaveholders are loyal citizens; a third deems it an unmitigated evil and nuisance. Each of these has a right to his own opinion, and to its free and hearty expression. But when the question of saving or losing the republic presents itself, all others must give way. If upholding slavery tends to insure and hasten the vindication of the national authority, the saving of the Union, then it may plausibly be unheld; otherwise, No.

II. The questions in issue concern the slaves of *rebels*, and those only. Loyal slaveholders are a class by themselves — "small but respectable." With them, we would have the government nowise interfere, unless for their protection. But rebel slaveholders should have been warned at the outset that they could not persist in treason without losing their slaves, and striking a heavy blow at slavery. And had they been thus warned, we believe many, if not most, would have stood aloof from rebellion. And now, had they been seasonably notified that no one may persist in rebellion after the first of January next without forfeiting his slaves, we think many would conclude that rebellion is not likely to pay, and would give it up.

III. On the side of the rebels, confiscation is the order of the day. *All* the property of loyalists — slave or otherwise — is mercilessly swept into the strong-box of Jeff. Davis and Company. There is no talk in *that* quarter of confiscating only the slaves who work on the Union defenses or are found serving in our armies — they go the whole hog. . . .

IV. But we are reminded by the New York *Times* that "the objects of legislation are *practical*." The suggestion may be profound, but its novelty is not striking. Let us, therefore, once more enlighten the *Times* and those whom it guides as to the *end* we would accomplish.

Four millions of sturdy bondmen, nearly all residents of the rebel States, stand waiting and wondering what is to be *their* part in this contest, what their advantage therefrom. They form a majority of the people of South Carolina and nearly or quite a majority of those of several other revolted States. They are about one-third the population of Jeff Davis's dominions. Their interest in the struggle *is practical* — very practical indeed. They want many things, but before all else, Liberty. They are willing to work for it, run for it, fight for it, die for it. There cannot be a rational doubt of the ability of the government to enlist the sympathies and the efforts of these four millions of Jeff's subjects on the side of the Union by simply promising them freedom. Talk of confiscation does not move them, for it involves the idea — to their minds, at least — of deportation and sale to new masters. Talk of confiscating, or even freeing, those only who have been employed in the rebel armies, does not much affect them; for it seems partial, timid, and selfish. But say to them that all whose masters are involved in the rebellion shall be Free, and they will feel that their day is at last dawning. They will not hasten to throw away their lives by mad, senseless insurrections; but they will watch for opportunities to escape and come within our lines, bringing information certainly and perhaps arms and other material aid. And the bare fact that their slaves are watching their chances to get away and over to the Union side will immensely weaken the rebels.

We are not proposing that Congress should take any particular action in the premises. We indicate no time at which decisive action would be desirable, or beyond which it would be likely to prove fruitless. We do not propose to abandon the ship unless it is sailed according to our chart. We shall render a hearty support to the war for the Union, whether conducted according to our views or otherwise. But our conviction is very strong that the Unionists cannot afford to repel the sympathies and reject the aid of Four Millions of Southern people.

THE AGRICULTURAL COLLEGE ACT[1]

New York *Tribune*, June 23, 1862

We print herewith the act recently passed by Congress providing, by grants of public lands, a fund in each State for the establishment of one or more colleges for the education of youth in agriculture and the mechanic arts, and the sciences auxiliary thereto. It is not often that a measure of such promise is carried by majorities so overwhelming as this — after years of struggle and debate — has commanded. We hail in this triumph an augury of wide and lasting good.

The benefits of such a measure cannot be speedily realized. Probably two years will elapse before any State will have so perfected its preliminary formalities and guaranties most wisely required by this act as to be able to avail herself directly and palpably of its benefits. Colleges must be organized, buildings erected, faculties chosen, etc., etc., before opportunities can be proffered under this act for the thousands of youths who would gladly combine Learning with Labor, and master the sciences which will make them eminent farmers and mechanics rather than those which would impel them into the already overcrowded professions. But the time *will* come — it will not be delayed beyond three years in some States, especially if institutions already commenced, such as the Farmers' College of Pennsylvania, shall be taken as the basis and nucleus of the larger and better seminaries which this act is intended and calculated to secure. Some States may possibly decline to accept the grant proffered them under the rather stringent conditions imposed by this act; some may fail even in hearty and well-meant efforts to popular-

[1] The Morrill Land Grand Act for the endowment of universities and colleges giving instruction in agriculture and the mechanic arts was passed by both houses in June, 1862, and signed by President Lincoln on July 2.

ize science and render the useful arts liberal and even learned pursuits; but it is not possible that *all* should fail. And if the net result of this measure is the establishment of *five* colleges in so many different States which shall within five years succeed in placing within the reach of our youth an education at once scientific and practical, including a knowledge of the sciences which underlie and control the chief processes of productive labor, all the cost of this measure will have been richly repaid.

[THREE HUNDRED THOUSAND MORE]

New York *Tribune*, July 3, 1862

We publish today a call from the President for 300,000 more men as an additional force to the armies of the Union. The President hopes that they "will be enrolled without delay, so as to bring this unnecessary and injurious civil war to a speedy and satisfactory conclusion." This wish will be responded to by every loyal heart in the land.

The call is made at the urgent request of all the Governors of the loyal States, with four exceptions. Whether these omissions are accidental, or because for some personal reason the signatures are withheld, we do not know; but these States, which have sent quite as large a number of their sons to the war, in proportion to their population, as the rest, will not, we are sure, be backward in responding to the President's call. The signers to the letter urging this appeal to the country very truly present, we have no doubt, the feeling of the people whom they represent. A "speedy conclusion" of the war is what the nation demands.

New York *Evening Post*, July 16, 1862 [1]

We are coming, Father Abraham, three hundred thousand more,
From Mississippi's winding stream, and from New England's shore;
We leave our ploughs and workshops, our wives and children dear,
With hearts too full for utterance, with but a silent tear
We dare not look behind us, but steadfastly before:
We are coming, Father Abraham, three hundred thousand more.

If you look across the hilltops that meet the Northern sky,
Long moving lines of rising dust your vision may descry;
And now the wind, an instant, tears the cloudy veil aside,
And floats aloft our spangled flag in glory and in pride,
And bayonets in the sunlight gleam, and bands brave music pour:
We are coming, Father Abraham, three hundred thousand more!

[1] Contributed to the editorial columns by the financial editor, John S. Gibbons.

THE TIME HAS COME[1]

The *Independent*, August 14, 1862

The way to make war is to destroy slavery. The way to secure peace after war is to destroy slavery. If any have scruples about interfering with Southern rights, their scruples are too late. We have already done it. War is supreme interference. We have violated State sovereignty as much as it can be done. What State sovereignty is there under an imposed military governor intruded upon New Orleans, Nashville, and Newbern?

The only question is whether we will use that lawful intrusion for the ends of health and peace, or whether we will go on with a timid and fatuous policy, designed to roll over upon future times tenfold greater disturbances than those which we have suffered.

Is it not time for us to ponder the meaning of God's providence?

With what energy did men resist the anti-slavery discussion of the past thirty years! But it prevailed and covered the land. With what desperate energy did the North resist the legislation of 1850 and the infamous Fugitive Slave law! But it was in vain. With what fierce indignation did the whole North resist the abrogation of the Missouri Compromise! But it was broken up and the Kansas volcano uncapped. Then came the fiery campaign between Frémont the Eagle, and Buchanan the Owl. In the days of him whom the Conservatives elected as safe and prudent, came Secession. When it was threatened, we refused to believe that it would happen. We were all mistaken. We then refused to believe that there would be war. But it has flamed over half a hemisphere.

Thus far, the conservative North has been striving to conduct this war so as not to meddle with the so-called Southern right of slavery. But in spite of every scruple, events have crowded men to the necessity of confiscation and emancipation. There is one more step. It is the last sublime step toward National safety and National Christian glory. It is IMMEDIATE AND UNIVERSAL EMANCIPATION!

Ah, men of America! Patriots! Christians! Could you but cleanse your native land of the inconsistency with her own vital principles, and give to her coming times undiseased with slavery, bright with the immortal beauty of liberty, would it not be worth all treasures and all suffering?

It may be done. Let every man in his place rise up and demand it! Each man's voice is but a breath. But let breath mingle with breath, and the current begin to move, as a storm marches which, gathering force as it goes, moves the very deep and shakes the land. Then, when the earthquake of War shall have been felt, and the

[1] By Henry Ward Beecher.

great and stormy voice of the People, our rulers will peradventure hear the still small voice of God, speaking with irresistible authority— "Let my people go!" — and bow down, and obey!

THE PRAYER OF TWENTY MILLIONS

New York *Tribune*, August 20, 1862

To Abraham Lincoln, President of the United States:

Dear Sir: I do not intrude to tell you — for you must know already — that a great proportion of those who triumphed in your election, and of all who desire the unqualified suppression of the Rebellion now desolating our country, are sorely disappointed and deeply pained by the policy you seem to be pursuing with regard to the slaves of Rebels. I write only to set succinctly and unmistakably before you what we require, what we think we have a right to expect, and of what we complain.

I. We require of you, as the first servant of the Republic, charged especially and preëminently with this duty, that you EXECUTE THE LAWS. Most emphatically do we demand that such laws as have been recently enacted, which therefore may fairly be presumed to embody the *present* will and to be dictated by the *present* needs of the Republic, and which after due consideration have received your personal sanction, shall by you be carried into full effect, and that you publicly and decisively instruct your subordinates that such laws exist, that they are binding on all functionaries and citizens, and that they are to be obeyed to the letter.

II. We think you are strangely and disastrously remiss in the discharge of your official and imperative duty with regard to the emancipating provisions of the new Confiscation Act. These provisions were designed to fight Slavery with Liberty. They prescribe that men loyal to the Union, and willing to shed their blood in her behalf, shall no longer be held, with the Nation's consent, to persistent, malignant traitors, who for twenty years have been plotting and for sixteen months have been fighting to divide and destroy our country. Why these traitors should be treated with tenderness by you, to the prejudice of the dearest rights of loyal men, we cannot conceive.

III. We think you are unduly influenced by the counsels, the representations, the menaces, of certain fossil politicians hailing from the Border Slave States. Knowing well that the heartily, unconditionally loyal portion of the white citizens of these States do not expect nor desire that slavery shall be upheld to the prejudice of the Union — (for the truth of which we appeal not only to every Republican residing in those States, but to such eminent loyalists as H. Winter Davis, Parson Brownlow, the Union Central Committee of Baltimore, and the Nashville *Union*) — we ask you to consider that slavery is everywhere the inciting cause and sustaining base of treason: the most slaveholding sections of Maryland and Delaware being this day, though under the Union flag, in full sympathy with the Rebellion, while the Free-Labor portions of Tennessee and of Texas, though writhing under the bloody heel of Treason, are unconquerably loyal to the Union. So emphatically is this case, that a most intelligent Union banker of Baltimore recently avowed his confident belief that a majority of the present Legislature of Maryland, though elected as and still professing to be Unionists, are at heart desirous of the triumph of the Jeff. Davis conspiracy; and when asked how they could be won back to loyalty, replied — "Only by the complete abolition of slavery." It seems to us the most obvious truth, that whatever strengthens or fortifies slavery in the Border States strengthens also Treason, and drives home the wedge intended to divide the Union. Had you from the first refused to recognize in those States, as here, any other than unconditional loyalty — that which stands for the Union, whatever may become of slavery — those States would have been, and would be, far more helpful and less troublesome to the defenders of the Union than they have been, or now are.

IV. We think timid counsels in such a crisis calculated to prove perilous, and probably disastrous. It is the duty of a government so wantonly, wickedly assailed by Rebellion as ours has been to oppose force to force in a defiant, dauntless spirit. It cannot afford to compromise with traitors nor with semi-traitors. It must not bribe them to behave themselves, nor make them fair promises in the hope of disarming their causeless hostility. Representing a brave and high-spirited people, it can afford to forfeit anything else better than its own self-respect, or their admiring confidence. For our government even to seek, after war has been made on it, to dispel the affected apprehensions of armed traitors that their cherished privileges may be assailed by it, is to invite insult and to encourage hopes of its own downfall. The rush to arms of Ohio, Indiana, Illinois, is the true answer at once to the Rebel raids of John Morgan and the traitorous sophistries of Beriah Magoffin.

V. We complain that the Union cause has suffered, and is now suffering immensely, from mistaken deference to Rebel slavery. Had you, sir, in your inaugural address, unmistakably given notice that, in case the Rebellion already commenced were persisted in, and your efforts to preserve the Union and enforce the laws were resisted by armed force, *you would recognize no loyal person as rightfully held in slavery by a Traitor*, we believe the Rebellion would therein have received a staggering if not fatal blow.   At that moment, according to the returns of the most recent elections, the Unionists were a large majority of the voters of the Slave States.   But they were composed in good part of the aged, the feeble, the wealthy, the timid — the young, the reckless, the aspiring, the adventurous, had already been largely lured by the gamblers and negro-traders, the politicians by trade and the conspirators by instinct, into the toils of Treason.   Had you then proclaimed that Rebellion would strike the shackles from the slaves of every traitor, the wealthy and the cautious would have been supplied with a powerful inducement to remain loyal.   As it was, every coward in the South soon became a traitor from fear; for Loyalty was perilous, while Treason seemed comparatively safe.   Hence the boasted unanimity of the South — a unanimity based on Rebel terrorism, and the fact that immunity and safety were found on that side, danger and probable death on ours.   The Rebels from the first have been eager to confiscate, imprison, scourge, and kill; we have fought wolves with the devices of sheep.   The result is just what might have been expected.   Tens of thousands are fighting in the Rebel ranks today whose original bias and natural leanings would have led them into ours.

VI.   We complain that the Confiscation Act which you approved is habitually disregarded by your generals, and that no word of rebuke for them from you has yet reached the public ear.   Frémont's proclamation and Hunter's Order favoring emancipation were promptly annulled by you; while Halleck's No. 3, forbidding fugitives from slavery to Rebels to come within his lines — an order as unmilitary as inhuman, and which received the hearty approbation of every traitor in America — with scores of like tendency, have never provoked even your remonstrance.   We complain that the officers of your armies have habitually repelled rather than invited the approach of slaves who would have gladly taken the risk of escaping from their Rebel masters to our camps, bringing intelligence often of inestimable value to the Union cause.   We complain that those who *have* thus escaped to us, avowing a willingness to do for us whatever might be required, have been brutally and madly repulsed, and often surrendered to be scourged, maimed, and tortured by the ruffian traitors who pretend to own them.   We complain that a large proportion of our regular army officers, with many volunteers, evince far more solicitude to uphold slavery than to put down the Rebellion.   And finally we complain that you, Mr. President, elected as a Republican, knowing well what an abomination slavery is, and how emphatically it is the core and essence of this atrocious Rebellion, seem never to interfere with these atrocities, and never give a direction to your military subordinates, which does not appear to be conceived in the interest of Slavery rather than that of Freedom.

VII. Let me call your attention to the recent tragedy in New Orleans, whereof the facts are obtained entirely through pro-slavery channels. A considerable body of resolute, able-bodied men, held in slavery by two Rebel sugar-planters in defiance of the Confiscation Act which you have approved, left plantations thirty miles distant and made their way to the great mart of the Southwest, which they knew to be in the undisputed possession of the Union forces. They made their way safely and quietly through thirty miles of Rebel territory, expecting to find freedom under the protection of our flag. Whether they had or had not heard of the passage of the Confiscation Act, they reasoned logically that we could not kill them for deserting the service of their lifelong oppressors, who had through treason become our implacable enemies. They came to us for liberty and protection, for which they were willing to render their best service; they met with hostility, captivity, and murder. The barking of the base curs of Slavery in this quarter deceives no one — not even themselves. They say, indeed, that the negroes had no right to appear in New Orleans armed (with their implements of daily labor in the cane-field); but no one doubts that they would gladly have laid these down if assured that they should be free. They were set upon and maimed, captured and killed. . . . It was *somebody's* fault that they were so murdered — if others shall hereafter suffer in like manner, in default of explicit and public direction to your generals that they are to recognize and obey the Confiscation Act, the world will lay the blame on *you*. Whether you will choose to bear it through future history and at the bar of God, I will not judge. I can only hope.

VIII. On the face of this wide earth, Mr. President, there is not one disinterested, determined, intelligent champion of the Union cause who does not feel that all attempts to put down the Rebellion and at the same time uphold its inciting cause are preposterous and futile — that the rebellion, if crushed out tomorrow, would be renewed within a year if slavery were left in full vigor. . . . that army officers who remain to this day devoted to slavery can be but at best halfway loyal to the Union — and that every hour of deference to slavery is an hour of added and deepened peril to the Union. I appeal to the testimony of your Ambassadors in Europe. It is freely at your service, not at mine. . . .

IX. I close as I began with the statement that what an immense majority of the Loyal Millions of your countrymen require of you is a frank, declared, unqualified, ungrudging execution of the laws of the land, more especially of the Confiscation Act. That Act gives freedom to the slaves of Rebels coming within our lines, or whom those lines may at any time enclose — we ask you to render it due obedience by publicly requiring all your subordinates to recognize and obey it.   The Rebels are everywhere using the late anti-negro riots in the North, as they have long used your officers' treatment of negroes in the South, to convince the slaves that they have nothing to hope from a Union success — that we mean in that case to sell them into a bitterer bondage to defray the cost of the war. Let them impress this as a truth upon the great mass of the ignorant and credulous bondmen, and the Union will never be restored — never.   We cannot conquer Ten Millions of people united in solid phalanx against us, powerfully aided by Northern sympathizers and European allies.   We must have scouts, guides, spies, cooks, teamsters, diggers and choppers, from the Blacks of the South, whether we allow them to fight for us or not, or we shall be baffled and repelled.   As one of the millions who would gladly have avoided this struggle at any sacrifice but that of Principle and Honor, but who now feel that the triumph of the Union is indispensable not only to the existence of our country but to the well-being of mankind, I entreat you to render a hearty and unequivocal obedience to the law of the land.

HORACE GREELEY.

New York, August 19, 1862.

PRESIDENT LINCOLN'S LETTER

New York *Tribune*, August 25, 1862

Executive Mansion, Washington
August 22, 1862.

Hon. Horace Greeley:

DEAR SIR: I have just read yours of the 19th, addressed to myself through THE N. Y. TRIBUNE.   If there be in it any statements or assumptions of fact which I may know to be erroneous, I do not now and here controvert them.   If there be in it any inferences which I may believe to be falsely drawn, I do not now and here argue against them.   If there be perceptible in it an impatient and dictatorial tone, I waive it in deference to an old friend, whose heart I have always supposed to be right.

As to the policy I "seem to be pursuing," as you say, I have not meant to leave anyone in doubt.

I would save the Union.   I would save it the shortest way under the Constitution.   The sooner the National authority can be restored, the nearer the Union will be "the Union as it was."   If there be those who would not save the Union unless they could at the same time *save* slavery, I do not agree with them. If there be those who would not save the Union unless they could at the same time *destroy* slavery, I do not agree with them. My paramount object in this struggle *is* to save the Union, and is *not* either to save or to destroy slavery. If I could save the Union without freeing *any* slave, I would do it; and if I could save it by freeing *all* the slaves, I would do it; and if I could do it by freeing some and leaving others alone, I would also do that. What I do about slavery and the colored race, I do because I believe it helps to save this Union; and what I forbear, I forbear because I do *not* believe it would help to save the Union. I shall do *less* whenever I believe what I am doing hurts the cause, and I shall do *more* whenever I shall believe doing more will help the cause. I shall try to correct errors when shown to be errors; and I shall adopt new views so fast as they shall appear to be true views. I have here stated my purpose according to my view of *official* duty, and I intend no modification of my oft-expressed *personal* wish that all men, everywhere, could be free. Yours,

A. LINCOLN.

Mr. Greeley's Response

DEAR SIR: Although I did not anticipate nor seek any reply to my former letter unless through your official acts, I thank you for having accorded one, since it enables me to say explicitly that nothing was further from my thought than to impeach in any manner the sincerity or the intensity of your devotion to the saving of the Union. I never doubted, and have no friend who doubts, that you desire, before and above all else, to reëstablish the now derided authority and vindicate the territorial integrity of the Republic. I intended to raise only this question — *Do you propose to do this by recognizing, obeying, and enforcing the laws, or by ignoring, disregarding, and in effect defying them?*

I stand upon the law of the land. The humblest has a clear right to invoke its protection and support against even the highest. That law — in strict accordance with the law of Nations, of Nature, and of God — declares that every traitor now engaged in the infernal work of destroying our country has forfeited thereby all claim or color of right lawfully to hold human beings in slavery. I ask of you a clear and public recognition that this law is to be obeyed wherever the national authority is respected. . . .

Mr. President, I beseech you to open your eyes to the fact that the devotees of slavery everywhere — just as much in Maryland as in Mississippi, in Washington as in Richmond — are today your enemies and the implacable foes of every effort to reëstablish the National authority by the discomfiture of its assailants. Their President is not Abraham Lincoln but Jefferson Davis. You may draft them to serve in the war; but they will only fight under the Rebel flag. There is not in New York today a man who really believes in slavery, loves it, and desires its perpetuation, who heartily desires the crushing out of the Rebellion. He would much rather save the Republic by buying up and pensioning off its assailants. His "Union as it was" is a Union of which you were not President, and no one who truly wished Freedom to All ever could be. . . .

That you may not unseasonably perceive these vital truths as they will shine forth on the pages of history — that they may be read by our children irradiated by the glory of our National salvation, not rendered lurid by the blood-red glow of National conflagration and ruin — that you may promptly and practically realize that Slavery is to be vanquished only by Liberty — is the fervent and anxious prayer of

Yours, truly,

HORACE GREELEY.

New York, Aug. 24, 1862.

THE PROCLAMATION OF FREEDOM[1]
New York *Tribune*, September 24, 1862

In sacred and profane poetry, the epitome of all human wisdom, there is no truth more clearly recognized than that in the lives of nations and of men there comes sometimes a precious moment, a mere point of time, on the proper use of which depends salvation for that life, whether temporal or eternal. That moment has come to us. The proclamation of the President, which gives in a certain contingency — almost sure to occur — freedom to four millions of men, is one of those stupendous facts in human history which marks not only an era in the progress of the nation, but an epoch in the history of the world. Shall we recognize and use it wisely, or shall we, blindly and foolishly, refuse to see that we have now our future in our own hands, and enter upon that downward career which leads eventually to ruin and oblivion? . . . .

While we rejoice and hope for the best, we still tremble. There are among us men whose foolishness will not depart from them though it be brayed in a mortar — other men who will not cease from wicked ways while in the flesh. But the emancipation which the President has proclaimed is the emancipation of more than four millions of black slaves; it is the freedom of well-nigh twenty millions from a thraldom they have been taught to reverence. Have they learned aright the lesson of these last two years? Do they know now that they also have been in bondage, and will they accept this

[1] Lincoln's proclamation announcing emancipation was issued, following McClellan's victory over Lee at Antietam, on September 22, 1862.

great boon of freedom which a wise ruler offers them? We hope so; we devoutly pray that wisdom may enter into the hearts of all the people. Let the President know that everywhere throughout all the land he is hailed as Wisest and Best, and that by this great deed of enfranchisement to an oppressed people — a deed, the doing whereof was never before vouchsafed to any mortal ruler — he re-creates a nation.

For such indeed is the fact. By a single blow he has palsied the right arm of rebellion. Slavery is the root of the rebellion; he digs it up by the roots. Property in slaves, the appalling events of the last two years show, is dangerous to the existence of the nation; he destroys such property. The Rebels are dependent for their daily subsistence upon their slaves; he makes these slaves freemen. As slaves they are the mere subjects of Rebels, to toil for them, to be used by them as beasts of burden; as freemen they are the loyal allies of a free government, asking only in return the protection which such a government gives to the humblest citizen. By a word the President transforms a State sunk in the semi-barbarism of a mediaeval age to the light and civilization of the Nineteenth Christian Century. As it is not extravagant to say that God had hid away this continent until the human race had reached its manhood and was fit to enter upon so fair an inheritance, so it is a simple statement of a truth to say that in all the ages there has been no act of one man and of one people so sublime as this emancipation of a race — no act so fraught with good for the sons of men in all time to come.

LEE AND HIS ARMY[1]

Richmond *Enquirer*, May 8, 1863

It is no disparagement to other great generals and gallant forces in our service to say that General Lee and his army of Northern Virginia may now be pronounced the most famous chief and army on earth at this day. No leader now in the world has won so many great battles. No army has stood so often or so long in such tempests of fire, nor borne off victory in the face of such terrible odds, and in the midst of such red carnivals of slaughter. The Confederacy may well be proud of such a host and such a leader: for the banners emblazoned with the names of the battles of Richmond, of Second Manassas, of Fredericksburg, and of the Rappahannock, fly higher at this day, and glow with a purer lustre than any battle standards that in this generation have been given to the winds over all lands and all seas.

[1] Published immediately after the battle of Chancellorsville, and before Lee's invasion of Pennsylvania.

The meagre and fitful snatches of news that have come to us from the last tremendous scene of conflict — gasped out, as it were, from amid the lurid war smoke and thunder, while our noble defenders are still panting and bloody with the desperate strife — inspire a feeling of proud and terrible joy, give a keen sense of the priceless value of that blessing that we pay for with oceans of so rich blood, and think it cheap. The events of such a war, stirring to the depths the inmost core of all hearts and kindling every generous and ennobling passion, cannot but elevate the whole character of a people, give it a higher purpose and a more intense love for all that is good and lofty in the world. It is war, not peace (war, we mean, waged in the righteous cause of liberty) that makes a nation great and good; that brings out the very best and purest qualities of manhood and womanhood, and intensifies that spirit of patriotism which is the true basis of a great national character. . . .

Who will not hereafter be proud to trace his descent from one of those who stood in the gaps at Fredericksburg with the glorious Lee? Will not the virtue and glory of such ancestors be a stimulus the more with their children's children even to the hundredth generation, to show themselves worthy of their forefathers? Even in our own day, when this horrible but needful work is done, and we can breathe freely with the sense that the land is redeemed and established forever, and is our own and our children's from the centre to the sky — who is there that will not feel within him a stronger spring of character, a purer impulse to the performance of all manly duty, from the very scenes of passionate struggle through which Providence has borne him safe; from the chivalrous friendships that will have been formed and cemented on the sanguinary fields where comrades have so often proved each other's manhood, relieved each other's weariness, and watched by one another's beds of pain!

Yes, our land shall be more opulent in every virtue, and one can scarce say whether she will be richer in her living or her dead, for it is by the dew of heroic blood that this ancient earth renews her youth forever, and by virtue thereof "the world is a world and not a waste." The daring imagery of Shelley holds a grand truth —

> "Still alive and still bold, shouted Earth —
> I grow bolder and still more bold —
> The Dead fill me ten thousand fold,
> Fuller of speed, of splendor, and mirth.
>
> "I was cloudy, and sullen, and cold,
> Like a frozen chaos uprolled,
> Till by the spirit of the mighty dead
> My heart grew warm —"

Such are the reflections that naturally throng upon us, as we seem to hear the crash of combat from behind the sulphurous clouds that cover the vale of the Rappahannock. — May God bless the banners of Lee and his immortal army!

HOW TO EDIT A SOUND CONSERVATIVE UNION PAPER

New York *Evening Post*, May 20, 1863

It is a mystery to many readers how certain Democratic journals, which profess the warmest devotion to the Union, nevertheless, manage to play into the hands of the Secessionists. But the thing is easy enough — quite as easy as lying if you will only consider it for a moment. The editors of such journals are of course compelled to parade their Unionism, because of the overwhelming sentiment of the North; at the same time, however, by observing any or all of the following rules, they are able to do very effective work for the other side. The rules we give, by the way, are without charge to the parties concerned.

1st. All the military successes of the rebel armies should be magnified in their effects, while those of the North should be depreciated. If we lose ten thousand men, set it down at twenty-three thousand; while, if they lose eighteen thousand, set it down at eight. In this manner the superior gallantry and pluck of the Southerners may be gracefully insinuated into the popular mind until in the end it comes to be believed as a fact.

2nd. The war reports of the Southern papers should be paraded at great length, especially those which swell the number of their army, or which extol the exploits of their generals. But care must be taken to exclude their inflated despatches and leading articles, which are evidently, on the face of them, monstrous Munchausenisms; for your readers must not be allowed to suppose that the rebel writers are ever guilty of inaccuracy or falsehood; as that would spoil their credit with the unsuspicious Northern public.

3rd. The efficient and energetic generals in the loyal service should be calumniated in every plausible way; insist upon it that they are plunderers and thieves; and above all, denounce them for utter incompetency. On the other hand, laud such Generals as have distinguished themselves for do-nothingism and a half-faced sympathy in the revolt; call them the master Generals of the age, whose prudence surpasses that of Fabius, while their impetuosity rivals Napoleon's; and above all, remark upon that pre-eminence of intellectual and moral quality which renders them the staunchest of conservatives.

4th. Whenever the Union army achieves a signal victory say very little about it; complain, perhaps, incidentally, at the slowness of the war, but whenever it suffers a reverse (as all armies do at times), ask boldly and indignantly whether it be not time that this patricidal and hopeless war should be brought to an end. Assert roundly that the people are weary of it; weary of paying their money and sacrificing the lives of their brothers; and that we can never hope to accomplish any result. It is scarcely necessary to suggest on this head that the fact that during the two years in which we have prosecuted the war we have made greater progress than during almost any other two years of war recorded in history, must be carefully concealed.

5th. The finances of the government may be made a fruitful topic of suggestion. Do not let your readers know, on any account, that our securities command better prices than they did in years of peace; do not show them what the exchequers of other nations have borne in times of war; do not appeal to the universal confidence our bonds inspire in commercial circles; but talk sneeringly of "greenbacks;" ask with a wink of the eye what has become of the gold; say that our debt must be two or three thousand millions by this time, is rapidly increasing, and can never be paid; and mutter of frightful times, bankruptcy, stock-jobbers, contractors and shoddy men. It would be well, if you could, to contrast the successful management of the rebel finances with ours; but as gold among them is about four hundred percent premium; as one of our notes will buy three of theirs; as their debt already equals ours; and as their taxation greatly surpasses ours, very little, we fear, could be made of the argument. Pass it over, therefore, in profound silence.

6th. In the abuse of Mr. Lincoln and his cabinet no regard need to be paid to the consistency of your charges. Pronounce them all weak, timid, vacillating, and utterly incapable, in one column; and in another, accuse them of tyranny, despotism, excessive rigor, and a determination to trample the rights of the masses into the dust. Some of your readers will believe one story, and some the other, and so the confidence of all sorts will be shaken. You need give yourself no concern about the truth of your charges, provided they look plausible, or can be made to stick. Be sure, however, to insinuate that the men in power are not attached to the Union, but that they prosecute the war only to compel the separation of the South. That part of the nation, it is well known, is so earnestly devoted to the national cause that nothing but the perverse obstinacy and hatred of the Administration keeps it from rushing into our arms in all the ecstacy of fraternal endearment. Mr. Lincoln and Mr. Seward do not wish the South to come back, and are fighting as hard as they can to keep it out. Claim for yourselves, at the same time, the title of the only true Unionists.

7th. As it does not hurt anybody very much in these days to call him a radical, while the bugaboo of abolitionism has lost its principal terrors, you cannot accomplish a great deal by reiterating those nefarious epithets. But you can protest vehemently against "nigger" brigades — against the atrocity of arming slaves against their masters, and against the still greater atrocity of putting black soldiers on a level with white. On that head you may be voluble, as considerable anti-negro prejudice still exists among our more ignorant classes. But in doing all this be somewhat adroit, and do not for the world let it slip out that the first negro troops were used by Governor Moore of Louisiana, that they are to be found in nearly all the rebel garrisons, and that their labors are sometimes assisted by Indians and blood-hounds. Should you reveal all the facts of the case, the common sense of the people might rush to the conclusion that, as negroes are to be used in the war inevitably by one side or the other, it will be better to use them on the side of the Union than against it, while it may also come to be considered that they are better adapted to the malarious regions of the semi-tropical climates. A few even may go so far as to calculate that the more negroes we put into the service the fewer white men will be exposed to the draft. Denounce, then, but avoid facts!

8th. The draft — the conscription — ah! That's your topic of topics, which can be played upon like "the harp of a thousand strings." Be careful, at the outset, not to imitate the foolhardy Fernando Wood and advise an open resistance to it: for Fort Warren frowns angrily in the distance. Nor yet let it be known that our enrolment act compared with the conscription laws of the rebels — of which there are three or more — is like the Sermon on the Mount compared to the Draconian code. But clamor against it in detail; intimate doubts of its constitutionality; concealing its benevolent exemption of all who have others dependent upon them, denounce the $300 clause; say that it make odious distinctions between the poor and the rich; and refer learnedly to the despotic military systems of Austria and France. As no man likes to be forced into any duty, and particularly into so dangerous an occupation as that of fighting, you will have a large audience to appeal to; their selfishness at least will be in your favor; and you may work not only upon that, but upon the affections of their wives and children, who very naturally desire to keep the head of the house at home. There is a fine field in which prejudices may be easily excited, and the law brought into the most unmitigated disgrace. Plough it and work it well, and it can scarcely fail to yield you much

"CINCINNATUS"

H. G. the farmer receiving the nomination from H. G. the editor

From *Harpers Weekly*, Feb. 10, 1872.

By Thomas Nast

fruit. The interests, the integrity, the honor, the glory of your country, can be quietly kept in the background, while you arouse the fears and touch the sensibilities of the mother and the wife.

By pursuing these rules, and others which we may hereafter prescribe, an excellent conservative journal may be published, orthodox in every respect at the North, and highly popular at the South.

"TWO YEARS HENCE"

Richmond *Enquirer*, June 16, 1863

In two years, as many persons hope, we may possibly have peace — that is, always provided we continue to repulse and defeat the invading enemy. The Yankee "Democracy" is certainly rousing itself and preparing for a new struggle (at the ballot-box) in the great cause of the "spoils," or, as they call it, the cause of constitutional liberty. Those Democrats are evidently beginning to raise a peace platform for their next Presidential election; and if they have the good luck to be helped on and sustained by more and more serious disasters of the Yankee army in the field, there is no doubt that the present devourers of the said spoils at Washington may soon be so discredited and decried that our enemy's country would be ripe for such peaceful ballot-box revolution.

It is sincerely to be hoped that those earnest champions of constitutional freedom will be helped on and sustained in the manner they require, namely, by continued and severe reverses in the field, and it is the first and most urgent duty of our countrymen so to help and sustain that Democratic party. It is nothing to us which of their factions may devour their "spoils"; just as little does it signify to us whether they recover or do not recover that constitutional liberty which they so wantonly threw away in the mad pursuit of Southern conquest and plunder. But it is of the utmost importance to us to aid in stimulating disaffection among Yankees against their own government, and in demoralizing and disintegrating society in that God-abandoned country. We can do this only in one way — namely, by thrashing their armies and carrying the war to their own firesides. Then, indeed, conscientious constitutional principles will hold sway; peace platforms will look attractive; arbitrary arrests will become odious, and habeas corpus be quoted at a premium. This is the only way we can help them. In this sense, and to this extent, those Democrats are truly our allies, and we shall endeavor to do our duty by them.

But armistice there will be none, and we are glad of it. Our sovereign independence is already won and paid for with treasures of brave blood. It shall not be sold by peddlers, to be built into a Yankee platform.

THE GOOD NEWS

Harper's Weekly, July 18, 1863

After a long period of gloom and discouragement, we can again congratulate our readers upon good news. On 3d July, at five p.m., the broken masses of Lee's rebel army, recoiling from the shock of Meade's veterans, were flying to the mountains, throwing aside their guns and cartridge boxes, and strewing the plains of southern Pennsylvania with the materials of war; while on the one side the Army of the Potomac, flushed with victory and believing in its commander, was hotly pressing the fugitives in their retreat *northward;* and on the other the yeomen of New York and Pennsylvania, under Couch, fresh from peaceful pursuits but as steady as veterans, were pressing down on their flank and converting their attempted retreat into a rout. Not only did the rebels leave dead and wounded in our hands. The skulkers and stragglers from Lee's army — who fill every farmhouse and thicket in southern Pennsylvania and Maryland — are alone said to number one-fourth of the effective force with which he entered Maryland. Of the guns lost by the rebels and taken by us, the reports are thus far so conflicting that we do not care to repeat them. It is evident, however, that Lee must have lost in his hasty and disorderly retreat a great portion of his artillery; and if, as is reported, Meade came up with him at or near Williamsport on the 7th, and engaged him while he was preparing to cross into Virginia, his loss of guns will probably prove irreparable. Men may ford the river even in its present swollen condition, but guns cannot; and without an adequate artillery force Lee's forces will never get back to Richmond as an army.

Within twelve hours after the defeat of the rebels under Lee the garrison of Vicksburg surrendered to General Grant. We have as yet no details of the event — nothing, we may say, but a very brief dispatch from Admiral Porter to Secretary Welles. On this account the authenticity of the news has been questioned by some rebel sympathizers. We can see no good reason, however, for assuming its incorrectness. On the contrary, the last letters from Vicksburg, dated up to the 28th ult., all foreshadow the early surrender of the place, partly from the effect of our bombardment and mining operations, and partly from the want of provisions. Before these lines are read all doubts will be removed by the receipt of fuller intelligence, and we take for granted that this intelligence will confirm the present belief that we have taken Vicksburg with all its garrison and artillery.

It is assumed by some of our papers and many of our people that the defeat of Lee's army and the fall of Vicksburg involve the collapse of the rebellion. This may be so in one sense, inasmuch as the reopening of the Mississippi which follows as a matter of course from the capture of Vicksburg, and the overwhelming defeat of the rebel army in northern Virginia, render the further prosecution of the contest by the pro-slavery insurgents absolutely hopeless. The capture of Vicksburg secures the capture of Port Hudson, bisects the rebel country, and leaves General Grant's army free to operate in conjunction with Banks against Mobile, or in conjunction with Rosecrans against Chattanooga — the geographical and strategical centre of the Confederacy; while on the other hand the defeat of Lee uncovers Richmond and the railroad system of Virginia, and if properly turned to account by our people, will compel the so-called government of the Confederacy to seek refuge in North Carolina — where, according to last accounts, they are not very likely to be welcome. In this point of view, the news which we have, if confirmed, may be said to involve, sooner or later, the collapse of the pro-slavery insurrection, and the restoration of the authority of the United States government over the whole territory of the United States.

But it will probably prove a mistake to expect the actual surrender of the rebels, so long as Bragg, Beauregard, and Johnston have armies under their control. By falling back into the uplands of Carolina and Georgia; by concentrating their forces and their supplies; by increasing their cavalry force and devoting their energies to cavalry raids into the North, and the destruction of the long lines of communication which we shall have to maintain with our armies in the heart of the South; by distributing guerrillas and partisan companies along the banks of the Mississippi and the other great rivers of the Confederacy; a contest may be carried on even for years which, though hopeless and ineffectual to produce any good result, may yet avail to prevent our being able to claim that the rebellion has been crushed or peace restored. This, we take it, will be the policy of the rebel leaders. They are not the kind of men who "give up." They know that they have nothing to gain by penitence. Disgrace and exile are the mildest rewards they can expect. A halter from their own outraged people will be a more likely end to their career. The authors of the greatest rebellion in history — a rebellion equally remarkable as being a rebellion not only against the government of their own country, but against the plainest principles of truth and justice and Almighty God himself — they will not, they cannot, sue for terms as other vanquished combatants might. They will fight to the bitter end; fight so long as they can persuade a single deluded white man or wretched negro to shoulder a musket in their cause.

THE DRAFT RIOTS

Harper's Weekly, August 1, 1863

The outbreak was the natural consequence of pernicious teachings widely scattered among the ignorant and excitable populace of a great city; and the only possible mode of dealing with it was stern and bloody repression. Had the mob been assailed with grape and canister on Monday, when the first disturbance took place, it would have been a saving of life and property. Had the resistance been more general and the bloodshed more profuse than it was, on Thursday, the city would have enjoyed a longer term of peace and tranquillity than we can now count upon.

It is about as idle now to argue the question of the $300 clause in the Conscription Act as it is to debate the abstract right of secession. Before Monday night the riot had got far beyond the question of the draft. Within an hour after the destruction of the Provost-Marshal's office the rioters had forgotten all about the $300 question, and were engrossed with villainous projects of arson, murder, and pillage. It was not in order to avoid the draft that the colored orphan asylum was burned; that private houses were sacked; that inoffensive colored persons were beaten, mutilated, and murdered; that Brooks's clothing establishment and a score of smaller stores were pillaged; that private citizens were robbed in the open daylight in the public streets, beaten, and maimed; that the metropolis of the country was kept for nearly a week in a state of agonizing terror and suspense. For these outrages the draft was merely the pretext; the cause was the natural turbulence of a heterogeneous populace, aggravated by the base teachings of despicable politicians and their newspaper organs.

Some newspapers dwell upon the fact that the rioters were uniformly Irish, and hence argue that our trouble arises from the perversity of the Irish race. But how do these theorists explain the fact that riots precisely similar to that of last week have occurred within our time at Paris, Madrid, Naples, Rome, Berlin, and Vienna; and that the Lord George Gordon riots in London, before our time, far surpassed the New York riot in every circumstance of atrocity? Turbulence is no exclusive attribute of the Irish character: it is common to all mobs in all countries. It happens in this city that, in our working classes, the Irish element largely preponderates over all others, and if the populace acts as a populace Irishmen are naturally prominent therein. It happens also that from the limited opportunities which the Irish enjoy for education in their own country, they are more easily misled by knaves, and made the tools of politicians when they come here, than Germans

or men of other races. The impulsiveness of the Celt, likewise,
prompts him to be foremost in every outburst, whether for a good
or for an evil purpose. But it must be remembered in palliation of
the disgrace which, as Archbishop Hughes say, the riots of last week
have heaped upon the Irish name, that in many wards of the city
the Irish were during the late riot stanch friends of law and order;
that Irishmen helped to rescue the colored orphans in the asylum
from the hands of the rioters; that a large proportion of the police,
who behaved throughout the riot with the most exemplary gallantry,
are Irishmen; that the Roman Catholic priesthood to a man used
their influence on the side of the law; and that perhaps the most
scathing rebuke administered to the riot was written by an Irishman,
James T. Brady.

It is important that this riot should teach us something more
useful than a revival of Know-Nothing prejudices. We ought to
learn from it — what we should have known before, but communities like individuals learn nothing from experience — that riots
are the natural and inevitable diseases of great cities, epidemics, like
smallpox and cholera, which must be treated scientifically, upon
logical principles, and with the light of large experience. In old
cities where the authorities know how to treat riots, and resort at
once to grape and canister, they never occur twice in a generation,
one lesson being sufficient for the most hot-blooded rioter; in other
places, where less vigorous counsels prevail, the disease is checked
and covered up for a time, but breaks out afresh at intervals of a
few months or years. The secret is, of course, that by the former
method the populace are thoroughly imbued with a conviction of
the power of the authorities, and of their ability and determination
to crush a riot at any cost — a lesson remembered through life;
while in the latter case, the half-quelled rioters are allowed to go
home with a sort of feeling that they may after all be the stronger
party, and the government the weaker. Hence it is that while the
baton is the proper weapon of the policeman in times of peace and
order, the rifle and the howitzer are the only merciful weapons in
times of riot.

[WARTIME PLEASURE–MAKING: THE RUSSIAN BALL]

Harper's Weekly, November 21, 1863

The Ball is over, the music is hushed, the dances ended, the wine
drunk, the costly laces and diamonds put back to their places. And
now that the sounds of the revel are dying out it occurs to us that
we have a headache, and we are saying wisely to each other that
the ball was not, after all, so very sensible a thing; and that, when

our brothers and our sons are dying on battlefields, and thousands of brave Union soldiers, prisoners at Richmond, are being starved to death by the Southern chivalry, it is hardly decent for us here to be dancing, and making merry, and throwing away fortunes on diamonds. There is something in the idea. Should this number of *Harper's Weekly* fall into the hands of some poor wounded fellow at Chattanooga, or some half-starved Union prisoner at Richmond, the contrast between his own condition and that of the scented and perfumed dancers who figure in the ball picture may not improve his temper. "They are fiddling while I am dying," is the remark which would not unnaturally occur to him, and it would leave a bitter taste behind.

"What then?" says Shoddy. "Are we all to put on sackcloth and ashes because of the war? Are Mrs. and the Misses Shoddy not to have an opportunity of displaying their beauty — to say nothing of the splendid dresses and the magnificent diamonds which I bought them with the proceeds of paper money — simply because we are engaged in a war? The notion is monstrous! I pay for the war: taxes on my income, taxes on my clothing, taxes on my house, horses, carriages, silver, and everything that I've got; I send my blood relations to the war to fight and die; I give money for bounties and money to the Sanitary Commission; I vote to support the government. Having done all this, I submit that my duty is fulfilled, and that I may, if I choose, get up balls for Mrs. and the Misses Shoddy, and that they may enjoy them as becomes their age, their means, and their spirits. Dancing and balls are not bad things, by any means. It is good that young people should enjoy themselves while they can. They will all find sorrow enough in life by and by. Besides, our Russian Ball had a political significance, and may render good aid to the Union cause."

Thus much Shoddy. And though his reasoning is likely to seem very shallow and very selfish to the brave suffering men on Belle Isle or in Castle Thunder, it must fairly be admitted that, in past time, balls and battles have often jostled with each other, and the dying sounds of the dance have often mingled with the blast of the bugle. "There was a sound of revelry by night" within a few hours of the battle of Waterloo, and the dance was never more popular in Europe than during the Napoleonic Wars. The Preacher gives the key to the apparent paradox when he says, "Let us eat, drink, and be merry; *for tomorrow we die.*"

And now — good Shoddy, fair Mrs. Shoddy, and sweet daughters of the Shoddy house — that you have had your dance, and flirted with your Cossack, and flashed your diamonds in a thousand envious eyes; now that you have spent, so they say, over a million of dollars for one night's enjoyment; have you time and do you care to think of a suggestion by which your pleasure and our suffering heroes' needs may both be satisfied?

There was a time, not many years ago, when a commercial crisis precipitated the poor of New York into great suffering. At that time large-minded men and women gave their thoughts to the subject, and while soup-kitchens were established by A. T. Stewart and others, fashionable ladies gave a series of calico balls, the rule of which was that every lady present donated the dress she wore to the poor. By this means thousands of poor girls and women, who would otherwise have gone half-clad that bitter winter, were furnished with clothing. What say you now, ladies, to a

DIAMOND BALL,

the jewels worn to be given after the ball to the Sanitary Commission, which has our wounded soldiers in charge?

If, as is stated, a million of dollars' worth of diamonds were worn at the Russian ball, a million of dollars might be procured by such a Diamond Ball as we suggest — enough money to secure every comfort required by our wounded soldiers, and probably to save hundreds of lives which are now sacrificed for want of suitable attendance, clothing, and food. Could the jewels be put to a nobler use? Would not their radiance, in such a cause, flash not only from wall to wall of the ballroom, but down through the vale of time to the most distant age, lighting the fame of New York women, and proving that they were worthy wives and daughters of the brave men who are dying for their country?

GETTYSBURG [1]

Harper's Weekly, December 5, 1863

The solemn ceremony at Gettysburg is one of the most striking events of the war. There are graveyards enough in the land — what is Virginia but a cemetery? — and the brave who have died for us in this fierce war consecrate the soil from the ocean to the Mississippi. But there is peculiar significance in the field of Gettysburg, for there "thus far" was thundered to the rebellion. This it is which separates it from all the other battlefields of this war. Elsewhere the men in the ranks have fought as nobly, and their officers have directed as bravely; but here their valor stayed the flood of barbarism, and like the precious shells that the highest storm tides strew upon the beach, showing how far the waters came, so the

[1] *Harper's Weekly* and the Springfield *Republican* were the two outstanding journals which recognized at once the greatness of the Gettysburg Address.

dead heroes of Gettysburg marked the highest tide of the war. Therefore shall their graves be peculiarly honored, and their memory especially sacred; and all that living men can bring of pomp and solemnity and significance to hallow their resting-place shall not be wanting.

The President and the Cabinet were there, with famous soldiers and civilians. The oration by Mr. Everett was smooth and cold. Delivered, doubtless, with his accustomed graces, it yet wanted one stirring thought, one vivid picture, one thrilling appeal.

The few words of the President were from the heart to the heart. They cannot be read, even, without kindling emotion. "The world will little note nor long remember what we say here, but it can never forget what they did here." It was as simple and felicitous and earnest a word as was ever spoken.

Among the Governors present was Horatio Seymour. He came to honor the dead of Gettysburg. But when they were dying he stood in New York sneeringly asking where was the victory promised for the Fourth of July? These men were winning their victory and dying for us all; and now he mourns, ex officio, over their graves.

When the war is over and the verdict of history is rendered, it is not those who have steadily perplexed the government in every way — those who first incited and then palliated massacre and riot — who will be known as the friends of the soldiers, but those whose faith was firmest in the darkest hours, and who did not falter though the foe were at the door.

THE UNION NOMINATIONS

Harper's Weekly, June 25, 1864

The Baltimore Convention met and organized on the 7th of June, and on the 8th, in one session, laid down its platform, nominated Abraham Lincoln and Andrew Johnson with enthusiastic unanimity, and adjourned.

There was never a convention which more truly represented the people, and upon the first opportunity offered, it showed its purpose in the most unmistakable manner. No one who watched its deliberations, or who has read its proceedings, but must feel that it expressed the strongest popular determination of the unflinching prosecution of the war by every efficient method. Its settlement of the Missouri question, by admitting the radical delegation from that State and excluding the other, by a vote of 440 to 4, was the indication that the vast mass of Union men in the country have parted company with the hesitating and doubtful course which has been associated with the name of Blair. The resolutions, clear, incisive, and full, are to the same result, and leave no doubt in any mind that the "Border State policy," having served its purpose, and a purpose with which we are not disposed to quarrel, is no longer the policy which the people of the country approve. This decision is emphasized by the nomination of Andrew Johnson, a lifelong Democrat, who has been educated by fire and sword straight up to the necessities of the crisis.

Of Abraham Lincoln we have nothing to change in the views often expressed in these columns. That he unites perfect patriotism and great sagacity to profound conviction and patient tenacity, and that his conduct of our affairs has been, upon the whole, most admirable and wise, we are more than ever convinced; and that no public man in our history since Washington has inspired a deeper popular confidence we have no doubt whatever that the result of the election will establish. Of Andrew Johnson it is enough to say that there is no man in the country, unless it be Mr. Lincoln himself, whom the rebels more cordially hate. He fought them in the Senate, when they counted upon his aid, and he has fought them steadily ever since and with untiring energy. It is pleasant to record, of our personal knowledge, that one of the wisest and truest patriots in the country, who has sacrificed not less than Johnson himself, says of the contingency of Johnson's succession to the chief magistracy, that the country and the cause of American liberty could then not be in safer hands.

The reception of the nominations is what might be expected of a people which had virtually ordered them to be made. The copperhead journals, the late supporters of John B. Floyd & Co., denounce the convention as a corrupt body; and seeing in the nominations the most tremendous proclamation of the loyal citizens of the United States to all enemies at home and abroad that the cause of the American Union is to be fought out along this line, they renew their old cry that our liberties have been lost in the effort to maintain them. The real copperhead regret is, not that liberty has been lost, but that slavery has not been saved. The Union journals which have considered Mr. Lincoln badly advised, timid, and hesitating, still cordially applaud the platform, which they properly regard as a body of instructions from the people for increased and continual vigor. They are entirely satisfied with the resolutions and Andrew Johnson, but wish the Presidential nomination had been left dependent upon the result of the campaign. That is a view of the situation which seems to us peculiarly erroneous, and fraught with the utmost danger. The reliance of every patriot is and must be upon the sturdy good sense and purpose of the people — a faith not to be shaken by disaster, and a purpose which demands that the

Chief Magistrate, in such a time as this, shall be a tried and not an untried man.

It is remarkable that journals which we have always supposed were truly and not technically "democratic," because believing in the general wisdom and instinct of the people, while they regret to see that Mr. Lincoln has been renominated, confess that he is beyond any question the man and the choice of the people.

LINCOLN

Richmond *Dispatch*, April 7, 1864

Lincoln alone harmonizes in himself all those qualities which are essential to a representation of average Yankeeism. He has no education beyond that of the common schools and the attorney's office, and is rich in moral and immoral features which distinguish the genuine son of the Puritan from the rest of mankind. He is shrewd, energetic, shallow, cunning, selfish, egotistical, hard-hearted, vulgar, hypocritical, and fanatical. Every one of these qualities he has manifested from the moment when he marched into Washington in a freight car, until the American people would be false to their own instincts if they did not recognize him as their true representative man. We shall be greatly mistaken if he is not the reëlected candidate for the Presidency.

THE PEACE BLONDINS AT NIAGARA

Harper's Weekly, August 6, 1864

The late Peace performance at Niagara Falls was not very mysterious. It was simply a movement of the rebels to help their friends the Copperheads. It was a notification, to whom it might concern, that if the government of the United States were handed over to the friends of the rebels, then the rebels would lay down their arms. It was a confession that the rebel leaders are sorely pinched, that they foresee disaster, and that they are perfectly willing to have us give them by our votes the victory which they despair of obtaining by their arms.

The conduct of the President was simple and proper. Informed that there were accredited agents from the rebel chiefs who wished to treat of peace, he consented that they should visit Washington. But when they confessed that they had no authority whatever, the President, in order that there should be no apparent justification even of the assertion that he had refused to listen to overtures from the rebels, issued a notice, to whom it may concern, that the government of the United States is always ready to hear and consider any authorized proposition from the rebel leaders involving the restoration of the Union and the abandonment of slavery. To this the discomfited and self-appointed rebel agents reply in a manifesto intended to represent the President as an autocrat and a despot, etc., and expressing their own resolution never to submit to conquest, etc. It is interesting to learn from this paper that in a region where every man between fifteen and sixty-five is dragged into the ranks, and exempt soldiers are legislated back to serve as long as they are wanted, there is no military autocrat; and that, in a section where the most hopeless terrorism prevails, social institutions, established constitutions, and priceless hereditary self-government are not overthrown, subverted, or bartered away. Mr. Clement Clay's letter is but a poor specimen of our own copperhead orations and editorials. But it is not without value, for it shows to the dullest mind the perfect sympathy in sentiment between Copperheads and rebels.

It is suggested that the Constitution does not authorize the President to make any condition such as the abandonment of slavery. Those who say so honestly are mistaken. There may be a question of policy, which we think the President has rightly resolved; but there is no constitutional question. The Constitution defines treason, authorizes making of war, appoints the President commander-in-chief, and authorizes the suspension of the writ of *habeas corpus* in case of rebellion and invasion. There is nothing in any of these provisions which deprives the government of the right of exercising its common sense, or compels it to lay down its arms at the will of rebels or foreign enemies. The government is the judge when a foreign war is over or a domestic rebellion quelled. Nor is there in the Constitution nor in reason any obligation upon the government to connive at its own destruction. The government of the United States is bound by every consideration to secure peace; and peace is impossible while the active cause for war remains, watching for its opportunity. The cry that the President can not constitutionally require the destruction of that cause as a condition of peace is but another effort of the enemies of the country to prolong the war indefinitely. When the government was established the cloud of slavery was as large as a man's hand. Four years ago it was a tempest, blackening the heavens and raining fire. And now we are told that it is proper to put up an umbrella to keep off the wet, but unconstitutional to erect a lightning rod to draw the fire harmless to the ground. It is idle to shirk the vital point of the whole war, and imagine that peace can be made with slavery. To that point the public mind has advanced. If a truce should be called and the question opened for debate, the truce would soon disappear in fresh cannon-smoke. Liberty and slavery are fighting for and against this government. Is he a wise man who affects to think that by omitting the name we can avoid the thing?

THE CHICAGO DEMOCRATIC CONVENTION

Harper's Weekly, September 10, 1864

The platform of the Chicago Convention will satisfy every foreign and domestic enemy of American Union and Liberty. It declares that the government of the United States is guilty of resisting rebellion, and that the American people cannot maintain the authority of their laws. It has no word of righteous wrath against the recreant citizens who have plunged the country in the blood of civil war, but lavishes its fury upon the constituted authorities which have steadily defended the Union. It has no censure for any act of rebellion, but the war measures taken by the Administration, under the authority of the Constitution, are branded as tyrannical and despotic. There is not a word in it that can cheer any soldier or sailor fighting for his country; not a syllable that stirs the blood of a patriot. It is craven, abject, humiliating. It confesses the defeat of the Union cause, and covertly implores the mercy of Jefferson Davis and his crew.

And this at a moment when stout old Farragut is thundering at Mobile; when the inexorable Grant clutches at the Weldon Road, which, as an officer of the army writes, is "like touching the cubs of a tigress;" when Early's Shenandoah invasion is too late for success; when Sherman is closing around Atlanta; when State after State is supplying its quota of fresh soldiers; when gold steadily declines; when a universal public confidence is awakening; and when the rebels are plainly, palpably struggling to hold out only long enough to see if the election, by the elevation of the Chicago candidate, will not turn to their advantage.

Never again will this nation have a fairer chance of maintaining its constitutional authority than it has now. For three years it has, at every disadvantage, battled against this formidable conspiracy, and never was the conspiracy in so desperate a strait. The country has it by the throat. A little more force, a closer pressure, and the monster falls strangled, dead forever. A little less force, a relaxed hold, a wavering purpose, and the scaly folds of rebellion thrill with hope to the extremity; it renews its strength, it recruits its venom, and darts a deadlier blow at the life of the country. . . . The issue is simple and sublime. It is the life or the degradation of the nation. It is to show that a government of the people is equal to every exigency — ready for taxation, ready for military service, ready for endurance, ready for forbearance — that it is as strong as any government in the world, and stronger — that in war it is as powerful and resolute and orderly as in peace it is industrious and prosperous. There seems to us but one way in which this can be shown, but one way in which utter national humiliation can be avoided, and that is by the steady and strong hand of war until the rebels confess the authority of the government. That is the policy which is personified in Abraham Lincoln and Andrew Johnson, and which we shall most strenuously support, for it is the cause of the peace and happiness of the American people.

[McCLELLAN'S CANDIDACY]
Springfield *Republican*, September 18, 1864

With respectable talents, a pure character, and patriotic purposes, he is wanting in that high moral sense that perceives the truest truth, and that high moral courage that does and dares in its behalf. He waits, he hesitates in the presence of great opportunities; he compromises with time and with truth; and he is no fit man to deal with the sharp exigencies and the sublime occasions of this hour. He wants and would try to save the country; but he would hinder rather than help the people, who *will* save it in the long run, despite their own occasional fickleness and faint-heartedness — because he fails to see and use quickly the moral and material agencies by which it is to be saved, and because he is no match for the men who are bent on its ruin. . . .

The platform is weak in words and wicked in intention. It lacks vigor, sharpness, and high principle. The breaking purpose shines through every sentence. Its words for the Union are hesitating, guarded, shuffling; while its clamor for experiments that would endanger it, its want of condemnation for those who have struck at it, and still hold aloft the bloody flag of disunion and destruction, and its petty arraignment of those who are wielding the power of the government to sustain and secure it, all show that the real sympathy of its authors is with the enemies rather than the defenders of the Union.

NEGROES AS REBEL SOLDIERS[1]
Richmond *Inquirer*, October 6, 1864

The general order for the revocation of details will be found in this issue of the *Inquirer*. This step has been taken by the government to fill up the army. It is necessary and proper, and if this

[1] The question of arming the slaves was increasingly discussed throughout the South during 1864; the Confederate Congress that autumn authorized the hiring of slaves from their owners; and President Davis's message of November, 1864, recommended that the government be empowered to buy them for war use, and, if it liked, to emancipate them at the end of the struggle. The Confederate Secretary of War at the same time went farther and advocated making soldiers out of large bodies of slaves. When this editorial was written, however, such a proposal was considered extreme doctrine.

order is properly enforced the increase of the army will be speedy and rapid. We should like to see steps taken to promptly enforce the law of Congress for the employment of negroes as teamsters, etc. The law of Congress on this subject is plain, and though it does not go far enough, yet by promptly enforcing its provisions, many soldiers will be returned to their commands, and the army very greatly strengthened. The details should come forward promptly; their services are greatly needed, and if they are speedily collected and sent to the front there will be no danger at Richmond, and the condition of the country will present the most encouraging aspect. It is useless to seek to conceal that more men are greatly wanted.

The President has emphatically announced the startling fact that two-thirds of the army are absent from the ranks. There would be no need of reinforcements but for this most disgraceful straggling and deserting. But as the fact exists, and the evil must be repaired, the details are called upon to do service. How long their service will be required cannot now be said. Sixty to ninety days will terminate the active operations of the campaign, and then details may be resumed; but, at present, all are needed, and all must come forward. Those that delay or shirk will be hunted down, and permanently sent to the army.

The law of Congress authorizing the employment of negroes, if fully carried out, would give ten thousand men to the Army of Northern Virginia. The slaves and free negroes can be impressed just as any other property, and the law provides for their support and clothing, and pays the owner soldier's wages.

The question of making soldiers of negroes, of regularly enlisting them, and fighting them, for their own safety as well as our own, must have presented itself to every reflecting mind. Because the Yankees have not been able to make soldiers out of their drafted negroes, it does not follow that we cannot train our slaves to make very efficient troops. We believe that they can be, by drill and discipline, moulded into steady and reliable soldiers. The propriety of employing negroes as soldiers we shall not at present discuss; but whenever the subjugation of Virginia or the employment of her slaves as soldiers are alternative positions, then certainly we are for making them soldiers, and giving freedom to those negroes that escape the casualties of battle.

We should be glad to see the Confederate Congress provide for the purchase of two hundred and fifty thousand negroes, present them with their freedom and the privilege of remaining in the States, and arm, equip, drill and fight them. We believe that the negroes, identified with us by interest, and fighting for their freedom here, would be faithful and reliable soldiers, and, under officers who would drill them, could be depended on for much of the ordinary service and even for the hardest fighting. It is not necessary now to discuss this matter, and may never become so, but neither negroes nor slavery will be permitted to stand in the way of the success of our cause. This war is for national independence on our side, and for the subjugation of the whites and the emancipation of the negroes on the side of the enemy. If we fail the negroes are nominally free and their masters really slaves. We must, therefore, succeed. Other States may decide for themselves, but Virginia after exhausting her whites, will fight her blacks through to the last man. She will be free at all costs.

THE FINAL RESULTS OF THIS WAR

Philadelphia *Public Ledger*, November 7, 1864

In the North no person can step into a railroad car but the rapid change which is going on will be apparent to him. Many are travelling who never travelled before on cars and steamboats, so that the character of the travelling masses is quite different from what it used to be. Formerly only merchants and professional men and persons of wealth and leisure travelled, but now the whole country, as soldiers, fathers, brothers, sisters, mothers of soldiers, are passing to and fro in every train. Those depths of society which are usually least disturbed by ordinary movements have been agitated and wakened into a life and activity unparalleled in history. There is hardly a family but has some of its sons with one or more of our armies in the South, and all this enlarges the mind and expands the ideas amazingly. What must and will be the result of such a war as the present, where soldiers go a thousand or two miles home on furlough and write letters by every post such as no other nation can parallel? Every newspaper conveys the latest telegraphic news and the minutest features in the domestic life of every town and village visited by our forces. Men are thrown together in masses who formerly lived sequestered, and by comparing their observations educate each other. All this may produce an intellectual activity for which the past affords no precedent. Already the best schools and institutions of learning, especially for young ladies, are crowded to excess, and academies and even colleges show such increased numbers that the effect of the draft is not felt upon them. The abundance of money is increasing the demand for education to such an extent that this war produces no injurious effect. This is, we believe, unprecedented.

What the effect of the war will be on the South eventually, who shall predict? But the masses of the poor whites will be much enlightened by all they have passed through, and by their contact with Northern minds. They will be no longer controlled by a few wealthy leaders. Northern energy and intelligence will be diffused in various ways throughout those Southern sections whose fertility is incalculable. When the present rebellion is put down the progress of the country as a whole will probably be very much more rapid than at any former period, and the history of a new life will begin from the present war. The whole world will be affected by it most sensibly. The wealth of Germany and the population of Ireland will be found transported to a wonderful extent to our shores. The privileged classes of the old world will see in our success, as Professor Goldwin Smith well remarked, their own downfall. But the masses of the people of all Europe will find it the prognostic of their own progress in liberty.

THE DEATH OF LINCOLN [1]

New York *Evening Post*, April 20, 1865

Oh, slow to smite and swift to spare,
Gentle and merciful and just!
Who, in the fear of God, didst bear
The sword of power, a nation's trust.

In sorrow by thy bier we stand,
Amid the awe that hushes all,
And speak the anguish of a land
That shook with horror at thy fall.

Thy task is done; the bond are free:
We bear thee to an honored grave,
Whose proudest monument shall be
The broken fetters of the slave.

Pure was thy life; its bloody close
Hath placed thee with the sons of light
Among the noble host of those
Who perished in the cause of right.

[1] Contributed to the editorial columns by the editor-in-chief, William Cullen Bryant.